STUDIA TRADIT

Explorations in Earl

Theology continually engages with its past: the people, experience, Scriptures, liturgy, learning and customs of Christians. The past is preserved, rejected, modified; but the legacy steadily evolves as Christians are never indifferent to history. Even when engaging the future, theology looks backwards: the next generation's training includes inheriting a canon of Scripture, doctrine, and controversy; while adapting the past is central in every confrontation with a modernity.

This is the dynamic realm of tradition, and this series' focus. Whether examining people, texts, or periods, its volumes are concerned with how the past evolved in the past, and the interplay of theology, culture, and tradition.

STUDIA TRADITIONIS THEOLOGIAE

Explorations in Early and Medieval Theology

36

Series Editor: Thomas O'Loughlin,
Professor of Historical Theology
in the University of Nottingham

EDITORIAL BOARD

Director
Prof. Thomas O'Loughlin

Board Members
Dr Andreas Andreopoulos, Dr Nicholas Baker-Brian,
Dr Augustine Casiday, Dr Mary B. Cunningham, Dr Juliette
Day, Dr Johannes Hoff, Dr Paul Middleton, Dr Simon Oliver,
Prof. Andrew Prescott, Dr Patricia Rumsey, Dr Jonathan Wooding,
Dr Holger Zellentin

THE LITANY
IN ARTS AND CULTURES

Edited by
Witold Sadowski and Francesco Marsciani

BREPOLS

© 2020, Brepols Publishers n.v., Turnhout, Belgium.

All rights reserved. No part of this publication may be reproduced, stored in a retrieval system, or transmitted, in any form or by any means, electronic, mechanical, photocopying, recording, or otherwise, without the prior permission of the publisher.

D/2020/0095/163
ISBN 978-2-503-58670-0
e-ISBN 978-2-503-58671-7
DOI 10.1484/M.STT-EB.5.118735
ISSN 2294-3617
e-ISSN 2566-0160

Printed in the EU on acid-free paper

TABLE OF CONTENTS

List of Plates and Illustrations — vii

Acknowledgments — xi

Abbreviations — xiii

Studies on Litanies in the Past and Present — 1
Witold Sadowski, Magdalena Kowalska, Magdalena Maria Kubas

Litanies in Ancient Egyptian Written Culture — 25
Roland Enmarch

Litanies in the Sumerian Liturgy of Ancient Mesopotamia:
A Typology of a 2,000-Year-Long Transmission History — 47
Uri Gabbay

Performative Aspects of Litanies in Sumerian Liturgical Prayers,
According to Selected Late Manuscripts — 71
Sam Mirelman

Aspects of Litany in the Old Testament — 89
Christos G. Karagiannis

TABLE OF CONTENTS

'Πολλὰ ἔτη εἰς πολλά': Some Litanic Practices in Byzantine Imperial Ceremonies?   101
Marie-Emmanuelle Torres

A Litany in the Rule of St Benedict: On the Mysterious Form of Chapter 4 of the *Rule* and Its Theological Implications   125
Bernard Sawicki OSB

Litanic Songs for the Virgin: Rhetoric, Repetition, and Marian Refrains in Medieval Latin Song   143
Mary Channen Caldwell

The Litany of Saints of the Easter Vigil in the Roman Rite   175
Joris Geldhof

Singing the Litany in Tudor England, 1544–1555   197
Magnus Williamson

When Music Takes Over: Sacramental Litanies in the European Music History   221
Karina Zybina

Sardinia's Funerary Lamentations – The *Attitos*, A Case of Litany?   255
Tiziana Palandrani

The Semiotics of Litanies From the Middle Ages to the YouTube Era: Interpretative, Intersemiotic, and Performative Issues   273
Jenny Ponzo, Francesco Galofaro, Gabriele Marino

Index   303
   Scriptural Index   303
   Index of Manuscripts   305
   Index of Ancient and Medieval Names   306
   Index of Modern Names   307

LIST OF PLATES AND ILLUSTRATIONS

Sam Mirelman, Performative Aspects of Litanies in Sumerian Liturgical Prayers, According to Selected Late Manuscripts

> Figure 1. Line drawing of an excerpt of a cuneiform tablet of a Sumerian liturgical prayer, demonstrating the division of the line into two halves.   77

Bernard Sawicki OSB, A Litany in the Rule of St Benedict

> Figure 1. Modalities within the Rule of St Benedict.   133
> Figure 2. Syllabic length of verses in Chapter 4 of the Rule of St Benedict.   134

Mary Channen Caldwell, Litanic Songs for the Virgin: Rhetoric, Repetition, and Marian Refrains in Medieval Latin Song

> Music Example 1. *Salve virgo virginum*, *Ave Maria virgo virginum*, and *Salva nos stella maris*, music.   159
> Music Example 2. *O summi regis mater inclita*, music.   160
> Music Example 3. Rhetorical and melodic modules in *O summi regis mater inclita*.   156
> Figure 1. Florence, Biblioteca Medicea Laurenziana, Pluteus 29.1, fol. 463r, historiated initial 'D'.   163
> Figure 2. Paris, Bibliothèque nationale de France, latin 5267, fol. 80r, Marian litany.   165
> Plate 1. Florence, Biblioteca Medicea Laurenziana, Pluteus 29.1, fol. 469v.   171

Plate 2. Florence, Biblioteca Medicea Laurenziana, Pluteus 29.1, fol. 470r.   172

Plate 3. Florence, Biblioteca Medicea Laurenziana, Pluteus 29.1, fol. 470v.   173

Plate 4. Florence, Biblioteca Medicea Laurenziana, Pluteus 29.1, fol. 471r.   174

Magnus Williamson, Singing the Litany in Tudor England, 1544–1555

Music Example 1. Rogationtide Litany refrain, *Kyrieleyson qui precioso* (square in Voice III with implied chant in Voice II, and Voice I singing a fourth above the chant).   198

Music Example 2. Anonymous Litany, Folger Shakespeare Library, STC 16237 (1544 × 49, reconstructed).   208

Music Example 3. Anonymous Litany, British Library, Additional MS 34191, f. 35 (*c.* 1549, reconstructed).   208

Music Example 4a. Anonymous Litany, 'Wanley' partbooks, #54.   210

Music Example 4b. Anonymous Litany, 'Wanley' partbooks, #73.   210

Music Example 5a. Thomas Tallis, vernacular Litany of 1544: *Kyrie*.   212

Music Example 5b. Anonymous, 'Peryn-Morley' Litany: *Kyrie*.   212

Music Example 6. Antonio Cabezón, Litany: Invocación (from Robledo (1989), 146).   214

Plate 1. Washington, DC, Folger Shakespeare Library, STC 16237   207

Karina Zybina, When Music Takes Over: Sacramental Litanies in the European Music History

Music Example 1. Giovanni Pierluigi da Palestrina, Litaniae Sacrosanctae Eucharistiae in F, Hab. XXVI.125, bars 90-2 (1st chorus).   228

Music Example 2a. Giovanni Pierluigi da Palestrina, Litaniae Sacrosanctae Eucharistiae in G, Hab. XXVI.133, bars 31–2, 34–5, and 37–8.   229

Music Example 2b. Giovanni Pierluigi da Palestrina, Litaniae Sacrosanctae Eucharistiae in G, Hab. XXVI.133, bars 40–1, 46–7, 48–9, 51–2, and 56–7.   229

LIST OF PLATES AND ILLUSTRATIONS

Music Example 2c. Giovanni Pierluigi da Palestrina, Litaniae Sacrosanctae Eucharistiae in G, Hab. XXVI.133, bars 59–60, 61–2, 65–6.   229

Figure 1. Georg Victorinus: *Thesaurus litaniarum* (Munich, 1596), fol. AAA1r (Tenor).   222

Figure 2. Georg Victorinus: *Thesaurus litaniarum* (Munich, 1596), fol. B4v (Discantus).   224

Figure 3. W.A. Mozart: autograph score of the *Litaniae de venerabili altaris sacramento* K. 243, fol. 1r.   237

Jenny Ponzo, Francesco Galofaro, and Gabriele Marino, The semiotics of litanies from the Middle Ages to the YouTube era: Interpretative, intersemiotic, and performative issues

Figure 1. Temple of Divine Providence, Warsaw. Map of the crypt by Francesco Galofaro.   301

Figure 2. '*Sancta Maria Ora Pro Nobis*', Table 6 from the treatise by Razzore and Mora (1931).   301

Figure 3. Inquisition-styled still image employed as the visual companion for the YouTube video '*Litanie dei santi*' (youtu.be/hOwNEtg7V94).   302

Figure 4. Apocalyptic stock image employed as a visual companion for the YouTube video '*Litanie dei santi*' (youtu.be/oEiSw-ZjEcI).   302

ACKNOWLEDGMENTS

For the inclusion of reproductions in this volume we would like to acknowledge permission granted to us by the following institutions: Firenze, Biblioteca Medicea Laurenziana (Mary Channen Caldwell's chapter, Figure 1 and Plates 1–4), Bibliothèque nationale de France (Caldwell's chapter, Figure 2), Folger Shakespeare Library (Magnus Williamson's chapter, Plate 1), Bayerische Staatsbibliothek München (Karina Zybina's chapter, Figures 1 and 2), and Staatsbibliothek zu Berlin – Preußischer Kulturbesitz, Musikabteilung mit Mendelssohn-Archiv (Zybina's chapter, Figure 3).

The Sardinian song 'E fizu ohi fizu meu', quoted in Tiziana Palandrani's chapter, is reprinted from *La musica sarda, canti e danze popolari*, edited by Diego Carpitella, Pietro Sassu and Leonardo Sole. Copyright 2011 by Nota. Reprinted by kind permission of Nota.

Further reproduction of this material by any means is prohibited.

ABBREVIATIONS

AMD	Ancient Magic and Divination
AOAT	Alter Orient und Altes Testament
AOS	American Oriental Series
AuOr	Aula Orientalis
CBQ	Catholic Biblical Quarterly.
CTMMA	Cuneiform Texts in the Metropolitan Museum of Art
DC	Constantine VII Porphyrogennetos, De Ceremoniis aulae Byzantinae; ed. J. J. Reiske, Bonn, 1829, 1830; trans. A. Moffat and M. Tall [2 vols], Canberra 2012
ETCSL	Electronic Text Corpus of Sumerian Literature
FAOS	Freiburger altorientalische Studien
GMTR	Guides to the Mesopotamian Textual Record
Grove	The New Grove Dictionary of Music and Musicians, ed. S. Sadie [29 vols; 2nd edn], Oxford 2001
HES	Heidelberger Emesal-Studien
HUCASup	Hebrew Union College Annual Supplements
JATS	Journal of Adventist Theological Society
JSOTSup	Journal for the Study of the Old Testament Supplement
MGG (Personenteil)	Die Musik in Geschichte und Gegenwart. Allgemeine Enzyklopädie der Musik, ed. L. Finscher [26 vols], Kassel [i.a.] 1999–2007
MGG (Sachteil)	Die Musik in Geschichte und Gegenwart. Allgemeine Enzyklopädie der Musik, ed. L. Finscher [9 vols; 2nd edn], Kassel [i.a.] 1994–1999

ABBREVIATIONS

MSL	Materialien zum sumerischen Lexikon
Or	Orientalia
RISM	Répertoire International des Sources Musicales
RSV	The Revised Standard Version of the Bible
Rule	The Rule of Saint Benedict
SANE	Sources from the Ancient Near East
SVT	Supplements to Vetus Testamentum
ZAW	Zeitschrift für die alttestamentliche Wisssenschaft

WITOLD SADOWSKI, MAGDALENA KOWALSKA,
MAGDALENA MARIA KUBAS

STUDIES ON LITANIES IN THE PAST AND PRESENT

In common parlance the term 'litany' is used to refer to an utterance based on a long, repetitive enumeration. For religious scholars, however, the litany is primarily a form of prayer with ancient roots, a prayer which not only consists of a list of acclamations and supplications addressed to God, angels or saints, but also involves acting through the different senses on all the basic attributes of man, that is through the body, the mind, the psyche and the soul. It seems probable that this latter dimension of the litanic prayer accounts for its popularity in various religious and cultural traditions.

However, what are the reasons for the popularity of the litanic prayer? These may be related to the still-unresolved issue of the influence of repetitive rhythm on spiritual focus, as well as on the internal integration of thought and emotion, both of which are synchronised with an individual's breathing and heartbeat. In past centuries, the litanic rhythm also served as a catalyst for collective experiences. Prayers were customarily performed by the clergy, together with their congregation, walking in procession through narrow, crowded city streets from church to church, often at night and not infrequently as a response to the danger posed by, for example, earthquakes, fires, or flooding. Litanies also contained a considerable amount of knowledge about the world and the supernatural. Much could be learnt about the hierarchy of the heavenly beings and the order of the creation, in addition to cosmic harmony and the spiritual dimension of the earthly reality, as well as a sense of history and the value of human labour or suffering. Believers could become familiar with the many names assigned to God, gaining an insight into the mystery of His inner life. They could also learn how to live in His presence and how to commune

Witold Sadowski • University of Warsaw, Poland
Magdalena Kowalska • Nicolaus Copernicus University in Toruń, Poland
Magdalena Maria Kubas • University of Warsaw, Poland

with the inhabitants of heaven. It comes as no surprise, therefore, that the litany, characterized as it was by its wide intellectual scope and its ability to penetrate what is impenetrable to human eyes and ears, had an impact on the organization of social rituals and was appropriated by not one, but many different fields of art, such as: poetry, music, sculpture, painting, and engraving, as well as being influential in the creation of stained-glass windows and the miniatures with which books were illuminated.

It is for this reason that in the present volume the litany becomes an object of study not only for theologians, but also for researchers from other disciplines. Indeed this book is written in response to the fact that, until the beginning of the twenty-first century, there was little interest in the litany among researchers of literature, music and the fine arts, with the academic focus being religious, a fact which created the impression that the litany is interesting merely from a theological perspective.

1. Litany and Ritual

In all probability, the first liturgical historian to publish a separate study on the litany was Manuel Vélez Marín.[1] In the eighteenth century, he examined the oldest examples of the Spanish Mozarabic liturgy, demonstrating that litanic prayers were present on the Iberian Peninsula before the conversion of the Visigoths to Trinitarian Christianity, i.e. before 589 CE.[2] However, with the exception of Marín's book, it was only in the twentieth century that systematic studies on the litany were conducted. Initially, it was historians of spirituality and ritual that showed an interest in the genre, either as the main subject of their research or while examining other liturgical genres accompanying the litany. Examples of the research in this field include studies on the earliest context in which the litany appeared and also those on the origins of the litanic prayers, studies conducted by scholars such as Theodor Schermann,[3] Anton Baumstark,[4] Louis Duchesne,[5] Ferdinand Cabrol,[6]

---

[1]   Vélez Marín (1758).
[2]   Piłat-Zuzankiewicz (2016b), 129.
[3]   Schermann (1903).
[4]   Baumstark (1904) and (1906). In his studies, the researcher examined, amongst others, the chairetismic tradition, which, as defined by Sadowski (2011), 25–68 and (2018), 98–224, is a constitutive element of the litanic genre.
[5]   Duchesne (1904).
[6]   Cabrol (1930).

Edmund Bishop,[7] Maurice Coens,[8] Josef Andreas Jungmann,[9] and Robert F. Taft.[10] A ground-breaking discovery was made by Baumstark who identified a probable prototype for the *Litany of the Saints* in the liturgy of the Church of Antioch. According to the researcher, the text that he discovered points to a tradition that probably dates to the fourth century. Many researchers have also referred to a description of a communal recitation of the litany in Jerusalem from the same century, a description which was included by a female pilgrim, Egeria, in her travel diary (*Itinerarium*) that was discovered at the end of the nineteenth century. Additionally, two works published in the second half of the twentieth century were of crucial importance in the study of the litany, namely those of Gilles Gérard Meersseman[11] and Michael Lapidge.[12]

Despite the detailed research carried out by scholars from different countries, the key term, that is 'litany', still remains an unresolved problem, as it has not yet been determined with which religious phenomena it should be associated. As noted by Armando Cuva, the term is frequently used in liturgical books of the Roman Catholic Church, but its scope is broad and general enough to cover various types of litanic structures.[13] The same term, for instance, is used with reference to two prayers of different origin: the *Litany of the Saints* and the *Litany of Loreto*. The presence of the former in the liturgy of the Catholic Easter Vigil is discussed in this volume by Joris Geldhof. Similar prayers, albeit without an enumeration of saints, are also found in Protestant churches, with examples including, amongst others, the Lutheran *Die Deutsche Litanei*, as well as the Anglican *The Letany*. The latter is discussed in this book by Magnus Williamson.

In the Western Church, however, the term 'litany' is also endowed with other meanings. It is, for instance, used with reference to certain junctures in the Eucharistic celebration (*Kyrie eleison*) and to processional supplications known as *rogationes*. It is frequently employed in a very broad sense too, with its scope extending to cover varied texts

---

[7] Bishop (1918).

[8] Coens (1936).

[9] Jungmann (1952) and (1969).

[10] See, amongst others, Taft (1977).

[11] Meersseman (1958–1960).

[12] Lapidge (1991). A more comprehensive bibliography of studies on the litany is provided by Sadowski (2018b), 19.

[13] Cuva (2006), 336.

aimed at either prayer or meditation, i.e. texts in which anaphoras or epiphoras, as well as enumerations of acclamations or deprecations, are arranged to create a repetitive rhythm. It is in this sense that the term is used in this book by Bernard Sawicki, who applies it to a chapter from the Rule of Saint Benedict. Taking into consideration the thematic and rhythmic dynamics of the text, Sawicki proves his hypothesis that framing the text in the form of a litany – in the broad sense of the word – is part of the pedagogical and humanistic strategy of its author.

Having said that, there is a marked difference in the terminology used in Orthodox churches, for within this branch of Christianity the term 'litany' is not applied to the text of a prayer, but instead to the procession during which the prayer is said.[14] The Byzantine litany, performed while walking, is discussed in the article by Marie-Emmanuelle Torres, who sets the typical repetitiveness of a litanic text alongside the vocal repetition in the songs of the aulic rituals at the imperial court. Her main source of information is the Book of Ceremonies compiled in the tenth century by emperor Constantine VII. Torres notes that the primary function of the litanic form was to enable a collective involvement in a ritual practice, thereby contributing to the collective experience of imperial authority.

As if this did not create enough problems, the difficulties connected with the 'litany' are not restricted to the somewhat different meanings of the term within the traditions of particular churches. This is because the term 'litany', derived from the Greek and long associated solely with a Christian prayer, is not in fact the exclusive domain of Christianity, as it appears in studies of Jewish prayers dating from the Talmud period,[15] and is also frequently used in texts about the ancient Sumerian,[16] Egyptian,[17] Hebrew,[18] and Ugarit[19] cultures.

In his article in this volume, Uri Gabbay examines the corpus of Mesopotamian litanies, litanies that were written in the Emesal register of the Sumerian language. The researcher describes a textual structure based on a juxtaposition of two axes, namely horizontal and vertical. The existence of the vertical axis enabled the prayer to be modified as a

---

[14] Sadowski (2018b), 83–97.
[15] Heinemann (1977), 144–52.
[16] Gabbay (2014), 38–58, Toboła (2016a).
[17] Assman (1980), 1062–66.
[18] Toboła (2016b).
[19] Toboła (2016c).

result of historical changes, such as the transfer of a cult from one city to another. Similar material is the basis of Sam Mirelman's examination of the musical dimension of the Mesopotamian litanies. The researcher discusses, amongst other issues, the role of the chorus and antiphonal song, as well as the choice and function of the musical instruments accompanying the prayer.

Roland Enmarch's paper, focusing on ancient Egyptian literature, should be read together with the essays on Sumerian litanies mentioned above. A comprehensive survey was undertaken of the main types of litanic texts that circulated within the Egyptian culture between the twenty-fourth century BCE and the second century CE. Christos Karagiannis also considers ancient times. Basing his analysis on an Orthodox understanding of the litany and using Old Testament texts as source materials, the author considers how the procession of the Ark of the Covenant has evolved through the ages from the time of Israel's Exodus to the postexilic era, the latter beginning in the sixth century BCE. By focusing, *inter alia*, on the way the believers moved, as well as the music and the litanic recitation of psalms, Karagiannis draws a connection between the changes that appeared in the ritual and the time when the Jews became confirmed in their monolatrous convictions.

The studies listed above are restricted to individual cultural domains, that is to say Sumerian, Egyptian, Ugaritic and Jewish litanies are examined independently of Christian litanies, with an additional division along confessional lines in the case of the latter. In recent years, however, attempts have been made to examine all these cultural variants as part of a common developmental process, with research undertaken that covers at least five millennia. The resulting hypothesis concerning the origins and evolutionary paths of the litanic genre is the work of Witold Sadowski.[20] One of the most conspicuous features of the litanic form is its syncretic character, a feature which brings together various religions and which pertains to each and every culture. It may be understood in different ways, but is invariably based on prayer, albeit prayer carried out through various means. Seen from this perspective, the litany is the combination of a number of ritual practices, practices different in different religions yet with the most important channel of meditation undoubtedly being music.

---

[20] Sadowski (2018b), 113–76. The outline of this process can be found in an earlier work: Sadowski (2011), 25–68.

2. Litany and Music

Surprisingly, the musical dimension of the litany has been the least researched. Very few scholars, for example, have discussed the importance of the role of the musical aspect of the oldest preserved litanies of the Middle East. The article by Sam Mirelman in this volume is a valuable exception. Rather more work has been published on the relationship between music and litanies from the Middle Ages[21] and indeed subsequent epochs, yet this area has also received far less attention from scholars than it deserves.[22]

Perhaps one of the reasons for the limited scholarly interest in the litanies of the great composers from Early Modernity onwards was due to the fact that the litany did not belong to the musical genres most frequently chosen by, for example, Mozart or Schubert.[23] As a result, the most interesting studies focused on the history of liturgical music. Consequently, there is no shortage of references to the presence of the litany, for example, in the rituals of monastic orders and congregations, in examinations of individual works of both primary and secondary importance, as well as in critical editions based on manuscripts and printed volumes containing the litanies of various rites from different historical periods.[24] And yet, with certain exceptions, until now these studies have not developed into a systematic assessment of the role of the litany, either in the history of sacred music[25] – including liturgical song[26] – or in the history of secular music.

---

[21] Among the early medieval works that have been preserved are anonymous litanies, with the oldest musical notation being recorded in eleventh-century manuscripts.

[22] Two exceptions are worth mentioning. In his doctoral dissertation, Blazey (1990) examines and documents how the musical litany flourished in seventeenth-century Italy. Kendrick (2013), in turn, addresses various types of the litany in Italy, as well as in other Catholic countries of Europe and also America.

[23] The most prolific author of litanies who is known by both first and surname is probably Giovanni Pierluigi da Palestrina. See Roth (1959). The composers of musical litanies included Thomas Tallis, William Byrd, Claudio Monteverdi, Leopold Mozart, Wolfgang Amadeus Mozart, Franz Schubert, Franz Liszt, Camille Saint-Saëns, Stanisław Moniuszko (see Dąbek 2011), Karol Szymanowski, Sergey Rachmaninoff, and Arvo Pärt. There are also numerous references to the litanic convention in contemporary singer-songwriting (see George Brassens's *La prière*).

[24] For instance, litanies in the Ambrosian rite: see Baroffio, Kim (2008). Early litanic prayers of the Mozarabic rite with musical notes, referred to as *preces*-type litanies, have been preserved on the Iberian Peninsula (see Meyer 1914), as well as in France. Another issue is the litany in the Eastern rites (see, among others, Taft (1975), McFarland (2011)), as well as in the Protestant rites (see e.g. Fisher 2015).

[25] See e.g. Schanzlin (1959), 259–61.

[26] See e.g. Duncan (1920).

An important aspect of litanic studies, but unfortunately an aspect that is not always comprehensively researched, is the twofold verbal-musical structure of the litany. The researchers who focus on the relation between text and music[27] tend to give priority to one, rather than both, of these layers. An attempt to analyze the litanic textual and musical patterns was undertaken by Magdalena Maria Kubas, who in the main examined music through its relation to words. In certain cases Kubas also distinguished the litanic markers found exclusively in the musical layers of the analyzed works.[28]

Studies devoted to the relations between text and music in litanic works are also included in this volume. Mirelman's essay on Sumerian litanies has already been mentioned, with further musicologically-oriented contributions to the book discussed below.

In her article on the four medieval *conducti*, Mary Channen Caldwell attempts to locate litanic markers within the interrelationship between text and melody. In her analysis of the texts, particular attention is paid to its rhetorical aspects, yet in her analysis of the melody, Caldwell draws upon information derived from the visual representations in the codex. This enables an analysis of performative features that reflect a litanic repetitiveness not only in the music, but also in the medieval styles of sacred dance.

Another contributor, Magnus Williamson, provides an insight into English culture at a moment of transition by examining when the vernacular litany replaced the Latin litany. This is addressed within the context of the religious changes that occurred during the English Reformation in the reign of Henry VIII, and the subsequent Recatholization in the reign of Mary I Tudor. Williamson is also interested in when the earlier compositional techniques disappeared due to being superseded by the polyphonic liturgical song. His analysis reveals the importance of the polyphonic version of *Letania Major* by Thomas Tallis. Having traced the chronology of the preserved texts, Williamson posits a hypothesis that the work by Tallis might have inspired the litany composed by Antonio Cabezón, whose work was previously considered to have been the ground-breaking composition.

Karina Zybina presents a comparative analysis of Eucharistic litanies, starting with Giovanni Pierluigi da Palestrina and the 'golden age' of polyphony, through Jan Dismas Zelenka's compositions, before

---

[27] Szczurko (2017), 127–49; Wilkus (2016), 214–27.
[28] Kubas (2018), 48–51, 103–07, 279–304.

addressing the work of Wolfgang Amadeus Mozart. Zybina demonstrates that the examined works enter into various relations with the litanic text. Following the initial stage, in which the text was most strongly connected with the responsorial technique of singing and the singing revealed the text, the musical aspect of the genre became independent from the text. This change was accompanied by the emancipation of the instrumental dimension of the musical work and the development of innovative performative elements, elements introduced by Mozart.

Tiziana Palandrani's study, in turn, centres around the folk funeral song. Even though the funeral song and the litany should be seen as two independent branches of the tradition, the unique Sardinian ritual of monodic *attitos* is examined as it contains repetitive rhythmic, melodic and verbal patterns which are analogous to those of the litany. Another similarity between the litany and the *attitos* of Sardinia is that both conventions employ identical rhetorical figures, such as enumeration, anaphora, and epiphora, even though in the case of the latter, emphasis is placed on the improvisational character of the song. A considerable part of Palandrani's article is devoted to the importance and function of repetitiveness in Sardinian folk culture.

It is to be hoped that further systematic and cross-sectional studies concerning the place of the litany within the history of music may become the first step in an examination of the influence of the litany on other musical genres, as well as any cross-genre contamination. Such studies may also lead to a definition of the concept of the litany in music and delineating the specificity of litanic musical schemes, which frequently permeate particular works, regardless of their composer's intentions.

3. Litany and Poetry

Although the litany has had an undeniable impact upon poetry, until the beginning of the twenty-first century the research on their relations was as limited as that regarding the litany and music. One of the first scholars to emphasize the fact that literary critics show surprisingly little interest in the litany, despite a much greater interest on the part of the authors themselves, was Isabelle Krzywkowski, who focused specifically on French research tradition. In her view, Anglo-Saxon and German research was rather more advanced, even though its primary focus was also on the litany as a part of the church liturgy.[29] More than a decade later, Krzywkowski's conclusion is shared to a large extent by Sadowski.[30]

The reasons behind this oversight may perhaps be found in *a priori* assumptions, assumptions adopted by the researchers of both medieval and modern literature, according to which the litany was accused of 'aesthetic weakness',[31] and classified as an 'apoetical' form, i.e. one in which lyricism becomes 'impossible'.[32] Some researchers even claimed that the litany did not appear in poetry until the nineteenth century, with its most artistically valuable examples being found in contemporary literature:

> Vernacular litanies appear in German, Italian, Old French, late Old Norse, and Provençal, but they are rarely of any poetic value. One need only consider modern poetry [...] to realize that this structural device and excellent poetry are not irreconcilable. Medieval authors simply perceived it as sub–literary, fit for supplication in times of plague or the like, but not for other religious purposes.[33]

Researchers of the poetic litany also show a willingness to return to a basic, but somewhat well-worn distinction between the form of a given work and its theme.[34] Those who adopted this approach may be divided into two groups, both of which perceived the litany as a problematic phenomenon, albeit for different reasons.

Researchers who focused on the litanic form faced difficulties that resulted from the lack of a common model of the church litany, i.e. a model that might serve as an inspiration for the poetic litany. As has been mentioned above, in different religious traditions the same term, that is 'litany', is used with reference to different prayers, with the shape of these prayers, depending as it does on their addressee or addressees,

---

[29] Krzywkowski (2002), 65.

[30] Sadowski (2018b), 19.

[31] According to Diehl (1985), 109, the 'aesthetic weakness' of the litany lies in its 'additive or accumulative' dimension.

[32] Astier (1996), 233, 249. The researcher also focuses on the accumulation of the characteristic features of the addressees, as well as on the constant confirmation of their (omni)presence, which results in a silencing of the voice of the addressers and in consequence in their inability to speak for and about themselves.

[33] Diehl (1985), 109.

[34] Maraud (1994), 185: 'l'esprit'–'la forme'; Astier (1996), 235: 'la forme'–'le motif'; see also the following German studies: Schwens-Harrant (2015), 355; Rakusa (2016).

changing over the centuries. Consequently, the same researchers who unanimously acknowledged the paramount importance of the litanic form were unable to agree when it came to defining the phenomenon. For instance, while Krzywkowski delineated three rather general features of the litanic form, that is prayer, repetition, and enumeration,[35] José Fradejas Lebrero perceived the litanic form as a poetic-musical structure, in which each line, performed by a soloist, is followed by a collective chorus.[36] The 'litanic form' has also recently been examined by Jana Juhásová, who, drawing on the functions of such stylistic devices as enumeration and accumulation, distinguishes 'three qualities of the litanic form': 'demonstration of totality', 'feeling of excessive tautology, emptying of the contents', and 'accumulation of expressions, which [...] points to the insufficiency of the language'.[37]

Numerous difficulties are also experienced by those researchers who treat the litany primarily as a literary theme, with attempts to answer the question posed by Clément de Bourmont proving particularly problematic, namely: how is it possible to find a common theme in prayers designed for such a variety of purposes?[38] Therefore, regardless of whether the litany is examined from the perspective of form or theme, there are a wide range of different features contained in the works that do not necessarily relate directly to religious traditions. Among the most intriguing studies on the litany are those whose authors – taking genre concepts and structures as their starting point – perceive the litany as a vehicle for conveying an attitude towards the world and also to the sphere of sacrum in specific epochs. Two such studies on the litany are discussed below.

In the case of Krzywkowski, the main criterion behind her selection of research material is based on the choice of, firstly, poems which

---

[35] Krzywkowski (2002), 65–66. The status of 'prayer' in Krzywkowski's article is not clear: although the author mentions prayer as one of the basic formal components of the litany, she also distinguishes the litany from prayer and other forms like lamentation, canticle, and psalm (66). Krzywkowski's approach corresponds with André Maraud's suggestion that the rather general 'prayer' should be replaced with a division specific to the litany, namely the call and the supplication. Maraud (1994), 183: 'la forme des litanies combine étroitement l'énumération (avec la succession des apostrophes) et la répétition (avec le retour de la supplication).'

[36] Lebrero presents his ideas on the litany with reference to Spanish and Ibero-American literature, examining poetry (including folk poetry) as well as theatre in several articles, see Lebrero (1981), (1988), (1996), (1999), (2001), and (2003).

[37] Juhásová (2018), 210.

[38] Bourmont (1971), 141.

have 'litany' in their title, and secondly, poems which take the shape of the litany.[39] Her research addresses decadent poetry in French and English.[40] Having demonstrated the primary importance of the polemical approach to the sphere of sacrum in the examined works, works whose importance is manifested in such poetic choices as sacrum *à rebours* (e.g. a prostitute or Satan as the addressees of the prayers), syncretism (addressing the litany to Diana or Cupid), as well as parody, Krzywkowski comes to an interesting conclusion about 'the death of the form'. She notes that when the litany is deprived of its exalted form and conventional addressee, what remains is merely vestigial litanic traits, such as repetition and enumeration. In this way, the poetic creation of the litany is reduced to 'a formal work which does not produce any sense'.[41] Indeed, the researcher goes as far as to call it 'a machine to construct a text'.[42]

In the light of Sadowski's theory, developed within a framework of the literary genre theory and formed from studies covering a wide cultural range (from ancient prototypes of the litany to poems composed in modern European languages), as well as spanning a vast time period (from biblical times until the mid-nineteenth century), it is said that the litany is based on a 'three-gene model of the generic structure'.[43] The genes (or genre components) in question are: an ektenial gene, a chairetismic gene, and a polyonymic gene.[44] Simultaneously, the litany is equipped with a unifying factor that moves beyond the strictly formal

---

[39] Krzywkowski (2002), 63 (this fact is indicated by the words below from the beginning of her article: 'textes intitulés *Litanie*, ou qui se réfèrent formellement à ce modèle'). Krzywkowski's article finishes with an appendix, entitled 'Titrologie', and yet even in this section, the examined works are divided into two separate columns, one containing those whose title and form both refer to the litany; the second to those whose affinity with the litanic form is attested in the title only (88–90).

[40] The framework of the appendix covers the years 1857–1926 in chronological order.

[41] Krzywkowski (2002), 87. Translation by Sadowski.

[42] Other researchers make more nuanced claims. Juhásová, for instance, in her studies of twentieth-century Slovak poetry, presents two trends in the evolution of the litany: the first may be referred to as traditional, for through this trend the litanic form is revealed in religious works, such as psalms and hymns; the second is similar to the trend described by Krzywkowski, which aims at 'deforming literary forms' through techniques such as 'experiment', 'decomposition of the whole', 'permutation', and 'combination' (Juhásová (2018), 211).

[43] Sadowski (2018b), 458.

[44] Sadowski (2018b), 100–37.

aspects of the work. As noted by Sadowski, 'the key factor in the tradition of litanic verse seems to lie in the generic worldview which results from a coherent vision of the litanic space-time'.[45] Accordingly, 'the perception of the concentric space-time is mirrored in the rhetorical devices characteristic of the litany [...], such as enumeration, parallelism, anaphoras and refrains'.[46] The stylistic devices enumerated above are treated as the qualities necessary for litanic verse in the numerous studies edited by Sadowski, studies whose scope extends over a significant part of European culture and includes the following literatures: French,[47] Italian,[48] Irish,[49] English,[50] Scottish,[51] Catalan,[52] Galician,[53] Spanish,[54] Portugal,[55] German,[56] Austrian,[57] Danish,[58] Norwegian,[59] Swedish,[60] Russian,[61]

---

[45] Sadowski (2018b), 457.

[46] Sadowski (2018b), 457.

[47] A volume devoted entirely to French poetry was written by Kowalska (2018). See also articles on French litanic verse: in the form of *lai* (Kowalska 2016), in sonnets (Kowalska 2017a), in Jules Laforgue's litany-poems (Sadowski 2016a) and in litanic paraphrases (Kowalska 2017b).

[48] A volume devoted entirely to Italian poetry from the Middle Ages until the 1930s was written by Kubas (2018); see also her detailed accounts of the litanic verse in *lauda*, such as Kubas (2015), (2016a), (2017a), in sonnets: Kubas (2017c) as well as in modern poetic genres: Kubas (2016b) and (2017b).

[49] Sadowski (2018b), 199–224. The researcher refers to Wright (1993), amongst others.

[50] Czarnowus (2016b) and (2016c); Ruszkiewicz (2016a) and (2016b); Dudek (2016), Czarnowus (2016a).

[51] Ruszkiewicz (2016a).

[52] Piłat-Zuzankiewicz (2016d); Woźniak (2016d).

[53] Piłat-Zuzankiewicz (2016d); Woźniak (2016d).

[54] Piłat-Zuzankiewicz (2016b), (2016c) and (2018); Woźniak (2016b) and (2016c). See also studies on the litanic verse in the poetic work of individual authors, such as Lope de Vega (Piłat-Zuzankiewicz 2016a), Miguel de Cervantes (Piłat-Zuzankiewicz 2017), and Juan Ramón Jiménez (Woźniak 2016a).

[55] Piłat-Zuzankiewicz (2016d); Woźniak (2016d).

[56] Fijałkowski (2016); Wantuch (2016a) and (2016b).

[57] Wantuch (2016b).

[58] Cymbrykiewicz, Wilkus and Zańko (2016); Cymbrykiewicz and Zańko (2016). See Cymbrykiewicz, Wilkus and Zańko (2015).

[59] Cymbrykiewicz, Wilkus and Zańko (2016); Wilkus (2016). See Cymbrykiewicz, Wilkus and Zańko (2015).

[60] Żmuda-Trzbiatowska (2016a), (2016b) and (2016c).

[61] Głażewski (2016).

Croatian,[62] Serbian,[63] Bulgarian,[64] Czech,[65] Hungarian[66] and Polish.[67] It is worth mentioning that the literatures examined also include cultures previously disregarded by earlier researchers as they were viewed as being of little interest in the context of poetic litany, as seen in Diehl's words quoted above,[68] cultures which in fact yielded abundant research material. Additionally, the scope of the studies with regard to the time periods covered, allowed the possibility to reconsider certain assumptions. For instance, one of the ideas questioned was a belief that exceptional achievements in the field of poetic litany did not appear until after the publication of the outrageously shocking litany in Charles Baudelaire's *Les Fleurs du mal* (1857).

4. Litany and Visual Arts

Some of the works analyzed in the studies on litanic verse revealed that their origins could be viewed as a relationship between literature and the visual arts. We have seen, for instance, litanic verse written after the author was inspired by a religious painting or a cathedral. This reminds us that the impact of the litany on various aspects of culture is not restricted to music and poetry, but also extends to other fields of art, the tradition of this relationship having a very old provenance.

Information concerning the dissemination of the litanic form in the visual arts can be found as early as certain classic studies on the place of the litany in the liturgy, studies written by Ernst Kantorowicz[69] and Mi-

---

[62] Prałat (2016c).
[63] Prałat (2016a).
[64] Prałat (2016b).
[65] Gorczyńska (2016).
[66] Czövek (2016).
[67] Sadowski (2011) and (2016b).
[68] Cultures, such as Old French and Provençal, were examined for the presence of litanic verse by Kowalska (2018). Kowalska's studies challenge the arguments concerning the exclusively accumulative, and thereby unsophisticated nature, of the old litanies (see the wealth of forms and genres examined in the first part of the book, e.g. *miracle*, *lai*, *dit*, Kowalska (2018), 25–110) and the unique role of decadent poetry. In fact, in French poetry, litanic verse appears frequently and is a constantly developing form that has experienced only short periods in which its popularity declined. Additionally, in the second half of the nineteenth century, litanic verse was appropriated by the revived tradition of Occitan poetry; see Kowalska (2018), 331–42.
[69] Kantorowicz (1946), 48. The author evokes Osieczkowska's study (1934).

chael Lapidge.[70] Kantorowicz examined three Byzantine ivory triptychs dating from 1521, which 'display a so-called Déesis', and 'represent a solemn suffrage, probably for the ruler, a suffrage in form of a Litany of Saints'.[71] However, the earliest visual representations of the litany in the Western world can be dated to long before the Renaissance. The oldest include the engravings on the coffin of Saint Cuthbert (died in the seventh century), which have been referred to by Ernst Kitzinger as a 'litany in pictures, invoking the protection of those represented for the relics inside',[72] as well as the miniatures in the Athelstan Psalter (dating from the tenth century), in which not only 'the choirs [...] are labelled with litanic formula *Omnis chorus angelorum*', but also 'the placement of these pictures suggest a litanic significance'. Since in the psalter 'the sequence of prayers approximates the order of the saints in a litany', the miniatures may be regarded as 'pictorial translations of the litany of the saints'.[73]

The researchers mentioned above played a fundamental role in the development of litanic studies and paved the way for later scholars. However, without doubt the most popular litany within the field of visual arts is the Marian litany. Ever since the publication of the chapter 'La Vierge entourée des symboles des litanies', written by the art historian Émile Mâle,[74] which appeared in a volume that was crucially important for French sacral art studies, research has been conducted on images of the Blessed Virgin Mary surrounded by the symbols from the *Litany of Loreto*, such as the engravings included in the earliest printed *Little Office*. It is believed that the first representation of this theme is to be found in Thielman Kerver's edition dating from 1 December, 1502.[75] Further vital work was conducted by Carme López Calderón, who estimates that the first emblem-decorated litany appeared in 1636.[76] The iconography of the Marian litany in Spanish art, in turn, particularly in the historic buildings of Granada, was examined by José Antonio Peinado Guzmán, including in his doctoral dissertation (2011), in which he considers information obtained from more than a dozen representations

[70] Lapidge (1991), 59–60.
[71] Kantorowicz (1942).
[72] Kitzinger (1956), 228–80.
[73] Deshman (1974), 176–79.
[74] Mâle (1908).
[75] Delaunay (2005), 30.
[76] López Calderon (2010–2012) and (2016); Montero (2004).

of the *Litany of Loreto* on the vaults and altars of the monuments of Granada, representations dating mainly from the eighteenth century.[77] The same artistic phenomenon, which was also developed in the Hauts-de-France region, was presented in a popular academic publication by Léa Vernier,[78] in which representations of the Marian litany in stained glass, sculpture and engravings are analyzed. However, it appears that this area of research was pioneered by Lionel Bataillon, whose studies centered on Norman works of art.[79]

Among the studies that do not primarily focus on the Marian litany, a late nineteenth-century work about the hierarchy of the litanic addressees in medieval painting[80] should be mentioned. This issue is also addressed by Sadowski, who underlines that both stained-glass windows and mosaics in Byzantine semi-circular vaults depict the same vision of a hierarchical and concentric space-time as found in the litany.[81] An entirely new direction of research is introduced by a study in this volume, a study undertaken by Jenny Ponzo, Francesco Galofaro and Gabriele Marino. Drawing on a repertoire of semiotic instruments, the researchers base their conclusions on a comparative analysis of the litany from three perspectives: when recited during contemporary public religious ceremonies within a specific sacred space (e.g. a circular crypt in a modern temple); nineteenth- and twentieth-century reflections on individual meditations and also interpretations in YouTube video files that were accessed after entering the term 'litanies of the saints' into the search field. The authors note that the recorded meditations, produced after the period in which the performance of particular litanies was accepted during public ceremonies, reveal a personal understanding of the litany, whereas the videos posted on the YouTube website testify to individual associations with particular fragments of the prayer, associations that are not infrequently surprising.

Even though as a whole the results of these studies reveal a diversity of artistic trends and tendencies that were inspired by the litany, a monograph dedicated to reflections on the litany in the various disciplines of the visual arts is yet to be written.

[77] Peinado Guzmán (2011), 1027–52. See also Peinado Guzmán (2015).
[78] Vernier (2013). The study also includes bibliography on the Marian litany in art.
[79] Bataillon (1923).
[80] Haseloff (1897).
[81] Sadowski (2018b), 247–53; see Sadowski (2016c) and (2018a).

Bibliography

Astier, C. (1996) 'Le lyrisme impossible, poésie et litanies,' in D. Rabaté, J. de Sermet, Y. Vadé (eds), *Le Sujet lyrique en question*, Bordeaux, 234–51.

Baroffio, G., Kim, E. J. (eds) (2008) *«Antiphonarium letaniarum» ambrosiano del 1492. Milano, Biblioteca dell'Università Cattolica del Sacro Cuore. Manoscritto UC MS 5*, Lucca.

Bataillon, L. (1923) *Les symboles des Litanies et l'iconographie de la Vierge en Normandie au XVIe siècle*, Paris.

Baumstark, A. (1906) *Die Messe im Morgenland*, Kempten.

— (1904) 'Eine syrisch–melchitische Allerheiligenlitanei,' *Oriens Christianus* 4.

Bishop, E. (1918) 'The Litany of Saints in the Stowe Missal,' in Idem, *Liturgica Historica: Papers on the Liturgy and Religious Life of the Western Church*, Oxford, 137–64.

Blazey, D. A. (1990) 'The Litany in the Seventeenth–century Italy' [unpublished doctoral dissertation, Durham University].

Bourmont, C. de (1971) 'Fonction et expression des prières d'intercession,' *La Maison–Dieu: cahiers de pastorale liturgique* 105, 134–49.

Cabrol, F. (1930) 'Litanies,' in Idem et al. (eds), *Dictionnaire d'archéologie chrétienne et de liturgie*, Vol. IX 2, Paris, 1540–1571.

Calderon, C. L. (2010–2012) '*Magna Dei Parens ac Virgo Maria est*: La apología mariana a través de la emblemática en una letanía seiscentista,' *Revista da Faculdade de Letras, Ciências e Técnicas do Património* 9–11, 82–107.

— (2016) 'Letanías emblemáticas: símbolos marianos de maternidad, virginidad y mediación en la Edad Moderna,' in J. Aranda Doncel, R. de la Campa Carmona (eds), *Regina Mater Misericordiae. Estudios históricos, artísticos y antropológicos de advocaciones marianas*, Córdoba, 413–30.

Chrulska, E. (2016) 'Litanic Verse in Latin,' in W. Sadowski, M. Kowalska, M. M. Kubas (eds), *Litanic Verse I. Origines, Iberia, Slavia et Europa Media*, Frankfurt am Main, 91–126.

Coens, M. (1936) 'Anciennes litanies des saints,' *Analecta Bollandiana* 54.

Cuva, A. (2006) 'Strutture litaniche negli attuali libri liturgici del rito romano,' *Salesianum* 67, no. 2, 335–64.

Cymbrykiewicz, J., Wilkus, A., Zańko, A. (2015) '"Stemmer, der veksler" — nogle bemærkninger om det dansk-norske litanidigt som fænomen fra middelalderen til 1600–tallet,' *Nordica* 32, 429–44.

— (2016) 'Litany Undercover: Denmark and Norway from the Middle Ages to the Eighteenth Century,' in W. Sadowski, M. Kowalska, M. M. Kubas (eds), *Litanic Verse I. Origines, Iberia, Slavia et Europa Media*, Frankfurt am Main, 181–96.

Cymbrykiewicz, J., Zańko, A. (2016) 'Litany in Retreat: Denmark from Romanticism to the 1930,' in W. Sadowski, M. Kowalska, M. M. Kubas (eds), *Litanic Verse I. Origines, Iberia, Slavia et Europa Media*, Frankfurt am Main, 197–211.

Czarnowus, A. (2016a) 'Litanic Verse in "Of on that is so fayr and bright" and the Harley Ms "The Five Joys of Mary",' *Terminus* 18 (1), 1–16.

— (2016b) '"Hail! The Heaven–born Prince of Peace!": The Eighteenth-Century and Romanticism in England,' in W. Sadowski, M. Kowalska, M. M. Kubas (eds), *Litanic Verse II. Britannia, Germania et Scandinavia*, Frankfurt am Main, 87–106.

— (2016c) '"That order of apostles is widely honoured by the nations": Pre–Chaucerian English Poetry,' in W. Sadowski, M. Kowalska, M. M. Kubas (eds), *Litanic Verse II. Britannia, Germania et Scandinavia*, Frankfurt am Main, 9–30.

Czövek, A. (2016) '"I gave night music to my heart from which deep litanies pealed": Hungarian Poetry,' in W. Sadowski, M. Kowalska, M. M. Kubas (eds), *Litanic Verse I. Origines, Iberia, Slavia et Europa Media*, Frankfurt am Main, 303–21.

Dąbek, S. (2011) *Twórczość litanijna Stanisława Moniuszki i jej konteksty*, Warszawa.

Delaunay, I. (2005) 'Le livre d'heures parisien aux premiers temps de l'imprimé (1485–1500),' *Gazette du livre médiéval* 46, 22–36.

Deshman, R. (1974) 'Anglo–Saxon Art after Alfred,' *The Art Bulletin* 56 (2), 176–200.

Diehl, P. S., (1985) *The Medieval European Religious Lyric. An Ars Poetica*, Berkeley.

Duchesne, L. (1904) *Christian Worship: Its Origin and Evolution. A Study of the Latin Liturgy up to the Time of Charlemagne*, London.

Dudek, K. (2016) 'Our Lady of Controversy: Defamiliarization of Litanic Verse in England between 1837 and 1937,' in W. Sadowski, M. Kowalska, M. M. Kubas (eds), *Litanic Verse II. Britannia, Germania et Scandinavia*, Frankfurt am Main, 107–32.

Duncan, J. M. (1920) 'The Preces, Responses, and Litany of the English Church: A By–Way of Liturgical History,' *The Musical Times* 932, 692–94.

Fijałkowski, M. (2016) 'From Merseburger Charms to Minnesang: The German Middle Ages,' in W. Sadowski, M. Kowalska, M. M. Kubas (eds), *Litanic Verse II. Britannia, Germania et Scandinavia*, Frankfurt am Main, 135–46.

Fisher, A. J. (2015) 'Thesaurus Litaniarum: the Symbolism and Practice of Musical Litanies in Counter-Reformation Germany,' *Early Music History* 34, 45–95.

Gabbay, U. (2014) *Pacifying the Hearts of the Gods: Sumerian Emesal Prayers of the First Millennium BC*, Wiesbaden.

Głażewski, J. (2016) 'A Separate World: Russian Poetry Between the Native and the Universal,' in W. Sadowski, M. Kowalska, M. M. Kubas (eds), *Litanic Verse I. Origines, Iberia, Slavia et Europa Media*, Frankfurt am Main, 265–82.

Gorczyńska, M. (2016) '"Krleš! Krleš! Krleš!". Litany and its Derivatives in Czech Literature to the 1930s,' in W. Sadowski, M. Kowalska, M. M. Kubas (eds), *Litanic Verse I. Origines, Iberia, Slavia et Europa Media*, Frankfurt am Main, 285–301.

Guzmán, J. A. P. (2011) 'Controversia teológica. Devoción popular. Expresión plástica: La Inmaculada Concepción en Granada' [unpublished doctoral dissertation, Universidad de Granada], 1027–52: http://o-hera.ugr.es.adrastea.ugr.es/tesisugr/2009937x.pdf.

— (2015) 'Simbología de las letanías lauretanas y su casuística en el arzobispado de Granada,' in J. A. P. Guzmán, M. del Amor Rodríguez Miranda (eds), *Lecciones barrocas: "aunando miradas"*, Córdoba, 159–90.

Haseloff, A. (1897) *Arthur Eine thüringisch–sächsische Malerschule des 13. Jahrhunderts*, Strasburg.

Heinemann, J. (1977) *Prayer in the Talmud*, Berlin and New York.

Juhásová, J. (2018) *Litanická forma od avantgardy po súčasnosť*, Ružomberok.

Jungmann, J. A. (1952) *Missarum Sollemnia. Eine genetische Erklärung der römischen Messe*, Wien.

— (1969) *Christliches Beten in Wandel und Bestand*, München.

Kantorowicz, E. (1942) 'Ivories and litanies,' *Journal of the Warburg and Courtauld Institutes* 5, 56–81.

— (1946) *Laudes Regiae: A Study in Liturgical Acclamations and Medieval Ruler Worship*, Berkeley and Los Angeles.

Kendrick, R. L. (2013) 'Litanies and their texts, 1600–1700,' in A. Addamiano, F. Luisi (eds), *Atti del Congresso Internazionale di Musica Sacra. In occasione del centenario di fondazione del PIMS, Roma, 26 maggio – 1 giugno 2011*, Roma, 703–10.

Kitzinger, E. (1956) 'The Coffin–Reliquary,' in C. F. Battiscombe (ed.), *The Relics of Saint Cuthbert*, Oxford, 228–80.

Kowalska, M. (2016) 'La forme de la litanie comme cadre: le cas du lai et d'autres genres littéraires médiévaux,' *Zagadnienia Rodzajów Literackich* 59 (2), 31–49.

— (2017a) 'Litanies of a Name. The Holy Name of Jesus in the Sonnets of Anne de Marquets and Gabrielle de Coignard,' *Journal of Academic Perspectives* 2017 (2).

— (2017b) 'Prière litanique — litanie poétique. Les paraphrases françaises jusqu'au XIXe siècle,' *Romanica Olomucensia* 29 (2), 223–34.

— (2018) *Litanic Verse III: Francia*, Berlin.

Krzywkowski, I. (2002) 'La litanie: une écriture sans fin de la fin,' in I. Krzywkowski, S. Thorel-Cailleteau (eds), *Anamorphoses décadentes. L'Art de la défiguration 1880–1914. Études offertes à Jean de Palacio*, Paris, 63–90.

Kubas, M. M. (2015) 'Litania come strategia retorica nelle *Laudi* del Bianco da Siena,' *Bullettino Senese di Storia Patria*, 76–90.

— (2016a) 'Forme e legame litanici in alcune laude mariane del Duecento,' in A. Pioletti, S. Rapisarda (eds), *Forme letterarie del Medioevo romanzo: testo, interpretazione e storia*, Soveria Mannelli, 255–70.

— (2016b) 'Un contrappunto visivo-sonoro: l'anafora metrica e sintattica ne 'La Libellula' rosselliana,' *Quaderni del '900* 16, 61–72.

— (2017a) 'Liturgia, preghiera e lauda spirituale nel libretto di *Betulia Liberata*,' *Studi sul Settecento e l'Ottocento* 12, 93–102.

— (2017b) '"Io ti percorro": gli spazi del misticismo di Alda Merini,' in S. Sgavicchia, M. Tortora (eds), *Geografie della modernità letteraria. Atti del XVII Convegno Internazionale della MOD 10–13 giugno 2015*, Pisa, vol. 1, 307–18.

— (2017c) 'La ripetizione anaforica nel sonetto boccaccesco,' in S. Zamponi (ed.), *Intorno a Boccaccio. Boccaccio e dintorni 2016. Atti del Seminario internazionale di studi (Certaldo Alta, Casa di Giovanni Boccaccio, 9 settembre 2016)*, Firenze, 51–63.

— (2018) *Litanic Verse IV: Italia*, Berlin.

Lapidge, M. (1991) *Anglo-Saxon Litanies of the Saints*, London.

Lebrero, J. F. (1981) 'La forma litánica hasta Berceo,' in C. G. Turza (ed.), *Actas de las III Jornadas de Estudios Bercanos*, Logroño, 63–72.

— (1988) *La forma litánica en la poesía popular*, Madrid.

— (1996) 'La forma litánica en la poesía del siglo XX,' *Revista de literatura* 58, no. 116, 399–425.

— (1999) 'La forma litánica en el mundo islámico,' in *Melanges Maria Soledad Carrasco Urgoiti*, Zaghouan, vol. 1, 37–44.
— (2001) 'La forma litánica en el teatro: Siglos XVI–XVIII,' *Revista de filología española* 81, 89–135.
— (2003) 'La forma litánica en Iberoamérica,' *Mar oceana: Revista del humanismo español e iberoamericano* 13, 41–56.
Łesyk, L. B. (2016) 'Byzantine Liturgical Litany,' in W. Sadowski, M. Kowalska, M. M. Kubas (eds), *Litanic Verse I. Origines, Iberia, Slavia et Europa Media*, Frankfurt am Main, 73–90.
Mâle, E. (1908) *L'Art religieux de la fin du Moyen Âge en France; étude sur l'iconographie du Moyen Âge et sur ses sources d'inspiration*, Paris.
Maraud, A. (1994) 'Litanies, rimes, refrain,' in S. Chaouachi, A. Montandon (eds), *La Répétition*, Clermont–Ferrand, 181–201.
McFarland, J. (2011). *Announcing the Feast: The Entrance Song in the Mass of the Roman Rite*, Colegeville, Minn.
Meersseman, G. G. (1958–1960) *Der Hymnos Akathistos im Abendland*, Volumes I-II, Freiburg.
Meyer, W. (1914) *Die Preces der mozarabischen Liturgie*, Berlin.
Montero, J. M. M. (2004) 'Emblemática e iconografía mariana. Imágenes emblemáticas de la Litaniae Lauretanae de Francisco Xavier Dornn,' in S. López Poza (ed.), *Florilegio de estudios de emblemática*, Santiago de Compostela, 541–52.
Morgan, N. J. (2012–2018) *English Monastic Litanies of the Saints After 1100*, Volumes I, II, III, London.
Osieczkowska, C. (1934) 'La mosaïque de la porte royale à Sainte–Sophie de Constantinople et la litanie de tous saints,' *Byzantion* 9, 41–83.
Piłat–Zuzankiewicz, M. (2016a) 'Tradición litánica en la obra de Lope de Vega,' *Hipogrifo. Revista de literatura y cultura del Siglo de Oro* 4 (2), 301–26.
— (2016b) 'Religious Poetry, *Religio Amoris* and Panegyric Poetry in Spain before the End of the Fifteenth Century,' in W. Sadowski, M. Kowalska, M. M. Kubas (eds), *Litanic Verse I. Origines, Iberia, Slavia et Europa Media*, Frankfurt am Main, 129–42.
— (2016c) 'Castilian Poetry and Autos Sacramentales during the Sixteenth and Seventeenth Centuries,' in W. Sadowski, M. Kowalska, M. M. Kubas (eds), *Litanic Verse I. Origines, Iberia, Slavia et Europa Media*, Frankfurt am Main, 143–56.
— (2016d) 'Praise, Litany and Cantigas: Catalonian, Galician–Portuguese and Portuguese Poetry up to the End of the Seventeenth

Century,' in W. Sadowski, M. Kowalska, M. M. Kubas (eds), *Litanic Verse I. Origines, Iberia, Slavia et Europa Media*, Frankfurt am Main, 157–67.

— (2017) 'Letanías poéticas en la obra de Miguel de Cervantes,' in M. Piłat-Zuzankiewicz (ed.), *En torno a Cervantes: Estudios sobre la época y la obra del autor del Quijote. Homenaje al Profesor Kazimierz Sabik*, Warszawa, 381–99.

— (2018) 'La estructura de chairetismo y polionimia en la tradición litúrgica y paralitúrgica mariana y sus huellas en la literatura religiosa hispana (siglos VII–XVII),' *'Ilu. Revista de Ciencias de las Religiones* 23, 239–62.

Prałat, E. (2016a) '"From besmeared lips, from hating heart, from unclean tongue": Writing and Rewriting of the Canon in Serbia,' in W. Sadowski, M. Kowalska, M. M. Kubas (eds), *Litanic Verse I. Origines, Iberia, Slavia et Europa Media*, Frankfurt am Main, 221–34.

— (2016b), '"The Words that feeds hungry human souls, the Word that gives power to your mind and heart": Bulgaria from Clement of Ohrid to the "September Literature" Circle,' in W. Sadowski, M. Kowalska, M. M. Kubas (eds), *Litanic Verse I. Origines, Iberia, Slavia et Europa Media*, Frankfurt am Main, 235–51.

— (2016c) '"Oh the blessed one, oh the most holy one, oh elevated above all the blessed ones": Litanic Patterns and Folk Inspirations on Croatian Poetry,' in W. Sadowski, M. Kowalska, M. M. Kubas (eds), *Litanic Verse I. Origines, Iberia, Slavia et Europa Media*, Frankfurt am Main, 251–64.

Rakusa, I. (2016) *Listen, Litaneien, Loops – zwischen poetischer Anrufung und Inventur*, München.

Roth, J. (1959) *Die mehrstimmigen lateinischen Litaneikompositionen des 16. Jahrhunderts*, Regensburg.

Ruszkiewicz, D. (2016a) '"O Lord, deliver us from trusting in those prayers": Early Modern England,' in W. Sadowski, M. Kowalska, M. M. Kubas (eds), *Litanic Verse II. Britannia, Germania et Scandinavia*, Frankfurt am Main, 51–86.

— (2016b) '"Thy name I sall ay nevyne": Fifteenth–Century England and Scotland,' in W. Sadowski, M. Kowalska, M. M. Kubas (eds), *Litanic Verse II. Britannia, Germania et Scandinavia*, Frankfurt am Main, 31–50.

Sadowski, W. (2011) *Litania i poezja. Na materiale literatury polskiej od XI do XXI wieku*. Warszawa.

— (2013) 'Prosodic Memory: Claudel – Eliot – Liebert,' *Prace Filologiczne. Literaturoznawstwo* 3(6), 11–30.
— (2016a) 'Le texte en dialogue avec son genre. Les litanies de Laforgue,' *Poétique* 179, 89–107.
— (2016b) 'Polish Litanic Verse until 1939. An Outside Perspective,' in W. Sadowski, M. Kowalska, M. M. Kubas (eds), *Litanic Verse I. Origines, Iberia, Slavia et Europa Media*, Frankfurt am Main, 323–46.
— (2016c) 'Wiersz litanijny w przekładzie na obraz,' in A. Stankowska, M. Telicki (eds), *Ikonoklazm i ikonofilia: Między historią a współczesnością*, Poznań, 61–72.
— (2018a) 'A Generic Woldview: The Case of the Chronotope of Litany,' in R. M. Erdbeer, F. Kläger, and K. Stierstorfer (eds), *Literarische Form: Theorien – Dynamiken – Kulturen. Beiträge zur literarischen Modellforschung*, Heidelberg, 347–74.
— (2018b) *European Litanic Verse. A Different Space–Time*, Berlin.
Schanzlin, H. P. (1959) 'Zur Geschichte der Litanei im 17. Jahrundert,' in A. von Gerald, S. Clercx–Lejeune, H. Federhofer, W. Pfannkuch (eds), *Bericht über den siebenten Internationalen Musikwissenschaftlichen Kongress Köln 1958*, Kassel, 259–61.
Schermann, T. (1903) 'Griechische Litaneien,' *Römische Quartalschrift für christliche Altertumskunde und für Kirchengeschichte* 17, 333–38.
Schwens–Harrant, B. (2015) 'Literatur als Litanei,' in T. Lörke, R. Walter–Jochum (eds), *Religion und Literatur im 20. und 21. Jahrhundert*, Göttingen, 353–66.
Szczurko, E. (2017) 'Litania do Marii Panny Jerzego Lieberta w kantacie Karola Szymanowskiego,' *Pro Musica Sacra* 15, 127–49.
Taft, R. (1975) *The Great Entrance. A History of the Transfer of Gifts and other Pre–anaphoral Rites of the Liturgy of St. John Chrysostom*, Roma.
— (1977) 'The Evolution of the Byzantine "Divine Liturgy",' *Orientalia Christiana Periodica* 43.
Taft, R., Winkler, G. (eds), (2001) *Acts of International Congress of Comparative Liturgy Fifty Years After Anton Baumstark (1872–1948)*, Roma.
Toboła, Ł. (2016a) '*In principio erat enumeratio*: The Origins of Litanic Patterns in the Ancient Near East,' in W. Sadowski, M. Kowalska, M. M. Kubas (eds), *Litanic Verse I. Origines, Iberia, Slavia et Europa Media*, Frankfurt am Main, 15–27.
— (2016b) 'Looking for the Origins of Biblical Litanies: the Hymn of Three Youths in Daniel 3: 52–90[deut],' in W. Sadowski, M. Kowalska,

M. M. Kubas (eds), *Litanic Verse I. Origines, Iberia, Slavia et Europa Media*, Frankfurt am Main, 29–39.

— (2016c) 'Three Short Litany-Like Texts from Ugarit: Translation and Commentary,' in W. Sadowski, M. Kowalska, M. M. Kubas (eds), *Litanic Verse I. Origines, Iberia, Slavia et Europa Media*, Frankfurt am Main, 41–49.

Wantuch, E. (2016a) 'Pietist Litanies in German Seventeenth- and Eighteenth-Century Poetry. The Case of Friedrich Gottlieb Klopstock,' in W. Sadowski, M. Kowalska, M. M. Kubas (eds), *Litanic Verse II. Britannia, Germania et Scandinavia*, Frankfurt am Main, 147–60.

— (2016b) '"You are the harp on which the player breaks in pieces": German and Austrian Poetry between 1797 and 1914,' in W. Sadowski, M. Kowalska, M. M. Kubas (eds), *Litanic Verse II. Britannia, Germania et Scandinavia*, Frankfurt am Main, 161–79.

Wilkus, A. (2016) '"Norway, Norway..." From the End of the Eighteenth to the Beginning of the Twentieth Century,' in W. Sadowski, M. Kowalska, M. M. Kubas (eds), *Litanic Verse II. Britannia, Germania et Scandinavia*, Frankfurt am Main, 214–27.

Woźniak, M. J. (2016a), 'Entre tradición y modernidad: modificaciones del poema litánico en la poesía de Juan Ramón Jiménez,' *Neophilologus* 3, 1–12.

— (2016b) 'On the Trail of Litany in Catalan, Galician, and Portuguese Poetry from the Eighteenth Century to the 1930s,' in W. Sadowski, M. Kowalska, M. M. Kubas (eds), *Litanic Verse I. Origines, Iberia, Slavia et Europa Media*, Frankfurt am Main, 197–204.

— (2016c) '"Thou, the most beautiful; thou, in whom the pink morning star shines": Castilian Poetry in the Eighteenth Century,' in W. Sadowski, M. Kowalska, M. M. Kubas (eds), *Litanic Verse I. Origines, Iberia, Slavia et Europa Media*, Frankfurt am Main, 171–81.

— (2016d) '"I do not know the name": Castilian Poetry from the Nineteenth Century to the 1930s,' in W. Sadowski, M. Kowalska, M. M. Kubas (eds), *Litanic Verse I. Origines, Iberia, Slavia et Europa Media*, Frankfurt am Main, 183–96.

Vélez Marín, M. (1758) *Dissertación sobre las letanías antiguas de la Iglesia de España*, Madrid.

Vernier, L. (2013) *Les litanies de la Vierge – dossier de présentation*, https://inventaire.hautsdefrance.fr/dossier/les-litanies-de-la-vierge-dossier-de-presentation/acf2580e-f240-405b-85d4-0a126f11010b.

Żmuda-Trzebiatowska, M. (2016a) 'Litany in Swedish Literature and Culture: Preliminary Remarks,' in W. Sadowski, M. Kowalska,

M. M. Kubas (eds), *Litanic Verse II. Britannia, Germania et Scandinavia*, Frankfurt am Main, 229–30.
— (2016b) 'Transformations of Litany in Swedish Poetry: From the Middle Ages to the Modern Breakthrough (1100–1879),' in W. Sadowski, M. Kowalska, M. M. Kubas (eds), *Litanic Verse II. Britannia, Germania et Scandinavia*, Frankfurt am Main, 231–41.
— (2016c) '"Why would you have to say a litany of your soul": Swedish and Swedish-Language Poetry in the Period 1879–1940,' in W. Sadowski, M. Kowalska, M. M. Kubas (eds), *Litanic Verse II. Britannia, Germania et Scandinavia*, Frankfurt am Main, 243–55.
— (2016d) 'På spaning efter en halvglömd genre: Litaniaminnen i "Bön till solen" av Karin Boye,' *Folia Scandinavica Posnaniensa* 19, 279–90.

Roland Enmarch

LITANIES IN ANCIENT EGYPTIAN WRITTEN CULTURE

The modern discipline of Egyptology sprang in the nineteenth century AD from the European cultural tradition. Early Egyptologists applied the term 'litany' to a range of texts in the realm of Ancient Egyptian culture which reminded them of the features of litanies known from the European tradition.[1] Working primarily from a European cultural context, Witold Sadowski has suggested that the 'litany' genre can be characterized more generally as texts (originally with a ritual compositional origin), marked by one or more of the following:[2]

1. repetitive elements such as anaphor (either as second-person apostrophe or third-person description)
2. a series of supplications, possibly as part of responsorial dialogue
3. repeated invocations of an (often divine) individual under many appellations.

The defining features of litany cross-culturally are thus not primarily dependent on prosody (the nature of which in Egyptian written culture remains contested),[3] but rather on semantic and verbal structure.[4]

---

[1] For an overview, see Assmann (1980), 1062–66.

[2] Sadowski (2016), 11.

[3] For an overview of differing suggested reconstructions of Egyptian prosody, see e.g. Burkard (2003), 207–20. The rhythms and possible metre of litanies and anaphoric poems have been discussed by Patanè (1983a and 1983b) and Mathieu (1994).

[4] Assmann (1969), 90, argues that the basic structure of Egyptian litany is the accretion of nominal and participial forms used appositionally, as names and epithets in an invocation or address. This definition works well for some offering litanies (*wdnw*),

Some of the features listed above are found commonly throughout the whole of Ancient Egyptian written culture, and many of these instances have little overlap with litanies as attested in other cultures. Repetitive syntactic structures, accompanied by variation of lexicon (*parallelismus membrorum*), were fundamental compositional techniques of Egyptian refined language,[5] and the use of repeated refrains (most usually anaphoric) is attested both within ritual texts, and well beyond them. Even within the realm of Egyptian ritual language, two basic rhetorical compositional forms are *proclamation* (where a god is identified under many guises, which in hymns serves to expound knowledge of royal/divine power), and *glorification* (expressed as wishes to the divine addressee, including what might be called 'supplications' on behalf of the ritual performer or other beneficiaries).[6]

1. Divine Names and Cult-topography in Offering Litanies

The primary context for Egyptian litanies was as a part of offering rituals in temple cult liturgies (often subsequently adapted for funerary use). Deities are offered to under varying names and cult-place specific epithets, all introduced simply with the preposition *n* 'to/for'.[7] These offering litanies were referred to by the Ancient Egyptian genre term *wdnw*, which simply means 'offering'.[8] At their very simplest, these are lists of divine names (e.g. 'to Shu, to Tefnut, to Geb, to Nut'). More frequently, however, they are elaborated by each name being combined with a specific cultic toponym in which the deity is being offered to, especially when the litany encompasses multiple forms of the same deity (e.g. 'to

---

but is less applicable to the more elaborate anaphoric strophic ritual texts, which are typically framed more as verbal actions (exhortatory or supplicatory wishes to a being or beings under a variety of names).

[5] Guglielmi (1996); Moers (2007).

[6] See Assmann (1996), who focuses on hymnic discourse, though this characterisation is applicable to many other kinds of religious texts.

[7] For example, the Ptolemaic ritual papyrus P. BM EA 10569, entitled 'To Osiris in all his names', is laid out in 34 columns of 26–28 horizontal lines each, with each litanic invocation occupying a single horizontal line. At the top of each column the preposition *n* 'to' is written just once in red, and is to be understood for the remaining divine names for each column. The invocations are divided into 'hours' presumably for liturgical performance. The entities invoked include not only gods in their specific cult-topographic forms, but also the blessed dead, the gates of the underworld, and terrestrial features such mountains, swamps, and cattle; see Faulkner (1958).

[8] Schott (1955).

Osiris in Anedjty, to Osiris in Sehtet, to Osiris in Nedjfet').[9] Some of the most baroque examples of these kinds of temple offering litany are monumentalized on the columns of the Temple at Esna in southern Egypt and date to the Roman era. The following example is directed to the god Osiris. This lengthy litany begins as follows:[10]

> To Osiris Wenen-nefer, true of voice, king of the gods, the great god dwelling in Esna.
> To Sokar-Osiris, dwelling in Esna.
> To Osiris-Sokar, dwelling in Shetyt.
> To Osiris, the great pillar, in Iunyt.
> To Osiris, for whom was opened the road of Ruty.
> To Osiris, lord of Khenty-ta, in the Region of the Two Chicks.
> To Osiris, lord of Aba, the great god dwelling in Per-netjer.
> To Osiris, lord of Per-khnum, Khnum foremost of his countryside.
> To Osiris, the mysterious image, in the Mansion of the Two Chicks.
> To Osiris, entering Per-netjer, every ten days. ...

The ritual performer offers repeatedly to Osiris, whose following epithets either allude to aspects of his mythology, or (more frequently) to his cultic topography and rituals connected to them.[11] This pattern, where gods are offered to under a combination of name and specific cult-

---

[9] Demonstrating the interpermeability of temple and funerary ritual text, the examples just quoted actually come a very lengthy offering litany found in funerary literature: *Book of the Dead*, spells 141 and 142; translation: Quirke (2013), 318–19. The spell titles in some New Kingdom manuscripts, such as the papyrus of Nu, imply that this litany also could be performed 'on the festivals of the West' by a man 'for his father or his son' in order to 'make him excellent in the heart of the sun-god'; Quirke (2013), 318.

[10] See Leitz (2008), 232–43. As with many of the Roman-era hieroglyphic texts at the Temple of Esna, the litanies are written in a deliberately elaborate version of the script, often characterized as 'cryptographic', where common signs and sign-values are replaced by more unusual signs and more esoteric derivations of sign-values. In the case of the Osiris litany, for example, the recurrent name 'Osiris' is written with different signs each time it occurs. Because of the pictoral nature of the script, individual signs can in many cases be taken to have symbolic meaning, wholly independent of their function as a component in the word or sentence of which they are part. Thus, for the erudite reader, the actual script in which the words of the Osiris litany are written can itself be additionally understood as a kind of purely visual litany, whose multifarious orthographies of the divine name underscore the deity's manifold manifestations; see Sauneron (1982), 56–58, and Ciampini (2015).

[11] For details, see Leitz (2008). Wenen-nefer is a common epithet of Osiris. Sokar is a god frequently identified syncretically with Osiris; Sokar's tomb is named Shetyt, and Osiris' tomb is named Aba. Iunyt, Khenty-ta, the 'Region of the Two Chicks', and Per-khnum are either alternate names for Esna, or for other nearby places.

toponym, can also be found in New Kingdom temple reliefs. Where pictoral reliefs accompany such offering litanies, the ritual performer (usually the king) is usually shown in the act of censing.[12] The text of the offering litany can actually be laid out in grid form, with an overlying horizontal introductory caption, under which come a series of vertical columns sub-divided by horizontal lines into a grid. The individual columns in each register are each devoted to a particular divine recipient, and are further subdivided into discrete boxes for their name, and their cult-site, respectively.[13] At the bottom of each column, a final formula identifies the royal donor. This example comes from the Abydos temple of Seti I, and is an extract from a composition which in total lists 130 divine name + cult-site combinations:[14]

Making an offering-which-the-king-gives for Ptah-Sokar-Osiris, foremost of the Westerners, dwelling in the Temple of Menmaatre,[15] and the Ennead in his entourage …

to Horus	in R[…]	being the gift of King Menmaatre.
to Isis	in Semdet	being the gift of son of Re Seti
to Thoth	in Sut-kau	being the gift of King Menmaatre.
to Sakhmet	in Hesau	being the gift of son of Re Seti
to Osiris	in Hut-ka-ptah	being the gift of King Menmaatre.

Directly opposite this particular offering list, on the other side of the temple corridor, is the famous Abydos kinglist, which is arranged in much the same way (the kings being recipients of ancestor cult offerings), though the kings are not allocated toponyms.[16] The great offering litany of Ramesses II in the Temple of Luxor is also laid out in a very similar way, though here each column begins *wdn n* 'offering to' rather than just *n* 'to'. The divine recipient of the offerings is in every case the god Amun-Re, but evoked under a different cult-site or epithet. While many of the designations are clearly site-specific, some epithets are rather more generic, or allude to the functions of the god. The introductory

---

[12] Schott (1955), 291–93.

[13] In fact, in Seti's example at Abydos and in similar examples, the vertical columns are further subdivided, creating two discrete registers of offering recipients (each with discrete boxes for name and cult-site).

[14] Mariette (1869), pl. 43–44; see also Quack (2008), 133.

[15] Menmaatre is the throne name of King Seti I.

[16] Quack (2008), 133.

caption describes the ritual as 'Making incense for Amun-Re King of the Gods, in all his names'.[17] Below are invocations 6–10 (out of a total of 82):

    Offering to Amun-Re   dwelling in the Theban nome.
    Offering to Amun-Re   lord of the Theban nome.
    Offering to Amun-Re   primeval one of the Two Lands.
    Offering to Amun-Re   establisher of Truth in the Theban nome.
    Offering to Amun-Re   lover of his City.
    (followed in each column by 'being the gift of King Usermaatre-setepenre/Son of Re Ramesses meriamun')

It is likely that litanies of this sort, extolling one god in many cult-topographical places, could be evoked in other ways in Egyptian temples: Amenhotep III famously commissioned hundreds of statues of the goddess Sakhmet (at least 365, perhaps as many as 730), the statues varying very slightly in the epithets inscribed on them. Parallels with later litanies to the goddess Sakhmet found in Egyptian temples of the Graeco-Roman Period suggest that Amenhotep III sought to create a monumental three-dimensional litany in statuary.[18] Similarly, in two-dimensional temple art, sequences of generic humanoid gods could be represented, but identified as discrete forms of the same deity, with differing epithets. An example of this can be seen on the exterior walls of the sanctuary of the contra-temple of Tuthmosis III at Karnak, where the king offers to 'Amun in all his names'.[19] Facing him are fifteen identical generic male humanoid gods (in three registers of five), who are only distinguishable by their accompanying captions. The better-preserved lower register of captions on the north outer side of the sanctuary reads:

    Amun-Re lord of thrones of the Two Lands
    Amun-Re lord of heaven
    Amun in Karnak
    Amun-Re king of the gods
    Amun-Re ruler of the Theban nome

---

[17] Daressy (1910), 62; Gardiner (1947), 49. Similar offering litanies to the gods could occur also in private tombs: see Bács (2004).
[18] Yoyotte (1980).
[19] Varille (1950), 144–45.

The tradition of *wdnw* offering litanies is ultimately derived from much older lists of divine names and cult-sites:[20] word lists (onomastica) play an important part in Egyptian written tradition as a form of codifying knowledge,[21] and lists of gods were probably already being transmitted in the Old Kingdom.[22] There is ample evidence in later time periods for lists of materia sacra, particularly lists of cult topographical details.[23] Already in the earliest large corpus of Egyptian ritual texts, the *Pyramid Texts* from the twenty-fourth century BC, there are utterances which incorporate lists of deities associated with lists of cult-topography. For example, Pyramid Texts utterance 601 aims to ensure the protection of the king's burial in perpetuity:[24]

> As the name of Shu, lord of Upper Menset in Heliopolis, flourishes,
> so shall the name of N flourish, and this his pyramid flourish accordingly, forever.[25]
>
> As the name of Tefnut, lady of Lower Menset in Heliopolis, remains,
> so shall the name of N remain, and this his pyramid remain accordingly, forever.
>
> As the name of Geb, belonging to the earth's soul, flourishes,
> so shall the name of N flourish, and this his pyramid flourish accordingly, forever.
>
> As the name of Nut, in the Enclosure of Shenit in Heliopolis, flourishes,
> so shall the name of N flourish, and this his pyramid flourish accordingly, forever.

The whole text comprises twelve such statements (above are statements 2–5), each time mentioning a different deity (the sequence addresses the

---

[20] The creation of litanies from such lexical lists is paralleled in Mesopotamian culture; see Tobola (2016).

[21] See Gardiner (1947).

[22] Baines (1988).

[23] See e.g. Kockelmann (2002), Quack (2008), 131–33, and Ragazzoli (2016).

[24] See Allen (2005), 199, 219, 269; further examples in Grapow (1936), 33. Firchow (1953), 192–215, gives a detailed discussion of the permutations of this kind of litanic repetition and listing in the *Pyramid Texts*.

[25] N represents the changeable name of the royal person in whose tomb, and for whose benefit, the Pyramid Texts are inscribed.

'Great Ennead', and in its first few invocations clearly follows the order of the Heliopolitan Ennead), followed by a cult-topographical epithet relevant to them. This litany, and related texts utilising the underlying formula 'may the name of X flourish just as divinity Y flourishes', went on to be used extensively in Egyptian temple and funerary ritual texts in later periods, being found (amongst other places) in New Kingdom temple cult,[26] and in funerary papyri from the Roman Period.[27]

A more famous example of the same basic rhetorical and list-based structure would be the 'negative confession' found in *Book of the Dead* spell 125 part B, where the deceased declares his sinlessness before a tribunal of 42 deities as his heart is weighed in the balance. Each deity is invoked with the generic formula 'O deity X, who came forth from cult-place Y, I have not done sin Z'.[28] On illustrated papyri, these declarations of innocence are often written in a tabulated format.[29]

2. Anaphora and Epiphora

The list-based litanies described in the previous section can be combined in Egyptian hymnody with standard brief anaphoric elements such as *jnd-ḥr:k* 'hail to you', creating a kind of eulogistic litany. The emphasis here is again on praising the god by listing their multifarious manifestations, with the following extract coming from a Late Period liturgy from a funerary papyrus:[30]

> Praise to you, Hathor, Lady of Thebes,
> Praise to you, Hathor, Lady of Herakleopolis,
> Praise to you, Hathor, Lady of Nehet,
> Praise to you, Hathor, Lady of Rehes,
> Praise to you, Hathor, Lady of Turquoise ...

---

[26] See e.g. Kitchen (2009).
[27] e.g. Herbin (2008), 90–96.
[28] Convenient translation: Quirke (2013), 271–73.
[29] Example: Faulkner (1985), 28–29.
[30] See Burkard (1995), 233. For a more complex New Kingdom example, elaborated with multiple mythological epithets, see Assmann (1999), 118–20. Further examples occur in solar hymns incorporated into the *Book of the Dead* (as 'spell 15'); for examples, see Assmann (1999), 126–28.

More complex permutations of the same tendency can occur in the ritual texts which enjoin or supplicate divine actors to act. These often take the form of repeated wishes, where the only variable element is the appellation of the addressee. In these texts, the emphasis on cult-topography is less prominent, and instead there are more terms of address that stress the mythical roles of the addressee. An early example is the morning cult-song (Morgenlied) found in a funerary liturgical context as utterance 573 of the *Pyramid Texts* (twenty-fourth century BC), which begins:[31]

> May you awake in peace, purified one, in peace!
> May you awake in peace, eastern Horus, in peace!
> May you awake in peace, eastern soul, in peace!
> May you awake in peace, Horus of the Horizon, in peace!

Here the deceased king is addressed under a four-fold sequence of divine and supernatural terms, but instead of simply enumerating, each term is incorporated into an anaphoric (and epiphoric) address, enjoining the king's resurrection as an empowered divine entity. The terms of address evoke the process of mummification and resurrection: the king has been 'purified' through dessication in natron, and is addressed as the sky-god Horus at dawn.[32] In this case, the variable appellations of the addressee are tightly hemmed in with anaphoric and epiphoric wording.

Not all Egyptian religious texts are so focussed on second-person forms of address, which lend themselves to this kind of baroque variation of appellations. Instead, many liturgical texts mobilize similar rhetorical styles in the third person, and can effectively be considered as poems divided into anaphoric strophes,[33] as for example in the following liturgical hymn to King Senwosret III:[34]

> He has come   to us, seizing the land of Upper Egypt, the Double Crown having united with his head.
>
>   having joined the Two Lands, having merged the sedge with the bee.

---

[31] See Allen (2005), 180.

[32] It should be noted that already in the Pyramid Texts the anaphoric refrain 'May you awake in peace' is used in a variety of discrete utterances, and continued to be used in a wide variety of temple and funerary ritual texts throughout the rest of Egyptian history; see Assmann (1999), 18–19, 364–65; Hays (2002), 159–60.

[33] See Goelet (2001).

[34] See Collier and Quirke (2004), 18.

> having ruled the Black Land, having put the Red Land in his portion.
>
> having protected the Two Lands, having pacified the Two Banks.

The layout above attempts to give some sense of the ancient layout on the papyrus, with each sentence occupying a separate horizontal line, and with every line from the second onwards being indented to show that the initial refrain 'He has come' should be repeated before each new sentence. The whole hymn comprises ten such sentences, and this hymn is only one in a cycle of similar anaphoric hymns to the king on the same manuscript. This text is not about extolling the addressee under multiple names. Instead, it lauds the king's actions, which essentially amount to one thing (having united Egypt). However, through tight use of semantic, lexical, and metaphoric parallelism, this is elaborated into a contrapuntal hymn of praise.[35] One of the hallmarks of litany in other cultural traditions is the presence of responsorial dialogue. Cult ritual in Ancient Egypt was not a mass participatory affair, and so it is perhaps unsurprising that the evidence for fixed repeated responses by a ritual 'audience' is weak. However, there are many cultic hymns which use the first person plural (as here), and many rituals involved more than one actor, leaving open the possibility of antiphonal elements in cult worship.[36] Unfortunately no evidence survives for the precise performative context of these hymns to Senwosret III, but in another of the anaphoric hymns from the same papyrus, there is a rubric at the end that says:

> Its refrain:[37] O Horus who broadens his boundary, may you repeat eternity!

This may imply that these words were meant to be spoken as an epiphoric refrain, which could conceivably have been spoken by a different group of liturgical performers. Beyond temple and burial ritual, there is some

---

[35] A similar example, spoken by the god Amun-Re to King Tuthmosis III (and emulated in several later royal inscriptions of the New Kingdom), features a similar anaphoric refrain: 'I have come that I might cause you to trample X', where X refers to foreign regions and peoples; see Goelet (2001), 82–84. In this case, the stela is actually laid out so that the repeated anaphoric refrain begins anew at the start of each horizontal line, strikingly arresting the viewer's attention.

[36] See discussion in Morenz (1973), 91–94.

[37] The word is *inyt*, a hapax, which literally means something like 'that which is brought back'.

evidence for the use of repeated refrains in other sung entertainments, such as the harpists' songs attested in New Kingdom tombs,[38] as well as for alternation in musical entertainment between orchestra and soloist.[39]

The anaphoric poetic style is not restricted to ritual and litanic texts, but is also found in fictional literary texts, particularly from the Middle Egyptian stage of the language, where it is particularly popular in lamentation. For example, in the *Dialogue of a Man with his Soul*, the man laments his lonely state:[40]

> To whom can I talk today?
>   Brothers are evil,
>   and friends of today do not love.
> To whom can I talk today?
>   Hearts are greedy,
>   and every man is seizing the property of his fellow.
> \<To whom can I talk today?\>
>   Mercy has perished,
>   and the hard-faced man falls upon everyone.

Similar repetitive rhetorical strategies can also be found in magico-medical incantations, as when a mother (or ritual practitioner on her behalf) questions the intent of the illness demons, the better to counter them:[41]

> Have you come to kiss this child?
>   I will not let you kiss him!
> Have you come to silence (him)?
>   I will not let you silence him!
> Have you come to harm him?
>   I will not let you harm him!
> Have you come to take him away?
>   I will not let you take him away from me...

These literary and magico-medical texts are not considered litanies by Egyptologists, and (other than the use of anaphora) they share little in common with most of the sorts of texts identified as litanies in non-Egyptian cultural traditions. They are included here to demonstrate

[38] See Fox (1977), 409.
[39] Hickmann (1975), 156–57.
[40] Parkinson (1997), 158. For anaphora in literary laments, see Enmarch (2008), 45–49.
[41] From P. Berlin 3027 spell C; see Yamazaki (2003), 14–15.

that there is no rigid formal distinction in Egyptian written culture between ritual litanies and other types of text.[42] The same lack of clear boundaries also holds *within* Egyptian ritual texts, where litanies can occur in widely varying types of ritual.[43]

3. The Litany of the Sun and Other Underworld Texts

Within Egyptology, perhaps the most prominent use of the term 'litany' has also been as the modern title for an entire composition, the *Litany of the Sun*, whose ancient title was the 'Book of Adoring Re in the West'.[44] This composition (which combines text and images) is first preserved in royal funerary contexts in the Valley of the Kings (fifteenth century BC). The overall purpose of this text is for the deceased king to assimilate himself to the sun-god's destiny, through knowledge of his forms, manifestations and activities over the 24-hour daily solar cycle. However, the introduction to the text proclaims that 'it is effective for a man on earth', and the conclusion gives instructions for how to recite this 'book', making it clear that the text should be recited in the middle of the night, and is a 'true remedy'. This, and the occasional occurrence of this text in a non-funerary, temple contexts, suggest that it had a ritual use for the benefit of the living too.[45] The characterisation of the whole composition as a litany derives primarily from its first section, the 'Great Litany'. This comprises a set of 75 invocations to the different manifestations of the sun-god, with

---

[42] For an example of this kind of anaphoric strophic compositional style in the Egyptian daily temple cult, see Quack (2008), 139.

[43] P. Greenfield, a twenty-first dynasty funerary papyrus, again demonstrates the interpermeability of discrete ritual traditions. As well as containing funerary texts from the *Book of the Dead* tradition, it includes a liturgical song as part of the solar cult, hymns to Osiris, a fumigation spell, three *wdnw* offering litanies, plus twelve litany-style solar hymns; see Assmann (1980), 1063, and Zaluskowski (1996).

[44] English translation: Darnell and Manassa Darnell (2018), 61–126.

[45] Darnell and Manassa Darnell (2018), 62. In later copies, from the Late Period, the *Litany of the Sun* is actually spliced with other compositions like the *Amduat*, forming a preface to the discrete 'hours' of the *Amduat*'s depictions of the underworld. This recalls the division into 'hours' of the offering litany in P. BM EA 10569 (see n. 7). Further evidence for liturgical performance may come from another discrete text, the *Litany of the Twelve Names of Re-Harakhty* (Gasse 1984). This originally stems from solar cult, and takes the form of a series of invocations to the sun-god under multiple names. It is attested in a private papyrus archive of the New Kingdom (there as a magical protective ritual for the performer), as well as on a funerary mythological papyrus of the Third Intermediate Period, and in two temples of the Graeco-Roman Period.

the terms by which he is addressed evoking different functions and activities of the sun-god at different points of his daily journey. On the walls of the royal tombs, the 'Great Litany' is complemented with a series of representations of each form of the sun-god invoked, standing in a row.[46] The following three invocations (nos 6–8) give a flavour of the overall tenor:[47]

> Praise to you, Re, exalted and powerful!
> Unique one, powerful of face,
> who unites with his corpse.
> This one who addresses his gods,
> as he passes his mysterious cavern.
> (Associated figure is a ram-headed humanoid): Powerful of face.
>
> Praise to you, Re, exalted and powerful!
> He whose eye summons, whose head addresses.
> This one who gives breath among the souls at their places,
> so that they receive their breath.
> (Associated figure is a generic mummiform humanoid): Giver of breath among the souls.
>
> Praise to you, Re, exalted and powerful!
> (He whose) soul arrives, who destroys his enemies,
> This one who ordains punishments among the dead.
> (Associated figure shows a sinner pinioned to a stake awaiting punishment): Punished one at the stake.

As these demonstrate, the standard structure of each invocation is an initial anaphoric refrain, followed by two or three epithets, followed by a further characterisation of the sun-god as 'this one who…'. Each invocation alludes to different aspects of the sun's nocturnal journey through the underworld: his nightly union with the god of the underworld, the 'corpse' Sokar-Osiris (#6), his enabling the souls of deceased righteous humans to breathe in the underworld (#7), and his punishment of deceased sinners (#8). The accompanying illustrations are not always meant to be pictures of the sun-god himself; in the case of #8, the image is of a rebel awaiting punishment, instead evoking the sun-god's activity for which he is praised. Hence, beyond being solely praise, the 'Great Litany' could be considered a mnemonic device for remembering eso-

---

[46] These are reproduced in Darnell and Manassa Darnell (2018).

[47] See Darnell and Manassa Darnell (2018), 78; Hornung (1975), I, 11–13; and Hornung (1976), II, 62.

teric information about the sun-god, which would potentially make the composition a kind of 'textual rosary of New Kingdom solar devotion'.[48]

After the conclusion of the 'Great Litany', the remaining sections of the *Litany of the Sun* (designated litanies 1–9) make explicit the goal of the deceased to be assimilated to the sun-god's destiny.[49] In litany 1, the ritual performer (or deceased king) proclaims their knowledge of the manifestations of the sun-god, while litany 2 requests that they 'make a path' for the speaker in the underworld. Some of these litanies are rather loosely structured, with only occasional repeated refrains. The following is from the beginning of litany 3, which constitutes a petition to the sun-god from the ritual performer:[50]

> May you guide me on the ways of the West
>   (on which) the souls of the Westerners pass.
> May you guide me on the ways secret of nature.
> May you guide me on the ways of the West,
>   so that I might traverse the caverns which are in (the land of) Igeret.
> May you guide me on the ways of the West,
>   so that I might adore this one in the Hidden Chamber.
> May you guide me on the ways of the West,
>   so that you might elevate me to the caves of Nun.
>
> Hail, Re, I am Nun!
> Hail, Re, I am you – and vice versa!
> Hail, Re, your soul is my soul,
>   your travels are my travels in the Underworld!
> Hail, Re, as I set into the Underworld, so I traverse the Beautiful West!

Litany 4 concerns the god Osiris, his nightly union with the sun-god, and his victory over his enemies. Litanies 5 and 6 focus once again on the sun-god, whereas litany 7 details the ritual performer's access to the regions of the underworld, and his divinisation through equation of his body parts with deities. Litanies 8 and 9 address the personified West, the land of the dead, with the ritual performer demonstrating his knowledge of her. These petitions and declarations take the form of an extended monologue spoken by the ritual performer (or, in some cases, the identity of the speaker is not given, and left neutral). The continual exaltations, exhortations,

---

[48] Darnell and Manassa Darnell (2018), 70.
[49] Abitz (1995), 56–72.
[50] Darnell and Manassa Darnell (2018), 103.

and petitions do not elicit a response from the sun-god, or from anyone else. Instead, their significance appears to be performative: by reciting these addresses, the ritual practitioner demonstrates their knowledge, and effectively enacts their assimilation into the barque of the sun-god.[51]

This concern with the ritual performer (or dead king) sets *The Litany of the Sun* somewhat apart from most of the other underworld compositions found in royal tombs from the New Kingdom onwards (the *Amduat*, the *Book of Gates*, etc.).[52] These are more diagrammatic in nature, with most of the text functioning as explanatory captions or speeches of the beings represented. A partial exception to this is the composition known to Egyptologists as the *Book of Caverns*, attested from the Ramesside Period onwards. While this composition also represents the sun's journey through the underworld as a series of six diagrammatic tableaux, it is distinguished by the addition of lengthy blocks of text that visually serve to divide up the tableaux.[53] These text blocks comprise 21 'litanies'. These are speeches either by the sun-god[54] to the underworld dwellers, or vice versa. Each litany is framed as multiple strophes with repeated elements; these can be anaphoric, epiphoric, or both. In some cases, the only element of variation is the name of the entity being addressed. For example, in the first litany, the inhabitants of the netherworldly caverns praise the sun in twelve strophes, the first three of which read:[55]

Litany 1
How beautiful is Re, when he passes through the darkness,
and his great sundisk rests in his entourage,
and N[56] is in Re's entourage!

How beautiful is Re, when he passes through the darkness,
and he travels over the cave, crosser of the Underworld,
and he travels over N, when he proceeds.

---

[51] For the underlying conception of ritual as participation by the ritual performer in the divine setting, see Assmann (1997).

[52] English translations in Darnell and Manassa Darnell (2018). Brief (often one-word) anaphoric elements are not wholly absent from these other underworld books, however; see Barta (1990), 104. It should also be noted that another, much shorter, solar litanic text, with similar anaphoric style to the *Litany of the Sun*, is known from the Osireion of Seti I and the tomb of Ramesses IX: see Roberson (2009).

[53] Abitz (1995), 104–20; Werning (2011), I, 6.

[54] Or rather, the ritual performer speaking in the first person as the sun-god.

[55] Werning (2011), II, 165.

[56] N refers once again to the name of the king in whose tomb the text occurs.

How beautiful is Re, when he passes through the darkness,
and he gives orders to the underworld-dwellers,
and he gives orders to N before the Great God!

By way of contrast, some of the later litanies in the *Book of Caverns* are much more repetitive, and only vary in terms of the divine being who is addressed. In the examples below, the variable elements in each strophe have been rendered in bold:

Litany 7[57]
O **Uraeus-wearer, Uraeus-wearer!**
Look, I pass through the Secret Chamber.
I go to greet my corpse,
to greet the corpse of N.

Litany 9[58]
O Tatenen,
who created births,
who begat the one who came forth from him, and the manifestations!

Litany 14[59]
Destroyed are the enemies of the Foremost One of the Underworld,
their heads have fallen into their cauldron,
destroyed are the enemies of N.

Litany 21[60]
O this manifestation of **Atum**,
his body, his image, his corpse!
N!
May you give the sweet breath (of) life to N.[61]

---

[57] 8 strophes with non-strophic conclusion; addressees are oblique terms for the Osirid king, referred to by the attributes he wears. The sun-god greets the corpse of Osiris as part of his nocturnal journey. See Werning (2011), II, 285–87.

[58] 13 strophes with non-strophic conclusion; the chthonic primordial god Tatenen is the addressee throughout, followed by two epithets describing him. See Werning (2011), II, 293–99.

[59] 14 strophes with non-strophic conclusion; variable statements as to how the enemies of the sun-god are mutilated/destroyed. See Werning (2011), II, 325–29.

[60] 34 strophes; each addresses a variable 'manifestation' (*b3*) of gods and other underworld entities. See Werning (2011), II, 445–57.

[61] The last line of each strophe cycles through three variants: the two others are 'May you protect N' and 'May you give N the sweet breath of the Northwind'.

The sheer variety of strategies deployed in these litanies is striking: some are essentially lists of divine names (litany 21), others address a single divine name with variable epithets (litany 9), whereas others are effectively anaphorically structured verse hymns of praise (litany 1).[62] Some litanies are petitions on behalf of the deceased king (litany 21), while others forcefully assert the carrying-out of the sun-god's proper actions in the underworld (litanies 7 and 14).

These New Kingdom underworld books contain examples of all three key traits of litanies enumerated at the beginning of this paper (anaphoric/epiphoric repetition; supplications; invocations of the divine under many names), but the ritual context of these works is poorly understood. Demonstrating *knowledge* of the names and attributes of the sungod (and the inhabitants of the underworld) appears to be the key aim of texts such as the *Litany of the Sun* and the *Book of Caverns*, but this does not preclude that the possibility that this was achieved through ritual performance. With some of the older Egyptian underworld books, such as the *Amduat*, there is considerable internal textual evidence that these texts possessed a non-funerary ritual/initiatory value for the living. Explicit indication of this is lacking in the text of the *Book of Caverns*, but the composition is well attested in non-funerary temple contexts for cults of a chthonic nature.[63] It is therefore tempting to speculate that the extensive litanies in the *Book of Caverns* may have been recited or performed in the rituals of these cults.[64]

---

[62] See Assmann (1980), 1064.

[63] Such as the Osireion at Abydos, and the Nilometer at Roda; see Hornung (1999), 83.

[64] The possibility of ritual performance of these texts is bolstered by the existence of another, related composition also dealing with the caverns of the underworld: *The Book of the Twelve Caverns*, erroneously labelled Book of the Dead spell 168, though a discrete composition in origin; Quirke (2013, 406–18). This composition is largely in litanic form, and is divided into twelve nocturnal 'caverns'. The composition makes repeated mention of offerings being make to the beings listed as residing in the caverns, and it is attested in temples as well as in funerary contexts; see Méndez Rodríguez (2017).

4. Conclusion

The examples cited in this paper (to which many more could have been added) demonstrate the breadth of types of ancient text to which the English language genre-label 'litany' has been applied by Egyptologists. The overlap with other cultures is only partial. Texts with litany-like traits are attested over virtually the whole chronological extent of Egyptian written culture, from the first known lengthy ritual texts, the Pyramid Texts of the twenty-fourth century BC, to the offering litanies such as those of the Temple of Esna dating to the second century AD. It is beyond the scope of this paper to speculate on whether Egyptian cultic litanic traditions had any impact on the cultures of the classical and later Christian worlds, though it should be noted that in places like Alexandria there conceivably may have been some cultural overlap. In broad terms, the litanic structure of hymns such as the *psalies*, found in the Egyptian Coptic church, shows considerable similarities with the pharaonic texts discussed in this paper, perhaps suggesting some continuity in Egyptian liturgical compositional techniques over many centuries.[65]

---

[65] See Haikal (2009).

Bibliography

Abitz, F. (1995) *Pharao als Gott in den Unterweltsbüchern des Neuen Reiches* [Orbis Biblicus et Orientalis 146], Freiburg and Göttingen.

Allen, J. P. (2005) *The Ancient Egyptian Pyramid Texts*, Atlanta, GA.

Assmann, J. (1969) *Liturgische Lieder an den Sonnengott: Untersuchungen zur altägyptischen Hymnik* I [Münchner Ägyptologische Studien 19], Berlin.

— (1980) 'Litanei,' in W. Helck and W. Westendorf (eds), *Lexikon der Ägyptologie III*, Wiesbaden, 1062–66.

— (1996) 'Verkünden und Verklären: Grundformen hymnischer Rede im Alten Ägypten,' in A. Loprieno (ed.), *Ancient Egyptian Literature: History and Forms*, Leiden, 313–34.

— (1997) 'Unio liturgica: Die kultische Einstimmung in götterweltlichen Lobpreis als Grundmotiv "esoterischer" Überlieferung im alten Ägypten,' in H. G. Kippenberg and G. Stroumsa (eds), *Secrecy and Concealment: Studies in the History of Mediterranean and Near Eastern Religions*, Leiden, 37–60.

— (1999) *Ägyptische Hymnen und Gebete: Übersetzt, kommentiert und eingeleitet* [2nd revised edn], Freiburg and Göttingen.

Bács, T. A. (2004) 'A Royal Litany in a Private Context,' *Mitteilungen des Deutschen Archäologischen Instituts, Abteilung Kairo* 60, 1–16.

Baines, J. (1988) 'An Abydos List of Gods and an Old Kingdom use of Texts,' in J. Baines, T. G. H. James and A. Leahy (eds), *Pyramid Studies and other Essays Presented to I. E. S. Edwards*, London, 124–33.

Barta, W. (1990) *Komparative Untersuchungen zu vier Unterweltsbüchern* [Münchener Ägyptologische Untersuchungen 1], Frankfurt am Main.

Burkard, G. (1995) *Spätzeitliche Osiris-Liturgien im Corpus der Asasif-Papyri: Übersetzung, Kommentar, formale und inhaltliche Analyse* [Ägypten und Altes Testament 31], Wiesbaden.

— (2003) *Einführung in die altägyptische Literaturgeschichte I: Altes und Mittleres Reich*, Münster.

Ciampini, E. M. (2015) 'Magic in the Sign: Iconic Writings in the Litany of Neith at Esna and the Performative Nature of the Divine Name [Esna 216.1–4],' in G. Bąkowska-Czerner, A. Roccati and A. Świerzowska (eds), *The Wisdom of Thoth: Magical Texts in Ancient Mediterranean Civilizations*, Oxford, 15–22.

Collier, M. and S. Quirke (2004) *The UCL Lahun Papyri: Religious, Literary, Legal, Mathematical and Medical* [BAR International Series 1209], Oxford.

Daressy, G. (1910) 'Litanies d'Amon du temple de Louxor,' *Recueil de travaux relatifs à la philologie et l'archéologie égyptiennes et assyriennes* 32, 62–69.

Darnell, J. C. and C. Manassa Darnell (2018) *The Ancient Egyptian Netherworld Books*, Atlanta, GA.

Enmarch, R. (2008) *A World Upturned: Commentary on and Analysis of The Dialogue of Ipuwer and the Lord of All*, Oxford.

Faulkner, R. O. (1958) *An Ancient Egyptian Book of Hours (Pap. Brit. Mus. 10569)*, Oxford.

— (1985) *The Ancient Egyptian Book of the Dead* [revised edn], Aylesbury.

Firchow, O. (1953) *Untersuchungen zur ägyptischen Stilistik II: Grundzüge der Stilistik in den altägyptischen Pyramidentexten* [Deutsche Akademie der Wissenschaften zu Berlin, Institut für Orientforschung, Veröffentlichung 21], Berlin.

Fox, M. V. (1977) 'A study of Antef,' *Orientalia* 46, 393–423.

Gardiner, A. H. (1947) *Ancient Egyptian Onomastica*, Oxford.

Gasse, A. (1984) 'La litanie des douze noms de Rê-Horakhty,' *Bulletin de l'Institut français d'archéologie orientale* 84, 189–227.

Goelet, O. (2001) 'The Anaphoric Style in Egyptian Hymnody,' *Journal of the Society for the Study of Egyptian Antiquities* 28, 75–89.

Grapow, H. (1936) *Sprachliche und schriftliche Formung ägyptischer Texte* [Leipziger ägyptologische Studien 7], Glückstadt.

Guglielmi, W. (1996) 'Der Gebrauch rhetorischer Stilmittel in der ägyptischen Literatur,' in A. Loprieno (ed.), *Ancient Egyptian Literature: History and Forms*, Leiden, 465–97.

Haikal, F. (2009) 'Performativité du nom divin en Égypte de l'antiquité à nos jours,' in P. Piacentini and C. Orsenigo (eds), *Egyptian Archives: Proceedings of the First Session of the International Congress Egyptian Archives*, Milan, 197–217.

Hays, H. M. (2002) 'The Worshipper and the Worshipped in the Pyramid Texts,' *Studien zur Altägyptischen Kultur* 30, 153–67.

Herbin, F. R. (2008) *Books of Breathing and Related Texts* [Catalogue of the Books of the Dead and other Religious Texts in the British Museum 4], London.

Hickmann, E. (1975) 'Alternierendes Musizieren,' in W. Helck and E. Otto (eds), *Lexikon der Ägyptologie I*, Wiesbaden, 156–57.

Hornung, E. (1975) *Das Buch der Anbetung des Re im Westen (Sonnenlitanei): Nach den Versionen des Neuen Reiches. Teil 1: Text* [Aegyptiaca Helvetica 2], Geneva.

— (1976) *Das Buch der Anbetung des Re im Westen (Sonnenlitanei)*: *nach den Versionen des Neuen Reiches. Teil 2: Übersetzung und Kommentar* [Aegyptiaca Helvetica 3], Geneva.

— (1999) *The Ancient Egyptian Books of the Afterlife* [D. Lorton (trans.)], Ithaca, NY.

Kitchen, K. A. (2009) 'Dumbing Down in a Former "Modernist Age": Literary Streamlining of Poetic Litany in Ancient Egypt,' in D. Magee, J. Bourriau and S. Quirke (eds), *Sitting Beside Lepsius: Studies in Honour of Jaromir Malek at the Griffith Institute*, Leuven, 267–72.

Kockelmann, H. (2002) *Edfu: Die Toponymen- und Kultnamenlisten zur Tempelanlage von Dendera nach den hieroglyphischen Inschriften von Edfu und Dendera* [Die Inschriften des Tempels von Edfu: Begleitheft 3], Wiesbaden.

Leitz, C. (2008) 'Les trente premiers versets de la litanie d'Osiris à Esna (Esna 217),' *Revue d'égyptologie* 59, 231–66.

Mariette, A. (1869) *Abydos: Description des fouilles exécutées sur l'emplacement de cette ville I*, Paris.

Mathieu, B. (1994) 'Études de métrique égyptienne, III: Une innovation métrique dans une "litanie" thébaine du Nouvel Empire,' *Revue d'égyptologie* 45, 139–54.

Méndez Rodríguez, D. M. (2017) 'The Transmission of the Book of the Twelve Caverns,' in G. Rosati and M. C. Guidotti (eds), *Proceedings of the XI International Congress of Egyptologists, Florence Egyptian Museum, Florence, 23–30 August 2015*, Oxford, 405–09.

Moers, G. (2007) 'Der Parallelismus (membrorum) als Gegenstand ägyptologischer Forschung,' in A. Wagner (ed.), *Parallelismus membrorum*, Fribourg and Göttingen, 147–66.

Morenz, S. (1973) *Egyptian religion* [A. E. Keep (trans.)], London.

Parkinson, R. B. (1997) *The Tale of Sinuhe and other Ancient Egyptian Poems, 1940–1640 BC*, Oxford.

Patanè, M. (1983a) 'À propos de la structure rythmique des litanies d'Esna,' *Göttinger Miszellen* 62, 63–66.

— (1983b) 'Analyse métrique des litanies égyptiennes,' *Göttinger Miszellen* 64, 61–65.

Quirke, S. (2013) *Going Out in Daylight – prt m hrw: The Ancient Egyptian Book of the Dead*, London.

Quack, J. F. (2008) 'Geographie als Struktur in Literatur und Religion,' in F. Adrom, K. Schlüter and A. Schlüter (eds), *Altägyptische Weltsichten: Akten des Symposiums zur historischen Topographie und Toponymie Altägyptens vom 12.–14. Mai in München*, Wiesbaden, 131–57.

Ragazzoli, C. (2016) 'Toponymie et listes: Un onomasticon fragmentaire de Basse Époque (P.BnF ms. Égyptien 245, 1–2),' in S. Dhennin and C. Somaglino (eds), *Décrire, imaginer, constuire l'espace*: *Toponymie égyptienne de l'Antiquité au Moyen Âge*, Cairo, 69–91.

Roberson, J. (2009) 'A Solar Litany from the Tomb of Ramesses IX,' *Journal of the American Research Center in Egypt* 45, 227–32.

Sadowski, W. (2016) 'Some Necessary Preliminaries,' in W. Sadowski, M. Kowalska, and M. M. Kubas (eds), *Litanic Verse I*: *Origines, Iberia, Slavia et Europa Media*, Frankfurt am Main, 9–12.

Sauneron, S. (1982) *L'écriture figurative dans les textes d'Esna*, Cairo.

Schott, S. (1955) 'Eine ägyptische Bezeichnung für Litaneien,' in O. Firchow (ed.), *Ägyptologische Studien*, Berlin, 289–95.

Toboła, Ł. (2016) 'In principio erat enumeratio: The Origins of Litanic Patterns in the Ancient Near East,' in W. Sadowski, M. Kowalska, and M. M. Kubas (eds), *Litanic Verse I*: *Origines, Iberia, Slavia et Europa Media*, Frankfurt am Main, 41–50.

Varille, A. (1950) 'Description sommaire du sanctuaire oriental d'Amon-Rê à Karnak,' *Annales du Service des Antiquités de l'Égypte* 50, 137–72.

Werning, D. A. (2011) *Das Höhlenbuch*: *Textkritische Edition und Textgrammatik* [Göttinger Orientforschungen 4. Reihe: Ägypten 48; 2 vols], Wiesbaden.

Yamazaki, N. (2003) *Zaubersprüche für Mutter und Kind*: *Papyrus Berlin 3027* [Achet 2], Berlin.

Yoyotte, J. (1980) 'Une monumentale litanie de granit: Les Sekhmet d'Aménophis III et la conjuration permanente de la déesse dangereuse,' *Bulletin de la Société Française d'Égyptologie* 87–88, 46–75.

Zaluskowski, C. (1996) *Texte außerhalb der Totenbuch-Tradierung in Pap. Greenfield*, Bonn.

Uri Gabbay

LITANIES IN THE SUMERIAN LITURGY OF ANCIENT MESOPOTAMIA

A Typology of a 2,000-Year-Long Transmission History

1. Introduction: Enumeration and Repetition in Ancient Mesopotamian Literature

One of the main features of litanies is the juxtaposition of enumeration with repetition: A list of elements – for example, names of divinities – is enumerated with a repeated phrase. Therefore, before examining the liturgical litanies of ancient Mesopotamia themselves, it is worth presenting a short survey of enumeration and repetition in other genres of ancient Mesopotamian literature.[1]

Enumeration in the form of lists plays an important role in the literature of ancient Mesopotamia, which includes not only *belles lettres* but also scholarly, scientific, and religious genres. Mesopotamian literature is preserved on many thousands of clay tablets written in cuneiform script, in the Sumerian and Akkadian languages. Discovered at various sites in Babylonia and Assyria in ancient Iraq, these tablets date from the beginning of cuneiform writing at the early third millennium BCE (and even earlier) up to the end of cuneiform culture at the first century BCE (and perhaps even later).

Lexical lists, one of the oldest genres of cuneiform literature, played an important role in ancient Mesopotamian scribal education. These lists enumerate long sequences of words, usually written in Sumerian; from the mid-second millennium BCE onwards an Akkadian translation is often included. Each list is arranged according to a certain criterion, which may be thematic or graphic (i.e. based on the shape of the cuneiform signs themselves).[2] For

---

[1] For this topic, see also Civil (1987); Toboła (2016); Wasserman, forthcoming.
[2] See Veldhuis (2014).

Uri Gabbay • Hebrew University of Jerusalem, Israel

example, a thematic list enumerating dozens of types of sheep, known from various tablets dating to the first millennium BCE, begins with the general term 'sheep', which is subsequently repeated with various qualifiers:[3]

(Text 1)
Sheep
Fattened sheep
Good (quality) fattened sheep

Another major genre of Mesopotamian literature consists of divinatory texts, known especially in Akkadian from the early second millennium BCE up to the end of cuneiform culture, which list various signs or omens followed by the event each omen predicts. These omens may be astral or terrestrial; they may appear in the entrails of sacrificial sheep or in other places. Similar to the thematically arranged lexical texts, the divinatory texts arrange related omens and their corresponding predictions in a sequence of entries.[4] Thus, for example, a sequence of entries in a collection dating to the early second millennium BCE is arranged in increasing numerical order according to the number of 'feet' (an anatomical feature) observed on the liver of a sacrificial sheep. Each entry begins with the phrase 'If there are *x* feet', and ends with a different prediction; three of these entries are cited here.[5]

(Text 2)
If there are five 'feet' – the king will tear down his own fortress.
If there are six 'feet' – your fortified city will become a wasteland.
If there are seven 'feet' – your army will drop its weapon in front of your enemy's army.

Enumeration and repetition is also a literary device that occurs in myths and epics, which often begin with a line that is repeated several times but with a different name or epithet in each iteration.[6] For example, the Sumerian myth 'Enlil and Ninlil', known from the beginning of the second millennium BCE, begins as follows:[7]

[3] Landsberger (1960), 7:1–3.
[4] See Koch (2015); Winitzer (2017).
[5] Winitzer (2017), 403:4–6.
[6] See the many examples in Streck (2002). See also Wilcke (1976), 214–17.
[7] *ETCSL* 1.2.1, lines 1–3; Streck (2002), 203.

(Text 3)
There was a city, there was a city – we live in it!
There was a city, (the city) Nippur – we live in it!
There was a city, (the city) Dur-ĝishnimbar – we live in it!

And of course, enumerations paired with a repetitive refrain are common in hymnic literature. An extreme example occurs in a Sumerian hymn to the goddess Inana, known from the beginning of the second millennium BCE: in a section containing almost sixty lines, dozens of nouns and infinitives are paired with the refrain '… are yours, Inana!'.[8]

The juxtaposition of enumeration and repetition occurs frequently in the large corpus of exorcistic and purificatory incantations written in Sumerian and Akkadian. For example, in an Akkadian section in a series of Sumerian and Akkadian incantations against demons, the anaphoric phrase 'I am Marduk' is repeated almost one hundred times, and each time it is paired with a unique epithet of that god.[9]

But the largest and most varied corpus of litanies is found, unsurprisingly, in liturgy, and the following sections will be dedicated to this corpus.

2. Liturgical Litanies

The main corpus of Mesopotamian litanies is found in a collection of prayers written in the Emesal register of the Sumerian language.[10] It was sung in the temple cult of ancient Mesopotamian cities from the beginning of the second millennium BCE (at least) up to the end of cuneiform culture (the latest dated liturgical tablet is from 86 BCE).

These prayers are known from close to two thousand cuneiform tablets, belonging to several native genres, especially the Balaĝ and Ershema genres (named after the musical instruments that were played when the prayers were performed); about two hundred individual prayers of varied length have been identified. The tablets stem from various cities in Mesopotamia, such as Assur, Nineveh, Babylon, Nippur, Ur, Uruk, and many others.

---

[8] *ETCSL* 4.07.3, lines 115–72.

[9] Geller (2016), 343–63.

[10] For these prayers, see, among other studies (in chronological order), Krecher (1966), Cohen (1974), Kutscher (1975), Cohen (1981), Cohen (1988), Maul (1988), Volk (1989), Black (1991), Maul (2005), Löhnert (2009), Gabbay (2014), Gabbay (2015), Delnero (2015), Mirelman (2018). The Emesal register of Sumerian was the subject of much scholarly discussion and debate, especially since there are indications that it may have been associated with women; see Whittaker (2002) (with previous literature).

According to ritual instruction texts written on dozens of cuneiform tablets, the Emesal prayers were the main verbal component of both the regular calendrical temple liturgy and of liturgies conducted on special non-calendrical occasions. They were usually sung by a particular priest in front of the cult image of the god, to the accompaniment of musical instruments.

The content of these prayers is usually lamentful, mourning over ruined temples and cities destroyed by the gods themselves. A deity – frequently the head of the pantheon, Enlil (and later Marduk) – becomes enraged and commands to destroy his or her own city, temple, and people. These descriptions of destruction should not be taken literally. The catastrophic events described in the prayers should be understood entirely theologically, as a depiction of the consequences that might occur if the raging god is not pacified. Therefore, later in the prayer, the god will be asked to calm down and look with favour upon his city.

A defining characteristic of these prayers, already attested in the earliest texts from the beginning of the second millennium BCE, is their inclusion of litanies. Although the litanies are a dominant element of these liturgies, in the past they were not subject to much study and analysis.[11]

2.a. *The Horizontal and Vertical Axes of Litanies*

Litanies, as they appear in written form, have two spatial aspects related to the concepts of repetition and enumeration: the horizontal and vertical axes.[12]

The horizontal axis is reflected in each individual line of the litany, which includes the same semantic, lexical, and syntactic elements as the other lines it is grouped with; the horizontal axis usually conveys the main message of the litany. One of those elements, however, is variable, and it is the enumeration of the variable element in each line that defines

---

[11] For the few studies on litanies, see Krecher (1966), 42–45; Black (1991), 29–31; Löhnert (2009), 52–54; Gabbay (2014), 38–58.

[12] Note that this horizontal-vertical spatial perception is found also in the study of omens; see Winitzer (2017), 28–30. It should also be noted that the vertical-horizontal scheme used here to describe litanies is based on the graphic layout of the written text (when performed, the litanies have an audible structure that unfolds along a temporal axis). Indeed, as discussed by Sadowski (2018a, 357–63; 2018b, 233–79), the litany, with its repetitive nature, and with the variable elements which can all refer to a single entity, can be visualized as a circular scheme, specifically (among other sub-schemes) as rays stemming from or culminating in one point or circle, an image that captures both the repetitive (and potentially endless) listing of diverse traits or epithets of a god and the idea that they all represent one divine entity (see also 2.e below).

the vertical axis of the litany. When isolated from the successive lines of the litany, the variable element usually forms a list of names or epithets which are all thematically connected but different from each other.

For example, in the following litany, the horizontal axis consists of the supplication 'O heart, turn, turn!', addressed to the deity and repeated numerous times (marked here in bold), while the vertical axis consists of a list of epithets and names of this deity (marked in italics):[13]

(Text 4)
O heart (of the god), turn (in forgiveness), turn! O heart, calm down, calm down!

Lord of the lands!	**O heart, turn, turn!**
Lord whose utterance is just!	**O heart, turn, turn!**
(The god) Mullil, father of the land!	**O heart, turn, turn!**
Shepherd of the black-headed (people)!	**O heart, turn, turn!**
He who observes everything by himself!	**O heart, turn, turn!**
Wild bull leading his troops!	**O heart, turn, turn!**
He who sleeps a false sleep!	**O heart, turn, turn!**

In the following, I will deal separately with the horizontal and vertical aspects of the litanies.

2.b. Features of the Horizontal Axis of Litanies

The horizontal axis usually contains a sentence or clause, comprising a series of syntactic elements. Generally, the single line, or in our terms, the horizontal axis, forms a syntactic unit; often it is an invocation or supplication, but it may also be a declarative or interrogatory sentence. In most cases the structure of the syntactic unit is fixed and contains a single variable element, a name or epithet, which forms part of the vertical axis. This variable element can be integrated into the rest of the syntactic unit of the horizontal axis in various degrees of connectivity, as will be discussed below (2.c.1).

Structurally, the horizontal axis follows one of two patterns: the common 'refrain' pattern, in which the fixed part of the line is found at its end, and the rarer 'anaphora' pattern, where the fixed part begins the line.

---

[13] Cohen (1988), 389, 395–96:b+112–26; 267, 270, v:16–22; 378, 382–83:a+48–53, 380:22–28; Gabbay (2015), 114, 117, no. 22:a+17–26. In the first-millennium BCE versions of this litany, the list of gods on the vertical axis is longer, and it is not cited here.

2.b.1. 'Refrain' Pattern

The 'refrain' pattern is the most frequent pattern of the horizontal axis in the litanies of the Sumerian Emesal prayers. In most cases, the divine name or epithet is the variable element forming the vertical axis, and the syntactic unit consists of an invocation of the god followed by a fixed refrain, which in performance may have acted as an antiphon.[14]

In most cases the variable element is syntactically independent of the rest of the clause. Frequently it takes the form of an exclamation (syntactically, a vocative) which can be separated from the rest of the invocation or supplication. For example:[15]

(Text 5)
May Heaven calm you! May earth pacify you!

Alas, lord!	May Heaven calm you!
(The god) Umun-ĝurusha!	May Heaven calm you!
Lord, great hero!	May Heaven calm you!
Governor of (the god) Mullil!	May Heaven calm you!
Lord, (the god) Urash!	May Heaven calm you!
Hero, (the god) Utulu!	May Heaven calm you!
Hero, lord of (the city) Nippur!	May Heaven calm you!
Lord of (the temple) Eshumesha!	May Heaven calm you!

…

In this litany, and in many others, the epithet of the god is a vocative phrase, syntactically independent from the rest of the clause, which stands as an independent sentence. In cases like this, the line can be divided into two elements: an invocation of a god by name or epithet, and a following refrain, in this case the supplication 'May Heaven calm you!'.

But the repeated phrase containing the variable element (the name or epithet) may also be syntactically integrated with the rest of the horizontal axis. For example, consider the following passage describing the goddess lamenting in the temple:[16]

---

[14] The performative aspects of the litany will not be dealt with in this article, for which see Mirelman, this volume.

[15] Gabbay (2015), 132–35, no. 28:b+15–22 (// 141–43, no. 31:a+1–8).

[16] Cohen (1988), 69, 72:b+61–71.

(Text 6)
The woman cried out in the holy House,
He (= the god) heard her cry in the holy House.
The lady of (the city) Tintir (= Babylon) cried out,
The mother of (the temple) Esaĝil cried out,
(The goddess) Panunaki cried out,
[(The goddess) ...] cried out,
The daughter-in-law of (the temple) Esaĝil cried out,
The foremost child of (the god) Urash cried out,
The foremost child of (the temple) E-ibbi-Anum cried out,
(The goddess) Gashan-gutesha-siga cried out,
(The goddess) Nanaya cried out.

In this litany, the horizontal axis is structured as a declarative sentence, and the variable element, namely the name or epithet of the goddess, is the subject of the sentence. Although Sumerian syntax allows a verb to stand alone without an explicit subject before it, dividing each line into an invocation (syntactically, a vocative) and a refrain (e.g. the invocation '(The goddess) Nanaya!' followed by the refrain 'She cried out!') does not seem to be the natural way of reading these lines.

Although in the refrain pattern, the variable part of the litany often begins the horizontal axis, it can also occur as part of a genitive construction following a repeated noun. For example:[17]

(Text 7)
It leans on earth like day(light), but its meaning is unfathomable!
His word leans on earth like day(light), but its meaning is unfathomable!
The word of (the god) great An leans on earth like day(light), but its meaning is unfathomable!
The word of (the god) Mullil leans on earth like day(light), but its meaning is unfathomable!
The word of (the god) Amanki leans on earth like day(light), but its meaning is unfathomable!
The word of (the god) Asarluḫi leans on earth like day(light), but its meaning is unfathomable!
The word of (the god) Enbilulu leans on earth like day(light), but its meaning is unfathomable!
The word of (the god) Muzebasa'a leans on earth like day(light), but its meaning is unfathomable!
The word of (the god) Dikumaḫa leans on earth like day(light), but its meaning is unfathomable!

[17] Cohen (1988), 122, 136:1–10.

In this litany the reference to the god's unfathomable destructive 'word' or order (a very common motif in the prayers) forms a genitive construction with the variable divine name that follows it. (Because the same phrase appears at the beginning of each line, this litany can also be considered as following the 'anaphora' pattern discussed in 2.b.2 below.) In this case, as in Text 6, this construction is integrated into the line, forming a syntactic unit with the following fixed phrase (the refrain), but the same genitive construction appears in other litanies as an invocation, syntactically independent from the following refrain.

A very common variation of the refrain pattern consists of a litany beginning with a phrase that does not contain a variable element, while the names and epithets that comprise the vertical axis of the litany are written simply as a list, without repeating the fixed phrase of the horizontal axis. For example:[18]

(Text 8)
Alas! Wise lord, counsellor!
Wise lord, counsellor, Alas!
Honoured one, lord, great (god) An,
Great (god) An, father of the great gods, great lord!
Honoured one, lord of (the city) Uruk,
(The one) from the shrine Eana, (the temple) Eĝiparimin,
Honoured one, lord of the lands,
Lord whose utterance is just, (the god) Mullil, father of the Land, great lord,
Honoured one, lord of (the city) Nippur,
Lord of (the temple) Ekur, lord of the Land,
Mighty storm of the father, (the god) Enlil,
Born in the mountain, lord of (the temple) Eshumesha.

This litany begins with an invocation of the god and continues with a list of epithets in which the phrase found in the first and second lines is not repeated. The question is whether the phrase was repeated as an antiphon when the litany was performed. This possibility is suggested by a few tablets that contain a remark in small script about an antiphon. One tablet preserving the litany above has a short paratextual remark in small script in the first line stating that the phrase 'Wise lord, counsellor' acts as the antiphon, probably indicating that the entire passage was performed with the refrain 'Wise lord, counsellor' (even though this is not indicated by the main text).

[18] Gabbay (2015), 58–60, no. 4:1–12.

A more complex variation of the refrain pattern features two alternating refrains that comprise the vertical axis of the litany. For example:[19]

(Text 9)
The manifest hierodule is not (manifest anymore),
(The goddess) Gashanana, what can one say to her?
The princess Gashanana, woe, she is not manifest (anymore),
The princess, Gashanana, what can one say to her?
Princess, lady of (the temple) Eana, woe, she is not manifest (anymore),
Princess, lady of the place, (the city) Uruk, what can one say to her?
Princess, lady of the place, (the city) Zabalam, woe, she is not manifest (anymore),
Princess, lady of (the temple) Hursaĝkalama, what can one say to her?
Princess, lady of (the temple) Eturkalama, woe, she is not manifest (anymore),
Princess, lady of (the city) Tintir (= Babylon), what can one say to her?

In this litany, the phrases 'what can one say to her?' and 'woe, she is not manifest (anymore)' comprise the horizontal axis and are alternately paired with the names and epithets of the goddess Inana (= Gashanana) that constitute the vertical axis.

2.b.2. 'Anaphora' Pattern

The 'anaphora' pattern of the horizontal axis is much rarer than the refrain pattern. In this pattern each line begins with a fixed phrase repeated throughout the litany, and the variable element – the name or epithet – follows it. For example:[20]

(Text 10)
Woe is me! Woe is me!
Woe is me!   (The god) Umun-ĝurusha!
Woe is me!   Lord of decisions!
Woe is me!   Governor of (the god) Enlil!
Woe is me!   Lord, great warrior!
Woe is me!   He *who leads* the land!
Woe is me!   Lord whose utterance cannot be altered!

[19] Cohen (1988), 653, 664: d+68–77.
[20] Cohen (1988), 277–78, 294:c+103–09.

In some litanies that follow the anaphora pattern, in addition to the fixed phrase at the beginning of the line another short fixed phrase (in the example below, the phrase: 'In ... are tears!') occurs at the end of the line, after the variable toponyms. Such litanies may be regarded as a combination of the anaphora and refrain patterns:[21]

(Text 11)
The mother in supplication! In her House are tears!
The mother in supplication! In (the city) Nippur, (the temple) Ekur are tears!
The mother in supplication! In (the temples) Ki'ur, Enamtila are tears!
The mother in supplication! In (the city) Sippar, (the temple) Ebabbar are tears!
The mother in supplication! In your city Tintir (= Babylon) are tears!
The mother in supplication! In (the temple) Esaĝil, (the city) Borsippa are tears!
The mother in supplication! In (the temple) Ezida, (the temple) Emaḫtila are tears!
The mother in supplication! In (the temple) Etemenanki are tears!
The mother in supplication! In (the temple) Edara'ana are tears!
...

Similar to what we saw in Text 9 above, the anaphoric element that precedes the names or epithets may consist of two alternating phrases. For example:[22]

(Text 12)
Elevated bull of the land, what can one know about you?
Honoured one, elevated bull of the land, what can one know about you?
Honoured one, lord, great hero,

Great hero,	governor of (the god) Mullil,
Honoured one,	lord Urash,
Great hero,	lord of (the temple) Eninnu,
Honoured one,	heir of (the temple) Eshara,
Great hero,	lord of (the temple) Eshumesha,
Honoured one,	lord of (the temple) Eshamaha,
Great hero,	lord of (the temple) E'ibishuba,

...

---

[21] Cohen (1988), 241–42, 250–51:c+359–81 (and parallels). Due to its length, only the first ten lines are cited here.

[22] Cohen (1988), 441–42, 450:1–32. The litany is long and only the first ten lines are cited here.

The litany begins with a phrase that is repeated in the second line, after the title 'honoured one'; the third line combines the titles 'honoured one' and 'great hero'. These two titles provide the anaphoric element in each line of the rest of the litany, where they are alternately paired with the sequence of names and epithets that forms the vertical axis. (It is also possible that the anaphoric phrases and the titles were combined in performance with the refrain 'what can one know about you?'; see Text 8 above).

2.c. Features of the Vertical Axis of Litanies

As noted above, the vertical axis of the litany is defined by the variable element in what are otherwise identical lines, and thus forms an independent list when isolated from the horizontal axis.

In Sumerian litanies it is possible to distinguish two patterns of vertical axis based on the content of the variable element. The regular and more frequent pattern enumerates names and epithets, while the other (rare) pattern employs a series of phrases (and not only personal nouns).

The regular pattern of litanies itself can be subdivided into two types: litanies that feature divine names and epithets, and litanies that feature toponyms – names of cities or temples, or of parts of temples. In each of these types, the variable element may consist of multiple names or epithets associated with the same god or toponym, or it may consist of multiple names or epithets that are each associated with a different god or toponym. These types are illustrated in sections 2.c.1–2.c.4.

2.c.1. Names and Epithets of a Single God

Several gods, especially important gods such as Enlil or Inana, have litanies addressed exclusively to them, in which their various epithets are enumerated on the vertical axis. For example, the litany in Text 4 above contains a very common sequence of epithets of the god Enlil (in the Emesal register of the litanies: Mullil), all combined with the phrase 'heart, turn!'.

On a semantic level, while the main message of the litany is conveyed in the horizontal axis's phrase 'heart, turn!', which is addressed to Enlil in every line, the antonomasia in the vertical axis delivers an extra message about Enlil, describing and detailing his characteristics and traits: He is honoured, his speech is always just, he is the father of the land and shepherd of its people, inspecting every part of the world by himself and leading his troops, and even though he, like other Mesopotamian gods, also sleeps, this is a 'false' sleep, because he remains alert for his people.[23]

---

[23] Kutscher (1975), 44–51. For the narrative and predicative function of the litanic antonomasia, see Sadowski (2018b), 331–343.

2.c.2. Names and Epithets of Several Gods

Litanies may also enumerate the names of several gods who are identified with each other through syncretism. Usually, the addition of gods in the vertical axis can be traced historically. For example, litanies originally containing the names of the traditional heads of the pantheon, An or Enlil (= Mullil), were often expanded in later versions to contain names and epithets of the god Marduk (Sumerian Asarluḫi), the new head of the pantheon, and even his son Nabû (Sumerian Emesal: Muzebasa'a); both Marduk and Nabû were identified with Enlil, as seen in Text 7 above.

In litanies that name several gods, the message delivered in the vertical axis is not as strong as in the antonomastic listing of epithets of a single god (see 2.c.1 above). Nevertheless, although the main message regarding all of the gods mentioned in this litany is the same, the litany implicitly contains an extra message, theological in nature, namely that all the gods mentioned in the litany actually refer to the same entity (see 2.e below).

2.c.3. Names and Epithets of a Single City

There are some litanies that mention a single city, along with its temples and other features such as its gates, as in the following example:[24]

> (Text 13)
> Oh, brickwork of (the temple) Ekur! Oh, brickwork of Ekur!
> That Ekur, House of (the god) Mullil,
> That (temple) Eki'ur, House of (the goddess) Ninlil,
> That (temple) Enamtila, House of Mullil,
> That (temple) Emitummal, House of Ninlil,
> That interior (of the temple) Edima, House of Mullil,
> That (temple) E'engurninnu, House of Mullil,
> It is the Exalted Great Gate, that House of Mullil,
> It is the Great Gate, that Place-of-the-Rising-Sun,
> It is that Great Gate, that (place) Facing-Ur!

Such litanies reflect the local nature of the prayer in which they appear, and often preserve the cultic topography of their performance (see 2.d.2).

---

[24] Gabbay (2015), 68–69, no. 8 (// 281–82, no. I):1–10.

2.c.4. Names and Epithets of Several Cities

As is the case with multiple gods, several cities may also be enumerated in litanies, and here too it is often possible to trace the historical circumstances in which the name of a given city was added to the litany (see 2.d.3). A very common enumeration of this sort is seen in Text 11 above, which lists the cities Nippur, Sippar, Babylon, and Borsippa, along with their temples.

2.c.5. Non-name Vertical Axis

As noted above, on rare occasions, the vertical axis consists of phrases that are not names. While these phrases are sometimes unique, they usually consist of stockphrases which often appear together, as in the following example:[25]

(Text 14)
Its (= the city's) bull in its cattle pen	– so that it returns [(...)]!
Its sheep in its fold	– so that it returns [(...)]!
Its possessions that were plundered	– so that it returns [(...)]!
Its treasures that were carried away	– so that it returns [(...)]!
Its goods that were removed	– so that it returns [(...)]!

The phrases paired with the refrain 'so that it returns ...' are clustered together in other litanies, often forming a vertical axis as in this example.[26]

In cases of non-name vertical axes, the message of the vertical axis is significant, as it communicates different details which are relevant to the message expressed in the horizontal axis.

2.c.6. Combination of Two Different Sequences

On rare occasions two different types of sequences can be combined in the vertical axis. Usually a sequence of divine names is combined with a sequence of toponyms. This combination can take various forms: The two sequences may appear one after the other, or interleaved in alternating horizontal axes, or even combined in the same line as two parallel vertical axes.

---

[25] Reisner (1896), 61, no. 32:17′–26′ (cuneiform text); see Maul (1991), 322; cf. the similar passage in Cohen (1988), 639:b+19–25.

[26] See Maul (1991), 321–25. It should be noted that the use of a set of essentially synonymous stock phrases containing verbs in the vertical axis can also be described as a type of varied horizontal axis as well, and indeed it can occur also with other sequences (see Text 17 below).

Although the phenomenon itself is rare, when it does occur, the sequences are usually placed one after the other. In the following litany, for example, a sequence of divine epithets is attached to a sequence of toponyms, forming a long vertical axis which is paired with the same refrain of the horizontal axis, 'turn!':[27]

(Text 15)
Important one, turn! Watch over your city!
Honoured one, important one, turn! Watch over your city!
Lord of the lands, turn!
Lord whose speech is just, turn!
(The god) Mullil, father of the Land, turn!
Shepherd of the black-headed (people), turn!
He who inspects (everything) himself, turn!
Bull leading his troops, turn!
He who sleeps a false sleep, turn!
...
Around your city Nippur, turn!
Around the brickwork of (the temples) Ekur, Ki'ur, Enamtila,
Around the brickwork of (the city) Sippar, turn!
Around the shrine Ebabbar, (the temple) Edikukalama,
Around the brickwork of (the city) Tintir (= Babylon), turn!
...

In this litany two sequences follow each other, combined with the refrain 'turn!' in different syntactical ways. In the first sequence, the divine names and epithets are vocative forms that identify the addressee of the imperative 'turn!'; in the second sequence, the place names have a locative function and refer to the place around which the god is to turn (the city or temple).

On rare occasions, the divine name sequence and the toponym sequence may be intertwined with each other, in alternating horizontal axes. For example:[28]

(Text 16)
In (the city) Enegi, the ... of the lads,
Where the hero, (the god) Umunazu lies;
In (the place) Arali ...,

---

[27] Cohen (1988), 227–28, 244–45:a+75–101; Gabbay (2015), 331–37, no. X. For another example, see Gabbay (2015), 185–87, no. 56:1–a+12.
[28] Cohen (1988), 675–76, 681–82:e+148–63.

Where the spouse of the goddess (Gashanana) lies;
In (the place) ...,
Where the lad, my (god) Damu, lies;
In (the city) Ĝishbanda, the land of sighs,
Where the son, (the god) Umunmuzida, lies;
In (the place) ...-mala, the path of the chariots,
Where (the god) Ishtaran of colourful eyes lies;
In (the place) Gamgamda(?), the steppe of (the city) Kuara,
Where my great ... lies;
In the House of the young bronze-cup-bearer,
Where (the god) Alla, lord of the net, lies;
In the road of the cemetery of tears,
Where the herald, (the god) Umunshude, lies!

In this litany, two relatively rare sequences of divine names and toponyms are combined, and each pair of items from the two lists is integrated into the alternating horizontal axes 'In ...', and 'where ... lies'.

Lastly, on rare occasions two sequences can be paired together in the same line. For example, the following litany combines a sequence of divine names with a sequence of non-name verbal phrases (which is rare in itself; see 2.c.5 above), forming a litany with a very laconic horizontal axis but with two parallel vertical axes, one for each sequence:[29]

(Text 17)
The great bull who stands fiercely, has been brought low in *my*(?) own place,
(In) the shrine Abzu, the House of (the god) Amanki,
Because of the brickwork of (the city) Uruzeb which has been destroyed,
Because of the House of (the god) Amanki which has been ruined,
Because of the House of (the goddess) Damgalnuna which has been defiled,
Because of the House of (the god) Asarluḫi which has been pillaged,
Because of the House of (the goddess) Panunanki which has been carried away,
Because of the House of (the goddess) Namma which has been seized,
Because of the House of (the goddess) Ara which has been handed over!

---

[29] Cohen (1988), 76, 85:a+29–37. For examples of this type of combination with sequences of divine names and toponyms, see, e.g. Cohen (1988), 210, 217:a+59–70; Krecher (1966), 60, vii:33–38.

Starting in the third line of this litany, a sequence of place names (a city in the third line, and 'House of the god ...' in the rest of the lines) is paired with a sequence of verbs ('destroyed', 'ruined', etc.), known from other texts as stock phrases comprising a sequence. As a result, two parallel vertical axes are combined within the phrase 'Because of ... which has been ...'.[30]

2.d. Principles of Organization of the Vertical Axis of Litanies

Aside from the thematic grouping together of several names, there are other principles that determine the sequence of the different elements that constitute a vertical axis, or that explain why certain elements are grouped together. Three such principles are described below.

2.d.1. Meter

Poetic meter in Sumerian is a relatively unexplored topic, in large part because Sumerian phonology is not completely understood.[31] Nevertheless, it is still possible to discern that in some litanies, each of the items in the vertical axis contains a more or less identical number of syllables (although it is difficult to identify the reasons for this specific number).

This grouping of elements on the basis of syllable count, for stylistic, rhythmic, and performative reasons, is found especially in the thematic category of names and epithets of a single god (2.c.1).

For example, in the common standard list of epithets of the god Enlil (Mullil in the Emesal register of Sumerian) (see Text 4 above), each of the epithets contains 5–7 syllables (mostly 5–6):

umun kurkura	lord of the lands	5
umun duga zida	lord whose word is just	6
Mullil ay(a) kanaĝa	Mullil, father of the Land	6–7
sipa saĝ ĝiga	shepherd of the black-headed (people)	5
ibi du nitena	he who inspects (everything) himself	6
am erina didi	bull leading his troops	6
u lula kuku	he who sleeps a false sleep	5

---

[30] As noted above (n. 26), the non-name nature of the second sequence can also be understood as a variation of the refrain of the horizontal axis.

[31] See Wilcke (1976), 227–31 (with previous literature).

Comparison with other texts underlines the relative consistency of the syllable count for the epithets in this unit. In some texts dating to the first millennium BCE (see 2.c.2, 2.e.3), other names related to the gods Marduk and Nabû have been added to this list for syncretistic and political reasons. The added names are conspicuous because they contain a different number of syllables.

2.d.2. Cultic Topography

A topographical sequence is discernible in some litanies which name temples and parts of temples located in one city. The sequence usually has a linear spatial aspect to it, which perhaps reflects the route of a procession during which the litany was performed. Thus, in Text 13 above, the litany begins with the main temples at the heart of the city of Nippur, continues with other temples, probably less central, and ends with the gates of the city. The litany thus maps a movement from the centre of the city outwards to its gates, which can be explained in the cultic context of processions and circumambulations. These cultic acts are associated with the Emesal prayers, especially in early periods; similar topographical rationales can be discovered in other litanies as well.[32]

2.d.3. Historical Context

When assessing the formal aspects of litanies, it is necessary to consider not only their literary structure and cultic context, but also their historical (both political and religious) context.

Litanies consisting of a vertical axis usually comprised of names of gods or cities could easily be modified by adding the name of a place or god. Such additions occurred in certain historical circumstances, for example, when a cult travelled from one city to another. The relocation of a cult might be caused, for example, by imperial ideology, migrations of priests, or other historical circumstances. The addition of a name to the list testifies that the litany has been adjusted to fit a new environment. For example, most litanies enumerating the cities of Nippur, Sippar, Babylon, and Borsippa (see Text 11 above) are attested in the first millennium BCE, when Babylon (and the cities of Borsippa and Sippar in the same region of north Babylonia) exercised political and cultural dominance. Earlier litanies naming only Nippur and its temples are known from tablets stemming from Nippur in the early second

---

[32] See Löhnert (2009), 55–61; Gabbay (2014), 170–71, 180–88.

millennium BCE,[33] and it is presumed that these litanies were expanded to include other cities when northern Babylonian cities, and especially Babylon, adapted this litany for their cult, usually for political reasons.[34]

In the last centuries of the first millennium BCE, especially in the late Achaemenid period and Seleucid period, some local changes and additions were made to the standard toponym and god name litanies, and these alterations likewise correspond to other local tendencies due to political, religious, and social circumstances.[35]

Thus, the listing of cities in a litany may often be seen as a record of the textual and performative transmission of the litany from its original place of performance to a new locality. By adding a city to an existing litany, it was possible to adapt an old liturgy to reflect a new performative setting, and thus a conservative traditional text could be preserved with minimal alteration.

2.e. Theology and Literary Genre

Using theories of Bakhtin and others on the correlation of certain genres or literary structures with certain temporal or spatial circumstances, Witold Sadowski (2018a; 2018b, 233–95) has examined the genre of litanies in Western culture within the worldview in which they developed. Is it possible to do the same with the Mesopotamian liturgical litanies? In the following I will attempt to connect the literary structure of litanies to the theological context in which they were written and performed.

The literary structure of litanies, in which one semantic unit is repeated several times, has implications for other, more conceptual aspects. The juxtaposition of unity, represented by the repeated single phrase of the horizontal axis, and diversity, represented by the enumeration of different names or epithets on the vertical axis, defines litanies as a place where unity and diversity – which are inherently in tension with each other – meet. Thus, litanies provide a context in which general theological elements related to the meeting point of and tension between unity and diversity may become apparent.

First, as seen above (2.c.2, 2.e.3), litanies were a convenient tool for adding new theological concepts to an existing system, and thus for identifying a new theological innovation with a traditional theology, or for incorporating a traditional local cult into the cult of a new city

---

[33] See Löhnert (2009), 183–85 (text N4).
[34] See Löhnert (2009), 273–77; Gabbay (2014), 208–09.
[35] Gabbay (2014), 215–25.

or temple. This was done in a very subtle way, without challenging the previous cult, by adding just one or two names to an existing list. The addition of names to the vertical axis of the litany followed the same pattern – specifically, the horizontal axis – of the traditional litany. Thus, the sense of unity created by the horizontal axis of the litany absorbed to some degree the diversity introduced on the vertical axis.

The very phenomenon of naming different gods in one litany has theological implications. In the litanies whose vertical axis contains various epithets of a single god, all the items refer to the same god, and serve as an antonomasia for this god (see 2.c.1). Similarly, the listing of different gods, either as additions to a litany comprising a standard list of epithets, or in an independent litany, encourages the perception that all these gods are actually one (see 2.c.2). This perception is further shaped by the fact that all these names were uttered and sung in performance in the cult of a single god, usually before the cultic image of this single god. In this context it is interesting to note that in earlier periods (specifically, the first half of the second millennium BCE) most of the additions to litanies occur in toponym sequences, while additions of names of gods to a single litany are most frequent in the first millennium BCE. The addition of gods to a litany has more radical implications than the addition of cities, and indeed, some scholars believe that the theological issues raised by speculation on unity and diversity in the realm of the divine were a growing concern in Mesopotamian theology and intellectual life during the first millennium BCE, and some even speak about this tendency in terms of emerging monotheism.[36] Indeed, when a litany mentioning Enlil, Marduk, and Nabû is sung before the cult statute of Marduk – or even of the god Shamash – this suggests a worldview in which Marduk or Shamash 'is' all these deities.[37] Thus, the litany, where unity and diversity meet, is a fitting structure for expressing monotheistic, or at least strongly syncretistic theological tendencies.

3. Conclusion

Litanies are one of the most prevalent characteristics of liturgical texts written in the Emesal register of Sumerian. These liturgies are known from a period of two thousand years (and may have existed even longer,

---

[36] See Pongratz-Leisten (2011).
[37] See Maul (1991), 306–09; Maul (1998), 190–94.

prior to their documentation in writing). The litanies they contain are not a popular subject of research in modern Assyriological scholarship, and at times are even regarded judgmentally as representing a somewhat lower or secondary stage of literature. However, as the history of additions to and changes in the litanies suggests, the ancient interest in litanies was very strong precisely because of their connection to the actual liturgical context in which they were performed. The repetitive nature of the litanies, combined with their variability, allowed them to accommodate both tradition and innovation. As such, litanies served as a mechanism that facilitated the preservation, transmission, and adaptation of liturgies throughout Mesopotamia for a remarkably long period of time.

Precisely because of the importance attributed to litanies at such an early point in the history of ancient Mesopotamia, litanies may have later travelled to other regions and influenced other liturgies, in the ancient Near East and beyond, as is the case with many other Mesopotamian cultural elements such as astronomy, mathematics, divination, and mythology. Perhaps the dominance of litanies in other Near Eastern liturgies, and especially in early Jewish and Christian liturgies, owes its origins to the rich litanic tradition of ancient Mesopotamia.

Bibliography

Black, J. A. (1991) 'Eme-sal Cult Songs and Prayers,' *AuOr* 9, 23–36.

Civil, M. (1987) 'Feeding Dumuzi's Sheep: The Lexicon as a Source of Literary Inspiration,' in F. Rochberg-Halton (ed.), *Language, Literature, and History: Philological and Historical Studies Presented to Erica Reiner* [AOS 67], New Haven, CT, 37–55.

Cohen, M. E. (1974) *Balag-Compositions: Sumerian Lamentation Liturgies of the Second and First Millennium BC* [SANE 1/2], Malibu, CA.

— (1981) *Sumerian Hymnology: The Eršemma* [HUCASup 2], Cincinnati, OH.

— (1988) *The Canonical Lamentations of Ancient Mesopotamia*, Potomac, MD.

Delnero, P. (2015) 'Texts and Performance: The Materiality and Function of the Sumerian Liturgical Corpus,' in P. Delnero and J. Lauinger (eds), *Texts and Contexts: The Circulation and Transmission of Cuneiform Texts in Social Space* [SANE 9], Boston, 87–118.

ETCSL: *Electronic Text Corpus of Sumerian Literature*, http://etcsl.orinst.ox.ac.uk/.

Gabbay, U. (2014) *Pacifying the Hearts of the Gods: Sumerian Emesal Prayers of the First Millennium BC* [HES 1], Wiesbaden.

— (2015) *The Eršema Prayers of the First Millennium BC* [HES 2], Wiesbaden.

Geller, M. J. (2016) *Healing Magic and Evil Demons: Canonical Udughul Incantations* [with the assistance of L. Vacín], Boston and Berlin.

Koch, U. S. (2015) *Mesopotamian Divination Texts: Conversing with the Gods. Sources from the First Millennium BCE* [GMTR 7], Münster.

Krecher, J. (1966) *Sumerische Kultlyrik*, Wiesbaden.

Kutscher, R. (1975) *Oh Angry Sea (a-ab-ba hu-luh-ha): The History of a Sumerian Congregational Lament*, New Haven, CT.

Landsberger, B. (1960) *The Fauna of Ancient Mesopotamia. First Part: Tablet XIII* [MSL VIII/1], Rome.

Löhnert, A. (2009) *'Wie die Sonne tritt heraus!' Eine Klage zum Auszug Enlils mit einer Untersuchung zu Komposition und Tradition sumerischer Klagelieder in altbabylonischer Zeit* [AOAT 365], Münster.

Maul, S. M. (1988) *'Herzberuhigungsklagen': Die sumerisch-akkadischen Eršaḫunga-Gebete*, Wiesbaden.

— (1991) '"Wenn der Held (zum Kampfe) auszieht ...": Ein Ninurta Eršemma,' *Or* 60, 312–34.

— (1998) 'Marduk, Nabû und der assyrische Enlil: Die Geschichte eines sumerischen Šu'ilas,' in S. M. Maul (ed.), *tikip santakki mala bašmu* [Festschrift R. Borger; Cuneiform Monographs 10], Groningen, 159–97.

— (1999) 'Gottesdienst im Sonnenheiligtum zu Sippar,' in B. Böck, E. Cancik-Kirschbaum, and T. Richter (eds), *Munuscula Mesopotamica* [Festschrift Johannes Renger; AOAT 267], Münster, 285–316.

— (2005) 'Bilingual (Sumerian-Akkadian) Hymns from the Seleucid Arsacid Period,' in I. Spar and W. G. Lambert (eds), *Literary and Scholastic Texts of the First Millennium BC* [CTMMA 2], New York, 11–116.

Mirelman, S. 'Text and Performance in the Mesopotamian Liturgical Tradition' [unpublished doctoral dissertation, New York University, 2018].

— (this volume) 'Sumerian Aspects of Sumerian (Emesal) Litanies'.

Pongratz-Leisten, B. (ed.) (2011) *Reconsidering the Concept of Revolutionary Monotheism*, Winona Lake, IN.

Reisner, G. (1896) *Sumerisch-babylonische Hymnen nach Thontafeln griechischer Zeit*, Berlin.

Sadowski, W. (2018a) 'A Generic Woldview: The Case of the Chronotope of Litany,' in R. M. Erdbeer, F. Kläger, and K. Stierstorfer (eds), *Literarische Form: Theorien – Dynamiken – Kulturen. Beiträge zur literarischen Modellforschung*, Heidelberg, 347–74.

— (2018b) *European Litanic Verse: A Different Space-Time* [Literary and Cultural Theory], Berlin.

Streck, M. P. (2002) 'Die Prologe der sumerischen Epen,' *Or* 71, 189–265.

Toboła, Ł. (2016) '*In principio erat enumeration*: The Origins of Litanic Patterns in the Ancient Near East,' in W. Sadowski, M. Kowalska, M. M. Kubas (eds), *Litanic Verse I: Origines, Iberia, Slavia et Europa Media*, Frankfurt am Main, 29–40.

Veldhuis, N. (2014) *History of the Cuneiform Lexical Tradition* [GMTR 6], Münster.

Volk, K. (1989) *Die Balaĝ-Komposition úru àm-ma-ir-ra-bi: Rekonstruktion und Bearbeitung der Tafel 18 (19'ff), 19, 20 und 21 der späten, kanonischen Version* [FAOS 18], Stuttgart.

Wasserman, N. (forthcoming) 'Lists and Chains: Enumeration in Akkadian Literary Texts'.

Whittaker, G. (2002) 'Linguistic Anthropology and the Study of Emesal as (a) Women's Language,' in S. Parpola and R. M. Whiting (eds), *Sex and Gender in the Ancient Near East: Proceedings of the 47th Rencontre Assyriologique Internationale, Helsinki, July 2–6, 2001*, Helsinki, 633–44.

Wilcke, K. (1976) 'Formale Gesichtspunkte in der sumerischen Literatur,' in S. J. Lieberman (ed.), *Sumerological Studies in Honor of Thorkild Jacobsen on His Seventieth Birthday, June 7, 19, 1974* [Assyriological Studies 20], Chicago, 205–316.

Winitzer, A. (2017) *Early Mesopotamian Divination Literature: Its Organizational Framework and Generative and Paradigmatic Characteristics* [AMD 12], Boston.

Sam Mirelman

PERFORMATIVE ASPECTS OF LITANIES IN SUMERIAN LITURGICAL PRAYERS, ACCORDING TO SELECTED LATE MANUSCRIPTS[1]

1. Introduction

From a musicological perspective which is oriented especially towards Christian liturgy, the litany may be generally defined as follows:

> A prayer form, usually characterized by the announcement of varying **invocations** (e.g. names of deities or saints) or **supplications** (Lat. *deprecationes*, *preces*, etc.) by a leader, each of which is followed by a fixed **congregational response**. This genre may be distinguished from other responsorial forms by the relative brevity, sometimes parity, of the call and response elements, giving it something of an **insistent quality**. Often quite rhythmic, litanies frequently accompany **processions**. Thus the term can signify the procession itself or the day upon which the procession occurs.[2]

As discussed below, the words which I have highlighted in the above passage resonate with the evidence for litanies in Sumerian liturgical prayers, or Sumerian liturgical prayers more generally.[3] Some Sumerian

---

[1] I wish to thank U. Gabbay for his comments to an earlier draft of this paper.

[2] Huglo, Foley, Harper and Nutter (2001).

[3] In the following 'Sumerian liturgical prayer' refers to the category of composition which is otherwise referred to as 'Emesal prayer' (referring to its use of the Emesal dialect of Sumerian) or 'ritual lament' (referring to its known ritual contexts of performance). In the following, 'Sumerian liturgical prayer' refers to the two main categories of Sumerian liturgical prayers, the *Balaĝ* and *Eršema*. Related categories of prayers were written in the same dialect of Sumerian (Emesal). These prayer types, namely the

Sam Mirelman • SOAS University of London, UK

The Litany in Arts and Cultures, ed. by Witold Sadowski and Francesco Marsciani, Turnhout, Brepols, 2020 (*Studia Traditionis Theologiae*, 36), pp. 71-87
© BREPOLS PUBLISHERS   DOI 10.1484/M.STT-EB.5.119207

liturgical prayers were performed in processions.[4] The litanies in such prayers certainly have an insistent quality, and they feature invocations and supplications. In addition, the litanies feature antiphonal performance (alternatively termed 'call and response' performance style(s)).[5] As outlined by Uri Gabbay in this volume, the litany is one of the principal defining features of Sumerian liturgical prayers. The following focuses on one crucial aspect of such litanies, namely the role of performance in their conception, transmission and ritual contexts. Before addressing this central question, it is necessary to briefly outline general performative aspects of Sumerian liturgical prayers.

2. The Performance of Sumerian Liturgical Prayers: General Aspects

2.a. Text and Performance

It is important to state at the outset that our knowledge regarding the performance practice of Sumerian liturgical prayers is limited by the available textual evidence, which dates to the second and first millennia BC. The interpretation of such sources is often difficult, and we do not possess any detailed descriptions or witnesses of performances. However, despite such limitations, we possess relatively detailed, selective information concerning the performance of Sumerian liturgical prayers. Numerous literary texts, including many hymns and prayers, are known from ancient Mesopotamia, and the ancient Near East. For the majority of such texts, the question of performance is a matter of speculation. For example, we do not possess specific information indicating whether the *Epic of Gilgamesh* was performed, and if so, in what manner and context(s). The two main exceptions with regard to this question, are incantations and Sumerian liturgical prayers, two categories of text for which we do have precise information concerning their performance. It is certain that in antiquity, both incantations and Sumerian liturgical

---

Eršahunga and *Šuila*, were normally recited, without musical instruments. For an overview of the genres of Emesal prayers see Gabbay (2014), 5–14.

[4] However, the available evidence suggests that entire prayers were performed during processions, not only the litanies. For the performance of Sumerian liturgical prayers during processions, see Gabbay (2013) and Gabbay (2014), 170–71.

[5] However, the term 'congregational' is not appropriate for ancient Mesopotamia, where the available evidence suggests that only the priesthood actively participated in liturgical performances.

prayers did not exist merely as written artefacts; they were performed. We are fortunate to possess specific information concerning the contexts and functions of performance of such texts; such information may be found within the manuscripts of the prayers themselves, particularly their colophons.[6] In addition, separate ritual texts refer to the performance of incantations and Sumerian liturgical prayers; in such ritual texts, compositions are normally referred to by their incipits. From such sources, it is certain that Sumerian liturgical prayers were not only recited; they were sung. This is indicated by the use of the Akkadian verb *zamāru* 'to sing' in references to the performance of Sumerian liturgical prayers. The widespread Semitic root *zmr* refers specifically to singing, in languages which are cognates of Akkadian, such as Hebrew and Arabic. In addition, it is certain that musical instruments accompanied the performance of such prayers. This is indicated by several sources; the native generic names for the two main categories of Sumerian liturgical prayer are *Balaĝ* and *Eršema*.[7] The *balaĝ* is the Sumerian name of the musical instrument which was associated with the performance of this category of prayer; its precise identity is disputed; most recently, U. Gabbay has made the case that it was originally a harp or lyre, but it became a drum in the later transmission of *Balaĝ* prayers.[8] The other main category of Sumerian liturgical prayer was the *Eršema*, which means literally 'lament of the *šem* (instrument)' in Sumerian. Again, it is unclear to which precise musical instrument the term *šem* refers to, although it is almost certainly a percussion instrument. Although the *Balaĝ* and *Eršema* were separate categories of compositions, they are closely related, and should be considered together, at least during the later transmission of such prayers. Indeed, during the first millennium BC both compositions were often written on the same tablet, and ritual texts confirm that they were performed together. *Balaĝ*s are multi-sectional compositions; during the first millennium BC, and perhaps earlier, each *Balaĝ* was typically followed by its shorter *Eršema*, with which it was paired.

[6] 'Manuscript' is used in the following, to refer to a clay tablet with cuneiform writing. Sumerian liturgical prayers were transmitted over a period of approximately 2000 years. Many individual compositions of Sumerian liturgical prayers are known in multiple manuscripts (tablets), which were written in different periods and locations within Mesopotamia. Each manuscript (tablet) is distinguished by minor and major features, in terms of content, detail, orthography, etc. See Gabbay in this volume and Gabbay (2014).

[7] ĝ indicates a nasalised g. Genre designations are capitalized, whereas instrument names are not. Thus, *Balaĝ* refers to the genre, and *balaĝ* refers to the musical instrument after which the genre was named.

[8] Gabbay (2014), 98–102.

Tablets of Sumerian liturgical prayers are known over a period of almost two millennia before the Common Era. Throughout this extremely wide historical period, the manuscripts of such prayers underwent significant changes. Some of these developments are directly relevant to the question of performance. Particularly in first millennium BC sources we possess relevant ritual texts, and colophons, which refer to the performance of such prayers. However, it is beyond doubt that Sumerian liturgical compositions were also performed from at least as early as the beginning of the second millennium BC onwards. This is indicated by several factors, including an important ritual text from the ancient city of Mari in western Syria, references within the texts themselves and external texts, and by certain details in the orthography of such compositions which suggest a performative context.[9] Numerous transformations took place in the later transmission of such prayers. In the latest phase, from the fifth or fourth century until the first century BC, an entirely new, sophisticated form of performative indications is introduced in the textual transmission of Sumerian liturgical prayers.[10] Directions for performance, such as the names of musical instruments, are added, often at the beginning and end of litanies. Most importantly, interpolated vowel sequences without semantic meaning are introduced; such sequences are likely to represent the transformation of the Sumerian text in sung form. Thus, for example, the Sumerian (Emesal dialect) word *eneĝ* 'word' may be followed by the vowel E; this additional vowel only appears in (some) late manuscripts, and it is likely to represent /eneĝe/ in performance, where the additional /e/ vowel does not have a semantic meaning; it indicates an additional vowel which is added for performative reasons. Many other performative indications are likely to indicate the addition of vowels, elongation of vowels, and melismas.[11]

2.b. *The Theological Role of Song and Performance*

Why were Sumerian liturgical compositions performed? Moreover, why were they sung, to the accompaniment of musical instruments, and not merely recited? I believe that we possess precise information which allows us to answer these questions. Sumerian liturgical prayers, including their litanies, were performed in the daily temple cult, as well as on occasions of perceived danger, such as an eclipse. It is clearly stated in the Mesopotami-

---

[9] See Delnero (2015) and Delnero (forthcoming, a).
[10] See Mirelman (2010) and Mirelman (2018).
[11] The term melisma refers to the performance of a single syllable with multiple pitches.

an sources themselves, that the performance of such prayers served to calm the anger of the gods. Indeed, Sumerian liturgical prayers were directed to deities; this is made clear especially in the regular temple performances of Sumerian liturgical prayers, which were sung by a particular priest (the *kalû*) in front of the cult statue of a deity in its cella. I consider the role of song, as opposed to recitation, to have played an important role in the perceived ritual function of Sumerian liturgical prayers. In ancient Mesopotamia the deity was typically conceived in anthropomorphic terms, in many ways similar to the king. Thus, the most powerful, emotionally persuasive form of performance is chosen for the deity; this is a model which is probably based on the use of music as a means of therapy. Thus, the manipulation of emotion by means of music is a paradigm which was transferred from a presumed human context, to the ritual context of a priest's prayer towards a deity (Mirelman, forthcoming). Such an emphasis on the role of song and performance, and its effects on emotion, are of great importance to an understanding of such prayers, including their litanies.

3. The Performance of Litanies Within Sumerian Liturgical Prayers

3.a. Memorisation of Litanies

As described by U. Gabbay in this volume, litanies in Sumerian liturgical prayers contain standardised sequences of deities, and/or their associated temples and cities. Such standardised sequences form the main content of litanies. Although the actual form of each litany in each composition is unique, the sequences of deities, temples and toponyms which occur in each litany is standardised throughout the corpus of Sumerian liturgical prayers. Such sequences were both standardised and memorised by the priests who were responsible for their performance. The memorisation of litanic sequences is indicated by the abbreviation of litanies, a practice which is known from the early second millennium BC, but which becomes widespread from the seventh century BC onwards. The use of abbreviation or summarization of litanies is a practice which is well known in Sumerian liturgical prayers. The implication of such manuscripts is that the performers of such litanies knew them well; thus, the manuscript is likely to have functioned as an Aide-Mémoire.[12] In such in-

---

[12] In the first millennium BC, and perhaps earlier, the priests responsible for the performance of Sumerian liturgical prayers (the *kalû*-priests) also wrote the prayers themselves. This is clearly shown by the colophons of such prayers, many of which in-

stances, long sections of litanies are routinely omitted from manuscripts, replaced by the annotation 'x (number of) skipped lines'. The abbreviation of litanies was not a consistent, universal practice. Indeed, we are able to reconstruct the skipped lines of such passages only by comparison with other manuscripts of the same litany, many of which write out the litany in full. In order to indicate which litany is intended, it is common practice to write the first line, followed by an annotation indicating the number of skipped lines, and followed by the final line of the litany. The number of skipped lines can range from only 4 lines, to over 100 lines.[13]

Such litanic sequences may occur together with a refrain which is repeated in each line; this refrain typically occupies the second half-line. However, such sequences may also consist simply of long lists of gods. For example, the following is an example of the standardised long god list which occurs in several Sumerian liturgical prayers, in slightly different forms. In this particular manuscript, the first and last lines are written in full. In between the first and last lines, the writer of this tablet indicates that 50 lines are skipped. Thus, in performance the total number of lines would be 52:[14]

(the god) An and (the god) Uraš, earth where barley sprouted
    50 skipped lines
gods of heaven, gods of the underworld

Example 1. Translation of an excerpt of a Sumerian liturgical prayer, where the writer annotates the omission of 50 lines of a 52-line list of gods (The Emesal Litany of the Gods).[15]

3.b. Performance, Syntax and Graphical Arrangement of Litanies

In addition to performative indications, which are included in late manuscripts of Sumerian liturgical prayers, a simple aspect of the performative nature of such prayers is reflected in the graphical arrangement of text on the manuscripts themselves. The graphical arrangement of text on

---

dicate that they were written by 'junior' *kalû*-priests. For the role of abbreviation and summarization in liturgical prayers and magical incantations in ancient Mesopotamia, see Gabbay and Mirelman (2017), 23–25.

[13] On the practice of skipping lines in some manuscripts of Sumerian liturgical prayers, see Gabbay and Mirelman (forthcoming).

[14] This manuscript includes some breaks, which are restored here. Note also Example 8 in this paper, which includes another example of the annotation 'skipped lines'.

[15] Reisner (1896), no. 23, reverse, lines 23–24.

manuscripts typically consists of two half lines, with a space before the half line. This graphical arrangement reflects the syntactical structure of the prayer. Thus, each physical line is normally a discrete phrase, divided into two half-phrases. This simple but important syntactical division of the line is characteristic of Sumerian liturgical prayers in general, but it is especially evident in litanies. The syntactical division of the line in the text coincides with the syntactical division of the line in performance. This assumption is reasonably certain, due to the fact that such performative syntactical divisions are not only indicated by the graphic arrangement of the line; they are reinforced by performative indications, specifically the addition of performative vowels in late manuscripts. Such additional performative vowels and vowel sequences typically occur in between each half line, at the end of a full line, or on the left edge before the beginning of the line; it is almost certain that performative vowels which occur at such natural syntactical breaks represent the elongation of final syllables, melismas and/or caesurae in performance. Thus, an important function of performative vowels consists of the delimitation of syntactical structures. This phenomenon has important implications for the metrical structure of such prayers, a topic which is beyond the scope of this article.[16] In addition, it is likely that the two half-lines in such litanies represent a call and response structure, performed by a soloist and choir, as discussed below. Examples 1–4 below illustrate the above points regarding graphical arrangement, prosody and syntax:

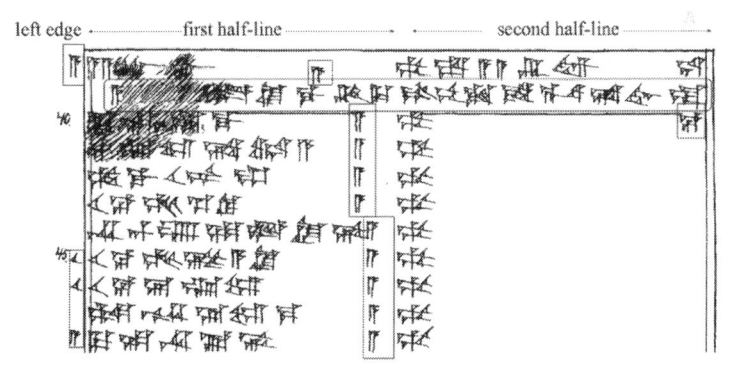

Figure 1. Line drawing of an excerpt of a cuneiform tablet of a Sumerian liturgical prayer to Nergal, demonstrating the division of the line into two halves. Square boxes indicate performative vowels. The rounded box in line 39 indicates an Akkadian translation (which was not performed) of the Sumerian line in line 38. From Reisner (1896), 19 (No. 9. Obverse, lines 38–48, annotated).

---

[16] Note the brief discussion of meter in the contribution of U. Gabbay in this volume.

| ᴬ a-a BU BU   ᴬ | gu₄-da a-a-re im-de₆ ᴱ |
| (*Akkadian translation*) | |

ᴬ ur-saĝ umun irigal-la ᴬ	gu₄-(da a-a-re im-de₆) ᴱ
ᵈmes-lam-ta-è-a ᴬ	gu₄-
am gal umun ir₉-ra ᴬ	gu₄-
umun-e gú si-sá ᴬ	gu₄-
en ᵈMES-SAĜ-UNUGᵏⁱ-ga ᴬ	gu₄-
ᵁ umun-e gú-du₈-aᵏⁱ ᴬ	gu₄-
ᵁ umun-e é-mes-lam ᴬ	gu₄-
bàd mah é-lam-ma ᴬ	gu₄-
ᴬ ur-saĝ en dag-ga ᴬ	gu₄-

Example 2. Transliteration of Figure 1, with performative vowels in capitals.[17]

| *ª* aya bubu-*ª* | guda a-are imde-*ᵉ* |
| (*Akkadian translation*) | |

ª ursaĝ umunirigala-*ª*	gu(da a-are imde)-*ᵉ*
meslamtaea-*ª*	gu(da a-are imde-*ᵉ*)
amgal umun irra-*ª*	gu(da a-are imde-*ᵉ*)
umune gu sisa-*ª*	gu(da a-are imde-*ᵉ*)
en bisaĝunuga-*ª*	gu(da a-are imde-*ᵉ*)
ᵘ umune gudua-*ª*	gu(da a-are imde-*ᵉ*)
ᵘ umune emeslam-*ª*	gu(da a-are imde-*ᵉ*)
bad mah elama-*ª*	gu(da a-are imde-*ᵉ*)
ª ursaĝ en daga-*ª*	gu(da a-are imde-*ᵉ*)

Example 3. Proposed transcription of Example 2, with performative vowels in bold italics[18]

---

[17] According to Mirelman (2018), Chapter 7.3. The text is simplified here, for illustrative purposes.

[18] This transcription attempts to represent the Sumerian text as it was pronounced. Our knowledge of the phonology of Sumerian is approximate, and therefore the phonological representation of the Sumerian text given here is provisional.

a	Father, *who roots out (the enemy)*!	*a*	Bull who brought glory! *e*

a	Hero! Lord of the underworld!	*a*	Bull (who brought glory!) *e*
	(god) Meslamtaea!	*a*	Bull (who brought glory! *e*)
	Great wild bull! Powerful lord!	*a*	Bull (who brought glory! *e*)
	O lord, who yokes/directs the oxen!	*a*	Bull (who brought glory! *e*)
	Lord Bisaĝunug!	*a*	Bull (who brought glory! *e*)
u	O lord of (the city) Kutha!	*a*	Bull (who brought glory! *e*)
u	O lord of (the temple) Emeslam!	*a*	Bull (who brought glory! *e*)
	Exalted wall of (the temple) Elama!	*a*	Bull (who brought glory! *e*)
a	Hero! Lord of dwelling(s)!	*a*	Bull (who brought glory! *e*)

Example 4. Translation of Example 2, including performative vowels in bold italics.[19]

3.c. Antiphonal Performance of Litanies

Several crucial aspects of the performance of Sumerian liturgical prayers remain unknown, or uncertain. For example, it is uncertain, but highly likely, that choirs were regularly employed in the performance of Sumerian liturgical prayers. Indeed, there is clear evidence for a differentiation between the choral performance of *Balaĝ* sections, versus the solo performance of an *Eršema*, in the early ritual from the city of Mari mentioned above. However, it is not explicitly stated within any Sumerian liturgical prayer, precisely which singer and/or choir sings which line(s) or section(s). As mentioned above, detailed performance instructions are included only in selected, late manuscripts. Furthermore, such directions, if included, highlight only selected aspects of performance. In all cases it seems that the written text served as a reference work and/or Aide-Mémoire, within the context of an oral tradition; thus, only selective aspects concerning performance were written down if at all.

Following the terminology used by U. Gabbay in this volume, in Examples 1–4 above, the refrain 'Bull who brought glory!' belongs to the horizontal axis, whereas the vertical axis consists of a list of epithets of the god Nergal. The refrain itself is written in an abbreviated form; at its

---

[19] According to Mirelman (2018), Chapter 7.3.

first appearance it is written in full, and in subsequent lines only the first word ('bull') is indicated, followed by a blank space on the tablet. This is a simple form of abbreviation which is found throughout the corpus of Sumerian liturgical prayers. It is highly likely that the refrain in Examples 1–4 was performed by a choir. This is suggested by several contributory factors. Firstly, one may expect such a performance style for this type of poetic structure. In various performative traditions, a refrain which occurs at regular intervals, is sung by a choir, contrasted with the solo performance of the main text (Clark 2001). Secondly, there are a small number of manuscripts which include an annotation signifying 'antiphonal refrain'. The instances of this annotation occur mostly at the beginning of compositions, or sections of compositions. For this reason amongst others, this annotation seems to refer to the antiphonal performance of a phrase which is written at the beginning of the section. An important question, which has already been highlighted by Gabbay in this volume, is whether this annotation refers to the antiphonal performance of this phrase throughout the composition or section in question. Continuing with Gabbay's 'Text 8' (in this volume), the following translation of the same section includes various performative indications, which occur in a single late manuscript:

Alas! Wise lord, " counsellor! **high (voice)** *u* **antiphonal refrain** *á* Wise lord, *u* counsellor!
Wise lord, counsellor, " Alas! *aeee* TA *aeeeá* **high (voice)**
Honoured one, " lord, *e* great (god) An, **high (voice)** *u*
Great (god) An, father of the great gods, great lord! *aee* TA *aeeá* **high (voice)**
Honoured one, " lord *e* of (the city) Uruk, **high (voice)** *u*
á (The one) from the shrine Eana, *á* (the temple) Eĝiparimin, *á* **high (voice)** *u*
Honoured one, " lord *e* of the lands, **high (voice)** *u*
á Lord whose utterance is just, (the god) Mullil, father of the Land, *á* great lord, *aee*

e TA *aeeeá* **high (voice)** *u*

Honoured one, " lord *e* of (the city) Nippur, **high (voice)** *u*
á Lord *á* of (the temple) Ekur, *á* lord of the Land, *aee* TA *aeeá* **high (voice)** *u*
Mighty storm of the father (god) Enlil, **high (voice)** *u*
Born in the mountain, " lord *e* of (the temple) Eshumesha. *á* **high (voice)** *u*

Example 5. Translation of the beginning of the Sumerian liturgical prayer 'Alas! Wise lord, counsellor!', according to a late manuscript which includes performative annotations (in bold, underlined) and vocalic indications (in italics).[20]

---

[20] Gabbay (2015), No. 4 (pp. 55–64), manuscript 'A', lines 1–12.

The above passage includes the annotation 'high (voice)', which perhaps indicates a heightened vocal performance style. The passage also includes vocalic performative indications, which in many instances I consider likely to represent interjections.[21] As discussed by Gabbay, the phrase 'Alas! Wise lord, counsellor!' occurs only in the first two lines of the passage. We would normally expect a refrain such as this to form the horizontal axis of the litany, as a complement to the invocations in the litany's vertical axis. The first line of the passage includes the annotation 'antiphonal refrain', followed by a repeat of the opening phrase 'Alas! Wise lord, counsellor!' in small script. Therefore, it is likely that in performance, this phrase was indeed performed as an antiphonal refrain throughout the section, probably by a choir.[22]

A further example of the annotation 'antiphonal refrain' suggests that a second refrain is performed, in addition to the refrain written in the horizontal axis ('whose rites are princely!'). This passage is directed to the god Enki, whose realm lay in the *Abzu*, a cosmic subterranean freshwater ocean. The annotation 'antiphonal refrain' is included in the following example, suggesting that the refrain '(Great hero,) honored one *awuu*' is performed as an antiphonal response, perhaps by a choir:

[Enlil...] Great hero [aá]		whose rites [e] are princely (and) lofty! [e]
	antiphonal refrain honored one *awuu*	
	Lord [a] Amanki [á]	whose rites [e] are princely! [honored one *awuu*]
[u]	Lord, [a] bull of (the city) Uruzeb [á]	whose rites [e] are princely! [honored one *awuu*]
[u]	Lord, [a] Asarluhi [á]	whose rites [e] are princely! [honored one *awuu*]
	antiphonal refrain	
[u]	Lord, Enbilulu [á]	whose rites [e] are princely! [honored one *awuu*]
	Lord Sukkalmaha [á]	whose rites [e] are princely! [honored one *awuu*]
	Lord Muzebasa'a [á]	whose rites [e] are princely! [honored one *awuu*]
	(god) Nabû, princely son [á]	whose rites [e] are princely! [honored one *awuu*]
	Heir of (the temple) Esaĝil [aá]	whose rites [e] are princely! [honored one *awuu*]

[21] TA represents a cuneiform sign, the reading of which is uncertain.

[22] It is perhaps of relevance that another tablet, which also dates to the late first millennium BC, lists incipits of sections of various Sumerian liturgical compositions; presumably, the tablet served as an Aide-Mémoire. One of the incipits listed on this tablet consists of the first two lines of the above passage 'Alas! Wise lord, counsellor!', 'Wise lord, counsellor, Alas!'. Furthermore, in this tablet the incipit includes an annotation specifying the use of a 'loud voice'. Perhaps this 'loud voice' refers to choral performance. For the text, see Gabbay (2015), No. 4 (pp. 55–64), manuscript 'B'.

	(He who) is full of awe in the Abzu *a*	whose rites *e* are princely!	honored one *awuu*
	In the sky *a* (are) your birds *a*	whose rites *e* are princely!	honored one *awuu*
a	On earth *a* (are) your birds *a*	whose rites *e* are princely!	honored one *awuu*
	In the abyss *a* (are) your fish *a*	whose rites *e* are princely!	honored one *awuu*
u	Princely lord *e*	*aaa* of the Abzu! *a*	
		honored one *awuu*	

Example 6 Translation, based on a late manuscript, of an excerpt of a Sumerian liturgical prayer to Enki, including performative annotations (in bold, underlined), vocalic indications (in italics), and an additional refrain (honored one *awuu*).[23]

3.d. Rhetoric and Emotion in the Performance of Litanies

The performative role of repetition and enumeration in litanies of Sumerian liturgical prayers is of fundamental importance to an understanding of this corpus in its ritual contexts. Such litanies, and the prayers in general, have often been considered to be unexciting as literature; indeed, some contemporary scholars consider this corpus to be of only minor interest as 'literature'; one of the principal reasons for such a low estimation is the inclusion of long litanies.[24] However, it is likely that such prayers were not primarily intended to be read, but to be experienced as performed works. What may appear on the page (or tablet) as a routine list of deities and/or toponyms, may have resulted in an insistent, impassioned, emotionally charged experience in performance. The experience of Sumerian liturgical compositions as performed works would have created an emotional response for the performers themselves, and the intended audience.[25]

Such an assumption regarding the emotive effect of Sumerian liturgical prayers is suggested firstly by the content of the prayers themselves. In addition, such an interpretation is supported by the inclusion of certain performative annotations and indications in late manuscripts. As mentioned above, some late manuscripts include not only performative vowels, but also

[23] Mirelman (2018), Chapter 7.2, lines 21–34a.

[24] For this history of scholarship on Sumerian liturgical prayers, see Gabbay (2014), 1.

[25] On the role of emotion and affect in Sumerian liturgical prayers, see Delnero (forthcoming, b). Regarding the question of audience(s), Sumerian liturgical prayers were directed primarily to the god(s); however, it is highly likely that the general public participated as spectators, at least in performances of processions in and around the city. For the role of processions in the performance of Sumerian liturgical prayers, see n. 4.

directions concerning performance. Unfortunately, the precise meaning of such directive annotations is often obscure. The following litany consists of a long, standardized list of gods. 25 lines of the list are omitted by the writer of this particular tablet. In addition, the writer includes three performative annotations towards the end of the litany. These annotations appear on the edge of the tablet, but in Example 7 they are written immediately before the lines to which they refer. This particular sequence of directive annotations occurs in several compositions of Sumerian liturgical prayers, towards the end of sections. Although their precise meaning is unclear, it is certain that these directive annotations involve the musical instruments *meze* and *šem*, which are both percussion instruments. When considered within its context, this sequence of performative directions may have represented a climactic crescendo of percussion, at the end of a litany:[26]

> Let prayers be addressed to the lord of prayers,
> Let petitions be addressed to the lord of petitions by:
> (the god) An and (the goddess) Uraš; Earth, where barley sprouted;
> **25 lines skipped**
> The faithful lady, (the goddess) Kiša, the charming woman;
> The father who begat you, (the god) Asalluhi;
> The mother who bore you, (the goddess) Panunanki;
> Your beloved spouse, (the goddess) Gašangutešasiga;
> The vizier of (the god) Anu, Gašanšubura; the lofty vizier who summons to counsel, (the god) Enšadu;
> **Throw down (the musical instrument) (?)**
> The Goat-fish, exalted priest of the Abzu; the great warrior Dugabšugigi;
> The counselor, Ennundagala;
> **Diminish (the sound of the) meze-instrument (?)**
> The counselor Gašanšudeana; the counselor Duganikirzal;
> **Make the šem-instrument resound (?)**
> The mother of the warrior, (goddess) Gašantinluba; the great warrior, the lord Dikumah: Lords of the secrets of heaven and underworld, gods of heaven and gods of the underworld.

Example 7 Translation, based on a late manuscript, of an excerpt of a Sumerian liturgical prayer to Nabû, featuring performative annotations involving the skipping of lines, and the playing of musical instruments (in bold).[27]

---

[26] Unfortunately the precise identity of the *meze* and *šem* cannot be established beyond their classification as percussion instruments. It is likely that they refer to a rattle or sistrum, and cymbals. See Gabbay (2014), 143–50.

[27] Mirelman (2018), Chapter 7.1, lines b+3–c+10. The question marks following the performative annotations indicate uncertain translations.

The emotive nature of litanic performance seems to be made clear in the following litany, which describes the destruction of the city and temple. Here, the sequence *ea*, and possibly *a*, must represent a sighing, lamentful exclamation:

The city is in sighs!	*ea* How long will it stay destroyed? *a*
My city, Nippur, is in sighs!	*ea* How long will it stay destroyed? *a*
The brickwork of (the temple) Ekur is in sighs!	*ea* How long will it stay destroyed? *a*
(The shrine) Kiur, the great place, is in sighs!	*ea* How long will it stay destroyed? *a*
The shrine Enamtila is in sighs!	*ea* How long will it stay destroyed? *a*
The brickwork of (the city) Sippar is in sighs!	*ea* How long will it stay destroyed? *a*
The shrine Ebabbar is in sighs!	*ea* How long will it stay destroyed? *a*
The brickwork of (the city) Tintir is in sighs!	*ea* How long will it stay destroyed? *a*
The brickwork of (the temple) Esaĝil is in sighs!	*ea* How long will it stay destroyed? *a*
The brickwork of (the city) Borsippa is in sighs!	*ea* How long will it stay destroyed? *a*
The brickwork of (the temple) Ezida is in sighs!	*ea* How long will it stay destroyed? *a*
(The shrine) Emahtila is in sighs!	*ea* How long will it stay destroyed? *a*
(The brickwork) of (the ziggurat) Etemenanki is in sighs!	*ea* How long will it stay destroyed? *a*
(The shrine) Edara'ana is in sighs!	*ea* How long will it stay destroyed? *a*

The city is in sighs, *a* if only it were able to hold (them) back! *eeae* The lady is in despair *a* over it!

Example 8 Translation, based on a late manuscript, of the beginning of a Sumerian liturgical prayer to Enlil, including performative vocalic indications (in bold italics).[28]

---

[28] Gabbay (2015), no. 50, manuscript 'A', lines 1–12. In Example 8 the translation has been simplified, including the reconstruction of passages which are broken, abbreviated or unclear in the original text.

4. Conclusion

This contribution has attempted to demonstrate the central role of performance in what is perhaps the earliest known tradition of litanies. This performative aspect is demonstrated by several features, which I have highlighted here. For example, the role of memorization (3.a.) demonstrates the oral tradition to which Mesopotamian litanies belonged. The practice of skipping lines is a practice which is highly unusual in cuneiform writing; it demonstrates the fact that such litanies belonged to the elementary repertoire of every *kalû*-priest in ancient Mesopotamia. Such litanies must have been taught orally and memorized. Several further performative features of such litanies include the fact that they conform to a bipartite structure, which implies antiphonal performance (3.b., 3.c.). Furthermore, although it is impossible to be completely certain of the nature of Mesopotamian litanies in performance, it seems likely that they were highly emotive occasions. Musical instruments and lamentful exclamations feature prominently (3.d.).

The historical context of Mesopotamian litanies within a wider history of music and liturgy was briefly referred to at the opening of this paper, as a means of defining the concept of the litany within the history of music and liturgy. This topic is an important avenue of research, which is ripe for exploration.

Bibliography

Clark, S. (2001) 'Refrain,' Grove Music Online (https://doi.org/10.1093/gmo/9781561592630.article.23058, accessed Feb. 2019).

Delnero, P. (2015) 'Texts and Performance: The Materiality and Function of the Sumerian Liturgical Corpus,' in P. Delnero and J. Lauinger (eds), *Texts and Contexts: The Circulation and Transmission of Cuneiform Texts in Social Space* [Studies in Ancient Near Eastern Records 9], Boston, 87–118.

— (forthcoming, a) 'Texts Before Texts: Orality, Writing, and the Transmission of Sumerian Laments,' in *Oral et écrit dans l'Antiquité orientale* [Proceedings, Collège de France, Paris – 27 May 2016].

— (forthcoming, b) 'Beyond Representation: The Role of Affect in Sumerian Ritual Lamenting'.

Gabbay, U. (2013) '"We are Going to the House in Prayer": Theology, Cultic Topography, and Cosmology in the Emesal Prayers of Ancient Mesopotamia,' in D. Ragavan (ed.), *Heaven on Earth: Temples, Ritual, and Cosmic Symbolism in the Ancient World* [Oriental Institute Seminars 9], Chicago, IL, 223–43.

— (2014) *Pacifying the Hearts of the Gods: Sumerian Emesal Prayers of the First Millennium BC*, Wiesbaden.

— (2015) *The Eršema Prayers of the First Millennium BC*, Wiesbaden.

Gabbay, U. and S. Mirelman (2017) 'Text and Performance: Tayyartu, "Repetition", in a Mīs Pî-type incantation and an Emesal prayer,' *Zeitschrift für Assyriologie und vorderasiatische Archäologie* 107, 22–34.

Gabbay, U. and S. Mirelman (forthcoming) 'MU.MEŠ GU$_4$.UD.MEŠ "Skipped Lines", in Balaĝ and Eršema Prayers.'

Huglo, M., E. Foley, J. Harper and D. Nutter (2001) 'Litany,' Grove Music Online (https://doi.org/10.1093/gmo/9781561592630.article.16769. accessed Nov. 2018)

Mirelman, S. (2010) 'Performative Indications in Late Babylonian Texts,' in R. Pruzsinszky and D. Shehata (eds), *Musicians and the Tradition of Literature in the Ancient Near East* [Wiener Offene Orientalistik 8], Vienna, 241–64.

— (2018) 'Text and Performance in the Mesopotamian Liturgical Tradition' [unpublished doctoral dissertation, New York University].

— (forthcoming) 'Mesopotamian Ritual Laments, "Music Therapy", and the Role of Song in the Conception of the Deity,' in *Music Beyond Cultural Borders. Proceedings from the Workshop of the 33rd Deutscher Orientalistentag. Jena, 19/20 September, 2017.*

Reisner, G. (1896) *Sumerisch-babylonische Hymnen nach Thontafeln griechischer Zeit*, Berlin.

Christos G. Karagiannis

ASPECTS OF LITANY IN THE OLD TESTAMENT

In the Christian Orthodox tradition the idea of the litany procession is inextricably linked to a sacred object that is carried by the faithful either to the remembrance of an event, to the glorification of God or as a prayer for the sending of its blessing. In this context, the liturgical life of the Orthodox Church included the liturgy ceremonies with a prominent example of the Epitaph liturgy held every year on Good Friday. But is this something new for the Christians or something that derives from the Old Testament?

The Old Testament biblical text speaks about the most holy object of ancient Israel which was made after the command of God during the wilderness in Sinai[1] and was carried by the Levites at the entrance to the Promised Land. That object was the ark of the covenant.[2] The Old Testament people of God venerated the ark of the covenant, a box of acacia wood adorned with winged cherubim and gilded with gold trimmings, which Moses fashioned upon God's command. Why would the Israelites venerate a gilded box crafted by human hands? Would that not be a violation of the First Commandment? Not so; what made the ark of the covenant an object of veneration were its contents, God's Word inscribed in stone tablets, a dish of manna and the staff of the high priest, Aaron.[3] These made the box divinely sanctified and an object of veneration. Scripture attests that God's holy presence, the Shekinah, covered

[1] Ex 19:11; Num 12:8. (The quotes are from RSV Bible).
[2] Karagiannis (2002).
[3] Benzinger (1894); Gressmann (1920); Gutmann (1971); Nielsen (1960); Fretheim (1968).

Christos G. Karagiannis • National and Kapodistrian University of Athens, Greece

over the ark like a cloud day and night as protector of Israel.[4] The location of the ark, among the Israelites, is designated as the centralized place of worship.[5] The ark was kept in the Tent of the Meeting during their forty-year journey in the desert, in a process of a litany led Israel across to the Promised Land as the waters of the Jordan parted before it for their crossing, and won victories for them in the conquest of Canaan. They were invincible in all their battles with the ark borne aloft by priests at the frontlines of every encounter.

As time passed the Chosen People repeatedly lapsed into infidelity to their Covenant with God. His presence that had been their protection–overshadowing the Tent of Meeting in their desert sojourn and the Temple of Solomon in Jerusalem–was disregarded by the people which brought on dire consequence of defeat, domination, and exile.

As it has been mentioned first of all, the concept of the litany of the ark appears at the entrance to the promised land. In this archetypal form of litany the ark is carried by the Levites in front of all the people of Israel. When the ark set out the people set out from their place as well and went after it. When the feet of the Levites dipped in the edge of the water, the waters were cut off and the people of God crossed over on dry ground.[6] The people followed the ark along its route, though at a respectful distance. Thus, when Israel crossed the Jordan, the ark was the central point. All eyes were turned towards it. The officers commanded the people, saying, 'When you see the ark of the covenant of the Lord your God, and the priests, the Levites, bearing it, then you shall set out from your place and go after it. And Joshua said to the people, "Sanctify yourselves, for tomorrow the Lord will do wonders among you"'.[7] So they crossed over, filing past the ark being held in the midst of the Jordan, and profoundly aware of the fact that only by means of the ark the entrance into the land had been opened to them.

The next incident, in the book of Joshua where the ark played an important part, was the conquest of Jericho. Having crossed the Jordan the people camped in Gilgal, near Jericho.[8] The city of Jericho was the stronghold of the enemy that now denied the Israelites further entry into the land. If Jericho the mighty would fall, they could march on un-

---

[4] Ex 40:31–34.
[5] Dt 12:5, 11, 21; 14:23–24; 16:2; 26:2.
[6] Jos 3:14–17.
[7] Jos 3:3–5.
[8] Jos 4:19; 5:10.

hindered.[9] The only thing the armed people had to do was to do a litany around the city in silence on six consecutive days.[10] On the seventh day, however, this silent procession had to go around the city seven times, the ark always being in the midst of the procession. The only sound heard was the sound of the rams' horns before the ark. The people themselves had to keep silent until the last time they marched around the city on the seventh day.[11] For the Lord would fight for them and they should hold their peace. Only on that last great day, after having marched around the city for the seventh time, acting a silent litany, they were allowed to raise a shout of joy – realizing that they owed the victory not to themselves, but to the ark of God.[12] And then, at the sound of the trumpets and the shouts of joy of the people the walls of Jericho fell down flat, leaving this once impregnable fortress open before the people of God.[13]

It is obvious that at this early stage of the history of Israel the transfer of the ark in a litany form takes place in a silent way, like a march without hymns or prays. The ark of God is considered as the symbol of the presence of the Lord among His people[14] and all the people of Israel remain silent before Him following His instructions and the His orders.

The wars of Israel with the Philistines after the conquest of the promised land led to the loss of Israel's holy object. When the ark was taken from them, the glory departed from Israel; thus, defeat in warfare was their lot.[15] Yet the retention of the ark in the Philistines only brought him to an end, bringing it back to the people of Israel. So the ark entered a new stage in its eventful history. Via Beth Shemesh, a Levitical city not far from Ekron, it returned to Israel and went to Kiriath Jearim. The story of the return of the ark, however, took a serious turn after the men of Beth Shemesh abandoned their initial reverent attitude towards the ark and wanted to have a closer look at it. Their attitude indirectly illustrates the way in which the typical litany worship return is defined.

The first attempt to bring the ark into the City of David, Jerusalem failed, because God's holiness was not sufficiently taken into account. The ark should have been returned in a litany typical way. The ark ought

[9] De Vaux (1978).
[10] Jos 6:8–14.
[11] Luerssen (1967).
[12] Gunn (1987).
[13] Jos 6:20–21.
[14] Ex 30:6; Lev 16:2; Jos 7:6; 1 Sam 4:22.
[15] 1 Sam 4:22; cf. 14:18f; 2 Sam 6:12,18.

to be carried on the shoulders of the Levites; it was not to be transported on a cart.[16] Nor were the Levites permitted to touch the ark and the other holy vessels. When the priests had covered them with several coverings and had inserted their poles, the sons of Kohath came to carry them. But they were not allowed to touch any holy thing, lest they died.[17] Both instructions were disregarded. As a result, this incident illustrates all the formalities and rules governing how to process a litany. For David had the ark transported on a new cart, and Uzzah put out his hand to the ark of God and took hold of it. The judgment announced in Numbers 4 was fulfilled and Uzzah died on the spot. So if it is Israel's sincere desire that God should dwell in its midst, it is necessary to take into account His demands. They failed to remember that the ark was the holiest object of their worship, the throne of God Himself. Probably driven by curiosity, they looked into the ark.[18] So their joy turned to grief and they lamented because the LORD had struck them with a great slaughter.

The ark of the covenant remained in Kiriath Jearim until King David gave it a central place once more in the midst of God's people, when he set up his theocratic reign in Jerusalem. David put the ark once again in the center of Israel's worship. Since the socio-political fortune of Israel and its religious fate were inseparable, a more functional and structured religious life of the people of God was inevitable.[19] This may be seen from David's attempt to build a temple for the ark of God, and appointment and assignment of sanctuary duties to the Levites.[20] The central place of worship on Mount Zion was now linked with the new seat of David's government over the people of Israel.

In the light of this it is an essential for the litany idea to look at the account of the bringing up of the ark to Mount Zion, as it is recorded in 2 Samuel 6 and 1 Chronicles 13, 15 and 16. The frequent references to the ark in 2 Samuel 6 suggest that YHWH is again identified with the ark. This bringing up of it to Jerusalem is a typical type of litany. The entry of the ark into the City of David was accompanied by music, dancing and songs of joy. This was suitable for the earthly people of God. For the people that worship God in spirit and truth[21] these things have a

---

[16] Num 7:9.
[17] Num 4:15–20.
[18] Num 4:19.
[19] 2 Sam 7:1, 9.
[20] 2 Sam 7:2–4; 1 Chr 15:1–16:43.
[21] Jn 4:24; Phil 3:3.

ASPECTS OF LITANY IN THE OLD TESTAMENT

spiritual meaning. The same applies to the sacrifices that were offered on the occasion of the bringing up of the ark.

The dancing of David before the Lord happened when the ark of God was being brought to Jerusalem.[22] The phrase 'dancing before the Lord' occurs only in 2 Sam 6:4, 16. The word 'dance' is the translation of the Hebrew *kārar*. It occurs twice in the Hebrew Bible.[23] In all of its occurrences literally means 'dancing', 'whirling'. Here it is referring to David's act before the Lord. This rendering may be supported by the phrase 'with all his might' in v. 14. This phrase signifies the tempo of his movement. Also, the accompanying instruments may make it more likely to be read as 'dancing' (vv. 5, 15). This dancing was before the Lord.[24] With this context in view, the meaning of the phrase, *dancing before the Lord*, is considered by first looking at its life setting and genre.[25]

The dancing of King David before the Lord[26] has been a concern for a number of biblical scholars and commentators. This dancing is considered religious since it sprouts from a religious event. David's dancing was an act of solemn and holy joy.[27] To an oriental of that day such an activity was a natural mode of expression, however strange it may seem to us today. By this means David expressed his grateful praise and thus gave honor and glory to God. David danced before the Lord probably because the Lord considered him worthy, considering his ordinary background, to rule over Israel.[28] To him, this favor meant a lot.[29] Therefore, it can be maintained that David danced before the Lord whose presence was symbolized by the presence of the ark, and his reason for this act in the presence of the Lord was personal.[30] David's dance of praise was a spontaneous one. There are many instances in the Old Testament in which there is either specific or general reference to some form of sacred dance or movement (Ex 15:20; 2 Sam 6:14; Ps 100:1–5, 149:3, 150:4). Dancing per se is favorably mentioned in more than seventeen instances in the Old Testament. Oesterley deems this fact as clear evidence that the dance played an extremely im-

[22] 2 Sam 6:1–4; 1 Chr 15:29.
[23] 2 Sam 6:14,16.
[24] Barchie (2014).
[25] Youngblood (1976).
[26] 1 Sam 6:14.
[27] Christian (2002); Knott (1992); Gillespie (1992).
[28] 1 Sam 16:7.
[29] Gordon (2004).
[30] 1 Sam 16:6–1.

portant part in the lives of the Israelites and thus is included in a litany procession.[31] At sacrificial gatherings it was the custom to encircle the sacred object as a sign that the object was to be devoted to God.

1 Chronicles 14 has stated that David in no way is to blame for the failure of bringing the ark to Jerusalem, so he begins his report of the *successful* transfer of the ark.[32] This is described not only in much more detail than the parallel description in 2 Samuel 6, but has also included with *extra* material. Thus, no less than three psalms have been inserted[33] and a number of liturgical prescriptions are expressly mentioned as well.[34] None of them are to be found in the parallel account in 2 Samuel. It should be stressed that (1) the theme of 'blessing the house of David' will again be a crucial item at the conclusion of 1 Chronicles 17, and (2) that one should pay attention to the fact that the formula 'to bless his house' in its new context[35] not only functions as the conclusion of the Chronicler's ark-narrative, but at the same time lays also the groundwork for the theme of 1 Chronicles 17. It must be considered, therefore, a crucial link between these two narratives.

The author of 1 Chronicles also gives the wording of the hymn that on this glad day of the entry of the ark was sung for the first time. It is a combination of verses from several Psalms[36] and they are of a teaching and prophetic character. David's song during the litany bringing of the ark is a thanksgiving which celebrates God's wondrous works in the history of Israel and also His universal glory as the Creator and Judge of all the earth. The Lord reigns, and He is coming to judge the earth.[37] This will be for the benefit of His people who will then be gathered together and delivered from the Gentiles.[38] Thus, the perspective of this song reaches to the end time, when Israel's elect will be gathered together from the four winds, from one end of heaven to the other.[39]

This idea appears clearly in Psalm 136, also known as the Great Hallel, which is presented in the form of a litany prayer. The first of each

---

[31] Oesterley (1923).
[32] 1 Chr 15:1–16:43.
[33] 1 Chr 16:7–36.
[34] 1 Chr 16:37–42.
[35] 1 Chr 16:43.
[36] Ps 105, 96 and 106.
[37] 1 Chr 16:31–33.
[38] 1 Chr 16:35.
[39] Mt 24:30–31.

verse recalls an act of God with the second line repeating the phrase 'for his steadfast love endures forever'. According to the researchers Psalm 136 is considered to be a single, unified composition.[40] Psalm 136 is a liturgical psalm in which elements of the Israelite thanksgiving hymn give expression to the celebration of the character and deeds of Yahweh. In the cult of ancient Israel this poem probably functioned as liturgy to express God's power over and against all other powers in creation and in history. In a polemic manner it serves as a remembrance and re-enactment of the incomparable God's power as the 'God of gods'. The psalm has a unique composition and structure in the Psalter. It also reflects a variety of poetic features that serve as literary vehicles to enhance the psalm's theological content. Although it is difficult to exactly date the text, there are indications in the psalm that it could be dated back to the end of the fifth or to the beginning of the fourth century BCE and as a result brings to the proscenium older traditions and ideas.[41]

Psalm 136 is an antiphon: a chant set to music, typically recited by two groups. This is reflected in the A-B form of the Psalm. Line A is a remembrance of an action of God in the Israelites' tradition, coupled with the B line, 'for his love endures forever'. 'The purpose of praise becomes clear [...] to respond to the experience of God's grace and power, to exalt what one has seen and known.'[42] Without the response, the Psalm tells a straightforward composition of God's actions in Israelite history. It enumerates the attributes of God, and consists of twenty-seven verses, each ending with the words 'For His love endures forever'. This repetition gives the whole psalm the effect of a litany.[43] In like manner we find in the Book of Daniel the canticle of the three youths in the fiery furnace; each verse ends with the words 'Praise and exalt Him above all for ever'. By including the repetition of the response, the audience is called to join in and affirm what the Psalmist has composed. This call and response was most likely used as a part of a worship service, perhaps the liturgy of the harvest festival. The harvest festival 'was celebrated in autumn, and likewise reflects the fundamental elements of the tradition of the feast, that is, the revelation of God's salvation in creation (vv. 5–9) and in history (vv. 10–24); the psalm ends in a thanksgiving to God for the blessing of the harvest.'[44] This

[40] Pröbstl (1997); Human (2004); Maloney (2011).
[41] Hakham (2003).
[42] Miller (1995).
[43] Herrick (2003).
[44] Weiser (1962).

concluding exhortation contains a title for God unique in the Psalter: the God of heaven. It highlights His sovereignty and was a favorite of the postexilic community.[45] Its occurrence here suggests a postexilic origin of this psalm, though it does occur three times in pre-exilic writings.[46]

Psalm 136 creates a particular national history for postexilic Israel, when stability, identity, and history are lacking. The movement in Psalm 136, from Genesis and Exodus to Numbers and Prophecy, takes the reader along on the journey of the Israel's salvation history within the frame of *hesed*. 'History is filled with evil, but Israel's faith was that the God of the covenant would not let the present evil of the world be the last word about creation.'[47] Finding hope in the covenant, the psalmist views history and the future within the context of a loving God.

But this Psalm shows a new way of litany worship and illustrates the manner in which the Jews used what we now call a litany. This Psalm was used in the public worship of the Temple, being recited alternately by priest and people, and was also employed in private devotions. The psalmist calls the people to be gathered under the one God. It is the same idea that occurred in 1 Chronicles 16. There the people gathered together around the ark. Now since the ark has been lost it is again the same God who was present in the ark, the Creator who is not defeated by the foreign deities but remains the one and only as time passes.

This idea will drive at the end of the days of the Old Testament, to Jesus Christ as the true center of His own who gather together around Him. He is the center of blessing, to Him are addressed the offerings, the praise and the worship. But then He also speaks to the people. Under the guidance of His Spirit a prophetic ministry of the Word of God is taking place, with a view to honoring God and teaching His people. Apostle Paul compares the ministry of the Word in the local gathering of believers to the playing of musical instruments.[48] Every instrument has its own distinct sound. Thus the service of the singers and the musicians as instituted by king David after the ark had reached its resting place in Zion,[49] points to a prophetic voicing of divine truth.

---

[45] 2 Chr 36:23; Esd 2:1; 5:11–12; 6:9–10; 7:12, 21, 23 Neh 1:4–5; 2:4, 20; Dan 2:18–19, 28, 37, 44.

[46] Gen 24:3, 7; Jon 1:9.

[47] Boring (2012).

[48] 1 Cor 14:7.

[49] 1 Chr 6:31.

Conclusions

To conclude, it has to be noted that according to the biblical text,
- At the early stage the concept of litany is depicted as a silent campaign in which the sacred object of the ark, under the shoulders of the Levites, is preceded by the people of Israel with the purpose of crossing the Jordan River and the conquest of Jericho.
- Later a litany form as a procession occurs in the attempt of the return of the ark from the Philistines which, due to the failure to observe the litany processesion, leads to the death of the persons involved. In this way, the biblical text points out the typical pattern to be applied for a litany procession.
- The transfer of the ark from Kiriath Jearim to Jerusalem by David constitutes a unique type of procession as it is accompanied by musical instruments and king's dancing. The procession of the ark in historical moments of Israel had as its point of reference the God Himself and the giving of the due honor to him. This presence of God in the midst of the people, in a form of a litany procession, is the link that relieves, protects and secures the salvation of the faithful people.
- The central position of the ark, which is identical to the presence of God, in a litany process is essentially connected with monolatry, the centralization of worship in one and only God. It is the Chronicler who associates the presence of God via the ark of the covenant with God's wondrous works in the history of Israel and also His universal glory as the Creator and Judge of all the earth.
- This approach is further constituted in the postexilic era with Psalm 136 which is presented in a form of a litany. The movement in Psalm 136, from Genesis and Exodus to Numbers and Prophecy, takes the reader along on the journey of the Israel's salvation history within the frame of *hesed*. Psalm 136 gathers Israel for the worship of God of heavens as Jesus Christ gathers all the faithful. Thus the spiritual meaning of the litany as the center of worship which gathers and unifies people derives from the ancient past to the era of the New Testament and functions as a fundamental point for the unity and salvation under Jesus.

Bibliography

Barchie, D. (2014) 'Dancing before the Lord,' *Catalyst* 9, 74.

Benzinger, I. (1894) *Hebräische Archaeologie*, Freiburg and Leipzig, 368.

Christian, E. (2002) 'The Christian and rock music: A review essay,' *Journal of Adventist Theological Society* 13 (1), 164–68.

Boring, E. M. (2012) 'Luke: Theologian, Composer, Historian,' in *An Introduction to the New Testament: History, Literature, Theology* [vol. 1], Louisville, 556–57.

De Vaux, R. (1978) *The Early History of Israel* [D. Smith (trans.)], London and Philadelphia: 608–12.

Fretheim, T. (1968) 'The Ark in Deuteronomy,' *CBQ* 30, 4.

Gillespie, T. (1992) 'Dancing to the Lord,' in S. Case (ed.), *Shall We Dance? Rediscovering Christ-Centered Standards*, Riverside, CA, 94.

Gordon, P. R. (2004) *I & II Samuel: A commentary*, Carlisle, 235.

Gressmann, H. (1920) *Die Lade Jahves und das Allerheiligste des Salomonischen Tempels*, BWANT NF, Berlin, Stuttgart and Leipzig, 17.

Gunn, M. D. (1987) *Joshua and Judges: The Literary Guide to the Bible*, Cambridge, MA, 108.

Gutmann, J. (1971) 'The History of the Ark,' *ZAW* 83, 27.

Hakham, A. (2003) *The Bible: Psalms with the Jerusalem Commentary, 101–50* [3 vols], Jerusalem, 385–86.

Herrick, A. J. (2003) *Does God Change? Reconciling the Immutable God with the God of Love*, Parkland, FL, 17.

Human, J. D. (2004) 'Psalm 136: A Liturgy with Reference to Creation,' in D. J. Human and C. J. A. Vos (ed.), *Psalms and Liturgy*, [JSOT-Sup 410], London, 74.

Karagiannis, C. (2002) 'The Ark of the Covenant,' *Theologia* 73, 245–304 and 649–94.

Knott, B. (1992) 'Shall we dance?,' S. Case (ed.), *Shall We Dance? Rediscovering Christ-Centered Standards*, Riverside, CA, 69; 75. M. L.

Luerssen, J. (1967) *The Evolution of Sacred Dance in the Judeo-Christian Tradition*, Bloomington, IL, 15.

Maloney, M. L. (2011) *Hermeneia*, Minneapolis, 503.

Miller, P. (1995) 'Between Text and Sermon' *Interpretation* 49 (1995), no. 4, 390–93.

Nielsen, E. 'Some Reflections on the History of the Ark,' *SVT* 7 (1960), 69.

Oesterley, E. O. W. (1923) *Sacred Dance: A study in comparative folklore*, New York, 44.

Pröbstl, V. (1997) *Nehemia 9, Psalm 106 und Psalm 136 und die Rezeption des Pentateuchs*, Göttingen, 180.

Youngblood, F. R. (1976) '1, 2 Samuel' in F. E. Gaebelein (ed.), *The Expositor's Bible Commentary with the New International Version of the Holy Bible* [vol. 3], Grand Rapids, MI, 554–55.

Weiser, A. (1962) *The Psalms: A Commentary* [H. Hartwell (trans.); vol. 5], Louisville, KY, 793.

Marie-Emmanuelle Torres

'ΠΟΛΛΑ ΕΤΗ ΕΙΣ ΠΟΛΛΑ': SOME LITANIC PRACTICES IN BYZANTINE IMPERIAL CEREMONIES?

A litany is 'a kind of prayer consisting of a long sequence of chanted supplications and responses; also, by extension, any prolonged or repetitive speech or written composition'.[1] It requires two participants: the sender of the request or invocation and the receiver, (and who can can meet the demand). More precisely, the prayer is split in two voices: the first one invokes the receiver by detailing his qualities, high facts... and the second one ends by pronouncing the request with a short and repetitive structure. In Byzantium, the κύριε ἐλέησον structure can be found in all the religious services, repeated several dozen times and addressed to God, to the *Theotokos* or to the saints.[2] So, litanic practice is one of the basics of Byzantine prayers. More broadly, by using two voices for the same request, the litany approaches the practice of ἀντίφωνον.[3] Since the fourth century, the Byzantine liturgy has been built on question-answer organized songs. Both parts of the choir share the lyrics and dialogue with the audience.[4]

The Byzantine Greek uses the term λιτανεία to refer to 'a series of short liturgical petitions'[5] and λιτή for the religious procession built on this litanic practice. Sometimes the term λιτανεία is metonymously used for the procession itself.[6] Indeed, λιτή is led by the patriarch in a anxious

[1] Baldick (2001), 140.
[2] Chițoiu (2013).
[3] Kazdan (1991), 120.
[4] Baldovin (1987); Taft (2006) and (1992); Brubaker (2013) and (2001); Manolopoulou (2013) and (2016).
[5] Kazdan (1991), 1234.
[6] Manolopoulou (2016), 28–30.

Marie-Emmanuelle Torres • Aix Marseille University, CNRS, LA3M, Aix-en-Provence, France

peregrination through the city to beg God to remove a danger or a natural disaster.[7] This is how the Akathist Hymn have been performed for the first time, during the siege of Constantinople in 626, at the instigation of Patriarch Sergius.[8] The λιτή was then also used for more serene celebrations and was practiced on almost all major religious feasts.[9]

At first sight, the litany appears to be a strictly religious practice. But in Byzantium, it is very difficult to isolate the sacred from the profane.[10] The emperor participates in many ecclesiastical λιταῖς and leads others ones, called πομπή and προέλευσις.[11] The very existence of specific terms to distinguish sacred processions from secular ones suggests that these celebrations were clearly different. But, pragmatic realties are much more difficult to distinguish. Indeed, at each imperial ceremony a brilliant ritual is mobilized. As during the religious λιτή, people have to occupy spaces, listen to the sound production and perform the endless repetition of acclamations and political songs. For the study of the aulic ritual, several sources can be used: the *Book of Ceremonies* compiled in the tenth century by the emperor Constantine VII, the Philotheus' *Kletorologion*, written from a banquet attendant in the ninth century and the *Book of Offices*, said to be written by the Pseudo-Kodinos during the palaeological palaiologan renaissance, not to mention the Peter the Magistros' fragments, kept at the end of the *Book of Ceremonies*. This chronological extent seems important but the Byzantines have always been very committed to perpetuating the tradition. Therefore, the pomp of the imperial power must always be perpetuate so that the Empire would be 'a cause of wonder to both foreigners and our own people'.[12] However, the *Book of Ceremonies* is much more detailed and precise than the other texts, probably because it is above all a compilation[13] intended to preserve what makes the lustre of the Empire. Consequently, it will be our priority source.

The litany corresponds to a long sequence of very repetitive requests addressed to the Divine. As the aulic rituals are also built on long sequences of songs and acclamations, one is entitled to wonder whether

[7] Lossky (2004); Kaldellis (2007).
[8] Limberis (2012).
[9] Berger (2000).
[10] Dagron (1996).
[11] Berger (2001).
[12] Constantine VII, *De Ceremoniis aulae Byzantinae* 1 (Reiske 3–4). Hereafter *DC*.
[13] Intimately mixing prescriptions from the sixth century of Peter the Magistros with others totally contemporary.

these rites would not also be of a litanic nature. Is there a litanic way of experiencing imperial authority in Byzantium? And if it is so, what does this vocal structure bring to this ritual? Would litanic practice also support aulic practice, and therefore, in the end, the whole Byzantine ritual practice? Would the use of litanic practice strengthen the connection between the sacred and imperial realms?

This is what we will try to demonstrate here by first studying the place of vocal repetition in these aulic rituals before analysing the requests made during these ritual songs. We would then study the contribution of this vocal practice to the collective experience of authority.

1. A Ceremony Based on Repetition

The ritual must be perfectly performed so that, seing 'what befits the imperial rule and what is worthy of the senatorial body [...], the reins of power will be managed with order and beauty'.[14] It can be considered as a real staging in which all political actors are involved and in which various voices can be heard. The sound implication is largely evident in the three ritual compilations distinguishing several kinds of ceremonies: the imperial audience, the great processional walk and the extras accompanying the great feasts. All of them are entirely built on repetition: each dignitary comes to acclaim the emperor, each ritual space is invaded for the same sequence of codified movements, adoration and acclamations. Here we find the very essence of the Byzantine aulic experience: statism, hieraticism, repetition, lengthy duration and spatial mobility.[15]

1.a. Repetition of Gestures

This practice of ritual repetition is very important during the greatest festivities such as wedding, coronation, religious feast. Thus the celebration of the imperial crowning lasts several days, mobilizing emperor, army, dignitaries, priesthood and mob. It is held at several sites: palaces, churches, hippodrome and Μέση. This magnificent and overwhelming celebration is organized into the προέλευσις, the imperial procession.[16] The emperor must hear the antiphonous songs and acclamations performed by the imperial choir and the crowd at each step.

[14] Constantine VII, *DC* 1 (R 4–5).
[15] Louth (2013).
[16] Dagron (2002).

For his crowning,[17] the emperor passes through the *Augusteon*, the *Onopodion* and the great Consistory to arrive at *Hagia Sophia*. In other words, during these celebrations the emperor inhabits spaces through his physical presence and through constantly repeated ritual gestures and sounds. Doing so, he also links the aulic and popular spaces of the city. Each ritual stage is marked by very long repeated vocalizations (antiphonous tropairs and acclamations). In *Hagia Sophia* the acclamation process is the longest: more than forty-six long-life cheers are shouted by the crowd, doubling those of the singers.

One might say that in such a collective celebration, especially in (semi-)open spaces such as the Μέση or the hippodrome, ritual behaviour would have been diverse, according to the space and the audience. But the basic political ideology always remains unchanged: only the endless repetition of specific gestures and vocalizations makes it possible to obtain an adequate performance. It is the only way to illustrate the harmony of the government. This is all the more important as it is repeated many times a year. In Byzantium, to remain in a certain harmony, one must bend to tradition and repeat the same gestures, the same words.

The constant repetition of these songs and acclamations is so important that it can also be found during the less ritualized moments of these great festivities. Indeed, all the great imperial events are also the occasion to banqueting, to races and theatrical performances. And during the official dinner, the soloists of *Hagia Sophia* come to sing again antiphon in honor of the emperor and to initiate the audience's acclamations.[18] This ritual combination is even more pronounced at the hippodrome. The games always begin with the cheers addressed to the emperor when he appears in the Κάθισμα. Since the sixth century, races have been organized only for the glory of the emperor and not for charioteer's fame.[19] Orchestra, mimes, dancers and choirs are required to perform the musical interludes and to initiate the cheerful songs and the crowd's acclamations. Whatever the occasion, all these imperial celebrations are built on this same repeated melodic structure. The antiphonated singing of the professional choirs is interspersed with the endless cheers of the crowd. In terms of performance, the πολλοὶ ὑμῖν χρόνοι occupies the same place in the aulic ritual as the κύριε ἐλέησον does during the ecclesiastical celebrations.

[17] Constantine VII, *DC* 1,38 (R 191) (R 194–196).
[18] Constantine VII, *DC* 1,65 (R 293–94).
[19] Dagron (2011); Cameron (1976); McCormick (1986).

1.b. Sound Productions

These aulic experiences are therefore particularly sonorous and vocalized. Various sound actors are required: emperor, master of ceremonies, choir, instrumentalists, court and crowd. Each of them acts at a precise moment, in a certain way, according to the ritual.

Professional singers, called ψάλται, are surely the most important ritual voices. According to the *Book of Ceremonies*, a group of professional singers, from the clergy of *Hagia Sophia* and the Holy Apostles, comes to sing religious services and aulic liturgies at the palace. Until the twelfth century, all of them were eunuchs.[20] Their voices had to be by their very nature, unique and quite different, and to produce a very specific effect during the aulic performance. In 1147, Odo of Deuil, who was following King Louis VII during the Second Crusade, acknowledged that these *castrati* made 'a favourable impression, because of their sweet chanting; for the mingling of voice, the robust with the graceful, to wit the eunuch's with the manly [...] softened the hearts of the Franks'.[21] Ignace of Smolensk, a Russian pilgrim who was attending the coronation of Manuel II in Constantinople on 11 February, 1392, echoed their 'indescribable, unusual music'.[22] These singers first initiate antiphonous songs and then conduct the crowd's response. This dialogue between the choir and the audience is coupled with the one of the two parts of the choir. In the preface to his edition of the *Book of ceremonies*, Albert Vogt explains that the cheers were interspersed with the indications of the singers and the short sentences of the people.[23] In other words, the edited text does not really reflect the liveliness of these sung exchanges that were questioning, answering and interrupting each other.

The mob must listen the complex chants of the ψάλται, and follow their indications to perform short and standardized answers. The audience is only evoked by the simple λαός. As Anthony Kaldellis pointed out,[24] this term is no really precise. It's certain that only dignitaries, clergy and sometimes also guests such as foreign ambassadors, could enter the confined spaces of the palace (*Chrysotriclinos, Augusteon...*). This crowd is composed of officials who are familiar with the aulic ritual. They know that the singers' instructions must be followed. But,

[20] Moran (2002), 9–11.
[21] Odo of Deuil, *De profectione Ludovici VII in orientem*, 4.
[22] Ignace of Smolensk, *Khozheniye v Tsargrad*.
[23] Vogt (1939), 10.
[24] Kaldellis (2013).

ceremonies hold in public spaces were opened to everybody. Esplanades, churches or even the large streets could have provided areas large enough to accommodate more people, but would have become quickly overcrowded,[25] and maybe, more difficult to canalize.

The last ritual expression is silent. The emperor remains totally silent, which intrigues foreigners a lot.[26] In Byzantium, the emperor is almost sacred, he is the God's lieutenant on Earth[27] and as such, he must manifest the distance that separates him from the world with complete silence, distancing and elevating the throne.[28] It is up to the master of ceremonies (πραιπόσιτος) to speak and to launch the singing and acclamation phases. Outdoors, the emperor keeps silent and the ritual dialogue is practiced by the singers and the crowd.

These vocal parts also alternate with instrumental phrases from trumpets, drums and organ. The latter is an imperial symbol:[29] it is located just beside the throne[30] and is played whereas everybody keeps quiet, but only when the emperor is there. Constantine V offered two of them to Pepin the Short in 757,[31] which is of great interest, but it would take some time for it to be used in the West,[32] and still, only in the religious sphere. At the beginning of the tenth century, Ibn Rustah passes on Harun Ibn-Yahya's story, who discovered the organ when he was kept prisoner in Constantinople in 867:[33]

> This is an object made out of a square of wood after the manner of an oil-press, covered with strong leather, into which sixty pipes of copper are put. The part of the pipes outside the leather is covered with gold [...] Two men now start to blow the organ, and the master comes and plays the pipes; and each pipe sings according to its length, sounding in honour of the Emperor, while all the people sit at their tables.

The ritual staging leaves nothing to chance to magnify the effect produced and clearly illustrates a very unequal discourse. Songs and accla-

---

[25] George Pachymeres, *De Michaele et Andronico Palaeologis libri tredecim*, 9,1.
[26] Drocourt (2015).
[27] Ahrweiler (1975).
[28] Dagron (2003).
[29] Dagron (2011); Maliaras (1991) and (2007); Wellesz (1961).
[30] Featherstone (2006).
[31] *Annales regni francorum*, 757.
[32] Herrin (1992); Bitterman, (1929).
[33] Ibn Rustah, *Kitab al-a laq al-nafisa*, 105–07.

mations produce a sound harmony to illustrate a social unity, but the use of the organ and the trumpets demonstrates clearly authority. The emperor is so far from the world that he no longer expresses himself through a human voice but only through the organ.

1.c. Antiphonous Pratique

This combination of repetition and dialogue is acoustically doubled by the combination of sound materials. All the sounds alternate, repeating themselves and dialoguing.

The first of these dialogues is built between the audience and the πραιπόσιτος. Only he can speak freely during the ceremonies. He always pronounces the same words: 'If you please' (Κελεύσατε), to initiate, like a conductor, the gestures and vocalizations of each of the ritual actors. This contains a form of rhetorical anaphora, an invitation, which receives various answers according to the stages of the ritual.

The second dialogue, between the organ (and thus the emperor) and the audience, is less obvious but quite real. The sound dramatization is remarkable for the reception at the Gold hippodrome Festival on Easter Monday:[34]

> After the deme's crying out the 'Holy!' when the organ also sounds in the fountain-court, the *praipositos* receives a sign from the emperor, and he signals with his hand three times and the organ stops. [...]. When the deme has cheered and shouted, the organ sounds, and when it has stopped the deme begins the apelatikos [...]. When the chant has been completed, the emperors stands up and immediately the organ sounds again.

The vocal play performed by the choir is certainly the most important, because it constitutes the basis of all these ceremonies. The choir sings and then initiates the response of the crowd. Let us take the example of the emperor's coronation.[35] It begins with the first reception of the patricians at the *Onopodion*, where the court sings 'for many good years'. Same thing with the Senate when one moves on to the Great Consistory. The procession then arrives at *Hagia Sophi*a and after two general cheers repeated three times, the great phase of antiphonous acclamation begins:

---

[34] Constantine VII, *DC* 1,64 (R 287–88).
[35] Constantine VII, *DC* 1,38 (R 191–96).

Glory to God in the highest and peace on earth – *The people likewise, three times.*
Goodwill to Christian people – *id.*
For God has shown mercy on his people – *id.*

We can only quote here for a very short moment from this imperial litany. To sum up, more than one hundred sentences will be sung in the same way, between the choir and the people, just for this moment of the ritual. Therefore, there is a real question-answer game between all the different sound actors alternating, as if each type of sound could evoke a part of the Byzantine society, acclaiming the emperor. Each time, the sound emission is divided between two actors and widely repeated.

It should also be noticed that all this sound orchestration takes on even greater meaning when it emphasizes silence in a negative way. In Byzantium the whole sonic world is orchestrated: the vocal phases constantly alternate with instrumental and silent ones. Thus, in the very controlled atmosphere of the palace (for example in the *Chrysotriclinos*), songs and acclamations suddenly are sung, and then suddenly replaced by a heavy silence. All the aural space is built by repetitive ceremonies.

2. Sung Dialogue: Forms and Functions

In the end, all these actors and all these sound materials intervene in a kind of stereotypical dialogue, so full of repetitions, to acclaim the emperor. Practically, one asks for divine benevolence: as a result, it is very close to litanic practice. The main component of these celebrations remains the songs developed by the imperial choir: it is a heterogeneous mixture of religious songs, such as the Τρισάγιον, psalms, imperial antiphonous tropairs and acclamations. All of them intimately combine the divine and the political.

2.a. Litanic Forms

For the 92 imperial celebrations described in the *DC*, 356 melodic items are chanted by choir, so more than 712 are sung in dialogue between choir and crowd. We will only study the imperial songs and acclamations and we can distinguish two forms (tropairs and acclamations). They are all built on an extreme practice of repetition, but can be performed in three different ways.

The songs of the ψάλται are similar to antiphonated tropairs. A long series of strophes details the celebration of the day, the imperial qualities, the link between Heaven and Empire. These verses are interspersed with pure acclamations, initiated by the choir to be repeated by the crowd. The structure seems not really different from that of the κοντάκια, like the Akathist. Cheers serve as a chorus. The way this basic structure is performed can vary in three types.

The first type, illustrated above by the example of the coronation, consists in making the crowd repeat each verse of each tropair of the singers one to three times in a row before moving on to the next verse. The assembly is therefore brought together in the same discourse that manifests through repetition the fact of having heard, understood and adopted the words of the singers. The result is quite heavy, very repetitive and impressive. Quite simply, the litanic, invocative and almost hypnotic aspect appears and considerably extends the duration of the ceremony. Even if the vocal request is split in two voices (choir and crowd), it remains uni-directional. All men sing the emperor's praises in two stages.

The second type keeps this shared voice but adds a question-answer game between singers and crowd. Let us see the acclamations sung during the birth of a Πορφυρογέννητος:[36] 'When the two factions go up to the fountain-court of the Sigma, the cheerleaders recite, "For the rulers". The people: "A good day for victories!" The cheerleaders: "What for them?" The people: "Give strength to them; yes, Lord, may you save them; yes Lord, a good day for victories!" …' The crowd's interpellation continues for the sake of the health of the *Augustae*, the Senate, the army and the Empire. It is clear that the general theme remains to sing the emperor and ask for divine benevolence in two voices. But this general demand is energized by the dialogue established between choir and crowd. The use of this oratory construction is very significant because it might provide a better involvement of the audience (perhaps also an adherence). Here the dialogue and direct questioning is perfectly tangible but keeps the litanic dimension of the responses. The effect is more dynamic, more lively.

The third type is built on cheers: some tireless repetitions of short and stereotyped words or patterns. Of the ninety-two imperial celebrations, the most frequently sung acclamations are: 'Holy, Holy, Holy' (160 times), 'Lord, save' (100), 'Many years to you' (90), 'Welcome' (75), 'Many, many, many' (23) and 'Many upon many years' (20). So the word πολλά or πολλοί can clearly be considered as the *leitmotiv* of imperial ceremonies. All these acclamations, repeated one to three

---

[36] Constantine VII, *DC* 1,42 (R 216).

times, punctuate the different songs of the choir. But but they can also be heard separately, during a very long sequence of cheering. For exemple, during the coronation of the emperor, numerous imperial antiphons alternated with acclamations and then the whole is concluded by a long series of cheers. The πολλοὶ ὑμῖν χρόνοι is repeated seven times:[37]

> The cheer-leaders: 'Many years to you, so-and-so and so-and-so, *Augoustai* of the Romans!' The people: 'Many years to you!' The cheerleaders:[38] 'Many years to you, the good fortune of the sceptres!' The people: 'Many years to you!' The cheerleaders: 'Many years to you, so-and-so, emperor of the Romans!' The people: 'Many years to you!' The cheerleaders: 'Many years to you, divinely crowned so-and-so!' ...

More generally, the audience endlessly repeats short structures sung to ask for divine benevolence. We are clearly in a litanic practice here, based on πολυχρονία and performed by choir and crowd.

2.b. Ritual Request

Whatever the form chosen, we find the same progression, which does not really differ from that of the Akathist. Let us look at the speech sung for the coronation of the *Augusta*,[39] keeping in mind that each item sung by the ψάλται is to be repeated three times by the crowd.

> For many good years – For many good years – Holy, holy, holy! Glory to God in the highest and peace on earth – Goodwill to Christian people – for God has had mercy on his people.
>
> This is the great day of the Lord. – This is the day of salvation for the Romans. – This day is the joy and the glory of the world – on which the crown of the imperial power has rightly been placed on your head.
>
> Glory to God who has proclaimed you empress – Glory to God who has crowned your head – Glory to God who has thus determined – having crowned you, so-and-so, with his own hand – may he guard you for a great number of years in the purple – to the glory and exaltation of the Romans – may God listen to your people.

---

[37] Constantine VII, *DC* 1,38 (R 196).

[38] Although the term may evoke a completely different register, ψάλται are indeed cheerleaders.

[39] Constantine VII, *DC* 1,40 (R 204–07).

Many, many, many! ...

Now may the creator and ruler of all – He who has crowned you with his hand – multiply your years, with the *augoustai* and those born in the purple – For perfect concord for the Romans.

Many years for the emperors.

There are some parallels with the structure of the sacred hymns and λιτανεία. In different verses, God is invoked, then the legitimacy, birth and high deeds of the members of the imperial family are made explicit. But above all, one can find the same request for divine benevolence. This demand is the essential element of these rituals: the whole people pray for the success and durability of the imperial family. In the προέλευσις or the aulic πομπή, one does not find the worried and feverish atmosphere of the begging practices of the λιτή. It is a time for brilliant celebration and not for worry about a siege or an earthquake. But this is still the register of the request, because, in the end, the preservation of the Empire also raises concerns shared by all, in a more long-term perspective. This is why this request is constantly reactivated by the litanic repetition, giving a rhythm but also an impression of incessant insistence.

However, in strictly structural terms, this litanic practice is unconventional. Indeed, it is clearly a singing request. All the audience, with two voices, invokes and asks for divine benevolence but not for itself. The two voices act as intermediaries of the imperial cause in front of God. On the oratory level, a third actor appears here (the emperor) who always remains silent. Consequently, it may be exaggerated to speak of an imperial litany in the strict sense. Nor is it a question of dialogue between the choir and the crowd, nor between men and the celestial sphere. However, it is clear that there is a complete 'litanization' of the aulic ritual leading to a hybrid form of litany.

The request is made by the audience to God, by imploring for the emperor. To a certain extent, the crowd contributes to the achievement of what they ask for. It is precisely through its voice that the social group must help the emperor and the Empire. It is by reminding God of the legitimacy and imperial qualities that the people hope to preserve divine kindness. This is not an unprecedented practice in Byzantium: in the synaxaries and the monastic τυπικά from the tenth century onwards,[40]

---

[40] Manuel of Stroumitza, *Typicon*, 6; Neilos of Tamasia, *Typicon*, 47; Gregory Pakourianos, *Typicon*, 42; Irene Doukaina, *Typicon*, 42; John II Komnenos, *Typicon*; Timothy Evergetinos, *Typicon*, 40; Michael Attaleiates, *Typicon*, 39.

prayers, songs and acclamations are prescribed for the health and durability of the emperor and Empire. The emperor is God's chosen one, but he must be careful to remain in his benevolence, otherwise he will lose the divine election and be replaced. In fact, even if these songs and acclamations are not intended to ward off an impending disaster, they serve to protect against a more general but equally important danger.

2.c. Polychronia and Imperial Legitimacy

So, all imperial rituals are performed on the acclamations, called πολυχρονία because they wish most of the time a long life (πολυχρόνιον or εὐφημίαν). The melody, which is known for the πολυχρονία of the fourteenth–fifteenth centuries,[41] as well as their lyrics, is quite simple, repetitive and built around the same idea, namely, to preserve divine benevolence. It is difficult to know if all the πολυχρονία were of the same kind as those found in the late period. But acclamation is an essential and mandatory element of imperial legitimacy.[42]

From the tenth century onward, the candidate for the Empire must be accepted by the Senate, acclaimed by the army and then sacred by the patriarch. The Senate no longer really played a real political role from the sixth century onwards[43]. On the contrary, the army has always played a major role in establishing and asserting imperial authority. The military acclamation also remains built on the same simple litanic practices as those pronounced in the morning by the army:[44]

> So-and-so and so-and-so, *augoustoi*, may you be victorious! – Heavenly emperor – Crown our emperors with victories! – Son of God, rule together with them – Divinely appointed – imitate God's love for mankind! – We, O armies, how shall we defeat the enemy? – By guarding the faith in God and the rulers' prudence. – May God make our emperors strong: yes, Lord, for many years!

During imperial ceremonis, through their voice, their sound affirmation and the endless repetition of the same πολυχρονία, the people took over the legitimizing function of the army and recognize the emperor. It is therefore vital for emperors to monitor or provoke this vocal legitimization. For Anthony Kaldellis, this is irrefutable proof of the political

---

[41] Tillyard (1912), 239–60; Wellesz (1961); Troelsgard (2011).
[42] Kaldellis (2013a).
[43] With the exception of the seventh-eighth centuries.
[44] Constantine VII, *DC* 1, 76 (R 372).

power of the demos. However, it might also be a ritualized expression which is recomposed by Byzantine historians. But we must recognize that these imperial rituals offer the people an opportunity to be heard. Several emperors or usurpers have taken a particular interest in this popular ritual voice, as if it clearly illustrates their popularity and their legitimacy.[45] During these ritual moments, the people of Constantinople is at the very centre of the attention.

It should not be forgotten that the political and ideological ideal in Byzantium remains harmony, equilibrium, moderation and control. It is surely necessary to see in this extreme meticulous ritual (and in the bureaucratic meticulousness that characterizes Byzantium) this absolute quest for order. The crowd is entitled in the Byzantine chronicles to only two possible expressions: the legitimate acclamation or the revolted expression. The latter is characterized by a deadly combination of screams, cries and moans. The definition of a totally codified ritual expression ultimately makes it possible to channel everyone's energy and avoid the chaos that seems to characterize it.

In the end, we observe in this litanic practice of the πολυχρονία both a double ritual function and a double request. It is as much the people intending to keep the emperor (and the Empire) in divine benevolence as the emperor searching for a continuous legitimacy. If ritual practice makes it possible to measure popular mood, it has yet to be properly analyzed. However, it might be also necessary to distinguish strict ritual expression from spontaneous expression, which could also use the ritual voice. This is obviously very difficult and Michael V was clearly lost by misunderstanding the meaning of this popular voice.[46] In 1042, he has been thinking indeed, for so long, to get rid of the Empress Zoe, who had given him access to the throne. But since he is afraid of the consequences, he wants to make sure of his popularity before acting. Thus he asks for a procession. Satisfied with the ritual warmness he hears, he decides to banish Zoe. He is totally confused when the people rise up in revolt. In the end, Michel V has made two mistakes: first, he has not imagined that popular expression could be totally fictitious. But above all, he has not understood that he only retains his legitimacy as long as he does the right thing (which is certainly not getting rid of a Πορφυρογέννητη Empress). Through this litanic practice of acclamation, all people can validate imperial legitimacy.

[45] Kaldellis (2013a); Cheynet (1990).
[46] John Skylitzes, *Synopsis historiarum* 417,1; Michael Psellos, *Chronographia* 5,5,23.26.30; Michael Attaleiates, *Historia* 4,4,12–13.

3. A Collective Experience of Authority

λιτή and πομπή are both collective celebrations: choir, court, army and crowd all are gathered in the same space. Therefore the choice of a litanic sung expression might be very useful because it quickly allows people to have a sense of unity in communication and ritual experience.

3.a. Political Propaganda

To attract and preserve divine benevolence, the people recall the qualities and achievements of the emperor. Doing so, it defines the ideal of government. However, these ritual songs are not created by the people but rather composed by official poets and melodes.

First of all, we recall its imperial function: it is the sovereign of the Romans, chosen, anointed and crowned directly by God, invested with divine royalty. God amply favors him by offering him many years, children, wife, military successes. He is also a great warrior, protected by God, as the ψάλται sing for the following day of the anniversary of his accession:[47] 'Incomparable soldiers, champions of the empire, who wear the crown, raised up by God to the throne of imperial power, you scattered foreign nations with divinely-inspired weapons of piety.' They further affirm his good government and the social consensus around his person.

So, the emperor appears to be the best possible leader. Its legitimacy and authority are affirmed by the general voice. Collective involvement demonstrates social commitment. We can observe that it is always a question of associating the divine and the imperial. First, one recognized the sacred dimension of the day, then one praised the emperor. All of the imperial qualities are detailed by making a constant comings and goings with the celestial example. It should not be forgotten that these great imperial celebrations take place at key moments in the liturgical calendar, such as Christmas. This obvious combination with the divine builds the real political propaganda. The emperor is praised for possessing the required qualities, piety, orthodoxy and legitimacy. Above of all, he is the emperor because he has been directly chosen and crowned by God. The link between Heaven and earth is constantly affirmed and reiterated.

This speech is not in itself unique or exceptional, but its staging is specific to Byzantium. Officially, political discourse is not imposed on the audience, nor is the emperor's authority. But collective expression is clearly

---

[47] Constantine VII, *DC* 1,63 (R 281).

oriented, even forced. The crowd must hear and sing these aulic chants. Everything is thought out to make the ritual political message more deeply integrated by the people. By affirming that the emperor is chosen by God and by jointly evoking the divine and imperial qualities, one demonstrates the emperor's special position, between Heaven and Earth. He has been chosen to rule and defeat Christ's enemies. He is indeed the lieutenant of God on earth whom it is necessary both to follow and to help with prayers. By taking place, silently, in these rituals affirming this delegation of power, the emperor appears as the visible avatar of divine power.

This rapprochement to the divine is also particularly strengthened by litanic practice. This includes the same ritual mode than in religious liturgies: litany, repetition, antiphonous and collective singing. The emperor does not interfere in the vocalizations and is not prayed to like a god. But it is presented by the people to God with elements of religious ritual. The choice of a hybrid form of litany gives him a specific position, between man and the divine. The constant reminder of his divine election obviously brings him closer to Heaven than to earth. This is all the more so since litanic practice unconsciously creates connections between sacred and secular domains, through the use of the same ritual gestures. The parallel with the Akathist is quite striking. The emperor is not the one who is prayed by the crowd, but in the end the sung speech juxtaposes the military functions of God and the emperor. The Akathist also details in detail the qualities of the Theotokos. Since the seventh century, she has been the protector of the Empire: a sacred and practical protection. By using the same sung style, the two protectors, one celestial and the other terrestrial, are intimately connected. The use of the litanic style makes it possible to illustrate in a concrete way the rapprochement of the imperial and divine spheres and to tint the ritual memory.

And we should not forget the consequences of a sort of vocal confusion in these endless repetitions. Slight changes in speech help to stimulate attention and practice. But the extreme duration of the sung phrases and the rebound play between the two parts of the choir, must have caused a certain vocal smoothing at best. Emperor and God are finally praised by the same means. This could trully make more tangible the political-religious association that defines Byzantine power.

3.b. Collective Unity

More broadly, for ritual, the idea is to develop all socio-political groups in the same ritual dance. Space and time are thus invested by the group.

The time investment, given the duration of the litanic phases, repeated at each station, each celebration, and each year, may be the most important. This temporal structuring gives rise to a habit that surely influences everyone's participation, and therefore the scope of such vocal practices. Litanic song and acclamation are ultimately the necessary response to a demonstration of power and perhaps even the primary expression of the collective. All revolts are accompanied by songs, shouts and cheer. Litanic singing and acclamation characterize the ritual expression of the collective.

Finally, if we go further into the reflection on repetitions in these ceremonies, it must be noted that it takes place on several levels. In the end, the entire year is built on a series of celebrations, rich in alternating requests, songs and acclamations. Litanic practice thus spreads in the acoustic space but also in time. The question then arises of the incidence of repetition itself,[48] the basis of any litanic practice: what is its purpose? Does it generate cognitive effects? Psychosocial ones? This collective participation is made more feasible by the fact that litanic practice simplifies vocalization as much as possible, energizes or even thrills attention and gives the necessary energy to bring this so static ritual to life. This vocal repetition clearly has an impact on collective practice. Simplification and repetition allow for better participation and therefore help to improve collective cohesion. In deed, the constantly repeated almost direct questioning by the singers' voices calls for a response or even support. Moreover, thanks to the songs of the ψάλται, the crowd knows perfectly well what to say and do. Michael Psellos[49] experienced the contagious effect of collective acclaim when he proposed a compromise to the rebellious Isaac Komnenos in front of his men. Step by step, even the most refractory of his soldiers started to sing like the others and ended up adhering to an opposite position. However, the importance of these ritual practices and the contribution of the litanic form can be measured. The participation of the crowd is energized by the use of antiphonous and litanic forms. With maximum simplification and stereotyping, its voice participation must more easily perform its political function.

The convocation of the group for a ritual experience clearly represents a demonstration of authority. The emperor is recognized as the es-

---

[48] Magri-Mourgues and Rabatel (2014); Olivési (1994); Clark, È. V. (2006); Clark, H. (1996).

[49] Michael Psellos, *Chronographia* 7,27.

sential actor of the power that one hurries to see and to sing, even to boo. In practice, all these experiences are ways of controlling this quickly versatile and easily agitated crowd. It is a way to control it, imposing a ritual attitude on it, such as obeying the instructions of the singers. The spontaneous aspect of the cheers might be only a facade and the voice of the people required at each ceremony does not reveal anything about the real enthusiasm. The fact that the cheerleaders themselves initiate the cheers of the crowd is effective enough to guide the spontaneous vocalizations. The volume of the ensemble's sound would also tend to mask any untimely interventions. This channels energy, exultation and even collective agitation. The ritual structure serves both to define the group that receives its only official expression there and to define the authority that can control ritual participation.

3.c. Aural Experience of the Group

The group is defined by its ritual role. However, its involvement cannot be strictly constant and homogeneous. Outside the confined spaces of the palace, the collective energy is only hardly circumscribed by the ritual voice. All the revolts prove it since they are all carried out with screams and ritual transvestites. Chroniclers discuss them in detail but without suggesting that it is unusual or inappropriate. Moreover, there is never any mention of any official reaction to parasitic voices, as long as it does not turn into a revolt. And, as it has been demonstrated by Nicolas Mariot,[50] it might be very difficult to determine the performative effectiveness of one popular legitimization. Ritual involvement can illustrate a full commitment of the participants who see it as a way to express it in an obvious way. But it may be a simple act of social routine. It can also only be part of the collective exaltation of the moment.

Nevertheless, it is through sound that the ceremonies are conducted and performed, but it is also thanks to these sounds that the involvement of all the participants can be achieved. Collective organization is defined by the orchestration of voices. Through the ritual the multiplicity of actors is unified. The ritual group is structured in different hierarchies to which very specific expression, behaviour and function are assigned. This illustrates the Byzantine τάξις,[51] or a quest for political, social and cosmic order, which explains the infinite complexity of the aulic ritual. We must recall the importance of the hierarchical vision

[50] Mariot (2006).
[51] Auzépy (2005).

of Pseudo-Dionysius Areopagite (sixth century).[52] The main idea is that Creation is organized by successive perfectly defined hierarchies, and that the organization of Earth imitates that of Heaven.[53] So each man must recognize his position, remain in his group and adopt the gestures, attitude and expression which define it. There is therefore a hierarchy in these aulic practices: at the top the emperor, divine avatar, in the middle the singers and the master of ceremonies, at the bottom the court and the people. Each level speaks differently: the emperor by his silence, the singers by the complicated modulations and melismas of their 'extra-human' voices (neither children nor men), the crowd by the repetition of simple words or expressions thrown by the singers. This hierarchy is combined with an idea of progression that is reflected in the framing of the popular voice by the voices of the singers.

But more generally, voice and sound create unity. Although it has only been studied extensively in the religious domain,[54] sound (voice, music and noise) is an essential part of the aulic ritual. Voices thus structure the ritual space. This is not just a simple topographical reality. As soon as we enter a space we fill it with our body, our senses, our emotions to make it a personal representation. These ritual spaces are both symbolic and sensory spaces. Raymond Murray Schafer has been the first to recognize the importance of sound in the interaction with space.[55] Indeed, by definition man is both a sound producer and a sensory receiver.[56] The atmosphere is only given by the sensations, and particularly by the sound. The impact of this spatial sound system cannot be forgotten because it particularly influences sound production[57] and the way this space is experienced. In Byzantium, if the atmosphere of the προέλευσις or πομπή is much calmer than that of the λιτή, the approach is the same: to bring the people together in a common and collective experience of imperial power. The emperor shows himself and establishes a dialogue with his people, a communication that is all the more stereotypical because it is litanic. But it goes even further than just connecting everybody: one must experience the union of the collective around the

---

[52] See Pseudo-Dionysius Areopagite, *De Coelesti Hierarchia* and *De Ecclesiastica Hierarchia*.

[53] Bornert (1966).

[54] Pentcheva (2017a), (2017b).

[55] Murray Schafer (1977).

[56] Sterne (2003); Thompson (2004); Faburel et al (2004); Emerit, Vincent, Perrot (2016).

[57] The singers adapt their practice in real time to the acoustics of the place.

same political actor. It is together that one must cheer and respond to the melodies of the singers. The ψάλται sing:[58] 'The world rejoices seeing you as sovereign emperor, and your City is delighted, divinely-crowned so-and-so. The order flourishes seeing you as head of the order, and the sceptres are fortunate in having you as the holder of the sceptre.' In fact, the sound harmony demonstrates the political harmony sung.

We must consider the symbolic impact of these ritual sounds. Singing mobilizes the body but collective practice gives a certain rhythm to the group. The soundspace comes to encompass all the audience in the same celebration, organized and fulled of symbolisms. On the one hand, as the ritual voices are hierarchical various spatial strata can be delimited: emperor, singers, court and people. But on the other hand, through this litanic repetition of imperial praise, the harmony of the whole is also illustrated. Harmony because each one keeps his or her assigned place, harmony because the divine is imitated, harmony because the cosmic order is renewed in the same way. Using the same practices in both sacred and secular rites brings these two collective experiences closer together. The stimulation of memory allows for a certain transfer of liturgical emotions. Little by little, the ritual space is populated with a multitude of meanings and symbols which are reactivated by ceremonial gestures. Imperial legitimacy remains a divine election: it is through aural ritual that it is felt and that authority is affirmed. The symbols which are used are clues to this quasi-divine power, and mark the minds as much as the weapons.

4. Conclusions

To conclude, it appears that all ceremonies involving the emperor are built on alternating sounds and vocal question-and-answer games. The space, bodies, voices and instruments are totally staged. More broadly, all the sound phrases alternate to build a dynamic and collective experience of authority. The vocal emission is divided into two parts, between singers and people, and between antiphonous songs and acclamations. All these ceremonies are therefore very sonorous and repetitive to ask for divine benevolence for the emperor. The πολυχρόνιον is repeated hundreds of times for his posterity. This is clearly a hybrid practice of the litany, in the sense that the request is addressed to God for a third per-

---

[58] Constantine VII, *DC* 1,63 (R 282).

son (the emperor) who is not involved in the voice exchange. This litany is more than a simple collective prayer: it is also an essential element of imperial legitimacy. Furthermore, these songs develop a political program: the emperor is the God's chosen one and the sword of Christianity. The choice of a litanic form makes palpable this in-between position occupied by the emperor, which benefits from the same ritual gestures as the divine. The highly repetitive dimension also allows for a collective union around the emperor and illustrates, through the voices, the social hierarchy. The sound space encompasses the assistance in the same experience of authority. It is therefore through the senses, ritual and emotion and the ritual litanization that political interlude can be achieved.

Bibliography

Ancient and Medieval Authors

Annales regni francorum; ed. and trans. F. Guizot, Paris, 1824.

Constantine VII Porphyrogennetos, *De Ceremoniis aulae Byzantinae*; ed. and trans. A. Vogt [4 vols], Paris, 1939; ed. J. J. Reiske, Bonn, 1829, 1830; trans. A. Moffat and M. Tall [2 vols], Canberra, 2012.

George Pachymeres, *De Michaele et Andronico Palaeologis libri tredecim*; ed. A. Failler, trans. V. Laurent [5 vols], Paris, 1984–2000.

Gregory Pakourianos, *Typicon*; ed. and trans. P. Gautier, *Revue Des Études Byzantines*, 1984 (42), 5–145.

Ibn Rustah, *Kitab al-a laq al-nafisa*; ed. M. J. De Goeje, Leiden, 1892; trans. A. A. Vasiliev, Bruxelles, 1932.

Ignace of Smolensk, *Khozheniye v Tsargrad*; ed. and trans. B. de Khitrovo, Genève, 1889; ed. and trans. G. Majeska, Washington, DC, 2007.

Irene Doukaina, *Typicon*; ed. and trans. P. Gautier, *Revue Des Études Byzantines*, 43 (1985), 5–165.

John II Komnenos, *Typicon*; ed. and trans. P. Gautier, *Revue Des Études Byzantines*, 32 (1974), 1–145.

John Malalas, *Chronographia*; ed. L. Dindorf, Bonn, 1831; trans. E. Jeffreys, M. Jeffreys and R. Scott, Melbourne, 1986.

John Skylitzes, *Synopsis historiarum*; ed. P. Lethielleux, trans. B. Flusin, Paris, 2003.

Liutprand of Cremona, *Antapodosis*; ed. P. Chiesa, Turnhout, 1998; trans. F. Bougard, Paris, 2015.

— *Relatio de Legatione Constantinopolitana*, ed. P. Chiesa, Turnhout, 1998; trans. F. Bougard, Paris, 2015.

Manuel of Stroumitza, *Typicon*; ed. and trans. Louis Petit, *Izvestiya Russkogo Archeologicheskogo Instituta v Konstantinopole*, 6 (1900), 1–153.

Michael Attaleiates, *Historia*; ed. I. Bekker, Bonn, 1853; trans. A. Kaldellis and D. Krallis, Cambridge, 2012.

— *Typicon*; ed. and trans. P. Gautier, *Revue Des Études Byzantines*, 39 (1981), 5–141.

Michael Psellos, *Chronographia*; ed. and. trans. É. Renaud [2 vols], Paris, 1926, 1928.

Neilos of Tamasia, *Typicon*; ed. I. Tsiknopoullos, *Kypriaka Typika*, 1969, 3–68, trans. A. Bandy, Washington, DC, 2001.

Odo of Deuil, *De profectione Ludovici VII in orientem*; ed. and trans. V. G. Berry, New York, 1948.

Pseudo-Dionysius Areopagite, *De Coelesti Hierarchia, De Ecclesiastica Hierarchia, De Mystica Theologia, Epistulae*; eds H. Günter and A. M. Ritter, Heidelberg, 2012.

Pseudo-Kodinos, *De Officiis*; ed. and trans. J. Verpeaux, Paris, 1966; eds and trans. R. Macrides, J. A. Munitiz and D. Angelov, Farnham, 2013.

Timothy Evergetinos, *Typicon*; ed. and. trans. P. Gautier, *Revue Des Études Byzantines*, 40 (1982), 5–101.

Modern Authors

Ahrweiler, H. (1975) *L'idéologie politique de l'Empire byzantin*, Paris.

Auzépy, M. F. (2008) 'Les aspects matériels de la taxis byzantine,' *Bulletin du Centre de recherche du château de Versailles* [http://journals.openedition.org/crcv/2253; DOI: 10.4000/crcv.2253; accessed Dec. 5, 2018].

Baldick, C. (2001) *The Concise Oxford Dictionary of Literary Termes* [2nd edn, original 1990], Oxford.

Baldovin, J. (1987) *The Urban Character of Christian Worship: The Origins, Development and Meaning of Stational Liturgy*, Rome.

Berger, A. (2000) 'Streets and Public Spaces in Constantinople,' *Dumbarton Oaks Papers* 54, 161–72.

— (2001) 'Imperial and Ecclesiastical Processions in Constantinople,' in N. Necipoğlu (ed.), *Byzantine Constantinople: monuments, topography and everyday life*, Leiden, 73–88.

Bitterman, H. R. (1929) 'The Organ in the Early Middle Ages,' *Speculum* 4, 390–410.

Bornert, R. (1966) *Les commentaires byzantins de la divine liturgie du VIIe au XVe siècle*, Paris.

Brubaker, L. (2001) 'Topography and the Creation of Public Space in Early Medieval Constantinople,' in F. Theuws, M. D. Jong, and C.V Rhijn (eds), *Topographies of Power in Early Middle Ages*, Leiden, 31–43.

— (2013) 'Processions and Public Spaces in Early and Middle Byzantine Constantinople,' in A. Ödekan, N. Necipoğlu and E. Akyürek (eds), *The Byzantine Court: Source of Power and Culture. Papers from the Second International Sevgi Gönül Byzantine Studies Symposium. Istanbul, 21–23 June 2010*, Istanbul, 123–28.

Cameron, A. (1976) *Circus Factions, Blues and Greens at Rome and Byzantium*, Oxford.
Cheynet, J. C. (1990) *Pouvoir et contestations à Byzance (963–1210)*, Paris.
Chițoiu, D. (2013) 'Repetition as Resumption: From Litany to Thinking in Byzantium,' *Revista Portugesa de Filosofia* 69, no. 2, 205–13.
Clark, E. V. (2006) 'La répétition et l'acquisition du langage,' *La linguistique* 42, no. 2, 67–80.
Clark, H. (1996) *Using Language*, Cambridge.
Dagron, G. (1996) *Empereur et prêtre. Recherches sur le 'césaropapisme' byzantin*, Paris.
— (2002) 'Réflexions sur le cérémonial byzantin,' *Palaeoslavica* 10, no. 1, 26–36.
— (2003) 'Trônes pour un empereur,' in A. Avraméa, A. Laiou, E. Chrysos (eds), *Βυζάντιο. Κράτος και Κοινωνία. Μνήμη Νίκου Οικονομίδη*, Athens, 179–203.
— (2011) *L'hippodrome de Constantinople: jeux, peuple et politique*, Paris.
Drocourt, N. (2015) *Diplomatie sur le Bosphore. Les ambassadeurs étrangers dans l'Empire byzantin des années 640 à 1204*, Leuven.
Emerit, S., A. Vincent, S. Perrot (2016) *Le paysage sonore de l'Antiquité*, Le Caire.
Faburel, G. et al (eds) (2004) *Soundspaces*, Rennes.
Featherstone, M. (2006) 'The Great Palace as Reflected in the De Cerimoniis,' in F. Bauer (ed.), *Visualisierungen von Herrschaft. Frühmittelalterliche Residenzen, Gestalt und Zeremoniell*, Istanbul.
Herrin, J. (1992) 'Constantinople, Rome and the Franks,' *Byzantine Diplomacy. Papers from the Twenty-Fourth Spring Symposium of Byzantine Studies, Cambridge, March 1990*, Aldershot.
Kaldellis, A. (2007) 'The Literature of Plague and Anxieties of Piety in Sixth-Century Byzantium,' in F. Mormando, T. Worcester (eds), *Piety and Plague: From Byzantium to the Baroque*, Kirksville.
— (2013a) 'How to Usurp the Throne in Byzantium: The Role of Public Opinion in Sedition and Rebellion,' in D. Angelov, M. Saxby (eds), *Power and Subversion in Byzantium*, Farnham.
— (2013b) 'The Military Use of the Icon of the Theotokos and Its Moral Logic in the Historians of the Ninth-Twelfth Centuries,' *Estudios Bizantinos: Revista de la Sociedad Española de Bizantinística* 1, 56–75.
Kazdan, A.P (1991) *Oxford Dictionary of Byzantium*, Oxford.
Khitrovo, B. de (1889) *Itinéraires russes en Orient*, Genève.
Limberis, V. (2012) *Divine Heiress*, London.

Lossky, A. (2004) 'La Litie, un type de procession liturgique byzantine – Extension du lieu de culte,' in C. Braga, and A. Pistoia (eds) *Les enjeux spirituels et théologiques de l'espace liturgique*, Paris, 165–78.

Louth, A. (2013) 'Experiencing the Liturgy in Byzantium,' in M. Jackson, and C. Nesbitt (eds) *Experiencing Byzantium*, New York, 79–88.

McCormick, M. (1986) *Eternal Victory. Triumphal Rulership in Late Antiquity, Byzantium, and the Early Medieval West*, Cambridge.

Magri-Mourgues, V., A. Rabatel (2014) 'Quand la répétition se fait figure,' *Semen* 38, 7–13.

Majeska, G. (1984) *Russian Travelers to Constantinople in the Fourteenth and Fifteenth Centuries*, Washington, DC.

Maliaras, N. (1991) *Die Orgel im byzantinischen Hofzeremoniell des 9. und des 10. Jahrhunderts*, München.

— (2007) *Βυζαντινά Μουσικά Όργανα*, Athens.

Manolopoulou, V. (2013) 'Processing Emotion: Litanies in Byzantine Constantinople,' in M. Jackson, and C. Nesbitt (eds) *Experiencing Byzantium*, New York, 153–72.

— (2016) 'Processing Constantinople' [unpublished doctoral dissertation, University of Newcastle].

Mariot, N. (2006) *Bains de foule*, Paris.

Moran, N. (2002) 'Byzantine Castrati,' *Plainsong and Medieval Music* 11, no. 2, 9–11.

Murray Schafer, R. (1977) *The Tuning of the World*, Rochester.

Olivési, S. (1994) 'De la politique du discours: éléments pour une analyse critique du discours politique,' *Quaderni: La revue de la communication* 24, 9–25.

Pentcheva, B. (2017a) *Hagia Sophia*, University Park.

— (2017b) *Aural Architecture*, London.

Sterne, J. (2003) *The Audible Past*, Durham and London.

Taft, R. (1992) *The Byzantine Rite: A Short History*, Collegeville.

— (2006) *Through Their Own Eyes: Liturgy as the Byzantines Saw It*, Berkeley.

Thompson, E. A. (2004) *The Soundscape of Modernity*, Cambridge.

Tillyard, H. J. W. (1912) 'The Acclamation of Emperors in Byzantine Ritual,' *The Annual of the British School at Athens* 18, 239–60.

Troelsgard, C. (2011) *Byzantine neumes*, Copenhagen.

Wellesz, E. (1961) *A History of Byzantine Music and Hymnography*, [2nd edn, original 1949], Oxford.

Bernard Sawicki OSB

A LITANY IN THE RULE OF ST BENEDICT

*On the Mysterious Form of Chapter 4 of the Rule
and Its Theological Implications*

1. General Background

Chapter 4 of the *Rule* of Saint Benedict has a specific character. As Adalbert de Vogüé observes:

> This catalogue of the 'instruments of good works' is without doubt the most unexpected part of the *Rule*. At first glance it astonishes the reader by its unusual make-up – a list of maxims – and by the lack of connection with the surrounding treatises. Upon further examination the reader is disappointed to find in this succession of little phrases little or no order. Moreover, it is a program of good works which are to be accomplished with an eye on eternal life.[1]

From the point of view of the history of form this chapter is a collection of sentences, a catalogue of virtues and vices, a list of sayings, with moral mnemonics that can be often repeated and thereby penetrate the heart and seize the whole person. Something of this is known in the Bible, the ten commandments, for example, or the book of Proverbs or the catalogues of virtues and vices. There are also apocryphal texts from the first century, containing similar collections of sayings, like the *Sentences of Sextus* or the *Passio Juliani*. In addition some liturgical rites, such as baptism and priestly ordination, use the form of short repetitive sentences

---

[1] Vogüé (1983).

Bernard Sawicki OSB • Pontifical Atheaneum of St Anselm in Rome, Italy

or invocations. These historical reasons as well as the formal structure allow us to classify the text of this chapter as a litany.[2]

The content of Chapter 4 of the *Rule* may be unexpected because of the wide range of themes and references. But does it not simply cover the matter of Christian life? If God gave us the grace and invitation[3] to the monastic life, so now conversion in everyday life should follow. Hence the list of good works is natural and helpful. The monastic profession is a consequence of baptism. This litany, in a way, refers to the ancient Christian baptismal instructions, obviously based on the Old and New Testaments. If the initiation into Christian life required some 'tools' that could be easily committed to memory, the more so did monasticism. Ancient Christianity knew a form of this kind, called 'Testimonia', i.e. scriptural florilegia such as that written by Cyprian (*Ad Quirinium, Ad Fortunatum*).[4]

The commentators note that Chapter 4 of the *Rule* is very different. According to some of them, although apparently different from other chapters, its doctrine is in harmony with the rest of the *Rule*.[5] Also the *Rule of Master* has small collections of such sentences.[6]

2. Parallels in Other Cultures

Looking at monastic texts written in other spiritual traditions, one can see some analogies. At the beginning of its text, after the declaration of 'taking refuge in Buddha, his law and Order', the Buddhist *Vinaya*, written in India, proposes a list of virtues – ten commandments announced by the spiritual master. In the course of this book we find two hundred and fifty minor prescriptions which apply the vows of the monk to the details of present life.[7]

At the beginning of the second and fourth books of the *Law of Manou* from the Brahma tradition, there are similar commandments

---

[2] We base this statement on the definition of the genre of litany given by Sadowski. He defines it as 'a heterogeneous phenomenon which comprises certain basic patterns, namely genes' making reference to 'the archaic past of litany. See Sadowski, Kowalska, Kubas (eds) (2016), 11.
[3] Benedict, *Regula, Prologue*, 19.
[4] Cf. Boeckmann, (2011), 209.
[5] Dreuille (2000), 125.
[6] Boeckmann (2011), 209–10.
[7] Dreuille (2000), 125–27.

addressed to hermits and young monks. Many of these commandments refer to non-violence and non-sensuality.[8]

Looking at the text of St Benedict in a wider cultural context, the phrases he uses in Chapter 4 of the *Rule* can be described as similar to mantras. The sentences taken from the Bible were often quoted by the Fathers in just this way. They contained a digest of all spiritual experiences and were conceived to be learnt by heart. St Benedict certainly knew this technique. He recommended not only to read the *Rule* often[9] but also to repeat frequently in one's heart certain Biblical phrases (*'dicat semper utilis frater in corde suo /he repeats always in his heart'*;[10] *'dicens sibi cum Propheta'*;[11] *'dicens cum Propheta'*;[12] *'dicens sibi in corde semper'*[13]). This list thus would appear as a catalogue of phrases which, often repeated advisedly, are like a hammer which breaks against Christ the bad thoughts and chisels into us the image of the Redeemer. Like in other tradition, it is a manual – but for both the Master and disciples, a set of tools for spiritual growth to help the brethren to discern what is coming from God. These are the words-keys which should work in the hearts to uproot egoism and to further the spiritual search.[14]

3. The Location Within the *Rule*

The position of Chapter 4 within the *Rule* shows its importance and its significance. St Benedict writes about 'the instruments of good works' at the beginning of the *Rule*, immediately after presenting the different categories of monks (ch. 1) and after outlining the governing system of the monastery (ch. 2 on the abbot and ch. 3 on his council). Chapter 4 appears immediately after this and precedes three chapters (5–7) that describe three principal virtues (attitudes) in Benedictine life: obedience, silence and humility. Thus, Chapter 4 of the *Rule* is a link between the general outline of structure and governance of the monastery and its main spiritual features. All these seven chapters constitute the first, 'spiritual' part of the *Rule*.

[8] Dreuille (2000), 128–30.
[9] See Benedict, *Regula* 66,9.
[10] Benedict, *Regula* 7,18.
[11] Benedict, *Regula* 7,50.
[12] Benedict, *Regula* 7,52.
[13] Benedict, *Regula* 7,65.
[14] Dreuille (2000), 139.

4. The Inner Structure

Apart from the external contextualization of the chapter under consideration its internal structure is also very interesting. Only by looking at it, can we begin a more thorough analysis of the chapter as a litany.

It is not easy to classify over seventy phrases put together by St Benedict in this chapter and find an unequivocal and clear key to the order of their composition. Different commentators distinguish various groups of these phrases but their divisions and criteria differ one from another.

Below are three attempts at such a classification. They attempt to order the phrases proposed by St Benedict with reference to the commandments of the Bible, other places in the *Rule* and the actions these phrases propose in reference to God, to neighbors, i.e. especially the confreres, and to the behavior of monks themselves. Even if these classifications are not sharp, at least they show an inner dynamism of this chapter, namely the integrating passages between theology and personal life, ascetic practices and prayer, relationships with God and neighbors. Simultaneously in all these phrases monastic ethos is very present.

> De Vogüé:
> 1–9 Two great commandments of the Old Law and of the Gospel
> 10–19 From Christ's teaching and example; generosity towards one's neighbor
> 20–33 The twofold movement of renunciation and attachment to Christ; relationship with the other; mortification of the irascible appetite
> 34–40 The parallel to the fourth degree of humility; a series of negative maxims
> 41–43 Invitation to hope and attention to God
> 44–54 Vigilance in eschatological perspective
> 55–58 From reading to prayer
> 59–61 Struggle against evil
> 62–63 A contrast to the possible discrepancy between the abbot's directives and his conduct
> 64–73 More fraternal relations[15]
>
> De Dreuille:
> 1–2 The love of God and neighbor
> 3–10 Non-violence commandments
> 11–33 Other 'monastic' precepts (mortification, charity, deepened charity)

[15] Vogüé (1983), 80–81.

34–40 Non-sensuality
41–50 Relation to God
51–74 Various injunctions

Boeckmann:
1–2 Love of God and neighbor
3–9 Old Testament
10–19 New Testament
20–21 Passage
22–33 Love of neighbor
34–40 Renunciation
41–50 Custody
51–58 Tools for custody
59–64 Renunciation of self
65–73 Importance of relation to neighbors
74–75 Love of God

In these three classifications it is evident that the phrases proposed by St Benedict deal with many spheres of spiritual and human life that he seeks to integrate. We will deal again with this aspect at the end of our analysis. On the other hand one can also get the impression that for St Benedict the particular *tools* (recommendations or virtues) in their specificity and concreteness are more important than all of them together.

This integrating and practical approach is also visible in the moral consequences (or rather perspectives) of St Benedict's proposals. He seems to ignore the anterior opposition non-violence vs. non-sensuality. Thus integrity may be regarded as a key to his morality, but it is the integrity of the Gospel, inspired by and modelled on Christ himself. In Chapter 4 Christ appears as a model of ascetic effort: St Benedict recommends his readers 'to deny one's self in order to follow Christ' (*'Abnegare semetipsum sibi, ut sequatur Christum'*),[16] 'to prefer nothing to the love of Christ' (*'Nihil amore Christi praeponere'*),[17] suggesting also a Christological development of the fourth step of humility[18] and, finally, to 'dash at once against Christ the evil thoughts which rise in one's heart' (*'Cogitationes malas cordi suo advenientes mox ad Christum allidere'*).[19]

---

[16] Benedict, *Regula* 4,10.
[17] Benedict, *Regula* 4,21.
[18] See Benedict, *Regula* 4,29–33.
[19] Benedict, *Regula* 4,50; see Dreuille (2000), 130–36.

In this litany there are also few thoughts original to and typical of St Benedict. De Dreuille calls them 'the gems incrusted in the whole text' mentioning the following ones: 'to honor all men' (*'Honorare omnes homines'*),[20] 'to honor the aged', 'to love the younger', 'to pray for one's enemies in the love of Christ', 'to make peace with an adversary before the setting of the sun', and lastly 'never despair of God's mercy' (*'elationem fugere, seniors venerare, iuniores diligere, in Christi amore pro inimicis orare, [...] et de Dei misericordia numquam desperare'*).[21] In these phrases one can find the whole human sensitivity and delicacy of St Benedict, the most powerful and meaningful features of his teaching. If that is the case Chapter 4 of the *Rule* has a particular relevance for Benedictine spirituality and theology.

5. Hidden Echoes of Other Parts of the *Rule*

Having considered the general theological characteristics of Chapter 4 we will now look at the internal connections of this chapter with other parts of the *Rule*. It turns out that Chapter 4 collects and interweaves many important themes which are present in other places in the *Rule*. Its first verses (3–7) make reference to the Ten Commandments. We can find echoes of the last six commandments there. Verses 14–19 refer to some 'works of mercy' (corporal: 'to clothe the naked', 'to visit the sick', 'to bury the dead' and spiritual: 'to console the sorrowing'). Verses 29–33 reflect the fourth step of humility ('if hard and distasteful things are commanded, nay, even though injuries are inflicted, he [the monk] accept them with patience and even temper, and not grow weary or give up but hold out [...]'[22]). In verses 34–38 there is an echo of some of the seven capital sins: pride, gluttony, drunkenness and drowsiness (which might be regarded as a practical form of laziness). There are also other allusions to the capital sins (lust, pride again and also anger). Verses 48–54 take up some themes of other steps of humility (the first, fifth, tenth and eleventh steps). Finally, besides these moral indications the litany of this chapter offers some suggestions concerning prayer which should be prepared by spiritual reading accompanied by tears and lead to conversion.

[20] Benedict, *Regula* 4,8.
[21] Benedict, *Regula* 4,69–71.73; see Dreuille (2000), 137–38.
[22] Benedict, *Regula* 7,35–36.

6. The Triple Thread

If we look more deeply at the external influences on the chapter we can see that they have three sources. They seem to create a sort of triple thread. First of all the text is woven with various biblical quotations. It is interesting to note the predominance of the New Testament. St Benedict quotes the Gospels of Matthew, Mark and Luke, as well as Romans, 1 Corinthians, Philippians, 1 Thessalonians, Titus, 1 Timothy and 1 Peter. The references to the Old Testament complete the list – first with quotations of the two most important commandments (Deut 6:5 and Lev 19:18) and then with three quotations from Ex 2:13–15. In addition there is one implicit reference to Tob 4:16.

St Benedict refers also to ancient, non-biblical authors, such as Augustine, Cyprian, Ambrose, Athanasius, Jerome, Cassian, Evagrius, Basil, Pelagius, Sulpicius Severus and two secular authors: Porphyry and Sextus. All this says something about his spiritual and literary culture but, above all, it confirms his human sensibility and ability to find the right measure both in description and teaching. It is another contribution to the particular and synthetic character of this chapter.

7. Rhythm of Logic and Expression

Having analyzed the structure and *timbre* of the text, we can now look at its movement which is connected with the character and sequence of all the verses. For this reason a special analytical operation has been undertaken: the verses have been grouped according to their character as it may be perceived by a reader. The whole litany is composed of three main modalities: 1) the presentation of different challenges (moral requirements, commandments, recommendations and so on); 2) direct references to God (Christ or God's Mercy); 3) encouragement or motivation (as a sort of balance to the *challenges*). The following diagram shows the configuration of these *modalities* and their distribution in the successive groups of verses. The font faces (i.e. regular, bold, italics) help to see the evolution and tendencies. The numbers show indicatively the level of positive undertones of these three modalities (-1 for the challenges, since being demanding, they are not always easy; 1 for the positive motivations; 3 for appearance of the person of Christ):

3–9 **Challenges** (against something) /the attributed value: −1/
10 Christ /the attributed value: 3/
11–20 **Challenges**,
21 Christ,
22–27 **Challenges**,
28 *Positive*, /the attributed value: 1/
29–40 **Challenges**,
41 God,
42–45 **Challenges**,
46 *Positive*,
47–49 **Challenges**,
50 Christ,
51–54 **Challenges**,
55–56, *Positive*,
57 God
58–62 **Challenges**,
63–64 *Positive*
65–69 **Challenges**,
70–71 *Positive*,
72 Christ,
73 *Positive*,
74 God's Mercy

Generally speaking the whole text is balanced with a fairly regular invocation of God. The verses on challenges, initially present and intense, gradually give place to the 'positive' ones, so that the whole message is ultimately positive and not devoid of a pedagogical sensitivity: St Benedict combines his requirements with promises and references to God. He intends to present the whole, integral perspective of monastic life in an honest but also encouraging way. He does not hide the difficulties but shows that they are only a part of a more splendid vision. The form of litany allows him to develop this pedagogical and human strategy. Its dynamism, built on the repetitive structure and on the alternation of the modalities mentioned above, is illustrated by the following diagram. In the diagram each verse with a challenge is assigned a negative value whereas the verses referring to God are assigned an eminently positive value (i.e. evaluated three times higher than the 'positive' verses). In Figure 1 we can see how much the positive undertone of the text is achieved and introduced in the structure of the whole litany:

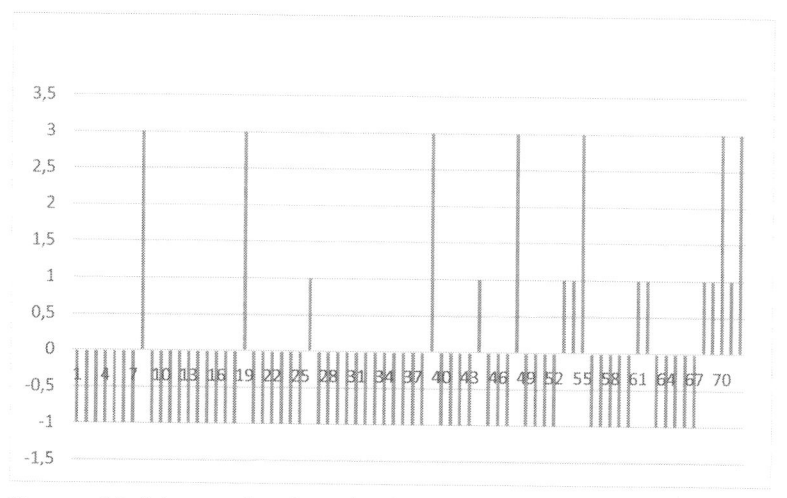

Figure 1. Modalities within the Rule of St Benedict.

The regularity strengthens the presence of challenging verses but at the end is somehow broken to give place to more positive messages. And even if, proportionally, the challenges prevail, the final effect remains positive because of the significant presence of verses with positive recommendations and dedicated to God.

Finally, there is still another, purely rhythmical aspect of this litany – also very significant. If we measure the number of syllables in each verse and then juxtapose them in a diagram we can see a very interesting phenomenon, namely a sort of play of syllables or, in other words, *irregular* waves created by them:

[3] 3+5, 6, 6, 6, 10, 9, 17, 16, 6, 8
[13] 7, 7, 5, 7, 7, 11, 7, 14, 11, 7
[23] 12, 9, 7, 10, 10, 13, 9, 19, 8, 21
[33] 13, 7, 5, 6, 5, 3, 6, 5, 9, 19
[43] 18, 8, 8, 22, 16, 14, 17, 37, 17, 9
[53] 13, 12, 11, 12, 31, 13, 12, 9, 63, 24
[63] 15, 7, 5, 6, 9, 9, 8, 8, 7, 14
[73] 18, 15

From this table we can see that the number of syllables gradually increases which means that the litany has its dynamic profile and character. Figure 2 shows it even better:

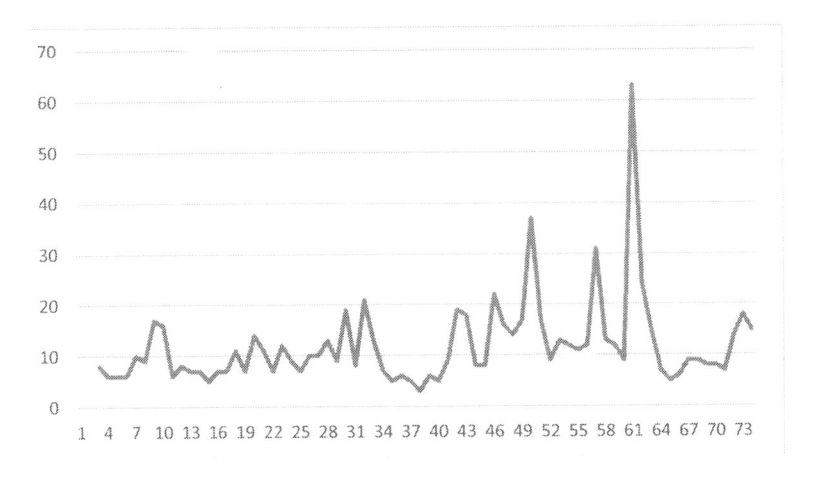

Figure 2. Syllabic length of verses in Chapter 4 of the Rule of St Benedict.

In a certain way, thanks to the rhythm of the syllables of the verses, the litany of Chapter 4 of the *Rule* seems to be alive and to move forward. The rhythm of the verses creates a sequence of movements in which longer and shorter sections alternate. Along with its progress, the intensity of this movement grows: more numerous, the longer verses simply bring more syllabic impulses and thus more movement. From the purely perceptual point of view such a situation increases, even subconsciously, the emotions of the reader. As a result the monotony of the litany repetitions is reduced and the reader remains, not only interested but perhaps also involved in the text. On this basis one can say that the integral, human aspect of this chapter finds here its complement: the text not only appeals by its content but also involves the reader by means of its rhythmic course. And it is exactly where the beauty and power of litany is revealed: in an integrated impact on the whole reader.

Summing up these observations one can say that Chapter 4 of the *Rule* of St Benedict is a very good example of both his spirituality and his humanity which are integrated internally and in unity one with the other. It is impossible to explain today why St Benedict gave this chapter the form of a litany, but clearly it makes the whole text of the *Rule* more attractive and it emphasizes the major themes. Primarily, however, it is attractive to the reader, inviting him or her, through its form to embrace the harmonious message of St Benedict.

Bibliography

Ancient and Medieval Authors

Benedict, *Regula*; *Die Benediktusregel. Leteinisch/deutsch* [Latin text according to Codex 914 of St Gallen library], Beuron, 1992; *The Rule of Saint Benedict* [English translation], Wyatt North Publishing, 1921.

Modern Authors

Boeckmann, A., (2011) *Christus hören. Exegetischer Kommentar zur Regel Benedikts. Teil 1: Prolog bis Kapitel 7*, Sankt Ottilien.

Dreuille, de, M., (2000), *La Règle de Saint Benoît et les traditions ascétiques de l'Asie à l'Occident*, Bégrolles-en-Mauges.

Sadowski, W., M. Kowalska, M. M. Kubas, M. M., (eds) (2016) *Litanic Verse I*, Frankfurt am Main.

Vogüé de, A., (1983) *The Rule of Saint Benedict. A Doctrinal and Spiritual Commentary*, [J. B. Hasbrouck (trans.)], Kalamazoo, MI [original French edn 1971–1977].

Appendix 1

Chapter IV of the Rule of St Benedict: The Instruments of Good Works[23]

1. In the first place to love the Lord God with the whole heart, the whole soul, the whole strength…
2. Then, one's neighbor as one's self (cf. Mt 22:37–39; Mk 12:30–31; Lk 10:27).
3. Then, not to kill…
4. Not to commit adultery…
5. Not to steal…
6. Not to covet (cf. Rom 13:9).
7. Not to bear false witness (cf. Mt 19:18; Mk 10:19; Lk 18:20).
8. To honor all men (cf. 1 Pet 2:17).
9. And what one would not have done to himself, not to do to another (cf. Tob 4:16; Mt 7:12; Lk 6:31).
10. To deny one's self in order to follow Christ (cf. Mt 16:24; Lk 9:23).
11. To chastise the body (cf. 1 Cor 9:27).
12. Not to seek after pleasures.
13. To love fasting.
14. To relieve the poor.
15. To clothe the naked…
16. To visit the sick (cf. Mt 25:36).
17. To bury the dead.
18. To help in trouble.
19. To console the sorrowing.
20. To hold one's self aloof from worldly ways.
21. To prefer nothing to the love of Christ.
22. Not to give way to anger.
23. Not to foster a desire for revenge.
24. Not to entertain deceit in the heart.
25. Not to make a false peace.
26. Not to forsake charity.
27. Not to swear, lest perchance one swear falsely.
28. To speak the truth with heart and tongue.
29. Not to return evil for evil (cf. 1 Thes 5:15; 1 Pet 3:9).

---

[23] The English text of the *Rule* is taken from http://www.holyrule.com/part1.htm [accessed Feb. 19, 2019].

30. To do no injury, yea, even patiently to bear the injury done us.
31. To love one's enemies (cf. Mt 5:44; Lk 6:27).
32. Not to curse them that curse us, but rather to bless them.
33. To bear persecution for justice sake (cf. Mt 5:10).
34. Not to be proud.
35. Not to be given to wine (cf. Tit 1:7; 1 Tim 3:3).
36. Not to be a great eater.
37. Not to be drowsy.
38. Not to be slothful (cf. Rom 12:11).
39. Not to be a murmurer.
40. Not to be a detractor.
41. To put one's trust in God.
42. To refer what good one sees in himself, not to self, but to God.
43. But as to any evil in himself, let him be convinced that it is his own and charge it to himself.
44. To fear the day of judgment.
45. To be in dread of hell.
46. To desire eternal life with all spiritual longing.
47. To keep death before one's eyes daily.
48. To keep a constant watch over the actions of our life.
49. To hold as certain that God sees us everywhere.
50. To dash at once against Christ the evil thoughts which rise in one's heart.
51. And to disclose them to our spiritual father.
52. To guard one's tongue against bad and wicked speech.
53. Not to love much speaking.
54. Not to speak useless words and such as provoke laughter.
55. Not to love much or boisterous laughter.
56. To listen willingly to holy reading.
57. To apply one's self often to prayer.
58. To confess one's past sins to God daily in prayer with sighs and tears, and to amend them for the future.
59. Not to fulfil the desires of the flesh (cf. Gal 5:16).
60. To hate one's own will.
61. To obey the commands of the Abbot in all things, even though he himself (which Heaven forbid) act otherwise, mindful of that precept of the Lord: 'What they say, do ye; what they do, do ye not' (Mt 23:3).
62. Not to desire to be called holy before one is; but to be holy first, that one may be truly so called.

63. To fulfil daily the commandments of God by works.
64. To love chastity.
65. To hate no one.
66. Not to be jealous; not to entertain envy.
67. Not to love strife.
68. Not to love pride.
69. To honor the aged.
70. To love the younger.
71. To pray for one's enemies in the love of Christ.
72. To make peace with an adversary before the setting of the sun.
73. And never to despair of God's mercy.

Behold, these are the instruments of the spiritual art, which, if they have been applied without ceasing day and night and approved on judgment day, will merit for us from the Lord that reward which He hath promised: 'The eye hath not seen, nor the ear heard, neither hath it entered into the heart of man, what things God hath prepared for them that love Him' (1 Cor 2:9). But the workshop in which we perform all these works with diligence is the enclosure of the monastery, and stability in the community.

Appendix 2

Caput IV: Quae sunt instrumenta bonorum operum[24]

1. In primis Dominum Deum diligere ex toto corde, tota anima, tota virtute;
2. deinde proximum tamquam seipsum.
3. Deinde non occidere,
4. non adulterare,
5. non facere furtum,
6. non concupiscere,
7. non falsum testimonium dicere,
8. honorare omnes homines,
9. et quod sibi quis fieri non vult, alio ne faciat.
10. Abnegare semetipsum sibi ut sequatur Christum.
11. Corpus castigare,
12. delicias non amplecti,
13. ieiunium amare.
14. Pauperes recreare,
15. nudum vestire,
16. infirmum visitare,
17. mortuum sepelire.
18. In tribulatione subvenire,
19. dolentem consolari.
20. Saeculi actibus se facere alienum,
21. nihil amori Christi praeponere.
22. Iram non perficere,
23. iracundiae tempus non reservare.
24. Dolum in corde non tenere,
25. pacem falsam non dare.
26. Caritatem non derelinquere.
27. Non iurare ne forte periuret,
28. veritatem ex corde et ore proferre.
29. Malum pro malo non reddere.
30. Iniuriam non facere, sed et factas patienter sufferre.
31. Inimicos diligere.
32. Maledicentes se non remaledicere, sed magis benedicere.
33. Persecutionem pro iustitia sustinere.

[24] The Latin text of the *Rule* is taken from: http://www.benediktiner.de/index.php/die-geistliche-kunst-2/die-werkeuge-der-geistlichen-kunst.html [accessed Feb. 19, 2019].

34. Non esse superbum,
35. non vinolentum,
36. non multum edacem,
37. non somnulentum,
38. non pigrum,
39. non murmuriosum,
40. non detractorem.
41. Spem suam Deo committere.
42. Bonum aliquid in se cum viderit, Deo applicet, non sibi;
43. malum vero semper a se factum sciat et sibi reputet.
44. Diem iudicii timere,
45. gehennam expavescere,
46. vitam aeternam omni concupiscentia spiritali desiderare,
47. mortem cotidie ante oculos suspectam habere.
48. Actus vitae suae omni hora custodire,
49. in omni loco Deum se respicere pro certo scire.
50. Cogitationes malas cordi suo advenientes mox ad Christum allidere et seniori spiritali patefacere,
51. os suum a malo vel pravo eloquio custodire,
52. multum loqui non amare,
53. verba vana aut risui apta non loqui,
54. risum multum aut excussum non amare.
55. Lectiones sanctas libenter audire,
56. orationi frequenter incumbere,
57. mala sua praeterita cum lacrimis vel gemitu cotidie in oratione Deo confiteri,
58. de ipsis malis de cetero emendare.
59. Desideria carnis non efficere,
60. voluntatem propriam odire,
61. praeceptis abbatis in omnibus oboedire, etiam si ipse aliter – quod absit – agat, memores illud dominicu praeceptum: *Quae dicunt facite, quae autem faciunt facere nolite.*
62. Non velle dici sanctum antequam sit, sed prius esse quod verius dicatur.
63. Praecepta Dei factis cotidie adimplere,
64. castitatem amare,
65. nullum odire,
66. zelum non habere,
67. invidiam non exercere,
68. contentionem non amare,

67. elationem fugere.
69. Et seniores venerare,
70. iuniores diligere.
71. In Christi amore pro inimicis orare;
72. cum discordante ante solis occasum in pacem redire.
73. Et de Dei misericordia numquam desperare.
74. Ecce haec sunt instrumenta artis spiritalis.
75. Quae cum fuerint a nobis die noctuque incessabiliter adimpleta et in die iudicii reconsignata, illa merces nobis a Domino recompensabitur quam ipse promisit.
76. *Quod oculus non vidit nec auris audivit, quae praeparauit Deus his qui diligunt illum.*
77. Officina vero ubi haec omnia diligenter operemur claustra sunt monasterii et stabilitas in congregatione.

Mary Channen Caldwell

LITANIC SONGS FOR THE VIRGIN

*Rhetoric, Repetition, and Marian Refrains
in Medieval Latin Song*

*Salve, virgo virginum,
Salve, sancta parens.*

(*Hail, virgin of virgins,
Hail, holy parent.*)

How many times, and in how many ways, can you 'hail' the Virgin Mary? Prayers such as the *Ave Maria* and the survival of numerous Marian litanies certainly gesture towards the limitlessness of Marian petitions in medieval devotional practices. Complementing the seemingly endless invocation of the Virgin in ritual contexts, medieval Latin song offers yet another avenue through which the Virgin can be petitioned dozens of times and by dozens of titles, often facilitated by refrains such that in the epigraph above.[1] Expressions of Marian devotion similar to this refrain saturate song across medieval Europe, traversing boundaries of language, place, and register. From vernacular songs such as the *Cantigas de Santa Maria* and motets to liturgical hymns and sequences, the Virgin stands as one of the most popular subjects for poets and composers. Her popularity increased significantly in the twelfth century, a fact witnessed by the proliferation of lyrics and songs in her name as

Manuscript Sigla
   F   Florence, Biblioteca Medicea Laurenziana, Pluteus 29. 1
   F-Pn lat. 5267   Paris, Bibliothèque nationale de France, latin 5267
   Tours 927   Tours, Bibliothèque municipale, MS 927
   St-M A   Paris, Bibliothèque nationale de France, latin 1139
   St-M D   London, British Library, Add. 36881

[1] *Salve virgo virginum*, in *F*, fol. 469v.

Mary Channen Caldwell • University of Pennsylvania, USA

well as the copying of one of the first extant Marian litanies from Western Europe.[2] It is no surprise, then, that within repertoires of rhymed, rhythmical Latin song produced from the twelfth to the fourteenth centuries under the labels of *versus*, *conductus*, and *cantio* – not to mention the modern label *nova cantica* – the Virgin figures prominently. Among *conducti* alone, at least a quarter of the repertoire explicitly venerates Mary, and many more celebrating feasts of the Temporale entreat the holy mother in passing.[3]

A striking feature of many Latin Marian songs is their relationship with the liturgy. *Ave Maria gratia plena*, for instance, is one of the most frequently referenced liturgical texts in the *conductus* repertoire, with several *conducti* citing this important prayer.[4] Other Marian texts find purchase in *conductus* poetry too in part or whole, including repeated references to or entire reworkings of Marion antiphons.[5] Modes of address range significantly across songs, although a petitionary register foregrounds the Virgin in her role as *mediatrix*; by contrast to vernacular traditions of Marian song, she is rarely allegorized in Latin poetry as a pastoral maiden, but instead receives treatment more in line with exegetical and mystical writings, such as those of Bernard of Clairvaux. Beyond noting specific examples or resonances with well-known sacred texts, the significance and reach of the Virgin's cult in Latin, as opposed to vernacular or – in the case of the medieval motet – bilingual, song has rarely been examined.[6]

In this chapter I take a series of four simple, monophonic *conducti* as a case study of Marian devotion in Latin song culture of the high Middle Ages: *Salve virgo virginum*, *Ave Maria virgo virginum*, *Salva nos, stella maris*, and *O summi regis mater inclita*. All transmitted within a

---

[2] For broad overviews of the cult of the Virgin and Marian devotion, see Graef (1963–1965) and Rubin (2009). A more context-specific study relevant to the songs discussed in this chapter can be found in Richards (2011).

[3] For approximate numbers of Marian *conducti*, see Everist (2018), 62–63.

[4] Everist (2018), 184–86. Contemporaneous reworkings of the *Ave Maria* are examined in Anderson (2010).

[5] See, for example, the polyphonic setting of the entirety of *Alma redemptoris mater* in I-Fl Plut. 29.1, fols 329r–330r and E-Mn 20486, fols 99r–100r.

[6] See, however, the studies of select Marian *conducti* (and motets) in Maschke (2013) and Anderson (2010). Angelo De Santi also cites a selection of what he terms litanically-influenced Latin 'laudes marianae' in his study of Marian litanies; see De Santi (1900), 167–68. Similarly, see also the Marian hymns and other sacred songs cited (and in some cases edited) throughout Meersseman (1958–60) On Marian themes in Latin lyrics and medieval and renaissance polyphony (in Latin and vernaculars), see Szövérffy (1985), 317–81; Carlson (2000 and 2003); and Rothenberg (2011).

few folios of a mid-thirteenth-century manuscript produced for (or in the milieu of) the famed Cathedral of Notre Dame in Paris, France (Firenze, Biblioteca Medicea Laurenziana, Plut. 29. 1; hereafter *F*), the lyric tetrad forms a strikingly coherent group due to their shared simplicity, high degree of repetition, and Marian focus. I argue that the four *conducti* are best understand through the interpretive lens of the litany, with each song embodying constituent elements of ritual litanies for the Virgin Mary. By means of repetitive structures, polyonymy, invocations, responsorial forms, and musical styles, the Marian *conducti* mirror the form, rhetoric, and performative mode of litanies. In what follows, I contextualize the manuscript transmission of the *conducti* before moving to detailed analyses of the poetry and music each work, illustrating the ways in which key features of litanies and litanic rhetoric and form manifest. I deal too with issues of performance, paralleling the repetitive and responsorial form of the songs to the likewise seemingly open-ended and responsorial form of the litany. Moreover, I suggest movement as a possible connection between song and litany, as each invokes embodied performance through processions or choreography. Finally, I close the chapter by situating the four *conducti* within the broader history of devotion to the Virgin in the form of Marian litanies.

1. Marian Songs in a Marian Manuscript

Among over 500 manuscript sources for medieval *conducti*, the manuscript *F* preserves the greatest number of works among several fascicles differentiated by number of voices and form.[7] In addition to *conducti*, the famed Parisian manuscript also preserves polyphonic music for Mass and Office, and Latin motets, largely reflecting the liturgy of Notre Dame of Paris.[8] Unsurprisingly, the Virgin and her feasts feature prominently throughout *F*, with at least 38 *conducti* in her name (not including references to Mary in other contexts).[9] Aside from the link to the Cathedral of Notre Dame, the copying of the manuscript between 1245 and 1255 falls at a moment when the cult of the Virgin had

---

[7] For an overview of the organization of *F*, see Roesner (1996), 24–32. On the *conductus* fascicles in *F* see Everist (2018), 14–16.

[8] Wright (1989), 235–72. See also Robertson (1995).

[9] For this number, see Everist (2018), 63. Perhaps the most famous Marian *conductus* is the widely transmitted and contrafacted *Beata viscera*, with poetry attributed to Philip the Chancellor and music to Perotin.

gained significant momentum across Europe, evidenced by increased numbers of institutional dedications, the increased creation of liturgical rites, and, of course, rising numbers of Marian poems and songs.[10] Even though the four *conducti* were likely composed prior to being copied in *F*, they nevertheless participate in the wide-spread cultivation of texts and music for the Virgin and complement other Marian music in the Parisian manuscript.[11]

Within *F*, the four Marian *conducti* are located in the final fascicle devoted principally to monophonic songs with refrains.[12] Paralleling the organization in other fascicles of *F* (as well as service books more broadly), the fascicle begins with works for Easter before moving to Christmas, a miscellaneous assortment, and then a small number of *conducti* for St Nicholas.[13] The sole Marian *conducti* in this fascicle occur amidst the miscellaneous section, copied in close proximity on fols 469v–471r (see Plates 1–4), with *Salve virgo virginum* and *Ave Maria virgo virginum* copied consecutively and *Salva nos stella maris* and *O summi regis mater inclita* separated by works for Christ's Nativity and Resurrection. The first two include notation only for the initial statement of the refrain, while the latter two include notation for the entirety of their first strophes. The remaining strophes (ranging from three in *Salve virgo virginum* to eight in *Ave Maria virgo virginum*) are copied text-only beside and below the notated portions of each song (the *residuum*); this is the normal layout for strophic *conducti* in *F* and most other sources.[14]

The *mise en page* of the manuscript, and this fascicle in particular, visually highlights the opening invocation of each song – *Salve, Salva, Ave*, and *O* – through large initials, red or blue ink, and delicate pen work. As is usual in the copying of *conductus* poems, the scribe greatly abbreviated the poetry (especially the *residuum*), visually signaled by interpuncts (indicating contractions and suspensions), macrons, and numerous stand-alone letters and letter dyads. The degree of abbrevia-

---

[10] On the dating of *F*, see Branner (1972); Baltzer (1972); and Everist (1989), 71–86.

[11] *Salve virgo virginum* is transmitted in the slightly earlier manuscript F-Tours 927, alongside other refrain-form *conducti*; the other three songs are *unica*. See Caldwell (2017), 117–19 and 148.

[12] On this fascicle, see Caldwell (2013), passim. While other Marian *conducti* are transmitted in *F*, only these four appear in the final fascicle and no other *conductus* in the manuscript features such repetitive forms.

[13] Caldwell (2013), 17–23.

[14] On issues of layout in strophic refrain songs, see Caldwell (2018), 282–92.

tion is especially heightened due to the refrains in three of the songs (*Salve virgo virginum*, *Ave Maria virgo virginum*, and *Salva nos stella maris*), and thoroughgoing repetition in *O summi regis mater inclita*. In each, repeated text is consistently abbreviated – the refrain line *Ave Maria virgo virginum* becomes, for example, '•ave•m•u•u•' (see Plate 1, bottom of folio), while the refrain in the epigraph, *Salve virgo virginum / Salve santa parens* becomes '•Salve•uir•u•S•S•parens'.[15] While the layout of the four songs allows them to blend smoothly with the other *conducti* of the eleventh fascicle, their Marian lyrics, textual structures, and devotional register distinguish them from surrounding songs.

2. Litanic Poetry for the Virgin

What makes a poem 'litanic' if it is neither labeled as one nor functions ritually as a litany? In the most recent work on non-liturgical litanies, a set of characteristics emerge as the most significant and shared among poems described as litanic: enumeration, usually of names (polyonymic), invocations and acclamations (chairetismic), petitions and supplications (ektenial), and, lastly, responsorial frameworks, which is often subsumed under the ektenial component of litanies.[16] As both the rhetorical and formal underpinning, repetition spans these characteristics of litanic verse and is one of the most recognizable features of litanies, regardless of language or function. The presence of each characteristic as part of the form, rhetoric, style and performance of verse strongly denotes poetry that takes litany as its central mode of composition and expression.

The four Marian *conducti* in *F* engage to varying degrees with the structural and rhetorical features of litanic verse, with repetition serving as the element linking song and litany. At the broadest level of form, the refrain functions as a central signal of repetition, recurring before, in the middle, and at the end of each strophe of *Salve virgo virginum*, *Ave Ma-*

---

[15] V and U are interchangeable; thus 'virgo' or 'uirgo'. On refrain abbreviation, see Caldwell (2018).

[16] See the discussion of generic components (polyonymic, chairetismic, and ektenial) of litanic verse in Sadowski (2016) that guides this volume (derived from Sadowski's article 'Geneza litanii w aspekcie formalno-kompozycyjnym', *Litania i poezja*, 25–59), and also the discussion of litanic poetry in Kowalska (2016 and 2017), Czarnowus (2016), in Latin poetry, Chrulska (2016). See also the discussion of vernacular 'litany types' in Gennrich (1932), 40–60.

ria virgo virginum, and *Salva nos stella maris*. The lack of a refrain in *O summi regis mater inclita* should not be taken as a sign of repetition's absence; rather, this *conductus* is the most repetitive of the four (see below). All the poems are *rithmi*, with rhythmical rather than metrical texts, featuring symmetrical structures, strophic structures, consistent rhyme schemes and syllable counts, and accents on either the penultimate syllable (paroxytonic accent) or antepenultimate syllable (proparoxytonic accent) of lines.[17]

The three refrain-form *conducti* are edited with translations in Table 1, with refrains italicized to clarify form. Like many of the *conducti* in the final fascicle of *F*, the refrain does not occur solely as a frame around strophes but is imbedded internally within each song. The resulting forms resemble the medieval *rondeau*, one of the French *formes fixes* and the only one to include a refrain in the middle of strophes.[18] The prototypical *rondeau* takes the shape of *ABaAabAB*, and in the three Marian *conducti* we find variations on this scheme. *Ave Maria virgo virginum* initially appears to conform to the prototypical shape but varies the refrain lines for strophes 5–7, converting *Ave Maria / Virgo virginum* into *Arens virgula / Yesse floruit*, lines that actually served as strophe 4 (the original refrain returns in strophe 8). *Salve virgo virginum*, on the other hand, repeats only the 'B' line of the refrain internally (resulting in the form *ABaBaBabAB*) and does so twice rather than the single iteration found in the *rondeau* form. *Salva nos stella maris* is the most conventional in appearance, its poetry corresponding to the form *ABaAabAB*; here, however, it is the music that subverts expectations (see below). While the refrain-form *conducti* in *F*, and especially this series of three *rondeau*-like works, have often been taken to be either contrafacts or predecessors of the French *forme fixe*, like their vernacular counterparts they present a developing form.[19]

---

[17] On the medieval *rithmus* see Norberg (2004), 81–155; Fassler (1987); Sanders (1995); and Everist (2018).

[18] On the development of the *formes fixes*, particularly the *rondeau*, see Butterfield (2002), 273–90.

[19] On the reception of these songs as *rondeaux*, see Spanke (1930) and Anderson (1979).

LITANIC SONGS FOR THE VIRGIN

Salve virgo virginum	Ave Maria virgo virginum	Salva nos stella maris	
1. Salve, virgo virginum, Salve, sancta parens, Genuisti filium, Salve, sancta parens, Creatorem omnium, Salve, sancta parens, Qui regit imperium, Omni labe carens; Salve, virginum, Salve, sancta parens.	1. Hail, virgin of virgins, Hail, holy parent. You have born a son, Hail, holy parent, Creator of all, Hail, holy parent, Who rules all the empire, Lacking all sin. Hail, virgin of virgins, Hail, holy parent.	1. Ave Maria Virgo virginum. Plaudant omnia Ave Maria Parit filia Mundi dominum Ave Maria Virgo virginum.	1. Hail Mary, Virgin of virgins. Let all cry, Hail Mary. A daughter has borne The Lord of the world. Hail Mary, Virgin of virgins.	1. Salva nos stella maris, Et regina celorum. Que pura Deum paris, Salva nos stella maris, Et per rubum signaris, Nesciens viri thorum; Salva nos stella maris, Et regina celorum.	1. Save us, star of the sea, And queen of heaven. Who, though pure, did bear God, Save us, star of the sea, And are signaled by the burning bush, Without knowing the swelling of man; Save us, star of the sea, And queen of heaven.
2. Tu Patrem ac Dominum Salve, sancta parens, Roga, salus hominum, Salve, sancta parens, Ut nutriat populum, Salve, sancta parens, Vite fundens poculum, Virgo, flos non arens. Salve, virginum, Salve, sancta parens.	2. Pray to the Father and Lord, Hail, holy parent, Salvation of man, Hail, holy parent, That he will nourish the people, Hail, holy parent, Spreading the cup of life, Oh virgin, flower without thirst. Hail, virgin of virgins, Hail, holy parent.	2. Parit filia Ave Maria Per quam gaudia Crescunt hominum Ave maria Virgo virginum.	2. A daughter has given birth, Hail Mary, Through whom joys Of men increase. Hail Mary, Virgin of virgins	2. O virgo specialis, Salva nos stella maris, Sis nobis salutaris, Imperatrix celorum. Salva nos stella maris, Et regina celorum.	2. Oh most special virgin, Save us, star of the sea, Be our salvation, Ruler of heaven. Save us, star of the sea, And queen of heaven.

Salve virgo virginum	Ave Maria virgo virginum	Salva nos stella maris	
3. Cordibus fidelium, Salve, sancta parens, Verum desiderium, Salve, sancta parens, Prestet et solatium, Salve, sancta parens, Nostrum refrigerium, Mundo lumen clarens. Salve, virginum, Salve, sancta parens.	3. In the hearts of the faithful, Hail, holy parent, Let true desire, Hail, holy parent, And solace prevail, Hail, holy parent, Our comfort Shining light in the world. Hail, virgin of virgins Hail, holy parent.	3. Crescunt gaudia Ave Maria Sordes vitia Cessat criminum Ave Maria Virgo virginum.	3. Joys increase, Hail Mary, And the filth and evils Of sin cease. Hail Mary, Virgin of virgins.
		4. Arens virgula Ave Maria Arens virgula Yesse floruit [Ave maria Virgo virginum.]	4. Though dry, the stem Hail Mary, Though dry, the stem Of Jesse flourishes. [Hail Mary, Virgin of virgins.]
		w	3. You, mother lacking equal, Save us, star of the sea, Did bear the manna of heaven, And the bread of angels. Save us, star of the sea, And queen of heaven.
		4. O parens expers maris, Salva nos stella maris, Partu non violaris, Paris sanctum sanctorum. Salva nos stella maris, Et regina celorum.	4. Oh parent lacking experience with man, Save us, star of the sea, And not violated by birth, You did bear the holy of holies. Save us, star of the sea, And queen of heaven.

Salve virgo virginum	Ave Maria virgo virginum		Salva nos stella maris	
	5. Parens primula Arens virgula, Viro fercula Dira prebuit Arens virgula Yesse floruit.	5. The first parent The dry stem, Offered dire Fruit to man; Though dry, the stem Of Jesse flourishes.	5. Celeste manna paris, Salva nos stella maris, Lux cecis, dux ignaris, Solamen angelorum. Salva nos stella maris, Et regina celorum.	5. You did bear the manna of heaven, Save us, star of the sea, Oh light of the blind, leader of ignorant, Solace of angels. Save us, star of the sea, And queen of heaven.
	6. Viro fercula Arens virgula Vere sedula Christi famula Christum genuit Arens virgula Yesse floruit.	6. To man is offered, The dry stem, Truly solicitous, Christ's handmaid Bore Christ. Though dry, the stem Of Jesse flourishes.		

Salve virgo virginum	Ave Maria virgo virginum	Salva nos stella maris
	7. Christi famula Arens Mortis vincula Fructu domuit Arens virgula Yesse floruit. 8. Illi gratia Ave maria Per quam venia Fit peccaminum Ave Maria Virgo virginum.	7. Christ's hand- maid The dry stem, By her offspring conquered The chains of death. Though dry, the stem Of Jesse flourishes. 8. Grace be unto her, Hail Mary, Through whom the pardon Of sins is made possible; Hail Mary, Virgin of virgins.

Table 1. Texts and translations of *Salve virgo virginum*, *Ave Maria virgo virginum*, and *Salve nos stella maris*.

Refrains not only signpost repetition, they also allude to the responsorial framing of the songs in concept, if not performance. Early studies of the *rondeau* and of vernacular refrains have frequently sought to relate such forms to responsorial performance, assuming the solo singing of strophic material and choral responses by means of refrains (or vice versa). While this has been disproven for most French *chansons* with refrains (including the *rondeau*),[20] a similar interpretation of the refrain in Latinate contexts has continued to lend them a performative identity as choral responses.[21] As I argue in a forthcoming monograph, however, the refrain-form songs of *F* and elsewhere were more likely to have been performed communally rather than responsorially, with an indeterminate group of singers serving as the collective *nos* in *Salva nos stella maris* and *nostrum* in *nostrum refrigerium* (*Salve virgo virginum*).[22]

Nevertheless, the instinctual association of refrains with responses is far from irrelevant when the lexical content of the refrains in these three songs is taken into consideration. Each of the three refrains serves as an invocation to the Virgin and, in one case, a request for intercession. Acclamations begin the refrains of *Salve virgo virginim* and *Ave Maria virgo virginum*, all familiar from Marian liturgical texts such as *Salve regina celorum* and *Ave maria gratia plena*, while *Salve nos stella maris* combines a petition with one of the Virgin's most common titles (*stella maris*) and the incipit of the widely-sung hymn *Ave maris stella* (see Table 1). Marked by chairetismic gestures ('hail' and *ave*) and petition (*salva nos*), the regular interjection of refrains into the strophic songs mirrors the repetitive structures of litanies, typically comprised of repeated invocations or petitions followed by responses. By contrast to liturgical litanies in which invocation and choral response are kept separate, however, the refrains in these *conducti* blend invocation, petition, and response.

The question remains as to whether the refrains functioned here as choral responses, resulting in a responsorial structure, or if strophe and refrain were sung by the same singer or group of singers – and whether this affects the interpretation of the songs as litanic in form. If, as is most likely, the songs were sung in a direct style by a soloist or group of singers than the function of the refrain as a response may seem attenuated. In

---

[20] Saltzstein (2013), 8–13.

[21] See my discussion of the performance of refrains in Caldwell, *Divine Refrains* (forthcoming).

[22] See note 21.

performance, however, this is not necessarily the case. The texture of a responsorial framework is achieved – regardless of specific performing forces – by number and regularity of repeats (no more than two lines of a strophe occur between refrain statements). With the same music sung for text of refrain and strophe, each return to the refrain text serves as a poetic, if not outwardly performative, response.

This works because the supplicative and invocational content of the refrain contrasts with the strophic content of each *conductus*. While the refrains offer a clear parallel in language and form to the chairetismic and ektenial features of litanies, the strophes themselves focus on naming the Virgin and detailing her sacred history, attributes, and role as intercessor. The set of polyonyms for the Virgin introduced and repeated by the refrains – *virgo virginum*, *sancta parens*, *virgula Yesse*, *stella maris*, *regina celorum* – are echoed and elaborated upon in the strophes. Among the four songs, twenty different titles, epithets, and descriptors are drawn upon, with two (*virgo virginum* and *stella maris*) occurring in more than one song (see Table 1). Most appear in popular and liturgical Marian texts such as hymns and sequences, while others reflect unusual or unique phrasings of otherwise common sentiments (as in 'lumen clarens').

Christi famula	Christ's handmaid
Creatorum omnium	Creator of all
Dux ignaris	Leader of the ignorant
Flos non arens	Flower without thirst
Imperatrix celorum	Ruler of heaven
Lumen clarens	Shining light
Lux cecis	Light of the blind
Mater expers paris	Mother lacking an equal
Mater inclita	Glorious mother
Nostrum refrigerium	Our refuge / consolation
Parens primula	First parent
Regina celorum	Queen of heaven
Sancta parens	Holy parent
Solamen angelorum	Solace of angels
Stella maris	Star of the sea
Virgo integra	Virgin intact

Virgo specialis	Special virgin
Viro virginum	Virgin of virgins
Virgo viri nescia	Virgin not knowing man
Virgula Jesse	Stem of Jesse

Table 2. Titles and epithets of the Virgin Mary in *Salve virgo virginum*, *Ave Maria virgo virginum*, *Salva nos stella maris*, and *O summi regis mater inclita*.

The Virgin's many namedness is exemplified in these four songs, with an emphasis on her virginity, her identity as mother, and her heavenly leadership.

Although polyonymy serves as the overriding lyrical conceit, the strophes also emphasize devotional aspects related to the Virgin. Chief among these is her purity, expressed in many of the epithets above (e.g. *virgo virginum*) as well as by lengthier descriptions in which she is described as bearing God 'without knowing the swelling of man' (in the first strophe *Salva nos stella maris*). Most importantly, the songs routinely frame the Virgin Mary as *mediatrix* and intercessor in her own right. The latter is conveyed succinctly in the second strophe of *Salva nos stella maris*, in which, as 'most special virgin', she is implored to be 'our salvation', while in the final strophe of *Ave Maria virgo virginum* she is the saint through whom 'the pardon of sins is made possible'. In terms of the former, her role as mediator between supplicant and her son Jesus is made clearest in the final two strophes of *O summi regis mater inclita* in which she is called upon repeatedly to 'beseech your son' (strophe 6) to 'spare your family' (strophe 5). Continuities in language and rhetoric poetically link the four *conducti* and further affirm their litanic identities. Achieved by means of repeated petitions, divine intercession is the desired outcome of litanic prayer, an outcome that is certainly foregrounded by the repetitive, petitionary, and polyonymic rhetoric of these Marian *conducti*.

By primarily discussing those songs with refrains first, I have left *O summi regis mater inclita* aside since its lack of a refrain makes it a formal outlier. Rather than a refrain, the repetitive structure of *O summi regis mater inclita* derives from lavish use of rhetorical figures of repetition (see Table 3):[23]

---

[23] In its music-poetic construction, *O summi regis mater inclita* is more comparable to Latin songs broadly termed *nova cantica* rather than the *conductus*; for a recent discussion of *nova cantica*, see Llewellyn (2018).

1. O summi regis mater inclita, O summi regis mater mater inclita, Inclita, Mater inclita.	1. O glorious mother of the highest king, O glorious mother, mother of the highest king, Glorious, Glorious mother.
2. O virgo virgo viri nescia, O virgo virgo virgo viri nescia, Nescia, Viri nescia.	2. O virgin, virgin not knowing man, O virgin, virgin, virgin not knowing man, Not knowing, Not knowing man.
3. O et post partum virgo integra, O virgo virgo virgo virgo integra, Integra, Virgo integra.	3. O virgin intact after birth, O virgin virgin virgin virgin intact, Intact, Virgin intact.
4. O stella maris nunquam turbida, O stella, stella, stella nunquam turbida, Turbida, Nunquam turbida.	4. O star of the sea never disturbed, O star, star, star never disturbed, Disturbed, Never disturbed.
5. O parce tuis, parce famulis, O parce, parce tuis, parce famulis, Famulis, Parce famulis.	5. O spare, spare your family, O spare, spare your, spare your family, Family, Spare your family.
6. O virgo, tuum roga filium, O roga, tuum, virgo, roga filium, Filium, Roga filium.	6. O virgin, beseech your son, O pray, virgin, beseech your son, Son, Beseech your son.

Table 3. Text and translation of *O summi regis mater inclita*.

The poem consists of a series of conventional Marian epithets, each elongated in the course of a single strophe through the application of rhetorical figures. In comparison with figures discussed in treatises contemporary with the mid-thirteenth-century copying of *F*, especially Geoffrey of Vinsauf's *Poetria nova* and *Documentum de modo et arte dictandi et versificandi*, the construction of *O summi regis mater inclita* emerges as a mélange of *figurae verborum* and *figurae sententiarum*.[24] In terms of the latter, the strophic *conductus* embodies the figure of *com-*

---

[24] These two treatises are edited and translated in Vinsauf (1968 and 2010). For a discussion of rhetorical figures in Latin song, including *O summi regis mater inclita*, see Caldwell (2013), 86–101.

memoratio by dwelling incessantly in individual strophes and across the poem on a limited stock of Marian prayers and epithets, expressed in a limited number of words per strophe. *Figurae verborum* are plentiful and include *repetitio* as well as *conversio* (also known as *anaphora* and *epiphora*), in which words are repeated at the beginning and end, respectively, of lines or clauses (which is also together referred to as *complexio*). *Anaphora* in particular is a central feature of litanic verse and in the other three Marian *conducti* is achieved through the inclusion of refrains.[25] *Gradatio* and *conduplicatio* are also employed in the repetition of words at the end of a phrase and beginning of following phrase and the repetition of words for emphasis or to invoke a particular emotion. Certainly, the repetition of 'virgo' thirteen times in *O summi regis mater inclita* qualifies as emphatic.

Although *O summi regis mater inclita* lacks the inherent repetition afforded by refrains, it more than compensates in its abundant play with rhetorical figures. By virtue of these repetitive features, litanic elements of the poem receive even greater emphasis. The final strophe, which places the Virgin firmly in the position of *mediatrix*, exemplifies the invocatory and supplicatory character of the litany with the phrase 'Oh Virgin, beseech your son' (*O virgo, tuum roga filium*), the sole text comprising the strophe. Infusing the line with rhetorical *figurae* morphs these ten syllables into a lengthier, meditative prayer, whose echoing quality evokes the responsorial effect of refrains.[26] Through the dip and sway of its wordy repetition, *O summi regis mater inclita* accesses the atemporality of litanies, described most eloquently by Alessandro Vettori in a discussion of the lyrical rhetoric of Franciscan Iacopone da Todi: 'Litany, with its repetitive element, challenges the limits of temporality, breaks the boundaries of rationality, and overflows into the realm of eternity. Its rhythmic scansion creates an interruption in the pattern of temporal sequence and transforms the text into atemporal circularity.'[27] While refrains certainly 'challenge' temporality by means of cyclical returns, the poetry of *O summi regis mater inclita* continually circles back on itself in such a way that the end seems to be continually elided – one can readily imagine the limitless variations that could follow these six strophes. Like many litanies

---

[25] Sadowski (2016), 11.

[26] On refrain-like repetition in Latin song, see Haug (2004), 93–96.

[27] Vettori (2007), 244. See also Paul Zumthor's definition of the litanic mode of composition as comprising *répétition indéfinie d'une même structure, syntaxique et partiellement lexicale*. Zumthor (1982), 116, cited in Kowalska (2016), 35.

whose petitions and responses proceed seemingly endlessly, *O summi regis mater inclita* has no perceivable conclusion beyond its material transmission.

In Witold Sadowski's definition of the essential components (or 'genes') of litanic verse, he argues that 'in the litany genre, the presence of at least one is obligatory', referring to the chairetismic, ektenial, and polyonymic genes. In the poetry of the four Marian *conducti* discussed here, each component can be located without difficulty – the songs feature anaphoric acclamations (*salve*, *ave*), repeated and potentially re-sponsorial petitions and supplications to the Virgin, and enumerations rooted in Mary's many namedness. It is, however, not solely the poetry of these songs that operates within the expressive mode of the litany – music reinforces the repetitive structures of the poems.

3. Singing Supplications

The melodies of the four Marian *conducti* (seen below in Music Examples 1 and 2) correspond to the strophic forms and (especially in *O summi regis mater inclita*) distinctive rhetoric of the poetry. Textures range from syllabic (*Salve virgo virginum*) to neumatic, with clusters of 3–4 pitches per syllable (*Salva nos stella maris* and *O summi regis mater inclita*). In keeping with the melodic style of the *conducti* in the eleventh fascicle of *F*, all four melodies privilege step-wise motion, with a preference for intervals of thirds and fifths when leaps occur.[28] Modally, an emphasis on G links the *conducti*, with the three refrain-form *conducti* centering on G and outlining no more than the range of a sixth (including a lower neighbor to F) while *O summi regis mater inclita* centers on D with an upper limit on G and a lower neighbor to C. In line with the repetitive nature of the texts, melodic material in each song is constrained to 1 to 3 phrases or motives – these are simple songs, made highly singable and memorable by means of their brevity.

The limited melodic material for *Salve virgo virginum*, *Salva nos stella maris*, *Ave Maria virgo virginum* accords with the underlying conceit of their *rondeau*-form, in which the music of the strophe comprises that of the refrain.[29] In other words, the variable strophes and unchanging refrain are sung to the same set of phrases (see Music Example 1).

---

[28] Caldwell (2013), 74–83.

[29] See the definition of *rotundellus* in Grocheio (2011), 68–69: 'we only call it a round, or *rotundellus* the parts of which do not have a *cantus* [melody] different from the *cantus* [melody] of the response or refrain.'

Music Example 1. *Salve virgo virginum*, *Ave Maria virgo virginum*, and *Salva nos stella maris*, music.

For *Salve virgo virginum* and *Ave Maria virgo virginum* this comprises two short phrases ending in open (on a) and closed (on g) position, resembling antecedent and consequent phrase construction. *Salva nos stella maris* differs only slightly by introducing a variant on the first phrase for the initial 'A' line of each strophe. While the reuse of musical material inherent to strophic structures and refrain forms clearly limits the potential for text expression, the repetition of text and music together serve to create the impression of formulae common to the musical form of litanies. Just as strophes and refrains are sung to the same music, so too are lines of litanies most often sung to identical musical phrases.

While similarly strophic, the relationship between poetry and musical expression is more finely wrought in *O summi regis mater inclita*, with compositional awareness of its rhetorical structures readily apparent.

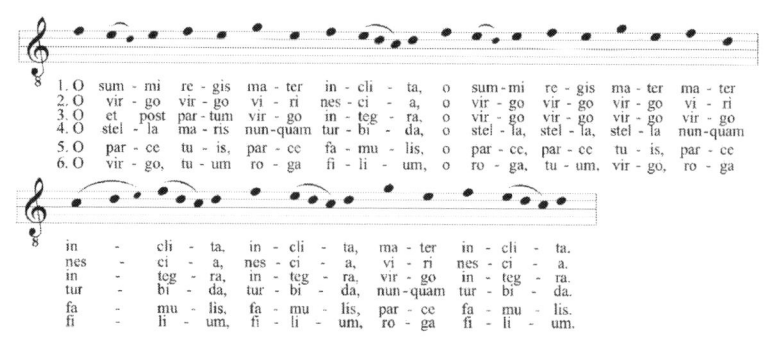

[Music Example 2: musical notation with text underlay]

1. O sum - mi   re - gis   ma - ter   in - cli - ta,   o   sum-mi   re - gis   ma - ter   ma - ter
2. O vir - go   vir - go   vi - ri   nes - ci - a,   o   vir - go vir - go   vir - go   vi - ri
3. O et   post   par - tum vir - go   in - teg - ra,   o   vir - go vir - go   vir - go   vir - go
4. O stel - la   ma - ris   nun-quam   tur - bi - da,   o   stel - la, stel - la, stel - la nun-quam
5. O par - ce   tu - is,   par - ce   fa - mu - lis,   o   par - ce, par - ce   tu - is,   par - ce
6. O vir - go,   tu - um   ro - ga   fi - li - um,   o   ro - ga, tu - um.   vir - go, ro - ga

in - cli - ta,   in - cli - ta,   ma - ter   in - cli - ta.
nes - ci - a,   nes - ci - a,   vi - ri   nes - ci - a.
in - teg - ra,   in - teg - ra,   vir - go   in - teg - ra.
tur - bi - da,   tur - bi - da,   nun-quam   tur - bi - da.
fa - mu - lis,   fa - mu - lis,   par - ce   fa - mu - lis.
fi - li - um,   fi - li - um,   ro - ga   fi - li - um.

Music Example 2. *O summi regis mater inclita*, music.

Unlike the three refrain-form *conducti*, *O summi regis mater inclita* eschews a refrain in preference for the layering of rhetorical figures, as discussed above. Aligning with the musical setting, the poetic text of the first strophe divides into three units, comprising *O summi*, *regis mater*, and *inclita*. Each is provided with its own musical material and repeated in turn, with the greatest emphasis and variability on the final word of each phrase – in the first strophe this is *inclita*. These three rhetorical and musical modules make up the entirety of the song:

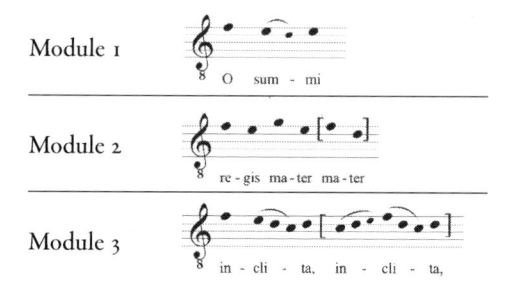

Module 1: O sum - mi

Module 2: re - gis ma - ter ma - ter

Module 3: in - cli - ta, in - cli - ta,

Music Example 3. Rhetorical and melodic modules in *O summi regis mater inclita*.

Narrow profiles and primarily conjunct motion characterize all three musical modules; when skips occur, they revolve around a third (this is the case especially for the melody of *regis mater*). Repetition is not exact for modules 2 and 3, although variation is subtle in each case (indicated with square brackets). The setting of *mater*, for instance, is transposed down a pitch on its third repetition of four total. *Inclita* varies more substantially, its second of four repetitions an inversion of its original form (featuring an ascending rather than descending step-wise descent), yet also including the same step-wise descent from F to D with a lower neighbor to C. Music is intimately and undeniable tied to the poetry in this *conductus*, with the limited melodic and textual materials inviting repetition and affording the opportunity for emphasis on key words, such as *mater* and *inclita* in the first strophe.

The strophic design, however, means strophes 2–6 vary in their relationship to the musical setting. In most cases, similar bonds result between word and melody. For instance, in all six strophes, the final word of the ten-syllable line always appears with the third melodic module in Music Example 3, above. Moreover, the first module, beginning with the anaphoric acclamation *O*, stays constant with an exception only in the third strophe where the text *et post partum* is substituted for *virgo* on the second occurrence of the melodic portion of the module. The tertian intervals characterizing the second module exhibit a looser relationship with the text, although there is a general concern to match word and melody.[30]

The aural effect of all four songs is of perpetual song and, by virtue of textual content, perpetual prayer.[31] Refrains and modular construction on the level of music and poetry serve to elide a listener's sense of finality – while the *conducti* do conclude, their repetitive structures offer the potential for an endless stream of Marian acclamations and petitions. In this way, the structuring of the Marian *conducti* alludes to the melodic settings of ritual litanies, which are principally sung to intonation formulae or are similarly repetitive in form.[32] While litanies can and were set to a variety of musical styles (including polyphonic settings) throughout the centuries, and could be recited silently as well as sung, most litanies take shape as fairly simple melodies or modal intonations.[33]

---

[30] The musical, textual, and rhetorical cohesion in *O summi regis mater inclita* parallels that in the related Latin *versus* repertoire: 'The textual-musical integration found in the *versus* suggests that poetic and musical language were shaped not independently but rather in conjunction, inspired by the same rhetorical principles and expressive desires,' referring to *Resonemus hoc natali* (St-M A, fol. 50v) and *De monte lapis scinditur* (St-M D, fol. 19v). Carlson (2006), 621.

[31] The idea of perpetual prayer is intrinsic to the litany; see, for example, the passage from Dan 3:56–87, which – in addition to featuring anaphoric petitions – repeats the dictum to 'praise and exalt him [the Lord] above all for ever' (*laudate et superexaltate eum in saecula*). Mershman (1913), 286.

[32] Hiley (1993). For a study of the music of litanies, especially the *Laudes regiae*, see Bukofzer's discussion in Kantorowicz (1946), 188–221 and Brockett (2006).

[33] For an example, see Hiley (1993), 53.

Although not formulae per se, the settings in Music Examples 1 and 2, above, are suggestive of a compositional response to the melodic style of litanies with narrow ranges, neumatic textures, and short, repeated phrases. Combined with the responsorial style conveyed by the refrain forms in Music Example 1 in particular, the music of the *conducti* underscores the litanic forms initiated by the poetry.

Finally, the processional aspect of litanies finds expression in the historiography, if not performance, of these four songs. Within the context of the liturgy and devotional rites, litanies were typically accompanied by processional movement, both within and outside of the church. As Alexander Fisher observes, litanies shared a special relationship with movement: 'The litany was most fundamentally connected… with the motion and the definition of space…Their repetitive, rhythmic profile, coordinated with the rhythms of breathing and walking, not simply expressed motion but induced it as well: they articulated lengthy journeys, helping to pace the procession and impel bodies through space.'[34] While rhythm in the case of the Marian *conducti* is supplied solely by the text and not music (the notation is non-mensural), the role of litanies as a natural accompaniment to the act of processing accords with the uncomplicated musical styles in Music Examples 1 and 2. One could easily sing these musical phrases while walking or processing.

Significantly, these *conducti* and the others in the final fascicle of *F* have long been associated in scholarship with a processional function.[35] Certainly, early sources from the late twelfth and early thirteenth centuries suggest a processional role for *conducti* (specifically in a series of thirteenth-century manuscripts preserving festive liturgies for the Feast of the Circumcision). While the wholesale association of the *conductus* genre with movement has been rightly overturned, connections with movement have persisted for the refrain-form *conducti* in *F*.[36] The label 'dance songs' assigned by numerous scholars to these simple, largely refrain-form songs is supported by the historiated initial that begins the fascicle (Figure 1).[37]

---

[34] Fisher (2015), 72.

[35] While some *conducti* served a processional function, many did not. For an account of the *conductus* as a processional genre, see Ellinwood (1941).

[36] See Everist (2018), 55–57.

[37] A similar depiction of clerics in motion appears in the frontispiece to *F*.

Figure 1. *F*, fol. 463r, historiated initial 'D'. Reproduced by permission of Florence, Biblioteca Medicea Laurenziana, MiBACT. Further reproduction by any means is prohibited.

In this much-discussed image, a group of tonsured clerics arrange themselves on either side of a central figure, appearing en masse to be in motion – the result is a clerical parallel to images of secular round dances, or *caroles*.[38] Over a century of interpretations of this image and the songs it introduces situate the repertoire as vocally and choreographically responsorial – the leader sings the strophes, the choir the refrain, with all performing a dance together in a line or circle.

In addition to the evidence of the image in Figure 1, the forms of the *conducti* in the eleventh fascicle have also been adduced as either imitating or foreshadowing the form of vernacular dance songs, notably the *rondeau* (see also above).[39] The circling motion initiated by the refrains has been read as a reflection of the choreographic patterns of round dances, and the light-hearted and exuberant texts as evocative of a culture of clerical play and festivity. At least one hypothesis explaining the development of the *carole* and its music and movement highlights a further link between the Latin *conducti* in *F* and vernacular traditions. In Margit Sahlin's seminal 1940 publication of her dissertation thesis as *Étude sur la carole médiévale*, she constructed an etymological path

---

[38] As Page (1987), 89, and others have suggested, the image is similar to ones in vernacular manuscripts of the *carole* or *corea*.

[39] Spanke (1930). Rightly so, the three Marian *rondeau*-form *conducti* – *Salve virgo virginum*, *Ave Maria virgo virginum*, and *Salva nos stella maris* – feature in discussions of the relationship between Latin and vernacular song forms, since these songs have an ostensibly 'late' *rondeau* form due to the repetition of the refrain at the head as well as end of each strophe.

from the liturgical acclamation and response *Kyrie eleison* to the vernacular *carole* as song and dance. Although critics have largely dismissed her argument,[40] Sahlin is far from the only scholar to search for, and locate, precedents for later refrain forms in responsorial liturgical practices.[41] If a link is to be made between responsorial chants such as the *Kyrie eleison* (and, by extension, litanies) and dance songs such as the *carole*, then the *conducti* in *F* would surely be implicated too as formal parallels to vernacular song forms. As such, the role of movement in the ritual enactment of litanies may find a counterpart in the embodied performance of the Marian songs *cum* litanies in the final fascicle of *F*.

4. Marian Litanies

Accessing the expressive mode of the litany through their poetry and music, the Marian *conducti* are, with one exception, unique to this thirteenth-century Parisian manuscript. Looking to the Virgin for intercession through repetitive prayers modeling many features of litanies is not uncommon, however, in late medieval song repertoires in Latin and the vernacular.[42] Rather, the Virgin is a frequent subject in songs whose forms and petitionary strategies resonate with litanies, although rarely to the degree of the four *conducti* discussed here. The popularity of addressing the Virgin Mary through litanic modes of discourse has a lengthy history reaching back to the Greek Akathist Hymn for Mary, whose repetitive supplications were translated into Latin by the ninth century.[43] By the twelfth century, Marian litanies began to be transmitted and newly-composed repertoires of Latin verse focus increasingly on the figure of the Holy Mother.[44] Among the earliest preserved Marian litanies is in a twelfth-century manuscript from southern France (see Figure 2); while unnotated, the string of polyonymic lines and the re-

---

[40] For a summary, see Mullally (2011), 12–14.

[41] See, for example, Fernandez (1976), 270, who cites *Salve virgo virginum* as a link between Latin chant and the vernacular *rondeaux*.

[42] Kowalska (2016), 34.

[43] On Latin translations of the Akathist hymn, see Huglo (1951).

[44] On Marian litanies, see De Santi (1900) and Huglo et al. (2001). As De Santi notes, the content of Marian litanies 'would seem to have been taken not so much from the Scriptures and the Fathers, at least directly, as from popular medieval Latin poetry'. De Santi (1913), 288. For a narrative of the Virgin's flourishing cult in the west up to the twelfth century and her ensuing popularity through to the fourteenth century, see Rubin (2009), 121–255.

sponsorial structure is clear in an incipient form. The *mise en page* with its repeated and emphasized initials and abbreviations bears a certain resemblance to the layout of the Marian *conducti* in *F*:

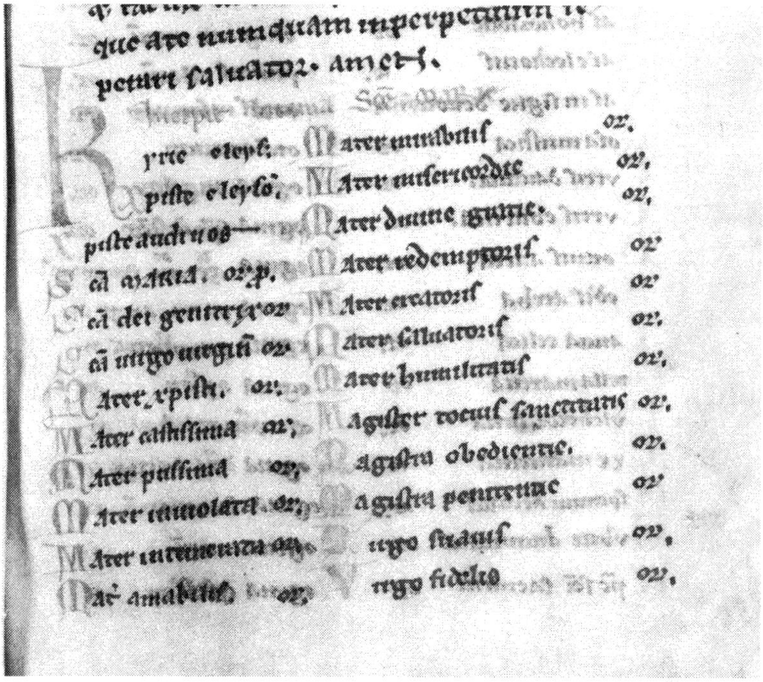

Figure 2. F-Pn lat. 5267, fol. 80r, Marian litany. By kind permission of the Bibliothèque nationale de France.

Beginning with a conventional acclamation (*Kyrie eleyson...Christe audi nos*), the subsequent lines offer familiar-sounding invocations – Mary is called upon as *virgo virginum, dei genitrix, inviolata*, etc. – and are responded to by the formulaic (and abbreviated) *ora pro nobis*.[45] Not only are these stock expressions of Marian devotion popularized in Latin liturgical and extraliturgical poetry (including the four Marian *conducti* in *F*), but the phrasing of this and other early litanies culminate in the standardized and sanctioned sixteenth-century Litany of Loreto.[46]

In light of the rising popularity of the Virgin as intercessor, and litanic prayer as one of the most popular mediums to access her power, it

[45] For an edition of the litany, see Meersseman (1960), 222–23.

[46] Text and translation of the Litany of Loreto can be found in Fisher (2015), 46–48; see also De Santi (1900) and Meersseman (1958–1960).

is fitting that four sung litanies found their way into a manuscript associated with the Cathedral of Notre Dame in Paris. How closely linked the creation of *Salve virgo virginum*, *Ave Maria virgo virginum*, *Salva nos stella maris*, and *O summi regis mater inclita* was with contemporary Marian litanies will likely remain unclear; nevertheless, as analysis of their poetry and music illustrates, the songs undeniably express Marian devotion by means of litanic forms, syntax, and rhetoric. Veneration of the Virgin Mary in these *conducti* draws inspiration from the rich poetic and performative resources of litany – repeated supplications, enumerations, acclamations, responsorial frameworks, and even movement. In this way, they endlessly entreat the *virgo virginum*, *sancta parens*, *stella maris*, and *mater inclita* using the power of song.

Bibliography

Ancient and Medieval Authors

Geoffrey de Vinsauf, *Documentum de modo et arte dictandi et versificandi (Instruction in the Method and Art of Speaking and Versifying)* (R. P. Parr, trans., 1968, Milwaukee).
— *Poetria nova: Revised Edition* (M. F. Nims and M. Camargo, trans., Medieval Sources in Translation vol. 49, 2010, Toronto).
Johannes de Grocheio. *Ars musice* (C. J. Mews, J. N. Crossley, C. Jeffreys, L. McKinnon, and C. J. Williams, eds and trans., 2011, Kalamazoo).

Modern Authors

Anderson, G. A., ed. (1979) *1pt Conductus–The Latin Rondeau Répertoire* [vol. 8, Notre-Dame and Related *Conductus* Opera Omnia], Henryville.
Anderson, M. A. (2010) 'Enhancing the *Ave Maria* in the Ars Antiqua,' *Plainsong and Medieval Music* 19, no. 1, 35–65.
Baltzer, R. A. (1972) 'Thirteenth-century Illuminated Miniatures and the Date of the Florence Manuscript,' *Journal of the American Musicological Society* 25, 1–18.
Branner, R. (1972) 'The Johannes Grusch Atelier and the Continental Origins of the William of Devon Painter,' *The Art Bulletin* 54, no. 1, 24–30.
Brockett, C. W. (2006) *Letania and Preces: Music for Lenten and Rogations Litanies*, Ottawa.
Butterfield, A. (2002) *Poetry and Music in Medieval France: From Jean Renart to Guillaume de Machaut*, Cambridge.
Caldwell, M. C. 'Singing, Dancing, and Rejoicing in the Round: Latin Sacred Songs with Refrains, circa 1000–1582' [Unpublished doctoral dissertation, University of Chicago, 2013].
— (2017) '"*Pax Gallie*': The Songs of Tours 927,' in C. Chaguinian (ed.), *The Jeu d'Adam: MS Tours 927 and the Provenance of the Play*, Kalamazoo, 87–176.
— (2018) 'Cueing Refrains in the Medieval *Conductus*,' *Journal of the Royal Musical Association* 143, no. 2, 1–52.
Carlson, R. G. (2000) 'Devotion to the Virgin Mary in Twelfth-Century Aquitanian Versus.' [Unpublished doctoral dissertation, University of North Carolina at Chapel Hill, 2000].

— (2003) 'Striking Ornaments: Complexities of Sense and Song in Aquitanian "Versus",' *Music & Letters* 84, no. 4, 527–56.

— (2006) 'Two Paths to Daniel's Mountain: Poetic-Musical Unity in Aquitanian *Versus*,' *Journal of Musicology* 23, no. 4, 620–46.

Chrulska, E. (2016) 'Litanic Verse in Latin,' in W. Sadowski, M. Kowalska and M. M. Kubas (eds), *Litanic Verse I: Origines, Iberia, Slavia et Europa Media*, Literary and Cultural Theory, vol. 45, Frankfurt am Main, 91–126.

Czarnowus, A. (2016) 'Litanic Tradition in *Of on that is so fayr and bright* and the Harley Ms *Five Joys of Mary*,' *Terminus* 18, no. 1 (38), 1–16.

De Santi, A. (1900) *Les Litanies de la sainte Vierge: étude historique et critique* [A. Boudinhon (trans.)], Paris.

— (1913) 'Litany of Loreto,' in C. G. Herbermann et al. (eds) *The Catholic Encyclopedia*, New York, 287–90.

Ellinwood, L. (1941) 'The Conductus,' *The Musical Quarterly* 27, no. 2, 165–204.

Everist, M. (1989) *Polyphonic Music in Thirteenth-Century France: Aspects of Sources and Distribution*, New York and London.

— (2018) *Discovering Medieval Song: Latin Poetry and Music in the Conductus*, Cambridge.

Fassler, M. E. (1987) 'Accent, Meter, and Rhythm in Medieval Treatises "De Rithmis",' *Journal of Musicology* 5, 164–90.

Fernandez, M.-H. (1976) 'Notes sur les origines du rondeau. Le "répons bref" – les "preces" du Graduel de Saint-Yrieix,' *Cahiers de civilisation médiévale* 19, no. 75, 265–75.

Fisher, A. J. (2015) '*Thesaurus Litaniarum*: The Symbolism and Practice of Musical Litanies in Counter-Reformation Germany,' *Early Music History* 34, 45–95.

Gennrich, F. (1932) *Grundriss einer Formenlehre des mittelalterlichen Liedes als Grundlage einer musikalischen Formenlehre des Liedes*, Halle.

Graef, H. C. (1963–1965) *Mary: A History of Doctrine and Devotion* [2 vols], New York.

Haug, A. (2004) 'Ritual and Repetition: The Ambiguities of Refrains' [J. Llewellyn (trans.)], in N. H. Petersen, M. B. Bruun, J. Llewellyn, and E. Østrem (eds), *The Appearances of Medieval Rituals: The Play of Construction and Modification*, Turnhout, 83–96.

Hiley, D. (1993) *Western Plainchant: A Handbook*, New York.

Huglo, M. (1951) 'L'ancienne version latine de l'hymne acathiste,' *Le Muséon: Revue d'études orientales* 64, 27–61.

Huglo, M., E. Foley, J. Harper, and D. Nutter (2001), 'Litany,' *Grove Music Online*. http:////www.oxfordmusiconline.com/grovemusic/view/10.1093/gmo/9781561592630.001.0001/omo-9781561592630-e-0000016769 (accessed October 14, 2017).

Kantorowicz, E. H. (1946) *Laudes regiae: A Study in Liturgical Acclamations and Mediaeval Ruler Worship, With a Study of the Music of the Laudes and Musical Transcriptions by Manfred F. Bukofzer*, Berkeley.

Kowalska, M. (2016) 'La forme de la litanie comme cadre: le cas du lai et d'autres genres littéraires médiévaux,' *Zagadnienia Rodzajów Literackich* 59, no. 118, 31–49.

— (2017) 'Prière litanique – litanie poétique. Les paraphrases françaises jusqu'au xixe siècle,' *Romanica Olomucensia* 2, 223–34.

Llewellyn, J. (2018) 'Nova Cantica,' in *The Cambridge History of Medieval Music*, M. Everist and T. F. Kelly (eds), Cambridge, 147–75.

Maschke, E. M. (2013) '"Porta Salutis Ave": Manuscript Culture, Material Culture, and Music,' *Musica Disciplina* 58, 167–230.

Meersseman, G. G. (1958–1960) *Der Hymnos Akathistos im Abendland* [2 vols], Freiburg.

Mershman, F. (1913) 'Litany,' in *The Catholic Encyclopedia*, C. G. Herbermann et. al. (eds), New York, 286–87.

Mullally, R. (2011) *The Carole: A Study of a Medieval Dance*, Farnham and Burlington.

Norberg, D. (2004) *An Introduction to the Study of Medieval Latin Versification*, [G. C. Roti and Jacqueline de La Chapelle Skubly (trans.)], Washington, D.C.

Page, C. (1987) *Voices and Instruments of the Middle Ages: Instrumental Practice and Songs in France, 1100–1300*, London.

Richards, J. (2011) 'Marian Devotion in Thirteenth-Century France and Spain and Interfaces Between Latin and Vernacular Culture,' in C. J. Mews and J. N. Crossley (eds) *Communities of Learning: Networks and the Shaping of Intellectual Identity in Europe, 1100–1500*, Turnhout, 177–212.

Robertson, A. W. (1995) 'Remembering the Annunciation in Medieval Polyphony,' *Speculum* 70, no. 2, 275–304.

Roesner, E. H., ed. (1996) *Antiphonarium, seu, Magnus liber de gradali et antiphonario: Color Microfiche Edition of the Manuscript Firenze, Biblioteca Medicea Laurenziana Pluteus 29. 1: Introduction to the 'Notre-Dame Manuscript' F*, Codices illuminati medii aevi vol. 45, Munich.

Rothenberg, D. J. (2011) *The Flower of Paradise: Marian Devotion and Secular Song in Medieval and Renaissance Music*, New York City.

Rubin, M. (2009) *Mother of God: A History of the Virgin Mary*, New Haven.

Sadowski, W. (2016) 'Some Necessary Preliminaries,' in W. Sadowski, M. Kowalska and M. M. Kubas (eds), *Litanic Verse I: Origines, Iberia, Slavia et Europa Media*, Literary and Cultural Theory, vol. 45, Frankfurt am Main, 9–12.

Saltzstein, J. (2013) *The Refrain and the Rise of the Vernacular in Medieval French Music and Poetry*, Cambridge.

Sanders, E. H. (1995) 'Rithmus,' in G. M. Boone (ed.) *Essays on Medieval Music: In Honor of David G. Hughes*, Cambridge, MA, 415–40.

Schlager, K., and M. Marx-Weber. (1996; online 2016) 'Litanei,' in L. Lütteken (ed.), *MGG Online*, Kassel, Stuttgart, and New York. https://www.mgg-online.com/article?id=mgg15646&v = 1.0&rs=mgg15646 (accessed September 10, 2018).

Spanke, H. (1930) 'Das lateinische Rondeau,' *Zeitschrift für französische Sprache und Literatur* 53, 113–48.

Szövérffy, J. (1985) *Marianische Motivik der Hymnen: ein Beitrag zur Geschichte der marianischen Lyrik im Mittelalter*, Leyden.

Vettori, A. (2007) 'Singing with Angels: Iacopone da Todi's Prayerful Rhetoric,' in T. J. Johnson (ed.) *Franciscans at Prayer*, The Medieval Franciscans, vol. 4, Leiden and Boston, 221–48.

Wright, C. (1989) *Music and Ceremony at Notre Dame of Paris, 500–1550*, Cambridge and New York.

Zumthor, P. (1982) 'Le rythme dans la poésie orale,' *Langue française* 56, 114–27.

Plates

Plate 1. *F*, fol. 469v. Reproduced by permission of Florence, Biblioteca Medicea Laurenziana, MiBACT. Further reproduction by any means is prohibited.

Plate 2. *F*, fol. 470r. Reproduced by permission of Florence, Biblioteca Medicea Laurenziana, MiBACT. Further reproduction by any means is prohibited.

Plate 3. *F*, fol. 470v. Reproduced by permission of Florence, Biblioteca Medicea Laurenziana, MiBACT. Further reproduction by any means is prohibited.

Plate 4. *F*, fol. 471r. Reproduced by permission of Florence, Biblioteca Medicea Laurenziana, MiBACT. Further reproduction by any means is prohibited.

Joris Geldhof

THE LITANY OF SAINTS OF THE EASTER VIGIL IN THE ROMAN RITE

1. Introduction

For many centuries the Roman rite has known an extensive litany, which was part of the liturgy of the Paschal vigil, celebrated on Holy Saturday. It is commonly called the 'litany of the saints'. Traditionally, the eve of Easter was the time established for the ceremony during which new Christians were baptized. While there have been significant modifications to the liturgy of Holy Week since the middle of the twentieth century,[1] the text itself of the litany is a remarkably stable given, even if there have been many local variations to the text throughout the centuries.[2] It is to the composition, liturgical function and theological meanings of this litany that the present contribution is devoted. The point of departure is the text as it appears in the 1570 *Missale Romanum*, where it is found after the rite of the blessing of the baptismal font (*benedictio fontis*).[3]

---

[1] For a detailed discussion as well as a lively account by an insider, see Amiet (1999).

[2] In the Roman missal, which is currently used in the Catholic Church, the litany of saints is still present as a part of the celebration of the Easter vigil. Under the influence of the encompassing liturgical reforms issuing from the Second Vatican Council, the text was revised. For the rationale behind the revision and a discussion of how it was carried out, see Bugnini (1990), 327–35.

[3] Sodi, Triacca (2012), 288–90; a full transcription of this text is added as an appendix. In the last edition of the 'Tridentine' missal before the second Vatican Council – i.e. the one which appeared in 1962 – the litany was split in two pieces, which was a direct consequence of the reform of the liturgy of Holy Week under pope Pius XII. What comes in between the two parts is the benediction of the baptismal water and the

Joris Geldhof • Catholic University of Leuven, Belgium

The Litany in Arts and Cultures, ed. by Witold Sadowski and Francesco Marsciani, Turnhout, Brepols, 2020 (*Studia Traditionis Theologiae*, 36), pp. 175-195
© BREPOLS PUBLISHERS DOI 10.1484/M.STT-EB.5.119212

This missal is known to be one of the major sources of the so-called 'Tridentine' liturgy, in addition to other official liturgical books such as the *Breviarium Romanum*, *Rituale Romanum*, *Pontificale Romanum* and *Caerimoniale Episcoporum*.[4] The missal is used for the celebration of the Eucharistic liturgy and comprises the general outline of the mass with the fixed prayers and rubrics (the Ordo Missae) as well as prayer forms for the entire temporal and sanctoral cycles, which cover all the feasts of the Lord, the Mother of God and the saints. The litany which forms the object of the present study has to be situated in the temporal cycle, in particular in a distinctive part of the very core of it, the celebration of the *triduum*.

In what follows I will first have a look at the external characteristics of the text of the litany itself, before I embark in a second section on a search for previous versions of it in earlier missals, and other liturgical sources.[5] The idea is to delve deeper from the sixteenth century to the fifteenth, the thirteenth, the tenth, and earlier. Not only will it turn out to be possible to do that, it will also become clear that the original context in which Christian litanic prayer came into being is as intriguing as it is difficult, in the sense of multi-layered. This historical survey of texts may not neglect the fact that, when interpreting them, one must always take into account the concrete liturgical contexts, i.e. ritual and ceremonial actions, in which they were used.[6] In doing so, at least to some extent, it will become possible to shed light on the fundamental significance of supplicatory prayer in Christian liturgy and faith.

The leading hypothesis underlying these reflections is that the litany of the Easter vigil in the Roman rite testifies not only of a noteworthy stability, which can be stretched to over one thousand years, but that it additionally offers an excellent illustration of what liturgy in general is.

2. The Text as it Appears in the 1570 Missale Romanum

The text of the litany of the Easter vigil in the *editio princeps* of the 1570 Roman missal is spread over just a little more than two pages: the full

---

renewal of baptismal vows. The text of the litany itself, however, shows only very few changes. See Sodi and Toniolo (2007), 198–99; 209–11.

[4] For some background to the promulgation of these books, see Geldhof (2018), 177–91.

[5] For some guidance into the complex world of ancient and medieval liturgical books, reference needs to be made to Vogel (1986) and Palazzo (1998). Both these reference works originally appeared in French. See also the very helpful contribution of Jeffery (1986).

[6] For a convincing defense of such a methodology, see Day (2014).

pages 228 and 229 and page 230 in the upper left corner only. The pages are made up in two columns, as (almost) everywhere in this edition of the missal. On pages 228 and 229 one finds a header which says in red letters *Litaniæ*; the font of this is the same in size and design as the full text. Unsurprisingly, the language throughout is Latin.[7] One also observes at a single glance relatively simple musical scores. Sometimes, i.e. especially in the first column, these scores have text below them, while most of them obviously indicate the chanting pattern of the supplicatory responses for the people who are expected to sing them. Every supplication starts with a capital in red; all the other words are in black and, except for proper names, in lower-case.[8]

As is common in medieval (liturgical) manuscripts and incunables, the words that are used are frequently abbreviated, but there is no consistency with respect to when exactly this happens and when not. The reason for abbreviating words is neither grammar nor spelling conventions but making optimal use of the space one has line per line. It is especially the letters 'n' and 'm' which are often omitted or replaced by signs on an adjacent letter. So one will find *Per morteʒ et sepulturam tuă* meaning *Per mortem et sepulturam tuam* (by your death and grave) next to the fully spelled out *Per sanctam resurrectionem tuam* (by your holy resurrection), *qui tollis peccata mŭdi* next to *qui tollis peccata mundi* ([you] who take away the sins of the world), *Ab omni malo* (from every evil) next to *Ab oĭ peccato* (from every sin), etc.[9] In addition, the text makes use of standard abbreviations for often recurring words, of which *dñe* for *domine* (Lord) is arguably the most common and emphatic one. The supplicatory response *te rogamus audi nos* (we ask you hear us) is abbreviated in many different ways, for which there seems no consistent

---

[7] In part to distinguish itself from Protestantism, and in spite of movements in the bosom of the Catholic Church which did promote the use of vernacular languages, albeit usually modestly, the highest authorities of the Church had firmly decided at Trent that Latin would remain the exclusive language for the celebration of the true 'Catholic' liturgy. See e.g. White (2003).

[8] Even the words *deus* and *trinitas* are put in lower-case. Exceptions to the aforementioned principle are the words *Martyres*, *Monachi* and *Eremitæ*. All other general categories of saints (such as *patriarchæ, apostoli, pontifices*, etc.) are not capitalized. There seems no logical explanation for this. – A transcription of the full text of the litany of saints in the 1570 *Missale Romanum* is included as an annex at the end of this contribution.

[9] When quoting from this litany, I will render the Latin original as it is in the text (i.e. with the abbreviations) and provide a translation of my own between brackets. When, further on, I quote from other editions of primary sources, I will proceed in a similar fashion, i.e. with an own translation between brackets.

pattern. Forms of the adjective *sanctus* (holy) are noteworthy, too, for the multifarious ways in which they are spelled.

It makes sense to discern a fivefold structure of the litany including an opening part, three series of supplications or entreaties and a concluding part. The opening part starts with two times four invocations addressed to God. The first one is *Kyrie eleison* (Lord have mercy), whereby it is likely that the 'Lord' mentioned here is Christ, the mediator between humanity and God, for the three following supplications are also directly addressed to him: *Christe eleison, Christe audi nos, Christe exaudi nos* (Christ have mercy, Christ hear us, Christ comply with us). The next four supplications have a clear Trinitarian outline, as they consecutively invoke the Father of the heavens, the Son redeemer of the world, the holy Spirit and the three of them together: *Sctă Trinitas un'de'* (Holy Trinity one God).

It is possible that somewhere in the course of history there has been a Trinitarian 'correction' here to the opening verses *Kyrie eleison, Christe eleison*, since from a dogmatic standpoint Christian prayer is ultimately, in principle, always addressed to God the Father (and no one else). The problem with immediately addressing Christ would have been the risk to deny his humanity. Traces of those discussions would have heavily impacted on liturgical prayer formulae,[10] both on the names used for the addressees at the beginning of the prayers and on the concluding doxologies.

The three series of supplications differ among themselves predominantly by the responses, and therefore by the grammatical constructions they entail. It is for these three responses that the text provides musical instructions (cf. supra); they were meant to be sung by the assembly. They are: *ora(te) pro nobis* (pray for us), *libera nos domine* (free us Lord) and *te rogamus audi nos* (we ask you hear us). The first response corresponds with a list of individual saints as well as collections of saints – whence there is the grammatical variation of *ora* (for an individual saint) versus *orate* (for a group of saints). The second response follows a series

---

[10] The issue of the ultimate addressee of Christian prayer, Christ or the Father, has been the object of intense research and debate among liturgical scholars. The groundbreaking position of Joseph Andreas Jungmann, who asserted that there had been a more or less straightforward liturgical evolution corresponding with doctrinal, particularly Christological, developments in early Christianity, is no longer held. Jungmann's reconstruction is not only too general, he had not looked at all the available evidence, which delivers a much more complex overall picture than he acknowledged. See Spinks (2008). Jungmann's original study *Die Stellung Christi im liturgischen Gebet*, of which there is an English translation from 1989 prefaced by Balthasar Fischer, dates from 1925.

of mysteries of faith, centered around the life, death and resurrection of Jesus Christ, as exemplified in the course of the liturgical year, with a strong emphasis on the saving capacity of these mysteries.[11] They liberate one from evil and prevent from eternal condemnation. The third response answers to a series of entreaties focusing on the beneficial effects which Christ's mysteries entail for all those who faithfully believe them. Moreover, the fact that all three responses have personal pronouns in the first person plural (*nobis, nos*) underlines the collective nature of the liturgical activity they are part of.

The concluding part of the litany addresses thrice the Lamb of God (*Agnus Dei, qui tollis peccata mundi*), but the supplications which follow slightly differ from the ones in the *Ordo Missae*, where one has twice *miserere nobis* and once *dona nobis pacem* (give us peace). Instead one here first has *parce nobis dñe* (be thrifty with us Lord), then *exaudi nos domine* (comply with us Lord) and finally, as in the Order of Mass indeed, *miserere nobis* (have mercy upon us). The final words of the litany constitute a kind of echo of the first addresses, as Christ is invoked twice: *Christe audi nos, Christe audi nos* (Christ hear us, Christ hear us).

3. Elements of a History of the Text

3.a. *The 1474 Missale Romanum*

When the question is asked where this text from the 1570 missal comes from, one has to look primarily to the first printed *Missale Romanum*, which ironically was not produced in Rome but in Milan almost one century before, in 1474.[12] Scholars have noted that the most important source for the one-and-only papally authorized missal issued in the immediate aftermath of the Council of Trent by Pope Pius V was the first-ever printed edition of the Roman missal.[13] The liturgical commission under the leadership of Cardinal Sirleto, which was installed by this pope to carry out the practical work, changed only minor elements.

---

[11] These mysteries are subsequently the incarnation, advent, nativity, baptism and fasting of Jesus, his cross and passion, death, resurrection, ascension and the coming of the Holy Spirit. It is possible to draw parallels here with the creed.

[12] *Missale Romanum Mediolani, 1474*. One finds the text of the litany of the Easter vigil on pages 190–93.

[13] Interesting surveys of the history of the Roman missal can be found in McCarthy (2013) and Sorci (2003).

This general observation applies without any problems to our litany. When comparing the two versions of the litany, one only notes spelling details in the introductory part (e.g. *Kyrieleyson* instead of *Kyrie eleison*). With respect to the concluding part of the litany, one sees that the abovementioned *inclusio* is much more evident in the 1474 Roman missal. Instead of two times *Christe audi nos* as in the 1570 missal, one here has *Christe audi nos. Christe exaudi nos. Kirieleyson. Christeleyson, Kirieleyson*, while the three preceding *Agnus Dei* acclamations are identical.

Most differences are found in the first part of the litany,[14] where the saints are invoked. There are no less than six groups of saints which, as a distinct category, are not mentioned in the 1474 text. Omitted are, consecutively, *Omnes angeli et archangeli* (all the angels and archangels), although the threefold Michael, Gabriel and Raphael are the same, *Omnes sancti discipuli domini* (all the holy disciples of the Lord), *Omnes sancti pontifices et confessores* and *Omnes sancti doctores* (all the holy pontiffs and confessors and all the holy doctors), which follow immediately after each other in the 1570 text, and *Omnes săctę viriginęs et viduę* (all the holy virgins and widows). In addition, the 1474 litany has the simpler general category *Omnes sancti confessores* (all the holy confessors) instead of the more extensive qualifications *Omnes sancti sacerdotes et levitę* and *Omnes săcti Monachi et Eremitę* (all the holy priests and Levites and all the holy monks and eremites).

As to individual saints, there are less deviations between the 1474 and 1570 litanies. The 1474 text does not have pope Sylvester before saints Gregory and Augustine and has Saint Clare instead of Saint Monica among the female saints. Also, the order and composition in the category of the 'confessors' (or, indeed, 'priests' and 'monks') is different. In the 1474 litany the sequence is Saint Martin, Saint Francis, Saint Anthony, Saint Dominic, whereas the 1570 text only has the following three: Saint Benedict, Saint Dominic, Saint Francis. There seems no reason why Saints Martin and Anthony are absent in the 1570 version, and why Saint Benedict was not part of the 1474 list.[15] All of them are of

---

[14] In the second part with the *libera nos domine* response the texts of the 1474 and 1570 missals are identical, too. In the third part with the *te rogamus audi nos* response, the 1570 version has added two *ut* clauses somewhere in the middle of them. The content of these clauses matches well with the defensive not to say polemical mode which the Church had taken on as a reaction to the Reformation. God is asked (*rogamus*) to take down the enemies of the Church and to give peace and true harmony to Christian kings and princes, but one can assume that one actually has mind 'Catholic' rulers.

[15] As is commonly known, Saints Benedict, Dominic and Francis are all founders of major religious orders which have co-shaped the identity of Christian religious

immense importance in the Catholic Church and were widely venerated throughout Europe in the Middle Ages.

The next question is what the sources were for the 1474 *Missale Romanum*. This question is much more difficult to answer than the previous one. The reason for that is the complexity of the history of the Roman missal as a book composed of many fragments from heterogeneous origins. Before Trent, it was not the case that there was only one singular version of the missal which was universally used in all the Catholic dioceses and monasteries of Europe (and beyond), and even after Trent it was by no means evident to have that one missal authoritatively implemented everywhere. To this is added the notoriously difficult liturgical history of the city of Rome, where one had the parochial or presbyteral regime in the so-called titular churches and, to a large extent independent of that, the papal ceremonies at the court of the Lateran palace. Since, moreover, the pope regularly traveled around the city for liturgical celebrations according to a fixed scheme, one speaks in this context of the stational liturgy.[16] The sources we have from both the presbyteral (parochial) and the papal (stational) regimes, however, have become conflated throughout the centuries.[17] When the liturgical models of Rome left the city for use elsewhere, they were adapted and modified in many ways, and when Rome had become culturally and politically weaker, some of those changed versions of the liturgy and its books were reintroduced in the eternal city.

---

life and culture in Europe, respectively the Benedictines, Dominicans and Franciscans. For church-political reasons it may have been important to keep a certain balance between them. On the other hand, with respect to the 1474 selection, one can comment that Saints Dominic and Francis are obviously there, and that Saint Anthony can count as the founder of monasticism, while Saint Martin was an indefatigable promoter of Christian faith in late antique Gaul. Among the saints he has a special role, because he was the first who was not a martyr but who instead gained much appraisal through his confession of the faith and missionary zeal. Apart from this, Saint Martin is also known to have been one of the most popular saints of the Middle Ages.

[16] For a comprehensive study of the stational liturgy in Rome (but also in Constantinople and elsewhere), see Baldovin (1987).

[17] An impressive attempt at reconstructing the parochial liturgy of Rome was undertaken by French scholar Chavasse (1957), who notes the absence of the *litania maior* in the old Gelasian sacramentary (p. 178), which he explains by saying that the litany was generally part of the stational liturgy, and that it therefore does not occur in a liturgical book for the presbyteral liturgy at Rome. Still, there were litanies performed in the titular churches on the occasion of baptisms (pp. 99–101). See also infra.

3.b. The 1244 Ordo Missalis Fratrum Minorum

Two phases of this particular history are relevant for our topic. The first one is when the newly founded religious congregation of the Franciscans relied on liturgical sources in use at Rome in the thirteenth century with a view to composing the missals and breviaries for its many friars traveling and settling all over Europe. The key figure in this development was Haymo of Faversham (*c.* 1180–1244), the fourth minister general of the Franciscan order. He knew the custom of praying the litany in the Easter vigil on Holy Saturday. In *Ordo Missalis Fratrum Minorum Secundum Consuetudinem Romane Curie* composed by him, dated 1243–44, he says:

> Thereafter one proceeds to the benediction of the fonts. [...] The priest, having taken off the chasuble, kneels before the altar together with the ministers and other friars stand upright and the litany is sung in the middle of the choir by two friars, with both choirs simultaneously responding to it. When one has arrived at [the line] *Peccatores te rogamus audi nos*, the priest and the ministers go back to the cloakroom and are solemnly vested. The lights around the altar are kindled with the blessed fire.[18] And when one has arrived at the [closing] *Kyrieleison* of the litany, the *Kyrieleison* for the mass is solemnly started by the cantors.[19]

Haymo of Faversham is aware of the litany of the saints in another context, too. He prescribes it as one of the ritual elements to be performed when a fellow brother has died. The *Ordo Commendationis Anime* (order of the commendation of a soul) opens with it. The fivefold structure of the text sounds familiar,[20] but the content is somewhat reduced as compared to the 1474 and 1570 versions of the litany from the Roman missal. One has the opening *Kyrieleison* and *Christeleison*, after which immediately the series of saints headed by *Sancta Maria* starts. Emphatic is the mention of Abel and the entire 'chorus of the just'. For the rest, one has the recognizable arrangement of subsequently patriarchs, prophets, apostles, evangelists, pontiffs, confessors, monks, eremites, and virgins, though individual names of saints are a little different from

---

[18] The blessing of fire was – and still is – another rite of the Easter vigil, usually at the very beginning of it. It is symbolically important that it is from this blessed fire that the Easter candle is kindled. It is for this candle that the *Exultet* is sung, a hymn of praise for the light of Christ and simultaneously a proclamation of the resurrection.

[19] *The Ordinals by Haymo of Faversham*, 247–48 (my translation).

[20] *The Ordinals by Haymo of Faversham*, 390–92.

the ones we already encountered. Evidently, Saint Francis is explicitly mentioned (but not Saint Dominic).[21] As to the second series of supplications, responded to with *libera*, one observes a specific adaptation to the death of someone,[22] but the evocation of the mysteries of Christ's life are more or less the same than the ones we encountered already. The third series of entreaties is here reduced to only one after *Peccatores, te rogamus audi nos*: *Ut ei parcas* (be thrifty with him). The conclusion of the litany is the simple threefold of *Kyrieleison, Christeleison, Kyrieleison*, as in the 1474 but unlike the 1570 one.

3.c. Ordo Romanus L and XXI

The second phase we must include in our reflections, is one which again takes us more than two hundred and fifty years earlier in history, which means that we enter into the first millennium of Christianity. Towards the middle of the tenth century, there was a great deal of activity around the production of liturgical books along the banks of the Rhine, where the Ottonian emperors ruled. Particular reference must be made to the abbey of Saint Alban in Mainz, which had a strong reputation as a center of learning – Rabanus Maurus had taught there – and which had been instrumental to the Carolingian renaissance. It is highly likely that it is in the scriptorium of this monastery that many liturgical prayers, rituals and customs were received from Rome and Gaul, elaborated upon, and passed on further. The monks and liturgists thus helped shape what scholars 1000 years later called the Romano-Germanic pontifical.[23] In the many sources giving access to this complex of texts from around the turn of the first to the second millennium of Christianity, we do find traces of our litany. Chief among those sources are the so-called *Ordines Romani*, representing the evolution of the liturgy of the Roman rite in Western Europe roughly between the eighth and the eleventh century,

---

[21] The founder of the Dominicans died in 1221 and was canonized in 1234, while the founder of the Franciscans died five years later (1226) but was canonized six years earlier (1228) than Saint Dominic.

[22] For their deceased brother the friars sing that he (and they themselves) may be freed 'Ab ira tua' (*from your anger*), 'A mala morte' (*from a bad death*), 'A periculo mortis' (*from the danger of death*), 'A penis inferni' (*from the torments of hell*), 'A potestate diaboli' (*from the power of the devil*), and 'Ab omni malo' (*from every evil*). Only the last one is part of the litanies in the 1474 and 1570 Roman missals. There is, moreover, no need to add that these supplications do reveal something about the religious life-world of medieval people.

[23] Vogel (1986), 225–47.

and carefully edited by the renowned and still highly esteemed French scholar Michel Andrieu (1886–1956).[24]

According to Andrieu, *Ordo Romanus* L, which was the last and the most comprehensive one in the volumes he took care of, can be dated around 950. The document contains liturgical instructions and fragments of hymns and prayers virtually covering an entire liturgical year. In that context it has several allusions and references to litanies. Interestingly, one of them is to be situated in the context of the celebrations on Holy Saturday. Instructions are given for the choir, which is to be split in a left and right part, a practice we encountered already in Haymo's instructions. The choir has to sing three times *Kyrie eleison* and *Christe eleison* and then pursue with seven repetitions back and forth. Mention is also made of supplications to be answered with *Christe audi nos*.[25] Elsewhere in this document, the compiler informs his readers of a custom stemming from the ancient diocese of Vienne (in southern France, i.e. Gaul), where the bishop instituted a practice of three days of 'rogations' (*dies rogationum*). They take place on Monday, Tuesday and Wednesday before the feast of the Ascension.[26] The compiler also explains that 'what is called *letania* in Greek corresponds in Latin with *rogation*'[27] – something which he is correctly informed about.

The text itself of our litany of the saints is part of the long chapter 36 of *Ordo Romanus* L. In that chapter there are also other litanies, which most probably originate from the abbey of Sankt Gallen in present-day Switzerland. One recognizes the overall structure we are already acquainted with. However, the introduction does not have a variant of *Kyrie eleison* but starts instead with a fivefold *Miserere nobis*, which nonetheless means the same. The five elements to which the miserere responses respond are strikingly similar to the divine titles we met above in the 1570 Roman missal litany: *Pater de caelis Deus* (Father from heaven, God), *Filius redemptor mundi Deus* (Son redeemer of the world, God), *Spiritus sancte Deus* (Holy Spirit, God),[28] *Qui es trinus et unus Deus* (who art the triune and one God) and *Ipse idemque benignus Deus* (He himself the same benevolent God). Clearly, there must have

[24] *Les Ordines Romani du Haut Moyen Âge* (1931–61).
[25] *Ordo Romanus L*, 29,71; *Les Ordines*, vol. 5, 288–89.
[26] *Ordo Romanus L*, 36,1; *Les Ordines*, vol. 5, 315–16.
[27] *Ordo Romanus L*, 35,1; *Les Ordines*, vol. 5, 314.
[28] Intriguingly, the Latin does not have the vocative form for Filius, which would be Fili, but it does have the vocative form for the adjective sancte accompanying Spiritus.

been an issue with the equal divinity of the three persons of the Trinity. Otherwise one cannot explain the insistent recurrence of *Deus* and the explanatory relative clause in this context (cf. supra).

Next follows a rather limited list of saints which is interrupted by only one acclamation of a category of saints, the apostles. The list starts with Mary, for whom there are two titles ('God-bearer' and 'virgin of virgins'), continues with the archangels, Peter, Paul and three more apostles, saints Lambert, Martin and Benedict, and finally six female saints (Perpetua, Cristina, Columba, Margarita, Iuliana and Anastasia).[29] It strikes one that saints who were important in Gaul (like e.g. Martin and Columba[30]) are inserted in the list. Before the concluding *Kyrie eleison – Christe eleison – Kyrie eleison* there are six entreaties with resemblances to ulterior contents; two are responded to with *Concede nobis, domine* (grant us, Lord), one with *libera nos*, one with *dona nobis* (give us), and two with the familiar *miserere nobis*.

Elsewhere in the corpus of the Ordines Romani we find a short *ordo* of hardly three pages, *Ordo Romanus* XXI, which is exclusively devoted to the *letania maior*, i.e. the litany of saints. According to Vogel, it 'is a Frankish arrangement of the Rogation procession of April 25 [...] which, at Rome, went with several stations from St Lawrence in Lucina to St Peter's basilica'.[31] 'It was composed after the introduction of the Roman liturgy in *Francia* [...] and before the Carolingian Renaissance [...]. It can therefore be dated 770–790'.[32] The ordo first describes some liturgical actions and then gets to the content of the litany. It is worthwhile to quote it in full:

> *Cyrie* [sic] *eleison* is thrice repeated, then *Christe audi nos*; *Saint Mary, pray for us*; *Saint Peter*; *Saint Paul*; *Saint Andrew*; *Saint John*; *Saint Stephan*; *Saint Lawrence*, or another saint in whose church the mass is celebrated; then *All saints may pray for us*; *Be well-disposed, be thrifty with us, Lord*; *Be well-disposed, liberate us, Lord*; *From every evil, liberate us, Lord*; *Through your cross, liberate us, Lord*; [being] *Sinners, we ask, hear us*; *Son of God, we ask, hear us*; *So that you may give peace, we ask, hear us*; and *Agnus Dei* all is repeated thrice; then *Christ hear us, Kyrie eleison*, also thrice, and then it's finished.[33]

---

[29] *Ordo Romanus L*, 46,79; *Les Ordines*, vol. 5, 334–35.

[30] Meant here is not Columba of Iona, who was a man, but a female saint and martyr from, or at least venerated in, the city of Sens in Burgundy.

[31] Vogel (1986), 170. Vogel summarizes Andrieu's findings.

[32] Vogel (1986), 170.

[33] *Ordo Romanus XXI*, 17; *Les Ordines*, vol. 3, 249 (my translation).

3.d. Two Litanies of Saints from the Nineth and the Tenth Century

It is meaningful to juxtapose this latter text from the *Ordines Romani* with other sources we have from roughly the same period (i.e. the late eighth until the early eleventh century), and which often consist of mere listings of saints with no or very little introduction. A good number of them have been published by Maurice Coens, a prominent scholar of the Bollandists, a notorious society which takes it on it to provide critical editions of lives of saints and thereby serve the Church. I limit myself to two examples.

The first example stems from a manuscript from the Dom at Cologne, can be dated at the outset of the nineth century and contains no less than 275 names of saints. The litany starts with *Kyrieleyson – Christe eleyson – Kyrieleyson – Christe audi nos* but then, somewhat deviantly, starts not with Mary but with the archangels Michael, Gabriel and Raphael. Mary comes next and is followed by Peter, Paul and the other apostles, early popes and a great many other saints.[34] Coens observes that there are some oddities in the list, since there are no general categories interspersing the listing and since some of the names of saints do not appear at those places where one would expect them – like Mary to begin with. At the end of the text, there are some supplications with elements which can be easily recognized, though the manuscript clearly omits certain wordings. One finds, among other elements, *Propicius esto* (be well-disposed), *libera, Peccatores, te rogamus* ([being] sinners, we ask you), *Agnus Dei* and the concluding *Kyrieleyson*.[35] It is difficult if not impossible to say what the relation may have been of this long litany with liturgical celebrations, even if the distinction of what is liturgy and what is not liturgy is hard to make with respect to the religious and devotional practices of people who lived over a millennium ago.

The second example comes from a manuscript from the second half of the tenth century and must be situated in Freising in Bavaria. The manuscript indicates at some point: *incipit laetania antiqua* (here starts the ancient litany). Then follows the introduction with *Kyrie eleison, Christe eleison* and four supplications addressed to Christ (*Christe*): hear us, protect us, save us, and liberate us.[36] Next come three addresses to *Salvator mundi* (Savior of the world) followed by entreaties: assist us, remove us, and have mercy on us when we leave this world. The subsequent

---

[34] Coens (1963), 140.
[35] Coens (1963), 144.
[36] Coens (1963), 169.

list of saints lead by Mary and the archangels is impressive; unlike the previous one, it is interspersed with general categories of saints. Among the angels, different divisions are mentioned: from the thrones up to the cherubim and seraphim. Then follow 16 patriarchs, 21 prophets, 17 apostles (but in addition to the classical twelve the list contains evangelists and collaborators of Paul, too), 138 martyrs (some of which did not die alone but had 'partners'), 77 confessors, 60 virgins (though Saints Felicitas and Symphorosa are mentioned *cum VII filiis* (with seven daughters/sons)), and 9 more categories of saints without specific names: widows, infants, innocents, priests, eremites, anchorites, cenobites and nuns.[37] This litany does not have other (concluding) prayer formulae, unlike the previous example, which makes it even more difficult to imagine any liturgical context. In the grouping of the saints itself, however, it clearly shows an advanced status.

4. A Brief Note on the Liturgical Uses of the Litany of Saints and the 'Litanic' Origins of the *Kyrie*

Digging into the history of the text of the litany of saints of the Roman rite has brought us so far somewhere at the edge of the eighth century.[38] It should not come as a surprise that the available sources amply show that Christians have known a practice of responsive supplications, and that they turned themselves to the one whom they confessed is their 'Lord' in that context. Whatever their doctrinal disagreements may have been about, they meant to explicitly address God and to seek for divine assistance amidst the vicissitudes of their lives. They also realized that doing this may require some mediation by trustworthy examples of faith, and that is where the saints come in. From our survey one may conclude that the use of *Kyrie* is one of the most consistent, if not the uttermost significant, building stone and characteristic feature of the litany of saints.

---

[37] Coens (1963), 170–74.

[38] Following a genealogical approach, it is possible to record the existence of litanies around the same time. On the basis of textual witnesses such as the writings of the Venerable Bede, the use of litanies must have been known in the British Isles by the late seventh and early eighth century. Moreover, according to scholars such as Edmund Bishop and Michael Lapidge, England was the first country where litanies were introduced, not through a steady evolution but directly from Syria. From England they would have been spread over Ireland and the European continent. See Lapidge (1991).

This raises the question where the *Kyrie* acclamation itself comes from. A prevailing opinion, which is largely due to Jungmann, is that that the litany of saints is an extension of the threefold *Kyrie eleison, Christe eleison, Kyrie eleison* which had become part of the celebration of the mass. There it was inserted in the opening rites preceding the readings from Scripture. In the last decade of the sixth century, pope Gregory the Great notes that the Greeks do not have the *Christe eleison* but that it is there in between the two *Kyrie eleison* in Roman usage, and also that there is a distinctive responsorial way of praying these supplications by the clergy and the people alternately.[39] There is compelling evidence, however, that the *Kyrie* was already used in the East, Milan and Gaul before it was adopted in Rome. In those regions it was always an intrinsic part of or accompanied by a litany.

As a consequence, one must reverse Jungmann's take on the matter. Peter Jeffery is very firm about this: 'Jungmann was wrong about the litany at the Paschal Vigil. It did not originate by adding names of saints to an originally christological Mass *Kyrie* – to suppose that it did is to ignore the way the text was used in liturgical action. In the oldest Roman sources the litany simply accompanies the procession to the font, then back to the altar. The Kyrie of the Mass grows out the litany, not the other way around'.[40] For Jeffery this is particularly important, for the Kyrie in the mass today should not primarily be seen as contributing to a confession of sins or penitential rite at the beginning of the Eucharist, but as a well-considered and prayerful putting oneself under the mild and merciful guidance of God, who listens to every human prayer and petition without exception.

Series of such prayers, in the context of which *Kyrie* occurs, are attested in two of the major sources of ancient Christian liturgy, the *Apostolic Constitutions* and Egeria's famous travel report about what she had experienced in the holy land.[41] The two of them reflect the situation of the late fourth century in Syria, in Antioch and Jerusalem to be precise. Gordon Lathrop aptly summarizes: 'The *Kyrie* probably began as a Kyrie litany, like the *ektenia* or συναπτή of the Eastern church, with a series of bids for the needs of the world and the church called out as the assembly gathers, the assembly responding repeatedly *kyrie eleison*, or

---

[39] This text is quoted at the beginning of a study by Capelle (1934), 127.

[40] Jeffery (2008), 183.

[41] Cf. Jeffery (2008), 150–56, with references there to accessible editions of these sources.

"Lord, have mercy'".[42] Realizing that the reasons or occasions for these liturgical gatherings could be diverse, Jeffery concurs:

> The true history of the Kyrie in the Roman Mass is to be traced through the litany of saints, sung at processions to stational Masses, Rogations, ordinations, and the procession to and from the font at the Paschal Vigil. With its long lists of saints, this litany retains the tradition of reciting names, and the Roman use of processional crosses may recall something of Egeria's procession to Golgotha. The individual petitions were typically doubled, alternated between the clerical cantors and the people, as Pope Gregory described.[43]

As such, the litany of saints embodied the important function of mediating between life and liturgy, marking important transitions of life in general and religious life in particular. In that capacity, the litany of saints can be said to be representative of the liturgy as a whole.

5. Conclusion

Taking the litany of saints of the 1570 *Missale Romanum* as a point of departure, it has been possible to trace its textual history back to the eighth century, while the practices reflected by it are still earlier and date from at least the fourth century. Put differently, there is considerable textual evidence of the litany and *Kyrie* supplications, on the basis of which one can conclude that it had a history of roughly one millennium before it attained to its version in the Tridentine missal.[44] Our brief investigations and presentations of a selection of primary sources have shown that it is above all its fivefold structure around three series of supplications with different responses preceded by an introductory *Kyrie* and winded up with another invocation of the Lord, that eventually warranted its stability and identifiability. The names of saints may change; there may or may not be mentions of groups of them; there may be greater or lesser variation in the supplications responded to with *libera nos domine* or *te rogamus audi nos* – or indeed with other

---

[42] Lathrop (2017), 119.

[43] Jeffery (2008), 192.

[44] When one realizes that a version of the same litany of saints still persists in the contemporary *Missale Romanum* which is used for masses in the Catholic Church according to the Roman rite (cf. footnote 2), one can extrapolate the reasoning and safely say that it currently has a history of around 1500 years.

responses still; but the structure is solid yet flexible. As to the invoked saints themselves, Mary and the archangels have always been there and have always been ranked first, followed by Saints Peter, Paul and other apostles, martyrs and Church leaders. Inasmuch as this litany is representative of the liturgy of the Roman rite as a whole, one can say with confidence that it offers a beautiful illustration of what the Christian liturgy is all about.

Bibliography

Medieval Sources

Les Ordines Romani du Haut Moyen Âge, ed. M. Andrieu [5 vols], Louvain, 1931–61, 5 vols, Specilegium Sacrum Lovaniense: Études et documents, vols 11, 23, 24, 28, 29.

Missale Romanum Mediolani, 1474, ed. R. Lippe [vol. 1: Text], London, 1899.

Sources of the Modern Roman Liturgy: The Ordinals by Haymo of Faversham and Related Documents (1243–1307), ed. S. J. P. Van Dijk [vol. 2], Leiden, 1963.

Modern Authors

Amiet, R. (1999) *La veillée pascale dans l'Église latine 1. Le rite romain: Histoire et liturgie*, Paris.

Baldovin, J. F. (1987) *The Urban Character of Christian Worship: The Origins, Development and Meaning of Stational Liturgy* [Orientalia Christiana Analecta 227], Rome.

Bugnini, A. (1990) *The Reform of the Liturgy 1948–1975* [M. J. O'Connell (trans.)], Collegeville.

Capelle, B. (1934) 'Le *Kyrie* de la messe et le pape Gélase,' *Revue bénédictine* 46, 126–44.

Chavasse, A. (1957) *Le sacramentaire gélasien (Vaticanus Reginensis 316): Sacramentaire presbytéral en usage dans les titres romains au viie siècle*, Paris.

Coens, M. (1963) 'Anciennes litanies des saints,' in *Recueil d'études bollandiennes* [Subsidia Hagiographica 37], Bruxelles, 129–322.

Day, J. (2014) *Reading the Liturgy: An Exploration of Texts in Christian Worship*, London and New York.

Geldhof, J. (2018) 'Trent and the Production of Liturgical Books in its Aftermath,' in W. François and V. Soen (eds), *The Council of Trent: Reform and Controversy in Europe and Beyond (1545–1700)*, vol. 1: *Between Trent, Rome and Wittenberg*, Göttingen.

Jeffery, P. (1986) 'Litany,' in J. R. Strayer (ed.), *Dictionary of the Middle Ages*, vol. 7, New York, 588–94.

— (2008) 'The Meanings and Function of *Kyrie eleison*,' in B. D. Spinks (ed.), *The Place of Christ in Liturgical Prayer: Trinity, Christology and Liturgical Theology*, Collegeville, 127–94.

Lapidge, M. (ed.) (1991) *Anglo-Saxon Litanies of Saints*, London.

Lathrop G. W. (2017) *Saving Images: The Presence of the Bible in Christian Liturgy*, Minneapolis.

McCarthy, D. P. (2013) 'Seeing a Reflection, Considering Appearances: The History, Theology and Literary Composition of the *Missale Romanum* at a Time of Vernacular Reflection,' in *Questions Liturgiques* 94, 109–43.

Sodi, M., A. M. Triacca (ed.) (2012) *Missale Romanum: Editio Princeps (1570)* [Monumenta Liturgica Concilii Tridentini 2], Città del Vaticano.

Sodi, M., A. Toniolo (ed.) (2007) *Missale Romanum: Editio typica 1962* [Monumenta Liturgica Piana 1], Città del Vaticano.

Palazzo, É. (1998) *A History of Liturgical Books from the Beginning to the Thirteenth Century*, Collegeville.

Sorci, P. (2003) 'Il Messale Romano come strumento della tradizione celebrativa,' in C. Giraudo (ed.), *Il Messale Romano: Tradizione, traduzione, adattamento* [Bibliotheca Ephemerides Liturgicae. Subsidia 125], Rome, 37–78.

Spinks, B. D. (2008) 'The Place of Christ in Liturgical Prayer: What Jungmann Omitted to Say,' in B. D. Spinks (ed.), *The Place of Christ in Liturgical Prayer: Trinity, Christology and Liturgical Theology*, Collegeville, 1–19.

Vogel, C. (1986) *Medieval Liturgy: An Introduction to the Sources*, Washington, DC.

White, J. F. (2003) *Roman Catholic Worship: Trent to Today*, Collegeville [2nd ed.].

Appendix

A transcription of the full text of the litany of the Easter vigil as it appears in the 1570 *Missale Romanum*

(1364)
Kyrie eleison
Christe eleison
Christe audi nos
Christe exaudi nos
Pater de cęlis, deus, miserere nobis
Fili redĕptor mŭdi, deus, miserere nobis
Spiritus săcte, deus, miserere nobis
Sctă trinitas vn'de': miserere nobis
Sctă Maria: ora p nobis

(1365)
Sancta dei genetrix	ora.
Sancta virgo virginum	ora.
Sancte Michael	ora.
Sancte Gabriel	ora.
Sancte Raphael	ora.

Omnes sancti angeli e[t] archangeli, orate pro nobis.
Omnes sancti beatorum spirituum ordines, orate.

Sancte Joannes baptista	ora.

Omnes sancti patriarchę e[t] prophetę, orate pro nobis.

Sancte Petre	ora.
Sancte Paule	ora.
Sancte Joannes	ora.

Omnes sancti apostoli e[t] euangelistę, orate pro nobis.
Omnes sancti discipuli domini, orate pro nobis.

Sancte Stephane	ora.
Sancte Laurenti	ora.
Sancte Uincenti	ora.

Omnes sancti Martyres, orate pro nobis.

Sancte Siluester,	ora.
Sancte Gregori	ora.

Sancte Augustine　　　　　　　　ora.

Sancte Hieronyme　　　　　　　　ora.

Sancte Ambrosi　　　　　　　　　ora.

Omnes sancti pontifices e[t] confessores, orate pro nobis.
Omnes sancti doctores, orate.

Sancte Benedicte　　　　　　　　ora.

Sancte Dominice　　　　　　　　ora.

Sancte Francisce　　　　　　　　 ora.

Omnes sancti sacerdotes e[t] levitę, orate pro nobis.
Omnes săcti Monachi e[t] Eremitę, orate pro nobis.

Sctă Maria Magdalena　　　　　　or. [*sic*]

Sancta Agnes　　　　　　　　　　ora.

Sancta Agatha　　　　　　　　　　ora.

Sancta Monica　　　　　　　　　　ora.

Omnes săctę virgines e[t] viduę, orate pro nobis.
Omnes săcti e[t] sanctę dei, intercedite pro nobis.

(*1366*)
Propitius esto: pce nobis dñe.
Propiti' esto, exaudi nos dñe.
Ab omni malo libera nos dñe.
Ab oĩ peccato, libera nos dñe.
A morte perpetua, libera nos.
Per mysterium sanctę incarnationis tuę, libera nos dñe.
Per aduentum tuum, libera.
Per natiuitatem tuam, libera nos domine.
Per baptismuʒ e[t] sanctum ieiunium tuum, libera nos dñe.
Per crucem e[t] passionem tuaʒ, libera nos domine.
Per morteʒ e[t] sepulturam tuă, libera nos domine.
Per sanctam resurrectionem tuam, libera nos domine.
Per admirabilem ascensioneʒ tuam, libera nos domine.
Per aduentum spiritus sancti paracleti, libera nos dñe.
In die iudicii, libera nos dñe.

(1367)
Pctōres, te rogamus audi nos.
Ut nobis p̱cas, te rog. au. nos.
Ut ecclesiam tuam sanctam regere e[t] cōseruare digneris, te rogamus audi nos.
Ut domnum apostolicũ e[t] omnes ecclesiasticos ordines in sancta religione cōseruare digneris, te rogam. audi nos.
Ut inimicos sãcte̱ Ecclesie̱ humiliare digneris, te ro. audi.
Ut regibus e[t] principibus christianis, pacem e[t] verã concordiam donare digneris: te ro.
Ut nosmetipsos in tuo sancto seruitio confortare e[t] conseruare digneris: te roga. audi.
Ut omnibus benefactoribus nostris sempiterna bona retribuas: te rogam' audi nos.
Ut fructus terre̱ dare e[t] conseruare digneris: te roga. audi.
Ut omnibus fidelibus defunctis requiem eternaʒ donare digneris: te rogamus audi.
Ut nos exaudire digners: te.

(1368)
Agnus Dei, qui tollis peccata mũdi: parce nobis dñe.
Agnus Dei, qui tollis peccata mundi, exaudi nos domine.
Agnus Dei, qui tollis peccata mundi, miserere nobis.
Christe audi nos. Christe audi nos.

Magnus Williamson

SINGING THE LITANY IN TUDOR ENGLAND, 1544–1555

This essay arises from some recent discoveries concerning a pair of polyphonic Litanies written in England in the 1540s and 1550s.[1] It was during these middle decades of the century that the musical and ceremonial implications of religious reform were first confronted head-on, and in this context the Litany was important for three reasons. Firstly, it was the first element of the old Latin rite to be translated for use within public worship: it was a pioneer, contested in the 1540s and debated more recently. Secondly, once introduced in 1544 the new vernacular Litany outlived successive waves of liturgical reform, partly because of the peculiarly legalistic temper of the English Reformation, and also because of the genre's liminal ritual status. Thirdly, because of its processional origins, the Litany was implicated in public campaigns of persuasion under Henry VIII and his daughter Mary. It is perhaps unsurprising that these early years of ritual reform gave rise to a cluster of polyphonic Litanies composed in the mid-sixteenth century.[2]

1. Before the Reformation

Within the pre-Reformation choral tradition, from the 1440s to the 1540s, Litanies were of tertiary importance. Within surviving and lost sources of

[1] On which, see the following essays from a recent issue of the periodical *Early Music*: Johnstone (2016), Skinner (2016) and Williamson (2016).

[2] The present essay is indebted to two excellent but contrasting studies: Bowers (2002) and Marsh (2007), 219–61. In broad terms, Marsh argues that the vernacular Litany was of greater ritual importance than Bowers admits, and more suggestive of a reformist direction in Henry VIII's religious policies. Bowers's hypothesis is adopted wholesale in Bernard (2005), 589–90.

Magnus Williamson • Newcastle University, UK

The Litany in Arts and Cultures, ed. by Witold Sadowski and Francesco Marsciani, Turnhout, Brepols, 2020 (*Studia Traditionis Theologiae*, 36), pp. 197-219
© BREPOLS PUBLISHERS   DOI 10.1484/M.STT-EB.5.119213

Latin polyphony, first priority was given to four genres: the Mass Ordinary, Propers for Lady Mass, the Magnificat and the 'votive antiphon' or motet of prayer and praise to a named saint (normally the Virgin Mary). Second priority was given to festal and seasonal Propers, such as hymns and responsories, music for Holy Week (including the Passions), and processional antiphons such as *Christus resurgens*. Some of these second-tier genres might be realised either through the semi-improvised method of faburden or as fully elaborated compositions, but the third layer of polyphonic activity was largely or wholly improvisatory. One of the notated legacies of the distinctive insular tradition of faburden is a corpus of 'squares' or melodic formulae which had originated as literal counter-melodies of the chant but then became embedded in singers' working repertories, in notated form. These mensural melodies were then used as the melodic foundations for improvised faburden, in place of the proper chants.[3]

The square for the Latin Litany refrain *Kyrieleyson qui precioso* provides an example of how the repertory of squares worked in practice (Music Example 1).

Kyrie Qui precioso (T139)

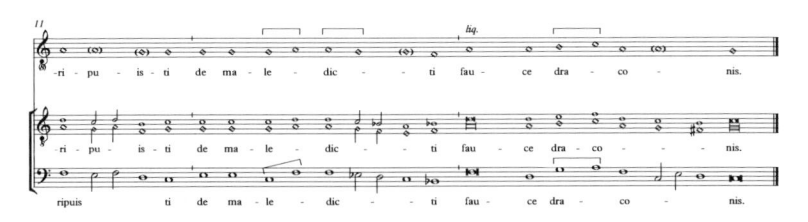

Music Example 1. Rogationtide Litany refrain, *Kyrieleyson qui precioso* (square in Voice III with implied chant in Voice II, and Voice I singing a fourth above the chant).

[3] Harrison (1962); Trowell (1980).

The uppermost stave shows the source melody found in the Salisbury *Processionale*. The lowermost stave (Voice III) shows the square as notated in one of its various sources, in this case a copy of the Sarum Processional printed in 1525.[4] The middle stave comprises the upper two voices in a typical three-voice realisation of the square: Voice II (shown here in lozenge-shaped notes) sings the chant, adjusted melodically to match the square which is sung in thirds and fifths below it, while Voice I (shown in small notes) sings in regular parallel fourths above the chant.[5] Following the normal rules of faburden, the square follows strictly in parallel intervals below the chant except at cadences; at these points, stylised mensurated cadences enable the square to glide in idiomatic steps down to a perfect concord (here a fifth) below the chant. Gregorian chants have a disobligingly frequent tendency not to cadence by step, textbook-style; a stock of melodic formulae enabled singers to circumvent this problem, and the principle of ornamentation then spread outwards from the cadence points to their surrounding melodic context, with a general bias towards stepwise movement. For this reason some of the notated squares are more elaborate than others (as is the case with the square *Kyrieleyson qui precioso*).[6]

Fully notated polyphony for the pre-Reformation Litany is found only in the Pepys manuscript, a choirbook of modest dimensions (180 × 125 mm) compiled in the 1460s as a miscellany, and probably not intended for use in performance *ad lectrinam*.[7] Otherwise, the Litany is represented exclusively in the form of squares such as *Kyrieleyson qui precioso*, added into pre-existing Processionals by their owners and us-

---

[4] Oxford, Bodleian Library, Auct. T inf. III.17: *Processionale...Sarum* (1525), sigs o.iii^v–o.iv^r; Trowell (1980), 71, #139. For source images see the Digital Image Archive of Medieval Music (https://www.diamm.ac.uk).

[5] In Auct. T inf. III.17 the square is notated in thirds and fifths below service book pitch; in another source (Bodleian Library, MS Rawl. liturg. e. 45) the same square is written a fifth lower, placing the chant conceptually in Voice I (in sixths and octaves above the square), shadowed by Voice II in parallel fourths *below* the chant.

[6] A slightly more elaborate form of the square *Kyrie qui precioso* is in two independent sources: London, Lambeth Palace Library, **H.5142.P.1545 (*Processionale... Sarum* (1545), fol. cxxx^v) and Dublin, Trinity College Library, KK.k.55 (*Processionale... Sarum* (1525), sigs m.8v–n. 1r; Trowell, 'Faburden – New sources', 71, #140. Source images on DIAMM.

[7] Cambridge, Magdalene College, MS 1236, fols 12v–13r (*Kyrie eleison qui precioso*), fols 17v–18r (*Kyrie: Christe audi nos*) and fol. 18r (*Kyrie: Christe audi nos*), and also the concluding verse in time of war, *Ab inimicis* (at fols 46v–47r): Curtis and Wathey (1994), 6: ## O285, O276, O277 and O2. Modern edition: Charles (1967), ## 8, 12, 13 and 46. On Pepys 1236, see Roger Bowers's description in Fenlon (1982), 111–14.

ers.[8] Most importantly, these semi-improvised Litanies belong exclusively to one specific genre, the repeating *prosae* of the Litanies *in revertendo*, which were sung as processions returned to their point of departure during Rogationtide.[9] The three days preceding the Ascension, which often comprised the feast of St Mark (25 April), were one of the main focuses of parish identity, well-attended, and with refreshments provided.[10] Rogationtide had a distinctive repertory of antiphons, Litanies, itineraries and visual symbols, chief of which was the dragon carried in procession, the shearing of whose tail on Wednesday served to banish evil spirits.[11] There are no pre-Reformation settings of the other kind of Litany, the Greater Litany that was recited on the outward leg of the Rogationtide processions (see Table 1).[12] This belonged to a family of Litanies that were sung during the year: on Wednesdays and Fridays during Lent;[13] the seven- and five-fold Litanies on Easter morning;[14] in *causa necessitatis*, as occasion demanded;[15] and in specific rites such as the coronation.[16] The earliest surviving polyphony for the Greater Litany dates from the mid-1540s and is, surprisingly, in English rather than Latin.

[8] See Trowell (1980), 71–72 and 76–78.

[9] The prose *Kyrie eleyson qui precioso sanguine* was sung during the first of these Litanies.

[10] Duffy (1992), 279; in 1533, Robert Peycoke of Kirkby St Peter (Lincs.), bequeathed funds for 'the Tuysday in rogacion weke to refreshe them that go in procession with bred and ale, xijd' (12 September 1532, probate granted 21/08/1533: David Hickman (2001), #76).

[11] Also the lion of St Mark; Bailey (1971), 52–58, 115.

[12] *Processionale…Sarum* (1545), fols cxxj^v–cxxiiij^r. The only known attempt to devise faburden-style squares for the Greater Litany is found in a copy of *Processionale… Sarum* (1545) now in Paris, Bibliothèque Nationale, Rés. B. 1852, online at https://gallica.bfr/fr), at fol. xcv, and in London, Lambeth Palace Library, **H.5142.P.1545 (fol. [ccxxvi]^v. These two related sources are discussed below.

[13] The Sarum Processional specifies *feria quarta* and *feria sexta*, but the Breviary provides also for daily recitation (Procter and Wordsworth (1879–86). II, cols 250–60); *Processionale…Sarum* (1545), fols xlj^v–xliiij^r.

[14] *Processionale…Sarum* (1545), fols xciiij^r–xcv^v. The Processional specifies recitation *sine nota* on Rogation days.

[15] *Processionale…Sarum* (1545), fols cciiij^v–ccv^v. Urgencies included need (undefined), tribulation, stormy weather, drought, pestilence, and war; the Litany *causa necessitatis* might also be sung *pro pace ecclesiae*.

[16] Marsh (2007), 235–36. Legg (1893), col. 687, where the Litany was begun by two bishops, kneeling, and followed by the seven penitential psalms.

		Quadragesima	Easter Sunday	Rogationtide	Causa necessitatis	Breviary[17]	Latin Books of Hours[18]	Cranmer 1544	Cranmer 1549
Seven Penitential Psalms				x	x	x	x		
Antiphon *Ne reminiscaris*				x	[19]	x	x	x[20]	x[21]
Kyrie eleison		x	x	x	x	x	x	x	x
Invocations to the Holy Trinity		x		x	x	x	x	x	x
Litany of Saints	Sancte/Sancta N.: *Ora pro nobis.*	x[22]	x[23]	x	x	x	x	[24]	
Deprecations	Ab/A _____: *Libera nos, Domine.*			x	x	x	x	x	x
Obsecrations	Per _____: *Libera nos, Domine.*			x	x	x	x	x	x
Intercessions	Ut _____: *Te rogamus audi nos.*			x	x	x	x	x	x
Agnus Dei				x	x	x	x	x	x
Kyrie eleison				x	x	x	x	x	x
Pater noster				x		x	x	x	x
Versicle(s) and response(s)				x		x	x	x	x
Prayers				x		x	x	x	x

Table 1. The Greater Litany, its variants and descendants to 1549

[17] *The Sarum Rite*: Latin Breviary: Psalter, 424–37. https://macsphere.mcmaster.ca/bitstream/11375/15874/19/A-12%20psalmi%20penitentiali.pdf.

[18] Sample: *An vniforme and Catholyke Prymer* (1555), sigs c.i^r–c.ii^r.

[19] Antiphon *Ne reminiscaris* replaced by alternative antiphons appropriate to the occasion.

[20] Antiphon 'Remember not Lorde our offences' (= *Ne reminiscaris*) now precedes Deprecations.

[21] Antiphon 'Remember not Lorde our offences' (= *Ne reminiscaris*) precedes Deprecations.

[22] Immediately after the Litany of Saints, the priest retires to vest and the cantor begins the Introit for Mass (*PS1545*, fol. xliiij^r).

[23] Immediately after the Litany of Saints, the priest retires to vest and the cantor begins the Introit for Mass (*Processionale…Sarum* (1545), fol. xliiij^r).

[24] In 1544 the 'Holye virgin Mary' alone is invoked by name; the Litany of Saints is compressed into two collective invocations: 'All holye Aungels and Archaungels, and all the holye orders of blessed spirites: *Praye for us*' and 'All holy Patriarches and Prophetes, Apostles, Martyrs, Confessors, & Virgins; and all the blessed companye of heaven: *Praye for us*'. In 1549 this vestige disappears.

2. The Greater Litany, Private Devotion and Religious Reform

If the Greater Litany was a discretionary rite, it was also highly adaptable and extensible – perhaps inevitably, given its form. The Litany of Saints, which followed the Invocations to the Holy Trinity, was particularly susceptible to customisation according to the needs of time and place: Nigel Morgan's encyclopaedic edition of monastic Litanies includes saints so localised as to appear in only one conventual Litany.[25] The same study has found isolated instances of particular Deprecations,[26] Obsecrations,[27] and Intercessions.[28] Mendicant Litanies had distinctive categories of saintly intercessors.[29] But this adaptability also enabled the Litany, particularly the Litany of Saints, to make the transition from corporate liturgies into the private devotional space and the Book of Hours. Any parishioner participating in the Rogationtide processions, or in one of the occasional processions *causa necessitatis*, would have been able to follow the contents of the Litany more or less verbatim from their personal Book of Hours (if they owned one). Like the Marian antiphons, the Office of the Dead and the seven penitential psalms, therefore, the Litany was encountered both in public worship, usually in procession, and in private domestic devotion, usually on the knees and often recited by women.[30] From the mid-thirteenth century de Brailes Hours onwards, the seven penitential psalms and Litany were a universal staple of Books of Hours, along with the Commendations (Ps. 118/119) and the fifteen Gradual Psalms.[31] No less than the *Salve regina*, the Litany stood at the cusp of private and public prayer;[32]

---

[25] From the letter W alone, Walaricus (Shrewsbury Abbey), William of Norwich (Norwich Cathedral Priory), Wistan (Evesham Abbey), Wulfhilda (Barking Nunnery), and Wulmarus (Abbotsbury Abbey): Morgan (2012–2018), III, 195–206.

[26] 'A persecucione inimici' (Westminster Abbey: Morgan (2012–2018), III, 14).

[27] 'Per angelorum ministrationem' (Amesbury, order of Fontevrault): Morgan (2012–2018) I, 56.

[28] 'Ut nos semetipsos in tuo sancto servicio confortare et conservare' (Gloucester Abbey): Morgan (2012–2018), I, 126).

[29] Sandler (1979), 65–80; the Austin Friars invoked 'All monks and hermits', naming Benedict, Francis, Anthony and Dominic.

[30] Erler (2003), 119; Donovan (1991), 183–200.

[31] British Library, Add. MS 49,999, fols 66r–89r. Donovan (1991), 110–14. Among printed Books of Hours, see *Hore* (1510), fol. lxxxv verso. The 'Golden Litany', first published in 1531, combined paraphrases of the Kyrie, Invocations to the Trinity with Obsecrations around the theme of Christ's Passion (*The golden letany* (1531)). Duffy (2006), 28.

[32] This observation counters Roger Bowers's suggestion that the Litany 'had never been an item of any more than the most minor significance' which had 'never formed part of standard parish practice' (Bowers (2002), 152 and 169n).

the well-thumbed Litany pages in Thomas More's Book of Hours suggest that this conventionally pious Henrician recited this devotion frequently.[33]

It was probably no coincidence that official reform of the English liturgy was first effected, albeit tentatively, in the Litany. The landmark date is June 1544, when Archbishop Thomas Cranmer's translation was mandated for use in public processions and prayers in aid of Henry VIII's French wars.[34] But purchasers of some of the more recent, officially-sponsored, Books of Hours would have noticed the shared paternity of Cranmer's text. Ten years earlier, William Marshall's 'aggressively Protestant' Primer, issued with the support of Secretary Thomas Cromwell had entirely omitted the Litany of Saints and its accompanying invocations, leaving only the seven penitential psalms which had traditionally preceded the antiphon *Ne reminiscaris*.[35] The omitted materials were restored in Marshall's next Primer (1535), but Henry VIII's distaste for Purgatory and the cult of saints, expressed in the Ten Articles of 1536, undermined the Litany of Saints.[36] The official Primer prepared in 1539 by John Hilsey, bishop of Rochester, excised all post-Biblical saints from the Litany.[37] Meanwhile, Cromwell's injunctions of 1538 had already provided cover for any clergy inclined to omit the saintly invocations altogether during public worship:[38]

> Item, where in tymes past men have used in dyvers places in their processions to synge *Ora pro nobis*, to so many saynctes, that they had no tyme to synge the good suffrages folowinge, as *Parce nobis Domine*, and *Libera nos Domine*, it muste be taughte and preached, that better it were to omytte *Ora pro nobis*, and to synge the other suffrages, beinge most necessary, and effectuall.

---

[33] Duffy (2006), 113.

[34] Bowers (2002), 157–63; Skinner (2016), 242–45; Marsh (2007) 237–43; Cuming (1982), 35–40; Mears (2013), 34–35.

[35] *A Prymer in Englyshe* (1534); Duffy (2007), 147.

[36] *A goodly prymer* (1535), sigs L.iij^v–M.ij^v; between the seven penitential psalms and *Ne reminiscaris*, Marshall printed a preface defending himself against 'diverse persones or small judgement and knowledge in holy scripture' who had complained about his omission of the Litany the previous year; he issued a disclaimer concerning some of the saints in the reinstated Litany who had been 'canonised and lade sayntes by such as have ben byshoppes of Rome, yet whether they be sayntes or no I committee to the secrete iudgement of god' (ibid., sigs L.ij^v–L.iij^r).

[37] *The manual of prayers* (1539).

[38] See, for instance, *Iniunctions* (1538).

When Thomas Cranmer produced his new vernacular Litany in aid of Henry VIII's military campaigns, therefore, he deployed the textual resources of the late-medieval Breviary and Book of Hours, but tempered by evangelical qualms over saintly intercession. He omitted the seven penitential psalms in favour of a long prose *Exhortation to Prayer* which preceded the opening Kyrie; he incorporated the prayer-like antiphon *Ne reminiscaris* into the body of the Litany where it followed a vestigial Litany of Saints; and, in his shortened selection of Deprecations, Obsecrations and Intercessions, he adapted traditional forms to serve the circumstances of 1544:[39]

> From all sedycion and privey conspiracie, from the tyranny of the bisshop of Rome and all his detestable enormyties, from all false doctrine and heresye, from hardnes of hearte, and contempt of thy worde and commaundemente:
>
> *Good lorde deliver us.*
>
> That it maye please thee to be his [Henry VIII's] defendour and keper, gyvyng hym the vyctorye over all his enemyes:
>
> *We beseche thee to here us good Lorde.*

The vernacular Exhortation and Litany of 1544 was re-issued the following year; but Cranmer's new text was also incorporated wholesale into the official Primer of 1545, where it was preceded by the seven penitential psalms and *Ne reminiscaris* – an acknowledgement of both the traditional form of the Book of Hours, and the close kinship between this first public vernacular liturgy and the private prayer books used by the laity.[40]

In its 1544 form, with only minor textual emendations, Cranmer's Litany was subsumed into the first fully-vernacular liturgy, the first Book of Common Prayer (1549), where it was appointed to be sung before Holy Communion twice weekly, on the traditional Litany days of Wednesday and Friday:[41]

---

[39] Complete edition at: http://justus.anglican.org/resources/bcp/Litany1544/Litany_1544.htm.

[40] *The Primer, in Englishe and Latyn* (1545), sigs g.i^v–g.[vi]^v.

[41] *The booke of common praier* (1549), sig. P.iii. verso.

> Upon Wednesdaies and Fridaies, the Englishe Letany shalbee saied or song in all places, after suche forme as is appoyncted by the kynges Maiesties Iniunccions ... And though there be none to communicate with the priest, yet these daies (after the Letany ended) the priest shall put vpon hym a plain albe or surplesse, with a cope, and saie all thynges at the Altare...vntill after the Offertory.

In the second Book of Common Prayer the same Litany immediately following the orders for Morning and Evening Prayer, and in this state the Litany became embedded within the Elizabeth Book of Common Prayer (1559) and its successors.[42] But Cranmer's Litany also continued to circulate in its original standalone form under Catholic Mary Tudor (r. 1553–8), shorn of Cranmer's long Exhortation and his anti-Papal Deprecation.[43] Mary's restoration of Catholicism proceeded in careful steps, initially through a legalistic reversion to the state of religion as it had stood at the death of Henry VIII in 1547:[44] as if an aberration, the Protestant reforms effected during the minority of Edward VI (r. 1547–53) were repealed under Mary – all, that is, except the vernacular Litany introduced by her father of famous memory. Marian editions of the vernacular Litany include intercessions on behalf of both Mary and her husband Philip, and so we can assume that performances of the vernacular Litany continued after the royal marriage on 26 July 1554 – that is, beyond the earliest phases of the Catholic restoration. Likewise, between the death of Mary Tudor in November 1558 and the re-introduction of the Book of Common Prayer in May 1559, the not-yet-abolished vernacular Litany was performed in the new queen's chapel (shortly before Christmas) and at her coronation in January. The vernacular Litany therefore provided a thread of liturgical continuity from Henry, through Edward and Mary, to Elizabeth.[45]

---

[42] *The boke of common praier* (1552), sig. B.iii. verso; 'Here foloweth the Letanie to be vsed vpon Sondayes, Wedensdayes, and Fridayes, and at other tymes, when it shalbe commanded by the Ordenarie'.

[43] STC 16453, without title page: British Library C.25.b. 10.(3.). Perhaps by an oversight, some of Cranmer's more Protestant formulations such as 'our onlye mediatoure and advocate, Jesu Christ' lingered in the Marian editions.

[44] On the legalistic tenor of royal religious policies in the 1550s, see Bowers (2000), 317–44.

[45] STC 16453.5 (no title page). This standalone Litany was published around New Year 1559 (Clay (1847), 10–22. Elizabeth is named in the intercessions, and the 'tiranie of the bishop of Rome, & all his detestable enormities' have returned to the Deprecation (but were expunged in the official Prayer Book Litany on 1559).

3. Early Polyphonic Settings of the Vernacular Litany

Cranmer's Litany of 1544 was published in three formats: the first with words only;[46] the second with words and monophonic chant derived from the old Sarum tone;[47] and a polyphonic setting 'as sung in the King's Chapel'. No printed copies survive of this latter polyphonic version, the only polyphony ever to be officially mandated by the Church of England, but Andrew Johnstone has convincingly identified the lost 1544 edition with the surviving five-part Litany by Thomas Tallis, by this time a Gentleman of Henry VIII's Chapel Royal.[48] Tallis's setting was a pioneering example, probably the first, of what would become the normative archetype for polyphonic vernacular Litanies: a fauxbourdon harmonization with the plainsong melody quoted literally in either the Tenor or the top voice (= Medius). Tallis's Litany is idiosyncratic, however, and will be discussed later on.

Immediately upon the publication of the new vernacular Litany, it was circulated, copied out, and set to polyphony by church musicians.[49] An anonymous setting can be found scribbled onto the back flyleaves of a printed Latin Processional now at the Folger Shakespeare Library in Washington, DC (Plate 1).[50] A single voice-part is given of what was probably a four- or five-part setting, and only the opening invocation is given, along with two short segments of untexted notation. This vernacular material supplements an annotation already made on the same verso, of the plainsong Sanctus from the Latin *Missa pro defunctis*, copied by the book's owner as a convenient if inelegant aide-memoire.[51] Like so many Proces-

---

[46] STC 10620–10621 (27 May 1544), 1622.5 (16 June 1544), 10623 (12 October 1544), 1623.3 (1544?), 10623.5 (1545?), 10624 (28 March 1545), 10625.3 (27 May 1546) and 10625.7 (8 December 1546).

[47] STC 10621.5 (n.d.), 10621.7 (16 June 1544) and 10622 (8 December 1546). There is no trace of any relationship between the chant provided for Cranmer's litany and contemporary Lutheran archetypes, for instance Johann Spangenberg's German Litany (*Cantiones ecclesiasticae Latinae* (1545), fols clxxxix^v–cxcii^v: https://reader.digitale-sammlungen.de/de/fs1/object/display/bsb10147756_00748.html).

[48] Johnstone (2016).

[49] For instance, at Exeter Cathedral, 1543–4: 'Item for pryckyng of bookes for procession, ij s...Item solutum pro libris chori nove letanie, iijs iiijd' (ex inf. Prof. Nicholas Orme); and at Durham Cathedral, 1544–5: 1544/5: 'Item paid to the chaunter of Westmynster for prykyng the new Latyny in .iij., .iiij. and .v. partes, xxd ... Item for xxiiij^{tie} Latines, wherof .j. dozen noted with playneson of fyve partes, at iijs the dozen, vjs' (Fowler (1903), 726).

[50] Washington, Folger Shakespeare Library, shelfmark STC 16237, a copy of *Processionale...Sarum* (1528).

[51] Because of their basic function as walking books, Processionals typically only contain the chants sung at the bringing of the bier into the quire (antiphon *Subvenite*, respond *Libera me* and antiphon *In paradisum*). My thanks to Dr Georgianna Ziegler,

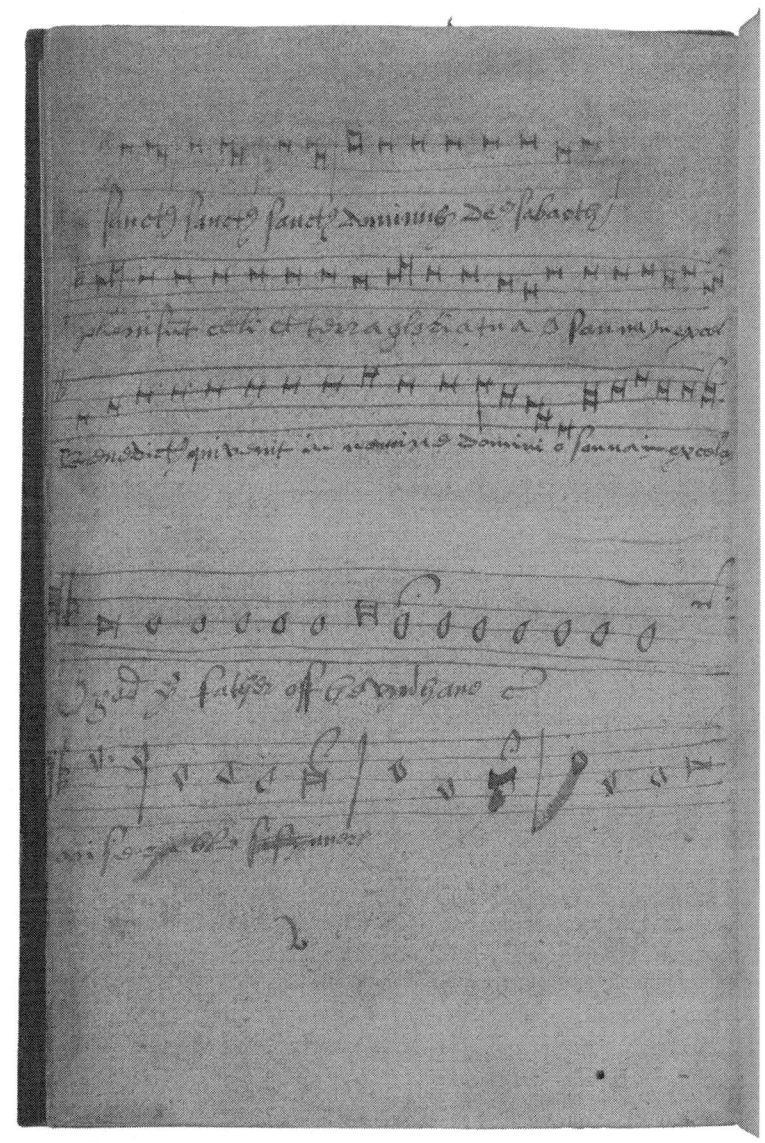

Plate 1. Washington, DC, Folger Shakespeare Library, STC 16237.

sionals the personal property of an individual singer, the Folger Shakespeare copy is customised so as to make it both a chant book and a *de facto* partbook; here, the polyphonic notation of the Litany transmits one of

Associate Librarian and Head of Reference at the Folger Shakespeare Library, for tracing this volume and providing images.

the harmonizing voice-parts, rather than Cranmer's chant. The surviving polyphonic voice-part is shown in a reconstructed four-part setting as Music Example 2; by deduction, Cranmer's chant is assigned to in the Medius voice, pitched with a reciting note of F (and shown in lozenge-shaped note-heads);[52] these two voices, one surviving and the other inferred, provide a matrix for two conjectured voice-parts (shown in small note-heads). Three observations can be made about this setting. Firstly, the surviving polyphonic voice-part aligns syllabically with Cranmer's chant, suggesting simple fauxbourdon. Secondly, the bi-syllabic setting of the word 'heaven' deviates from the published form of Cranmer's Litany, suggesting an early date of composition, before Cranmer's chant had become familiarised. Thirdly, we can assume that the untexted three-note snippet Bb-G-A was intended for the response 'Pray for us' (equivalent to *Ora pro nobis*'); Cranmer included three iterations of this relic of the old Litany of Saints in his Henrician Litany, but excised it entirely from the revised Litany he provided for the first Book of Common Prayer in 1549; we can therefore date the Folger Shakespeare setting to between May 1544 and June 1549.

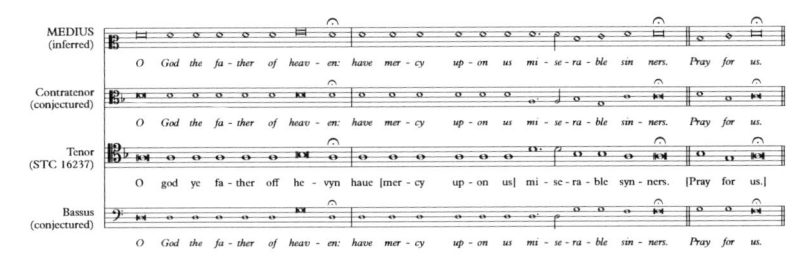

Music Example 2. Anonymous Litany, Folger Shakespeare Library, STC 16237 (1544 × 49, reconstructed).

Music Example 3. Anonymous Litany, British Library, Additional MS 34191, f. 35 (*c.* 1549, reconstructed).

[52] The chant can be accommodated an octave lower, but at the cost of weak part-writing at 'miserable sinners'.

The absence of the response 'Pray for us' enables us to date another early vernacular Litany to the next phase of liturgical reform, 1549–52. This is found in British Library, Additional MS 34191, fol. 35v (Music Example 3). Like the previous setting, this is copied into a pre-existing source, in this case a Bassus partbook of Latin polyphony originally copied before 1530.[53] The partbook was re-purposed after the abolition of Latin worship in June 1549, and the Litany comes first in a layer of vernacular music copied for the new prayer Book liturgy. The reconstruction given here is very speculative: it assumes four-part scoring for men's voices (but could have been in five parts for men and boys, like the pre-existing Latin polyphony in 34191), and it assigns Cranmer's chant to the Tenor rather than an upper voice.[54] Nevertheless, the surviving voice-part in 34191 suggests simple homophony very similar to the Folger Shakespeare setting, although the reciting note here is C rather than F.

Copied contemporaneously with the 34191 additions, the Wanley partbooks are a pioneering compendium of mainly four-part polyphony for the new Prayer Book of 1549; some of their contents would be rendered obsolete on the publication of Cranmer's more circumscriptive second Book of Common Prayer in 1552.[55] Although these books contain some contrafacta of old Latin polyphony hastily adapted to vernacular texts, they comprise mostly new pieces in two idioms: chanson-style settings, often comprising short-winded *fuga*;[56] and homophonic pieces frequently redolent of established methods of improvisation.[57] Wanley has two settings of the 1549 Litany, both of them with the chant in the Tenor. The first setting, with F as its reciting note, restlessly attempts to avoid simple harmonization (Music Example 4a).[58] The second setting, on reciting note C, adheres more closely to the established homophonic archetype, and is more successful as a result; it appeared in

---

[53] On the manuscript, see Summerly (1989), and Gibbs (2018), 131–48.

[54] This piece has also been reconstructed by Edmund Fellowes and Sydney Nicholson with the chant in the Medius and by Nicholas Temperley with the chant in the Tenor (Summerly (1989), 28 and 38).

[55] Oxford, Bodleian Library, MSS Mus. Sch. e. 420–22 (= 'Wanley Partbooks'), copied in or after 1549 and edited in Wrightson (1995).

[56] On the English absorption of the chanson style, see Milsom (2007), 1–31.

[57] Aplin (1980), 245–65.

[58] Wanley Partbooks: e. 420, fol. 58r, e. 421, fol. 29v and e.422, fol. 57v. The Tenor, lacking in the polyphonic source, is inferred from Thomas Cranmer's Litany of 1544. (Wrightson (1995), 142–44).

print in the 1560s and subsequently circulated in manuscripts (Music Example 4b).[59]

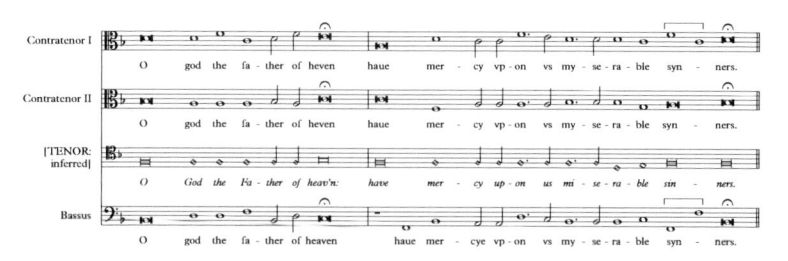

Music Example 4a. Anonymous Litany, 'Wanley' partbooks, #54.

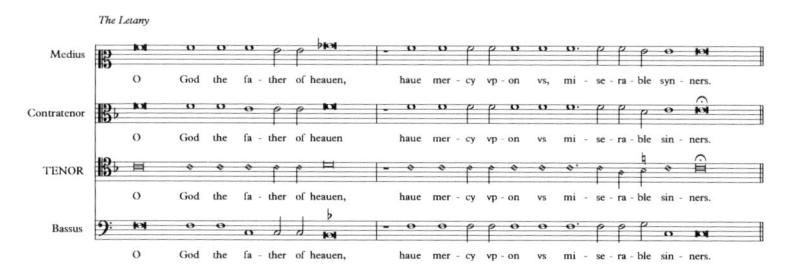

Music Example 4b. Anonymous Litany, 'Wanley' partbooks, #73.

4. Tallis, an English Emulator and Antonio Cabezón

So far, perhaps the most important and widely-circulated Tudor polyphonic Litany has been discussed only in passing. This is Thomas Tallis's setting, edited in its putative 1544 form by Andrew Johnstone at http://www.eecm.ac.uk/eecmsubsidia/twotudorlitanies/tallislitany/. It is richly scored for five voices (Medius, Contratenor I & II, Tenor and Bassus); combined with Tallis's use of ornamented suspensions and melismata in the Contratenor parts, this distinguishes it stylistically from the other early vernacular Litanies. William Byrd has long been recognised as an emulator of Tallis and, true to type, the older composer's influence has

---

[59] Wanley Partbooks: e. 420, fol. 83v ('The Prossessys'), e. 421, fol. 86v ('Prossessyon'), and e. 422, fol. 82r ('The Prossyon' [sic]); again, Cranmer's chant was in the now-lost Tenor partbook. Concordances: *Mornyng and euenyng prayer* (1560/1565); Brasenose College, Oxford, UB/S III 18/1–4; and Queens' College, Cambridge, G. 4. 17, fol. 58 (see Johnstone (2016), 221).

been detected in Byrd's five-part vernacular Litany;[60] the Tallis Litany is otherwise remarkable for its lack of Elizabethan emulators.[61] Perhaps paradoxically, the closest emulation of Tallis is found not in another vernacular setting, but in a Latin Litany almost certainly written for use in 1554–5, at the height of Mary Tudor's Catholic restoration.

This Litany and its most likely performance context have been discussed elsewhere.[62] It is found, unattributed, in the bindings of two copies of the Latin Sarum *Processionale* printed in Antwerp in 1545: one in Paris, the other in London.[63] Both of these copies belonged to members of Westminster's new-foundation cathedral in the first half of the 1550s: Alexander Peryn, minor canon and owner of the Paris copy, and Robert Morley, lay vicar (i.e., singing man) and owner of the Lambeth copy. Peryn's book has the Bassus part, and Morley's the Medius, and so the two books convey the two outer voices of what was almost certainly a five-voice setting of the *Letania Major* (as is suggested in Peryn's copy where the Litany is followed in immediate succession by the Bassus part of Thomas Tallis's five-part motet *O sacrum convivium*). In both copies, the Peryn-Morley Litany is complemented with additional Intercessions praying for a safe, timely and painless outcome for Queen Mary's pregnancy.[64] It could have reshaped Europe's geopolitical future, but the pregnancy was a crushing illusion; nevertheless, the clear allusion to it in both of these Processionals enables us to pinpoint a performance date between the first announcement of the assumed pregnancy in November 1554 and the abandonment of hope in August 1555.

The Peryn-Morley Litany bears a striking resemblance to Thomas Tallis's vernacular Litany of 1544. Although only two voices survive, one of them incomplete, they can be combined with the Sarum tone in the Tenor; the two Contratenor parts can be reconstructed with some

---

[60] Monson (1979); Monson (1980).

[61] This was possibly because Elizabethan composers showed no interest in the Litany (Harley (2015), 157).

[62] 'Queen Mary I, Tallis's *O sacrum convivium* and a Latin Litany'. A reconstruction by Jason Smart has been recorded in *Queen Mary's Big Belly: Hope for an Heir in Catholic England*, Gallicantus/Gabriel Crouch (SIgnum SIGCD464, 2017).

[63] Paris, Bibliothèque Nationale, Rés. B. 1852 and London, Lambeth Palace Library, **H5142.P.1545 respectively.

[64] Ut mariam reginam gravidam protegas: [*Te rogamus audi nos*]; Ut proles quam in utero gerit feliciter in lucem prodeat: *Te rogamus audi nos*; Ut in pariendo dolorem misericorditer evadat: *Te rogamus audi nos*; Ut prolem justo tempore pariat: *Te rogamus audi nos*.

confidence, because the polyphonic framework is, more or less, the same as Tallis's.[65] Music examples 5a and 5B show the Kyrie from each setting:

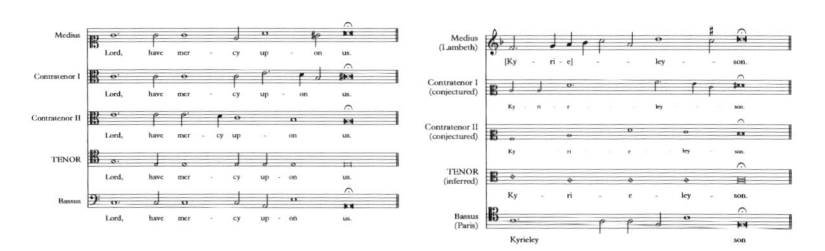

Music Example 5a. Thomas Tallis, vernacular Litany of 1544: *Kyrie*

Music Example 5b. Anonymous, 'Peryn-Morley' Litany: *Kyrie*

There are two obvious differences: the Latin Litany begins with an initial melisma in the Medius, and the two settings have divergent clef combinations (the Peryn-Morley Litany is set at service-book pitch, while the Tallis is, more pragmatically, transmitted in most of its sources down a perfect fourth).[66] But the polyphonic structure and concept are the same in both settings, and Tallis's distinctive cadence types are replicated in the anonymous Latin setting.

Who was emulating whom? Thomas Tallis was an occasional borrower: the *Credo* of his Mass for Four Voices is a contrafact of a composition by a Chapel Royal colleague, the Creed from John Sheppard's vernacular First Service;[67] Tallis had previously emulated the work of the elder John Taverner in the Mass *Salve intemerata*, having already alluded to Robert Fayrfax's *Ave Dei patris filia* in his own setting of the text.[68] But the Latin Litany is found only in sources that postdate the first performance of Tallis's vernacular Litany in 1544 (albeit by only one year), and both the Paris and Lambeth copies contain a *second* Latin setting of the Greater Litany, this time using the old tradition of

---

[65] A full reconstruction by Jason Smart is at http://www.eecm.ac.uk/eecmsubsidia/twotudorlitanies/latinlitany/.

[66] One seventeenth–century source presents the Tallis at the higher service-book pitch and attributes it to 'Mr Persons' (New York Public Library, MSS Mus. Res. *MNZ (Chirk)); the misattribution is ingeniously interpreted in Johnstone (2016), 222–23.

[67] The relationship between the Tallis and Sheppard pieces will be discussed by Stefan Scot in his edition of Sheppard's vernacular polyphony.

[68] Harley (2015) 39–41 and 25–27; Gibbs (2017), 81–83.

squares.⁶⁹ This other setting probably sounded somewhat old-fashioned and cumbersome to ears accustomed to Tallis's recent fauxboudon-style setting of the vernacular Litany. Back in 1544, Tallis's setting had been entirely unprecedented, the first of numerous homophonic harmonizations of Cranmer's chant attempted by mid-century musicians. A comparison of Tallis's setting with the surviving voices of the Peryn-Morley Litany suggests a tighter and more convincing fit in the English than the Latin (see Music Examples 5a-5b), and hence a greater likelihood that the vernacular setting came first. It was surely Tallis who set the precedent and the anonymous composer (or arranger) of the Latin Litany who followed it.

I have argued elsewhere that the Peryn-Morley Litany was performed in Westminster, and particularly as part of a grand procession organized by Hugh Weston, dean of Westminster, which proceeded from Westminster, through Whitehall Palace to Temple Bar on Sunday 27 January 1554.⁷⁰ Public processions were an important expression of the Catholic restoration, especially during the first two years, 1553–5; there are likely to have been numerous occasions on which the Latin Litany, with special Intercessions on behalf of the expectant queen, would have been sung outdoors. In November 1553, within a few months of Mary's accession, 'a general prossessyon with the old Latene [= Litany]...with *ora pro nobis*' had taken place at St Paul's Cathedral, and the Privy Council subsequently attempted to enforce general attendance at processional Litanies on Mondays, Wednesday and Fridays.⁷¹ Processions and Litanies were therefore ingrained in the culture of Marian Catholicism and, when the queen entered her bed of confinement after Easter 1555, her husband's household led some of these processions in her absence.⁷²

Public processions and petitions were mirrored by more private prayers within the walls of the royal palace during the queen's confinement. Here we consider the final piece of evidence, a Latin Litany by the Spanish composer Antonio Cabezón.⁷³ Cabezón was in the *capilla* of Philip of Spain when it sailed with him to England for the prince's

---

⁶⁹ See above, n. 12.
⁷⁰ Williamson (2016), 261–62.
⁷¹ Duffy (2009), 131.
⁷² Edwards (2005).
⁷³ Robledo (1989), 143–52; my thanks to Prof. Owen Rees for first drawing my attention to this piece.

marriage to Mary in July 1554; Cabezón returned to the continent in August 1555, after the royal couple's dynastic disappointment. Only this small fragment survives of his Litany which, although not based on the Litany tone, is fauxbourdon in style:[74]

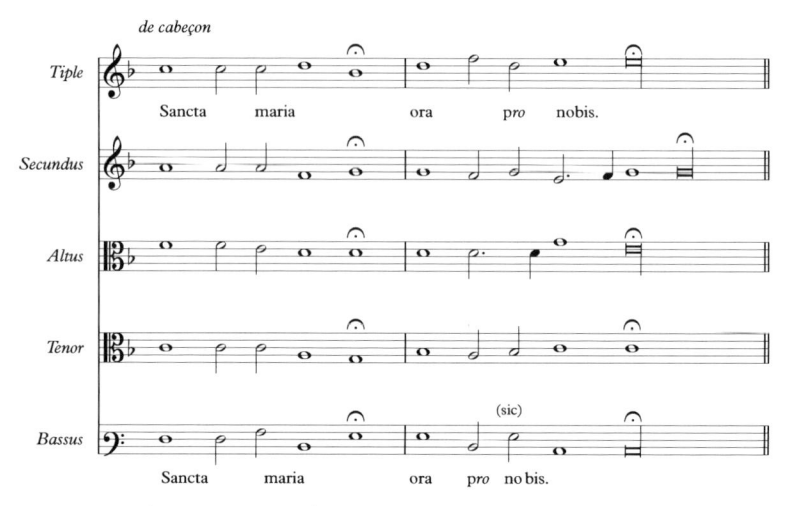

Music Example 6. Antonio Cabezón, Litany: Invocación.

The piece could easily be overlooked but for two factors. Firstly, Cabezón is regarded as one of the foremost and prolific keyboard composers of the Renaissance, whose likely impact on the English keyboard tradition has been postulated, but not thoroughly investigated. Cabezón is not regarded as a composer for voices; indeed, this Litany fragment is his only known piece of liturgical polyphony. Secondly, if this is an exceptional piece in Cabezón's oeuvre, the equally unusual circumstances of its composition were recorded in detail in 1601:[75] 'There is a Litany composed by Antonio Cabezón in fauxbourdon *pro regina gravida* that was sung in England daily in procession through the corridors of the palace, after it was understood that the queen entered the month.'

It was in Hampton Court Palace, 35 km upstream from Westminster, that Mary entered her confinement in April 1555. Cabezón's Litany

[74] Madrid, library of Don Bartolomé March Servera, MS 6829 (861), fol. 107, reproduced in Robledo (1989), 146.

[75] Robledo, 'Sobre la letanía', p. 144, citing Archivo General del Palacio Real de Madrid, Seccion Real Capilla, caja 78 (dated 26 August 1601): 'Ay vna letania compuesta por Ant. Caveçon en favordon pro regina grauida quese canto en ingalaterra haciendo proçesioncada día, despues que se entendio quelaroyna entraua enelmes, por loscorredores de Palaçio'.

must therefore have been composed for use while the queen was out of circulation, and when her husband played a more active role as the public face of this dynastic union. In parallel with the native singers' public performances of Tallis's Litany in Westminster, members of Philip's *capilla* performed Cabezón's Litany in the privacy of Hampton Court, no doubt to the queen's comfort as they circumnambulated the palace's cloister within earshot of her gloomy birthing chamber.

5. Conclusions

Thomas Tallis's vernacular Litany is the first known setting of its kind in the English repertory. Before 1544, no English composer is known to have made a polyphonic setting of the Greater Litany. This is surprising, perhaps, given how pervasive this liturgical form had become, in part because of its wide availability in Books of Hours. Instead, musicians had focused on the specific Rogationtide Litanies whose repeating refrains were more easily adapted to established traditions of improvisation. Tallis's setting was therefore innovative in the fact of its very making, while its texture and idiom also reflected the temper of modest reform that characterised the late-Henrician church. Beyond England, fauxbourdon-style liturgical settings of the *Letania Major* are also conspicuously scarce before Cabezón. Although Latin Litanies were published later in the sixteenth century, there are no obvious continental precedents for either the Tallis or the Peryn-Morley Litany.[76] Instead, in a reversal of the normal flow of traffic at this time, it may have been Cabezón who took his cue from the English tradition.

---

[76] For instance, Porta (1575): https://stimmbuecher.digitale-sammlungen.de/view?id=bsb00001894.

Manuscripts and Books Printed Before 1600

The booke of common praier and administracion of the Sacramentes, London, March 1549 [STC 16275].

The boke of common praier, and administracion of the sacraments, London, August 1552 [STC 16285].

Cantiones ecclesiasticae Latinae, Magdeburg, 1545 [USTC 613390].

The golden letany in englysshe, London, 19 June 1531 [STC 15707].

A goodly prymer in englyshe, London, 16 June 1535 [STC 15988].

Hore beatissime virginis marie, London, 1510 [STC 15908.5].

Haym, J., *Litaniae textus triplex*, Augsburg, 1582 [USTC 553585].

Iniunctions exhibited the ____ day of ____ anno M. D. XXXVIII, [London], 1538 [1538; STC 10087].

The manual of prayers or the prymer in Englysh and Laten, London, 15 July 1539 [STC 16009].

Mornyng and euenyng prayer and communion, London, 1560/1565 [STC 6418 and 6419].

Porta, C., *Litaniae Deiparae Virginis Mariae...cum musica octo vocum Constantii Portae*, Venice, 1575 [USTC 850951].

A Prymer in Englyshe, London, 1534 [STC 15986].

The Primer, in Englishe and Latyn, set foorth by the Kynges maiestie, London, 6 September 1545 [STC 16040].

Processionale ad usum insignis ac preclare ecclesie Sarum, Rouen, 1525 [STC 16236.6].

Processionale ad vsum Sarum, Antwerp, 1528 [STC 16237].

Processionale ad vsus [sic] insignis ecclesie Sarum, Antwerp, 1545 [STC 16243].

Processionale ad usum insignis ac preclare ecclesie Sarum, Rouen, 1555 [STC 16248].

An vniforme and Catholyke Prymer in Latin and Englishe, London, 4 June 1555 [STC 16060].

The 'Wanley Partbooks': Oxford, Bodleian Library, MSS Mus. Sch. e. 422–22.

Bibliography

Aplin, J. (1980) '"The Fourth Kind of Faburden": The Identity of an English Four-Part Style,' *Music and Letters* 61, 245-65.

Bailey, T. (1971) *The Processions of Sarum and the Western Church* [Pontifical Institute of Mediaeval Studies: Studies and Texts, 21], Toronto.

Bernard, G. W. (2005) *The King's Reformation: Henry VIII and the Remaking of the English Church*, New Haven and London.

Bowers, R. (2000) 'The Chapel Royal, the first Edwardian Prayer Book, and Elizabeth's Settlement of Religion, 1559,' *The Historical Journal* 43, 317-44.

— (2002) 'The vernacular Litany of 1544 during the reign of Henry VIII', in G. W. Bernard and S. J. Gunn (eds), *Authority and Consent in Tudor England*, Aldershot, 151-75.

Charles, S. R. (ed.) (1967) *The Music of the Pepys MS 1236* [Corpus Mensurabilis Musicae, 40], Neuhausen.

Clay, W. K. (1847) *Liturgical Services: Liturgies and Occasional Forms of Prayer set forth in the Reign of Queen Elizabeth* [Parker Society, 30], Cambridge.

Cuming, G. J. (1982) *A History of Anglican Liturgy* [2nd edn], Basingstoke.

Curtis, G., and Wathey, A. (1994) 'Fifteenth-century English liturgical music: a list of the surviving repertory', *Royal Musical Association Research Chronicle* 27, 1-69.

Donovan, C. (1991) *The de Brailes Hours: Shaping the Book of Hours in Thirteenth-Century Oxford*, London.

Duffy, E. (1992), *The Stripping of the Altars: Traditional Religion in England, c. 1400-c. 1580*, New Haven and London.

— (2006) *Marking the Hours: English People and their Prayers 1240-1570*, New Haven and London.

— (2009) *Fires of Faith: Catholic England under Mary Tudor*, New Haven and London.

Edwards, J, (2005) 'Corpus Christi at Kingston upon Thames: Bartolomé Carranza and the Eucharist in Marian England,' in J. Edwards and R. Truman (eds), *Reforming Catholicism in the England of Mary Tudor: the achievement of Friar Bartolomé Carranza*, Aldershot, 139-51.

Erler, M. C. (2003) *Women, Reading, and Piety in Late Medieval England*, Cambridge.

Fenlon, I. (ed.) (1982) *Cambridge Music Manuscripts, 900–1700*, Cambridge.

Fowler, J. T. (ed.) (1903), *Extracts from the Account Rolls of the Abbey of Durham*, [Surtees Society, 103; vol. 3], Durham.

Gibbs, D. M. (2017) 'The Transmission and Reception of the Marian Antiphon in Early Modern Britain' [unpublished doctoral dissertation, Newcastle University].

— (2018) 'England's most Christian king: Henry VIII's 1513 campaigns and a lost votive antiphon by William Cornysh,' *Early Music* 46, 131–48.

Harley, J. (2015) *Thomas Tallis*, Aldershot.

Harrison, F. Ll. (1962) 'Faburden in practice,' *Musica Disciplina* 16, 11–34.

Hickman, D. (ed.) (2001) *Lincoln Wills 1532–1534* [Lincoln Record Society, 89], Woodbridge.

Johnstone, A. (2016) 'Thomas Tallis and the five-part English Litany of 1544: evidence of "the notes used in the king's majesty's chapel",' *Early Music* 44, 219–32.

Legg, J. W. (ed.) (1893) *Missale ad Usum Ecclesie Westmonasteriensis*, [Henry Bradshaw Society, 5; vol. 2], London.

Marsh, D. (2007) 'Music, Church, and Henry VIII's Reformation' [unpublished doctoral dissertation, University of Oxford].

Mears, N., 'Special nationwide worship and the Book of Common Prayer in England, Wales and Ireland, 1533–1642,' in N. Mears and A. Ryrie (eds), *Worship and the Parish Church in Early Modern Britain*, Aldershot, 31–72.

Milsom, J. (2007) 'Caustun's Contrafacta,' *Journal of the Royal Musical Association* 132, 1–31.

Monson, C. (1979) 'The Preces, Psalms and Litanies of Byrd and Tallis: another "virtuous contention in love",' *Music Review* 70, 257–71.

— (ed.) (1980) *The English Services* [Byrd Edition, 10a], London.

Morgan, N. J. [2012–18] *English Monastic Litanies of the Saints after 1100* [Henry Bradshaw Society, 119–20 and 123; 3 vols], London.

Procter, F., and C. Wordsworth (1879–86) *Breviarium ad Usum Insignis Ecclesiae Sarum* [3 vols], Cambridge.

Renwick, W. (2006), *The Sarum Rite*, Hamilton [https://hmcwordpress.mcmaster.ca/renwick, accessed 13 December 2018].

Robledo, L. (1989) 'Sobre la letanía de Antonio de Cabezón,' *Nassarre: Revista Aragonesa de Musicologia*, 5/ii, 143–52.

Sandler, L. F. (1979) 'An early fourteenth-century English Psalter in the Escorial,' *Journal of the Warburg and Courtauld Institutes* 42, 65–80.

Scot, S. (ed.) (forthcoming) *John Sheppard IV: Vernacular Church Music* [Early English Church Music], London.

Skinner, D. (2016) '"Deliuer me from my deceitful enemies": a Tallis contrafactum in the time of war,' *Early Music* 44, 233–50.

Summerly, J. (1989) 'British Library, Additional 34191: its Background, an Index and Commentary' [unpublished Master of Music dissertation, King's College London].

Trowell, B. (1980) 'Faburden – New sources, new evidence: a preliminary survey,' in E. Olleson (ed.), *Modern Musical Scholarship*, Stocksfield, 28–78.

Williamson, M. (2016) 'Queen Mary I, Tallis's *O sacrum convivium* and a Latin Litany,' *Early Music* 44, 251–70.

Wrightson, J. (ed.) (1995) *The Wanley Manuscripts* [Recent Researches in the Music of the Renaissance; 3 vols], Madison, WI, 99–101.

Karina Zybina

WHEN MUSIC TAKES OVER

Sacramental Litanies in the European Music History

1. Introduction: From the 'Golden Age' of European Polyphony Onwards

The sixteenth century occupies a special place in the European music history. Known as the 'Golden Age' of polyphony, this period is marked by an overwhelming dominance of the polyphonic texture. In vocal music in particular, one or another combination of two and more independent voices served as a basis for a musical texture in both secular and religious genres, among others masses, motets, offertories, hymns, and madrigals. During the last third of the century, this list was expanded to include polyphonic litanies: large-scale musical adaptations of a sequence of petitionary prayers and responses.

The new era of polyphonic litanies commences in 1575, when Giorgio Angelire, an Italian printer based in Venice, published a sample of double-choir settings (*Litaniae deiparae virginis ariae*)[1] composed by

---

[1] *Litaniae Deiparae Virgis ex sacra scriptura depromptae quae in alma domo Lauretana omnibus diebus sabbati, vigiliarum & festorum eiusdem Beatae Virginis decantari solent, cum musica octo vocum*; compare a short description of the volume in the general catalogue of musical sources printed until 1800, The *Répertoire International des Sources Musicales* (RISM, number P5179). In 1583, one of the settings from this volume, the *Litaniae Deiparae Virginis Mariae*, was reissued by Adam Berg in Munich and ascribed to another Italian composer, Costanzo Festa (see the RISM catalogue record F 643; compare also the digital version of this edition:http://daten.digitale-sammlungen.de/0009/bsb00091147/images/index.html?fip=193.74.98.30&seite=48&pdfseitex [online scan provided by the Bavarian State Library Munich, last accessed on 27.11.2018]); in 1977, this setting was published as a part of the edition of Festa's complete works (Festa (1977), 80–103; see Nutter and Harper (2001), 881). For a discussion about the authorship of these compositions see Seay (1977), XV–VI; Marx-Weber (2004), 211.

Karina Zybina • Paris Lodron University of Salzburg, Austria

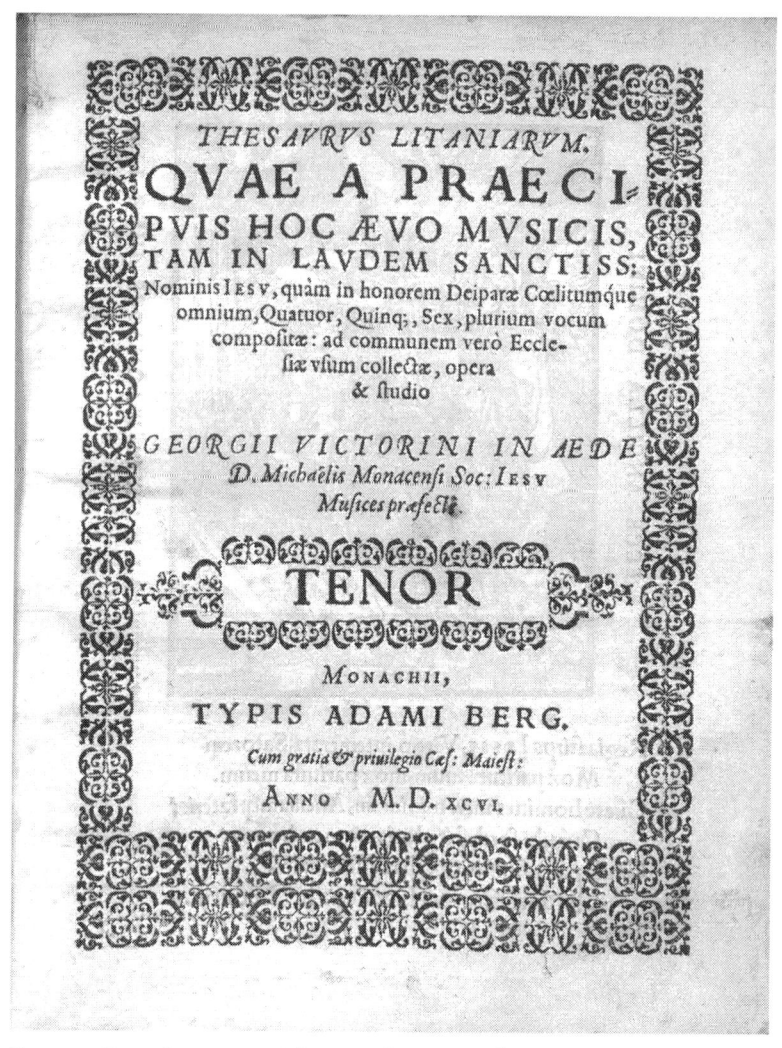

Figure 1. Georg Victorinus: *Thesaurus litaniarum* (Munich, 1596), fol. AAA1r (Tenor). Courtesy of Bavarian State Library Munich (Bayerische Staatsbibliothek München), shelfmark 4 Mus.pr. 59.

Constanzo Porta.[2] Later in 1596, the first large anthology of litanies was issued by Adam Berg in Munich: the *Thesaurus Litaniarum* or *Treasury of Litaniae* (see Figure 1).[3] This volume comprised of ca. 70 polyphonic litanies created in the preceding 25 years by some of the most prominent European composers of the time: Orlando di Lasso, Giovanni Pierluigi da Palestrina, and Hans Leo Hassler.[4]

The editor, Georg Victorinus – a music director at the Jesuit church of St Michael in Munich – divided his collection into three books focused on 1) litanies in the Name of Jesus, 2) Marian litanies, and 3) Sanctoral litanies respectively.[5] Moreover, he extended this list by adding the anonymous *Litaniae pro defunctis*[6] and the *Litaniae de venerabili Sacramento* by Cesare de Zacharia (see Figure 2),[7] a German musician of Italian origin.[8] Whereas the former remains unique in its setting this particular text to music, the latter, on the contrary, initiates a long tradition of musical settings that I aim to explore in this paper.

Known variously as *Litaniae de venerabili altaris sacramento, Litaniae corporis Christi, Litaniae sacrosanctae Eucharistiae* (in the English-speaking tradition – the Sacramental litanies, Eucharistic litanies, or the litanies of the Blessed altar sacrament),[9] this particular subgenre underwent numerous changes and mutations. Its text – which, similarly to other species of the litany, consists of several litanic 'patterns', the ektenial and the polyonymic[10] - has never been fully accepted into

---

[2] An Italian composer and teacher, mostly active in Padua, for detailed information about his life and works see Pruett (2001), 177–78; Kuhl (2005), 791–94. In fact, Porta's litany was preceded by a sample of litanic-motets composed between 1481 and 1490 by an Italian theorist, composer, and choirmaster Franchinus Gaffurius, see Blackburn (2001), 410–11; Nutter, Harper (2001), 881; Kreyszig (2002), 393–96. Two settings by Gaffurius, *Virgo dei digna* and *O beate Sebastiane*, are discussed in Chiu (2017), 117–22.

[3] RISM 1596².

[4] For a detailed description of this volume and its contents, see Roth (1959), 9–18; Fisher (2015), 71–91.

[5] The contents of this volume are listed in Fisher (2015), 92–95.

[6] The last litany setting of the third book.

[7] The sixth composition of the first book.

[8] Zacharia, also known as Zaccaria and Zachariis, was mainly active in several towns and cities of southern Germany, for detailed information see Bradshaw (2001), 709–10; Kraner (2007), 1291–2.

[9] For a full list of possible litany titles, see Federhofer, Federhofer-Königs (1969), VII; Petersen (2012), 118.

[10] Both terms have recently been proposed by Sadowski (2016), 11.

Figure 2. Georg Victorinus: *Thesaurus litaniarum* (Munich, 1596), fol. B4v (Discantus). Courtesy of Bavarian State Library Munich, shelfmark 4 Mus.pr. 59.

the Roman liturgy,[11] but only allowed for private worship. This led to a constant flux of structures shaped by different local traditions and practices. In a similar vein, the tradition of setting this form to music was profoundly influenced by the then current tendencies, trends, and local musical styles predominant in a particular area. As a result, the overall

[11] Until mid-nineteenth century, only Marian and Sanctoral litanies were officially accepted by the Roman church, see Schlager (1996), 1367.

structure, with its repeated alternation of invocations and responses, was often overtaken by other (more traditional for that time) musical forms and organisational principles prevalent in arias, ensembles, and choruses.

In order to illustrate this ever-changing tradition of the Sacramental litany, I shall undertake a voyage all across the European history of the sixteenth-eighteenth centuries, bringing to the foreground three examples, each a milestone in the history of this genre: first, two settings by a Renaissance composer Giovanni Pierluigi da Palestrina, both intended to be performed in Rome; second, two Dresden versions by a Czech musician of the Baroque period, Jan Dismas Zelenka; finally, two Wolfgang Amadeus Mozart's *Litaniae de Venerabili Altaris Sacramento* composed in and for Salzburg. By comparing the textual bases of these musical settings and analyzing their musico-textual relationships, I shall draw a multifaceted portrait of the Sacramental litany in the sixteenth-eighteenth centuries, one in which the changing faces of this genre reflect different local traditions and personal styles.

2. The First Stop: Rome

In 1577, Carlo Borromeo, the Archbishop of Milan, published his *Avvertenze per l'oratione delle quaranta hore*, a number of guidelines for a specific ceremony: the Devotion of the Forty Hours.[12] The main purpose of this ceremony consisted in a forty-hour display of the host (Eucharist), which had first to be carried in a procession leading from the main altar to the desired place of exposition, and then carried back after the end of the ceremony. Various prayers and orations, as well as a number of litanies, accompanied this ceremony and were recited by the congregation in the kneeling position.[13]

Borromeo's instructions summarize the ceremony that took place in different Milanese churches throughout the sixteenth century.[14] In 1592, Pope Clement VIII adopted it for the Roman practice in his con-

---

[12] *L'oratione delle quarant'ore*; the number of hours alludes to the period of Christ's entombment, see more in Weil (1974); DeSilva (2015), 138.

[13] The relevant excerpt from Borromeo's *Avvertenze* is quoted in Petersen (2012), 116.

[14] The ceremony was officially approved in 1539 by Pope Paul III, see Petersen (2012), 116.

stitution *Graves et diuturnae*. Seeking to make the congregation pray 'for peace and for the protection of Catholic Christendom against the danger of heresy and the Turks',[15] he contributed to the rising interest in musical litanies and their integration into the celebration of the Eucharist. It is not surprising then, that the end of the sixteenth century saw a dramatic increase in the number of polyphonic litanies.[16]

Two *Litanies del Sacramento*[17] in F[18] and in G[19] by the then Roman *maestro di capella* of the Capella Giulia in St Peter, Giovanni Pierluigi da Palestrina,[20] were presumably written at nearly the same time.[21] As the two compositions set rather different combinations of ektenial patterns to music, they must have been written for different occasions, albeit both certainly formed part of the Forty Hours Devotion. The initial set of *Kyrie* invocations, the Trinitarian formula (lines 1–5 and 6–9 respectively), and the concluding incarnational formula (John 1:14, *And the Word became flesh*: see lines 25–26 [= 23–24]) frame a number of individual prayers that emphasize the Catholic Eucharist theology; the prayers are mostly followed by a repeated response, *have mercy upon us*[22] (the structure of the textual basis is given in Table 1; for English translation see Appendix 1).[23]

---

[15] Quoted by Petersen (2012), 117.

[16] See Roth (1959), 11–17.

[17] These settings are also known as *Litaniae Sacrosanctae Eucharistiae, Litaniae sacrae Eucharistiae*, and *Litaniae Sanctissimi Corporis Xpi*.

[18] Hab. XXVI.125; as in all Palestrina's compositions, these litanies are referred to the numbers assigned to them in the first edition, see Palestrina (1968), 125–32.

[19] Hab. XXVI.133. Both settings remained unpublished until the end of the nineteenth century. They are preserved in two manuscripts from the Biblioteca Apostolica Vaticana, shelfmarks MS Barberini lat. 4184 (*olim* XLVII.55) from the late nineteenth century and MS Capella Guilia XIII. 24 (*olim* Cod. 60); for a detailed description of these manuscripts, see Marvin (2001), 109 and 111. In this paper, I examine the modern edition by Bianchi (1955), 144–53 and 154–60.

[20] Palestrina first served as Maestro di Capella from 1551 to 1554 and then from 1571 until his death on 2 February 1594. For more information, see Heinemann (1994), 23–25 and 39–61; Reynolds (1989), 69; Atlas (1998), 588–89; O'Regan (2006), 78.

[21] Alongside with a number of Marian litanies and litanies of the Holy Name; see a list of Palestrina's litanies in Heinemann (1994), 270–71. Significantly, several Marian settings were published during Palestrina's lifetime in the two-part collection Litaniae Deiparae Virginis RISM P 744 (Rome 1593 [lost] / Venice, 1600). See also Blazey (1990), 62, Schlötterer (2002), 207–10 and Marx-Weber (2004), 212–13.

[22] The texts of these settings are also discussed in Petersen (2012), 119–20.

[23] For an analysis of this structure, based on the litany of the Saints, see Blazey (1990), 139–41.

Meaning	Line	Invocations and responses	
		Hab. XXVI.125	Hab. XXVI.133
Opening	1.	Kyrie eleison	Kyrie eleison
	2.	Christe eleison	Christe eleison
	3.	Kyrie eleison	Kyrie eleison
	4.	Christe audi nos	Christe audi nos
	5.	Christe exaudi nos	Christe exaudi nos
Trinity invocations	6.	Pater de Coelis Deus	Pater de Coelis Deus
	7.	Fili Redemptor mundi Deus	Fili Redemptor mundi Deus
	8.	Spiritus Sancte Deus, miserere nobis	Spiritus Sancte Deus, miserere nobis
	9.	Sancta Trinitas, Unus Deus, m.n.	Sancta Trinitas, Unus Deus, m.n.
Main part	10.	Hostia sancta, m.n.	Panis vivus qui de Coelo descendisti, m.n.
	11.	Calix benedictionis, m.n.	Deus absconditus, et Salvator, m.n.
	12.	Misterium fidei, m.n.	Frumentum electorum, m.n.
	13.	Praecelsum et venerabile Sacramentum, m.n.	Vinum germinans virgines, m.n.
	14.	Sacrificium omnium sanctissimum, m.n.	Panis pinguis et delitiae Regum, m.n.
	15.	Vere propitiatorium pro vivis et defunctis, m.n.	Juge sacrificium, m.n.
	16.	Coeleste antidotum, quo a peccatis praeservamur, m.n.	Oblatio munda, m.n.
	17.	Stupendum super omnia miracula, m.n.	Agnus absque macula, m.n.
	18.	Sacratissima passionis Domini commemoration, m.n.	Mensa propositionis, m.n.
	19.	Donum transcendes omnem pulchritudinem, m.n.	Mensa purissima, m.n.
	20.	Memoriale praecipuum divini amoris, m.n.	Angelorum esca, m.n.
	21.	Divinae affluentia largitatis, m.n.	Manna absconditum, m.n.
	22.	Sacrosantum et augustissimum misterium, m.n.	Memoria mirabilium Dei, m.n.
	23.	Pharmacum immortalitatis, m.n.	
	24.	Tremendum ac vivificum Sacramentum, m.n.	
Conclusion	25 (=23)	Panis omnipotentia, m.n	Panis supersubstantialis, m.n.
	26 (=24)	Verbi caro factus, m.n.	Verbum caro factum habitans in nobis, m.n.

Table 1. Latin texts of G. P. da Palestrina's Sacramental litanies

For the most part, both texts are set to simple chords that sound almost like a slightly animated homophony,[24] except for several melismas, intended to adorn single words (e.g., *caro* in the invocation *Verbi caro factus* or the concluding *miserere nobis* in the litany Hab. XXVI.125; see Music Example 1).

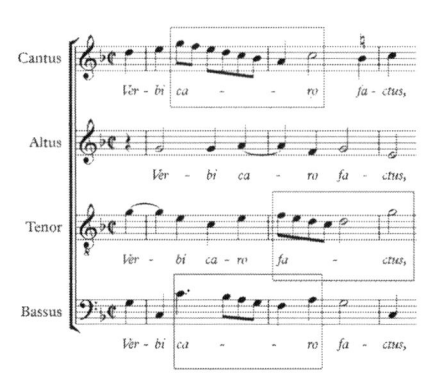

Music Example 1. Giovanni Pierluigi da Palestrina, Litaniae Sacrosanctae Eucharistiae in F, Hab. XXVI.125, bars 90–92 (1st chorus).[25]

In both settings, Palestrina divided the invocations and responses between the two choirs, each of eight singers, following the performance practice of the Papal Chapel.[26] This creates a simple responsorial structure.

For instance, in the central part of the litany in G, Hab. XXVI.133, all prayers are essentially dialogical in their structure: the initial invocation, *Panis vivus qui de Coelo descendisti*, is sung by the second choir; the second invocation (*Deus absconditus, et Salvator*) – by the first choir; the third invocation (*Frumentum electorum*) – again by the first choir, and so on. All invocations are concluded by the response *miserere nobis*. The composer tends to emphasize the repetitive structure of this textual basis, using identical or similar melodic formulas in a number of refrain statements: e.g., see slightly different variations (either rhythmic or harmonic or both) of three motives in the responses at the end of lines 10–12, 13–17, 19, and 20–22 (the letters B, F, and P, written in bold in Table 2; see also Music Examples 2a-c).

---

[24] Ironically characterized by Allan Atlas as 'let's-get-through-the-long-text-quickly tradition', see Atlas (1998), 594. See also a brief description of this technique in Brown (1976), 295.

[25] The transcription is based on Bianchi (1955), 153.

[26] For a more comprehensive study of the performance practice in the Papal Chapel in the sixteenth century, see Sherr (1987), 456–57.

Music Example 2a. Giovanni Pierluigi da Palestrina, Litaniae Sacrosanctae Eucharistiae in G, Hab. XXVI.133, bars 31–32, 34–35, and 37–38.[27]

Music Example 2b. Giovanni Pierluigi da Palestrina, Litaniae Sacrosanctae Eucharistiae in G, Hab. XXVI.133, bars 40–41, 46–47, 48–49, 51–52, and 56–57.

Music Example 2c. Giovanni Pierluigi da Palestrina, Litaniae Sacrosanctae Eucharistiae in G, Hab. XXVI.133, bars 59–60, 61–62, 65–66.

[27] The transcriptions are based on Bianchi (1955), 156–60.

first choir	second choir	motive
	Panis vivus qui de Coelo descendisti	A
	miserere nobis	**B**
Deus absconditus, et Salvator,		C
miserere nobis		**B'**
	Frumentum electorum,	D
	miserere nobis	**B'**
Vinum germinans virgines,		E
miserere nobis		**F**
	Panis pinguis et delitiae Regum,	G
	miserere nobis	**F'**
Juge sacrificium,		H
miserere nobis		**F''**
	Oblatio munda,	I
	miserere nobis	**F'''**
Agnus absque macula,		J
miserere nobis		**F''''**
	Mensa propositionis,	K
	miserere nobis	L
Mensa purrissima,		M
miserere nobis		**F'''''**

	Angelorum esca,	O
	miserere nobis	**P**
Manna absconditum		R
	miserere nobis	**P'**
Memoria mirabilium Dei,		S
miserere nobis		**P"**
	Panis supersubstantialis,	T
	miserere nobis	U

Table 2. The structure of the central part of the Sacramental litany by G. P. da Palestrina, Hab. XXVI.133 (bars 27–60).

As a result, Palestrina splits the central part of his litany into three sections, each a juxtaposition of constantly varying invocations with a textually and musically stable refrain. By doing that, he created an individual structure in which the remnants of the old monophonic tradition are merged together with some of his own original ideas.

3. The Second Stop: Dresden

In the first half of the eighteenth century, the celebration of the Eucharist grew in popularity in the Royal-Polish Residential City of Dresden. The Forty Hours Devotion, often accompanied by musical settings of litanic verses, soon became an integral part of Dresden's liturgical year. Take, for instance, this short description of the 1719 celebration of the Xavier feast on third of December:

> On the first day the father confessor of the Serene Princess performed, with co-celebrants, Solemn Mass which was enlivened by beautiful pieces of music produced by the Italian and other musicians of the King. In the afternoon, after Vespers, Exposition of the Blessed Sacrament. The Litany of Loreto was sung, followed by collects, among which were collects of St [Francis] Xavier, and finally, Solemn Benediction. The same was done on the other Sundays and

feast-days which fell during the octave. On the ferial days, Exposition of the Blessed Sacrament from ten o'clock in the morning, with the same number of candles [...] two private Masses were said by the court chaplains, the Xavier litany was recited in the vernacular and, after a private Benediction, devotions came to an end. At four o'clock in the afternoon, litanies were sung as on the feast-day itself. The octave was concluded with a sung votive [Mass] to the saint and, in completion of the litanies towards evening, Benediction followed.[28]

The so-called *Diarium Dresdae*,[29] one of our main sources of information about daily life in Dresden between 1710 and 1738, mentions a number of polyphonic litanies in the repertoire of the Dresden Clerici in 1721. Four years later, in 1725, this document referred to a performance of a certain Litany of the Holy Name of Jesus on fourth of March during the Pontifical High Mass.[30] Then, between 1723 and 1729, the court musician Jan Dismas Zelenka[31] enriched this collection with his *Litaniae Xaverianae*,[32] Marian,[33] and two Sacramental litanies (in C major ZWV 147 and in D major ZWV 148).[34]

These two last settings were first performed during the solemn Corpus Christi celebrations on 12 June 1727 and 18 June 1729 respectively.[35] Their textual basis seems to merge the two Roman versions used by Palestrina together, and expand it even further by adding a completely new section. Here, the opening *Kyrie* invocations and the Trinitarian formula (lines 1–5 and 6–9) are followed by a long sequence of

---

[28] The quotation is taken from Stockigt (2000), 81.

[29] The location of the original exemplar is unknown; a microfilm copy of this source is held at the Domstift und Bischöfliches Ordinariat, Bibliothek und Archiv, Bautzen, Germany.

[30] Information provided in Reich (1997), 47.

[31] See more about Zelenka's life and his activities in Dresden in Horn (1987), 52–58, Stockigt (2000).

[32] According to the catalogue (ZWV) in Reich (1985), these compositions are numbered Z 154, 155, 156.

[33] Z 149, 150, 151, 152 in Reich's catalogue. All settings are also listed in the Zelenka's handwritten catalogue, *Inventarium rerum* held in the Saxon State and University Library Dresden (shelfmark Bibl.-Arch. III H b 787^d); see a facsimile edition in Horn, Kohlhase (1989).

[34] Unpublished; my analysis is based on two autograph manuscripts (scores) currently in the Saxon State and University Library Dresden (shelfmarks Mus. 2358-D-55 and Mus. 2358-D-56).

[35] See also Horn / Kohlhase (1989), 130, 132, 301.

Eucharistic invocations (see lines 10–49 in the text presented in the Appendix);[36] similar to Palestrina's litanies, all Eucharistic prayers are alternated with the refrain *miserere nobis*. To this, Zelenka adds several acclamations to Christ with the refrain *libera nos, Domine* (God, save us) (lines 50–60), prayers for various needs followed by the response *Te rogamus, audi nos* (Lord, hear our prayer) (lines 61–67), and invocations to the Lamb of God. As a result, the Latin text of the Dresden Sacramental litany is shaped as a large-scale six-part composition (see Table 3).

Part	Meaning	Lines	Invocations
1.	Opening	1–5	Kyrie eleison [...] Christe exaudi nos
2.	Trinity invocations	6–9	Pater de Coelis Deus [...] Sancta Trinitas, Unus Deus
3.	Eucharistic invocations	10–49	Panis vivus de caelo descendens [...] pignus futurae gloriae
4.	Invocations to Christ	50–60	propitius esto [...] per quinque vulnera hujus tui Corporis sacratissimum, quae pro nobis suscepisti
5.	Invocations for various needs	61–67	peccatores [...] Fili Dei
6.	Invocations to the Lamb of God	68–70	Agnus Dei

Table 3. The structure of the Dresden version of the Sacramental litany.

Since it was originally supposed to be played by an impressive ensemble of performers (soloists and a choir accompanied by a full orchestra),[37] Zelenka divides this sequence of invocations and prayers into a series of arias, ensembles, and choruses: eleven in the earlier litany in C major, and nine in the second in D major. These movements correspond to, or

---

[36] Compared to the second Roman version set to music by Palestrina in his litany in G, this version lacks the invocation *Mensa propositionis*.

[37] The litany in C major is scored for two violins, viola, basso continuo and two oboes; in the second setting in D major this ensemble is reinforced by two trumpets and timpani.

contrast with, each other in terms of meter, tempo, key, instrumentation, and thematic content (see Table 4).

Movement number	ZWV 147	Movement number	ZWV 148
1.	Kyrie	1.	Kyrie
2.	Pater de Coelis Deus	2.	Panis vivus
3.	Praecelsum	3.	Praecelsum
4.	Sacrificium	4.	Sacrificium
5.	Panis omnipotentia	5.	Panis omnipotentia
6.	Spiritualis		
7.	Proprius esto		
8.	Ab indigna Corporis	6.	Ab indigna Corporis
9.	Peccatores	7.	Peccatores
10.	Fili Dei	8.	Ut nobis fidem
11.	Agnus Dei	9.	Agnus Dei

Table 4. The structure of the two Sacramental litanies by J. D. Zelenka.

All repetitions of the three refrains (*miserere nobis*; *libera nos, Domine*; and *Te rogamus, audi nos*) are reduced to a minimum, used only sporadically in order to conclude a movement, a section, and/or a subsection. For instance, in the second movement of the litany ZWV 147, *Pater de Coelis Deus*, written in A minor and performed by the ensemble of soloists, the pattern *miserere nobis* emerges only four times (compare B sections in Table 5), splitting the sequence of 21 invocations into four thematically contrasted sub-sections (lines 6–9, 10–11, 12–19, and 20–26).

invocations	response	motive	key
Pater de Coelis Deus		A	A minor
Fili redemptor mundi Deus			
Spiritus Sanctus Deus			
Sancta Trinitas unus Deus			
	miserere nobis	B	E minor
Panis vivus qui de Coelo descendisti		C	E minor
Deus absconditus, et Salvator			
	miserere nobis	B'	**G major**
frumentum electorum		D	G major
vinum germinans virgines			
panis pinguis et deliciae regum			
juge sacrificium			
oblatio munda			
agnus sine macula			
mensa purissima			
angelorum esca			
	miserere nobis	B"	**D minor**
manna absconditum		E	D minor
memoria mirabilium Dei			
panis supersubstantialis			
verbum caro factum, habitans in nobis			
hostia sancta			
calix benedictionis			
mysterium fidei			
	miserere nobis	B'"	A minor

Table 5. The structure of the Pater de Coelis Deus from the Sacramental litany in C major, ZWV 147, by J. D. Zelenka.

The overall structure is thus marked by a fourfold repetition of the refrain in different keys, from E minor to A minor (see the column 'key' in Table 5). This seems to be a variation and elaboration of Palestrina's approach to the same text (compare Table 3),[38] although it is rather unlikely that Zelenka actually knew Palestrina's pieces.[39]

Zelenka's settings of the Sacramental litany belong to a transitional phase: it fluctuates between the Renaissance approach towards these litanic verses, still deeply rooted in the responsorial structure of the Latin original, and a more modern tradition of polyphonic Sacramental litanies. The tradition in which music (with its compositional power) finally takes over.

4. The Third (and Last) Stop: Salzburg

This tradition is located in a small town north of the Alps, Salzburg, and is inextricably linked to the famous Salzburg composer from the second half of the eighteenth century, Wolfgang Amadeus Mozart.[40] While working for prince-archbishops of Salzburg until 1781, Mozart composed and brought to performance two versions of the Sacramental litany: in B flat major, K. 125, and in E flat major, K. 243,[41] completed in 1772 and in 1776, respectively.[42] The original occasions for these works remain unknown; there is some evidence that might shed light into the practical circumstances of the first performances though.

---

[38] Thomas Kohlhase characterizes this approach to text as the 'mixed church style' (*'vermischte Kirchen-Stylus'*), referring to a connection between the old and new principles of organisation in Zelenka's settings, see Kohlhase (1993).

[39] Several scores by Palestrina, including some of his masses, were preserved in Zelenka's private collection, however: see Horn (1993).

[40] In fact, a large number of Salzburg composers set to music the text of the Sacramental litany; during the period of Mozart's activity in Salzburg, the settings of this kind were produced by Johann Michael Haydn, Anton Cajetan Adlgasser, and Leopold Mozart. For more information about the Sacramental litanies written by Mozart's predecessors and contemporaries, and the Salzburg eighteenth century litany tradition in general, see Rosenthal (1941), Catanzaro (1990), Kircher (2005), Marx-Weber (2010), Zybina (2017).

[41] This numbering is based on the Köchel catalogue of Mozart's works created in 1862 by Ludwig von Köchel; the entries of this catalogue are abbreviated K. and KV.

[42] Mozart's litany collection also includes two Marian litanies, in B flat major K. 109 (74e), composed in 1771, and in D major, K. 195 (186d), written in 1774; these compositions are discussed in Federhofer-Königs (1967), Federhofer, Federhofer-Königs (1970), Krutmann (1992), Schick (2005), Marx-Weber (2006), Zybina (2020).

The autographs from the Berlin State Library[43] contain significant remarks that indicate that both works were composed in March (see the relevant note 'nel Marzo 1776' in the upper-right corner of the first page of the second litany in Figure 3). Coincidentally, the Easter both in 1772 and 1776 was celebrated next month, either in the early or mid-April. The main source of information about everyday life in the eighteenth-century Salzburg, the so-called *Salzburg Church- and Court Calendar*, reports that in 1772 the Easter fell on the nineteenth April; in 1776, on the seventh April.[44]

Figure 3. W. A. Mozart: autograph score of the *Litaniae de venerabili altaris sacramento* K. 243, fol. 1r. Courtesy of Berlin State Library, shelfmark Mus. ms.autogr. Mozart, W. A. 243.

The same source informs us that the Easter celebration was preceded by a grandiose Forty Hours Devotion which took place in the Salzburg Cathedral from Palm Sunday to Tuesday. According to the detailed description given in the Calendars, litanies - more precisely, the musical

---

[43] Staatsbibliothek zu Berlin – Preußischer Kulturbesitz, Musikabteilung mit Mendelssohn-Archiv, shelfmarks Mus.ms.autogr. Mozart. W. A. 125 and Mus. ms.autogr. Mozart, W. A. 243. Both settings have recently been published as a part of the second edition of Mozart's complete works: Mozart (1978).

[44] See the calendar part of the 1772 and 1776 issues.

settings of the Sacramental litany - served as a climactic point of the Forty Hours Devotion. The 1772 note reports on a performance of a litany on Palm Sunday, the twelfth April. The litany was played 'in the evening around 7 o'clock on the great choir with a collaboration of numerous musicians.'[45] The same chronicle specifies a performance of a new litany of the Blessed altar sacrament on Monday, 13 April, 'around 7 o'clock as a part of this honorable worship.'[46] On Tuesday, 14 April, a litany of the Blessed sacrament is mentioned as well, again 'around 7 o'clock' in the evening.[47] An identical description is encountered yet again in 1776. Consequently, Mozart's settings were intended to be performed during the Holy Week in the Salzburg Cathedral.

The text set to music by Mozart represents a reduced version of the Dresden Sacramental litany. More homogeneous, it includes 52 invocations altogether, which are divided into four sections: the opening *Kyrie*, the Trinitarian formula, and the Eucharistic prayers, immediately followed by the final *Agnus Dei* (see Table 6; compare lines 1–49 and 68–70 in the text presented in the Appendix); all invocations, except for lines 1 to 5 and 51–52, are followed by the refrain *miserere nobis*.

Part	Meaning	Lines	Invocations
1.	Opening	1–5	Kyrie eleison [...] Christe exaudi nos
2.	Trinity invocations	6–9	Pater de Coelis Deus [...] Sancta Trinitas, Unus Deus
3.	Eucharistic invocations	10–49	Panis vivus de caelo descendens [...] pignus futurae gloriae
4.	Invocations to the Lamb of God	68–70	Agnus Dei

Table 6. The structure of the Salzburg version of the Sacramental litany.

[45] German: 'Abends aber gegen halbe 7. Uhr auf dem grossen Chor unter zahlreich- und wohlbesetzter Music ein Litaney gehalten', quotation from the *Hochfürstlich-saltzburgischer Kirchen- und Hofkalender auf das Jahr 1772* [...], fol. B2r.

[46] 'Gegen 7. Uhr wird bey dieser hochlöblichen Anbetung deß Höchsten Altars-Sacrament eine Litaney anwiderum, wie gestern, gehalten', *Kirchen- und Hofkalender* (1772), B2r.

[47] 'Gegen 7. Uhr ist anwiderum die Litaney von dem Allerhöchsten Sacrament', *Kirchen- und Hofkalender* (1772), B2v.

Mozart's approach towards this sequence of prayers and responses is similar to the Zelenka's strategy discussed earlier. He splits the Latin original into nine self-contained movements, but with a different starting point for the sixth movement: in the later version, he extended the dramatic *Tremendum* by merging it with all invocations up to *Dulcissimum convivum* (see Table 7).[48]

Movement number	K. 125	Movement number	K. 243
1.	Kyrie	1.	Kyrie
2.	Panis vivus	2.	Panis vivus
3.	Verbum caro factum	3.	Verbum caro factum
4.	Hostia sancta	4.	Hostia sancta
5.	Tremendum	5.	Tremendum
6.	Panis omnipotentia		
		6.	Dulcissimum convivum
7.	Viaticum	7.	Viaticum
8.	Pignus	8.	Pignus
9.	Agnus Dei	9.	Agnus Dei

Table 7. The structure of the Sacramental litanies by W. A. Mozart.

He also reduced a number of refrain repetitions, using the same response *miserere nobis* only as a concluding formula. In the second movement of the litany in B flat major, the tenor aria *Panis vivus*, the refrain occurs after the invocations *Deus absconditus et Salvator, panis pinguis, Agnus absque macula, manna absconditum,* and *panis super substantialis,* splitting 13 invocations of the Latin original into five sub-sections separated from each other (see Table 8).

---

[48] The structure of both Mozart's litanies is discussed in more detail in Marx-Weber (2006), 208–16, Zybina (2020), 35–36 and 76–77.

part	invocations	response	motive	key
1.	panis vivus qui de Coelo descendisti		A	B flat major
	Deus absconditus, et Salvator			
		miserere nobis	B	B flat major
	frumentum electorum		C	B flat major
	vinum germinans virgines			
	panis pinguis et deliciae regum			
		miserere nobis	D	F major
2.	juge sacrificium		E	F major
	oblatio munda			
	agnus sine macula			
		miserere nobis	F	F major
	mensa purissima		G	G minor
	angelorum esca			
	manna absconditum			
		miserere nobis	H	E flat major
	memoria mirabilium Dei		I	E flat major
	panis supersubstantialis			
		miserere nobis	D'	**B flat major**

Table 8. The structure of the Panis from the Sacramental litany in B flat major, K. 125, by W. A. Mozart.

Taking this formal principle as his basis, Mozart creates a different structure, however. By adding an orchestral interlude in the centre of the movement, he groups these five sub-sections into two complementary sections which are related to each other thematically and harmonically: the first section starts in B flat major (the tonic) and then modulates to F major (the dominant); the second moves in the opposite direction, from the dominant to the main key (see the column 'key' in Table 8). This structural 'rhyme' is signaled by a repetition of the same thematic material in both concluding segments of the two sections (see the column 'motive'). As a result, the characteristic feature of the original text – the sequence of varying invocations, each followed by a fixed response – disappears, giving way to a standard musical structure of the time, the so-called binary form.[49]

By doing that, Mozart concludes a gradual transformation of the polyphonic Sacramental litany that lasted for ca. two hundred years: one in which we can discern a progressive shift of focus from a purely textual basis to independent and idiosyncratic musical forms. With Mozart's settings, the tradition of the polyphonic Sacramental litany is effectively brought to an end: apart from a few settings by Mozart's Salzburg colleague, Johann Michael Haydn, no other polyphonic litany of the Sacrament has ever been written in the following two centuries.

5. Afterword: Polyphonic Sacramental Litanies in the Modern World

The 'after-life'[50] of the Sacramental litanies discussed in this paper is significant, too. Palestrina's settings fell into oblivion soon after his death: there is no documented evidence for any occasional performance of these compositions. They remain little-studied and little-performed even nowadays. Only one of Zelenka's two Sacramental litanies (ZWV 147) was regularly performed throughout the eighteenth and nineteenth centuries: in 1789 (by Kapellmeister Joseph Schuster), in 1814 (by the church composer Franz Anton Schubert), and in 1820 (by Kapellmeister Francesco Morlacchi), all in the Dresden court chapel.[51] In 2002, it was recorded by Robert King in cooperation with the Choir of the King's Consort and The King's Consort.[52] The second litany, on the other hand, remains neglected and is still buried in archival dust of the Dresden State Library.

Mozart's compositions, however, have never been forgotten. They were repeatedly performed in the eighteenth century: e.g., in 1778, 1779, and 1783 in the Salzburg Cathedral,[53] in 1775 in the Frauenkirche in

---

[49] Also known as '*Ritornellform*', '*Konzertmittelsatz*', 'double-exposition sonata form', see more about this structure and its specific design in Mozart's compositions in Rosen (1988), 29, Schmid (1993), 185, Caplin (1998), 87–93.

[50] The term coined by Walter Benjamin and used in Dahlhaus (1983), 155.

[51] See more about these performances in Stockigt (2000), 275.

[52] The recording was published in 2003 on the British Hyperion Records Limited label.

[53] References to these performances can be found in extant diaries of Mozart's sister, Maria Anna (Nannerl) Mozart, and of his friend, Joachim Ferdinand Schiden-

Munich,[54] and in 1778 in the Holy Cross Church in Augsburg.[55] They could still be heard in the nineteenth century: e.g. in 1839–41 in Klagenfurt (K. 125),[56] in 1873 in Salzburg (K. 125),[57] in 1880,[58] and in 1887[59] in Munich (both K. 125 and K. 243). From 1955 onwards, a number of interpretations of both settings was produced by different conductors, including Peter Neumann (K. 243)[60] and Nikolaus Harnoncourt (both K. 125 and K. 243)[61] (for the full list of recorded versions see Appendix 2).

Characterized by the 'call-and-response' dialogical structure with its constant alternation of verses between the leader and the congregation, the litany has always remained an attractive and engaging liturgical genre in so far as it allowed the congregation to participate actively in the service, even if for a short period of time.[62] The musical life of this genre outlined in this article, however, tells a rather different story: for composers, the mesmerizing and almost hypnotizing effect of this dialogical structure proved to be challenging and potentially monotonous.

It is unsurprising therefore that Palestrina's and Zelenka's polyphonic renderings of this text, in which the relation of textual and musical structures is surely more palpable, fell from favor as soon as this peculiar musical structure became something of an archaism. Equally unsurprising is the fact that Mozart's compositions, in which an inherently musical structure took over the basic dialogical form of the text, enjoyed a longer afterlife in the European music history.

hofen, as well as in the correspondence of Mozart family, see Bauer, Deutsch (1962, II), 337, Geffray, Angermüller (1998), 32, Federhofer, Federhofer-Königs (1969), IX, Angermüller, Angermüller (2006), 14–15.

[54] Bauer, Deutsch (1962, I), 505 and 509.

[55] Bauer, Deutsch (1962, II), 136. It still remains unknown which composition was performed during these ceremonies.

[56] According to the remark in a contemporary copy of the work now in the Salzburg Dommusik Archive (shelfmark A 1127, Canto conc., fol. 163).

[57] See a handwritten remark in the trombone voice in the Salzburg copy mentioned above; see also Federhofer, Federhofer-Königs (1978), a/10.

[58] According to a manuscript addition from the copy kept in the Munich State Library (shelfmark Mus.ms. Mm 781).

[59] See handwritten remarks in the copy from the Munich State Library (shelfmark Mus.ms. Mm 779).

[60] In cooperation with the Collegium Cartusianum and Kölner Kammerchor; the recording was issued in 1988 on EMI, 567-749379-2.

[61] In 1991 and 1992 with the Concentus Musicus Wien and the Arnold Schönberg Chor (Teledec, 9031-72304-2 and 4509-90494-2).

[62] For more information, see Willa (2014), 63.

Manuscripts and Books Printed until 1800

Jhs Diarium seu Protocollum Missionis Societatis Jesu, À Serenissimo ac Potentissimo Poloniarum Rege, et Sacr: Rom: Imperij Electore FRIDERICO AUGUSTO, Dresdae, in urbe sua Electorali institutae. Scribi coeptum anno salutis humanae 1710, die 16 Januarij, quô Missioni huic, Authoritate Admodùm Reverendi Patris Nostri Generalis, per Rdum Patrem Provincialem Prov: ae Bohemiae, constitutus est Superior P. Georgius Klein, Microfilm copy, Batzen, Domstift und Bischöfliches Ordinariat, Bibliothek und Archiv.

Festa, Costanzo, *Litaniae Deiparae Virginis Mariae, ex sacra scriptura collectae, quae diebus sabbathi, virgiliarum & festorum eiusdem B. Virginis ... cantari solent*, München, 1583 [RISM F 643].

Hochfürstlich-salzburgischer Hof-Kalender oder Schematismus, Salzburg, 1773-85.

Hochfürstlich-saltzburgischer Kirchen- und Hofkalender auf das Jahr [...] *sambt beygefügten Schematismo*, Salzburg, 1750-72.

Inventarium rerum Musicarum Authorum Ecclesiae servientium, quas possidet Johannes Dismas Zelenka, Augustissimi Poloniarum Regis et Electoris Saxaniae à Camera Musicus. Inchoatum Anno 1726, die 17. Januarii, Dresden, Saxon State and University Library, MSS Bibl.-Arch. III H b 787^d.

Palestrina, Giovanni Pierluigi da, *Litaniae Deiparae Virginis ... cum quatuor vocibus; additae litaniae, quae in sancta ecclesia Lauretana utuntur, auctore Orlando Lasso*, Venezia, 1600 [RISM P 744].

Porta, Costanzo, *Litaniae Deiparae Virgis ex sacra scriptura depromptae quae in alma domo Lauretana omnibus diebus sabbati, vigiliarum & festorum eiusdem Beatae Virginis decantari solent, cum musica octo vocum*, Venezia, 1575 [RISM P5179].

Thesaurus litaniarum. Quae a praecipuis hoc aevo musicis, tam in laudem sanctiss. Nominis Iesu, quàm in honorem deiparae coelitumque omnium, quatuor, quinque, sex, plurium vocum compositae: ad commune verò Ecclesiae usum collectae, opera & studio Georgii Victorini in aede D. Michaëlis..., München, 1596 [RISM 1596^2].

Bibliography

Angermüller, H., R. Angermüller (2006) *Joachim Ferdinand von Schidenhofen. Ein Freund der Mozarts. Die Tagebücher des Salzburger Hofrats*, Bad Honnef.

Anonymous (1850) *The Golden manual: being a guide to Catholic devotion, public and private*, London.

Atlas, A. W. (1998) *Renaissance music. Music in Western Europe, 1400–1600*, New York and London.

Bauer, W. A., O. E. Deutsch (1962) *W. A. Mozart. Briefe und Aufzeichnungen. Gesamtausgabe* [Internationalen Stiftung Mozarteum Salzburg; 2 vols], Kassel.

Bianchi, L. (1955) 'Le Litaniae a (3), 4, 5, 6, e 8 voci, secondo la ristampa del 1600 c i diversi codici manoscritti,' in G. P. da Palestrina, *Le Opere Complete*, vol. 20, Roma, 144–60.

Blackburn, B. J. (2001) 'Gaffurius, Franchinus,' *Grove* 9, 410–14.

Blazey, D. A., 'The Litany in Seventeenth-Century Italy' [unpublished doctoral dissertation, University of Durham, 1990].

Bradshaw, M. C. (2001) 'Zacharia, Cesare de,' *Grove* 27, 709–10.

Brown, H. M. (1976) *Music in the Renaissance*, New Jersey.

Caplin, W. E. (1998) *Classical Form: A Theory of Formal Functions for the Instrumental Music of Haydn, Mozart, and Beethoven*, Oxford.

Catanzaro, Ch. D., 'Sacred music in Mozart's Salzburg: Authenticity, chronology, and style in the church works of Cajetan Adlgasser' [unpublished doctoral dissertation, University of North Carolina, 1990].

Chiu, R., (2017) *Plague and music in the Renaissance*, Cambridge.

Dahlhaus, C. (1983) *Foundations of music history*, Cambridge.

DeSilva, J. M. (2015) *The Sacralization of Space and Behavior in the Early Modern World: Studies and Sources* [St Andrews Studies in Reformation History], Surrey.

Federhofer, H., R. Federhofer-Königs (1969) 'Zum vorliegenden Band,' in *Wolfgang Amadeus Mozart. Neue Ausgabe sämtlicher Werke*, Serie I: Geistliche Gesangwerke, Werkgruppe 2: Litaneien, Vespern, Bd. 1: Litaneien, Kassel, VII–XVIII.

— (1970) 'Eighteenth-Century Litaniae Lauretanae from the repertory of the Viennese province of the Franciscan order,' in H. C. Robbins Landon (ed.), *Studies in Eighteenth-Century music. A tribute to Karl Geiringer on his seventieth birthday* [collaborating editor R. E. Chapman], New York, 108–212.

— (1978) 'Kritischer Bericht,' in *Wolfgang Amadeus Mozart. Neue Ausgabe sämtlicher Werke*, Serie I: Geistliche Gesangwerke, Werkgruppe 2: Litaneien, Vespern, Bd. 1: Litaneien, Kassel.

Federhofer-Königs, R. (1967) 'Mozarts Lauretanische Litaneien KV 109 (74e) und 195 (186d),' *Mozart-Jahrbuch* 1967, 111–20.

Festa, C. (1977) *Opera omnia*, vol. 6 [A. Seay (ed.); Corpus Mensurabilis Musicae 25], Neuhausen and Stuttgart.

Fisher, A-J. (2015) 'Thesaurus Litaniarum: The symbolism and practice of musical litanies in counter-reformation Germany,' *Early Music History* 34, 45–95.

Geffray, G., R. Angermüller (1998) *Marie Anne Mozart – 'meine tag ordnungen': Nannerl Mozarts Tagebuchblätter 1775-1783; mit Eintragungen ihres Bruders Wolfgang und ihres Vaters Leopold*, Bad Honnef.

Heinemann, M. (1994) *Giovanni Pierluigi da Palestrina und seine Zeit*, Laaber.

Horn, W. (1993) 'Zelenkas Bearbeitung und Ergänzung von Palestrinas Missa Nigra sum,' in Th. Kohlhase (ed.), *Zelenka-Studien I* [in cooperation with Hubert Unverricht], Kassel, 352–55.

Horn, W. (1987) *Die Dresdner Hofkirchenmusik 1720–1745. Studien zu ihren Voraussetzungen und ihrem Repertoire*, Stuttgart.

Horn, W., Th. Kohlhase (1989) *Zelenka-Dokumentation. Quellen und Materialien* [2 vols], Wiesbaden.

Kircher, A. (2005) 'Vorwort,' in A. C. Adlgasser, *Litaniae de venerabili altaris Sacramento in B-Dur (WV 3.53)*, Stuttgart, 2–10.

Kohlhase, Th. (1993) 'Der Dresdner Hofkomponist Jan Dismas Zelenka und der "vermischte Kirchen-Stylus",' in Th. Kohlhase (ed.), *Zelenka-Studien I*, [in cooperation with Hubert Unverricht], Kassel, 348–51.

Kraner, J. G. (2008) 'Zacharia,' *MGG (Personenteil)* 17, 1291–2.

Kreysizg, W. (2002) 'Gaffurio,' *MGG (Personenteil)* 7, 393–96.

Krutmann, J. (1992) 'Wolfgang Amadeus Mozarts Litaneien,' in H. Schützeichel (ed.), *Mozarts Kirchenmusik*, Freiburg im Breisgau, 52–72.

Kuhl, A. (2005) 'Porta, Costanzo,' *MGG (Personenteil)* 13, 791–94.

Lesure, F. (1960) *Recueils imprimés, XVIe-XVIIe siècles. I: Liste chronologique*, München.

Marvin, C. (2001) *Giovanni Pierluigi da Palestrina. A Guide to Research*, New York and London.

Marx-Weber, M. (2004) 'Römische Vertonungen der Lauretanischen Litanei. Palestrina – Cifra – Graziani – Foggia – Cisarini,' in

M. Engelhardt and Ch. Flamm (eds), *Musik in Rom im 17. und 18. Jahrhundert: Kirche und Fest / Musica a Roma nel sei e settecento: Chiesa e festa*, Laaber, pp. 211–33.

— (2006) 'Litaneien,' in Th. Hochradner and G. Massenkeil (eds) *Mozarts Kirchenmusik, Lieder und Chormusik*, Laaber, 201–20.

— (2010) 'Die Litaneien von Leopold Mozart,' in F. W. Riedel (ed.), *Mozart und die geistliche Musik in Süddeutschland. Die Kirchenwerke von Leopold und Wolfgang Amadeus Mozart im Spannungsfeld zwischen klösterlicher Musiktradition und aufklärerischem Staatskirchentum*, Sitzig, 171–92.

Mozart, W. A. (1978) *Neue Ausgabe sämtlicher Werke* [Serie I: Geistliche Gesangwerke, Werkgruppe 2: Litaneien, Vespern, Bd. 1: Litaneien], Kassel.

Nutter, D., J. Harper (2001) 'Polyphonic litanics before 1600,' *Grove* 14, 881–82.

O'Regan, N. (2006) 'Italy, 1560–1600,' in J. Haar (ed.), *European Music 1520–1640*, Woodbridge, 75–90.

Palestrina, G. P. da (1968) *Drei Bücher Litaneien zu vier, fünf, sechs und acht Stimmen und sechs zwölfstimmigen Motetten und Psalmen* [F. X. Haberl (ed.); Gesammtausgabe der Werke von Pierluigi da Palestrina 26], Leipzig.

Petersen, N. H. (2012) 'The Quarant'Ore: Early Modern Ritual and Performativity,' P. Gillgren and M. Snickare (eds) *Performativity and Performance in Baroque Rome*, Surrey, 115–33.

Pruett, L. P. (2001) 'Porta, Costanzo,' *Grove* 20, 177–80.

Reich, W. (1985) *Jan Dismas Zelenka: thematisch-systematisches Verzeichnis der musikalischen Werke (ZWV)*, Dresden.

— (1997) 'Das Diarium Missionis Societatis Jesu Dresdae als Quelle für die kirchenmusikalische Praxis,' in W. Reich and G. Gattermann (eds) *Zelenka-Studien II. Referate und Materialien der 2. Internationalen Fachkonferenz Jan Dismas Zelenka (Dresden und Prag 1995)*, Sankt Augustin.

Reynolds, Chr. (1989) 'Rome: a City of Rich Contrast,' in I. Fenlon (ed.), *The Renaissance. From the 1470s to the end of the 16th century*, New Jersey, 63–101.

Rosen, Ch. (1988) *Sonata forms*, New York, NY.

Rosenthal, K. A. (1941) 'Mozart's Sacramental Litanies and Their Forerunners,' *Musical Quarterly* 27 (4), 433–55.

Roth, J. (1959) *Die mehrstimmigen lateinischen Litaneikompositionen des 16. Jahrhunderts*, Regensburg.

Sadowski, W. (2016) 'Some necessary preliminaries,' in W. Sadowski, M. Kowalska, M. M. Kubas (eds) *Litanic Verse I: Origines, Iberia, Slavia et Europa Media*, Frankfurt am Main, 9–12.

Schick, H. (2005) 'Die geistliche Musik,' in S. Leopold (ed.) *Mozart Handbuch* [collaborating eds J. Schmoll-Barthel and S. Jeffe], Metzler, 164–247.

Schlager, K. (1996) 'Litanei,' *MGG (Sachteil)* 5, 1364–68.

Schlötterer, R. (2002) *Der Komponist Palestrina. Grundlagen, Erscheinungsweisen und Bedeutung seiner Musik*, Augsburg.

Schmid, M. H. (1993) 'Kyrie der c-moll-Messe KV 427. Textdarstellung und Form in Mozarts Vertonungen des ersten Messensatzes,' M. H. Schmid (ed.), *Mozart Studien 2*, Tutzing, 181–230.

Schlager, K. (ed.) (1971–81) *International Inventory of Musical Sources. Einzeldrucke vor 1800*, Kassel [u.a.].

Seay, A. (1977) 'The Litaniae,' in C. Festa, *Opera Omnia*, vol. 6, Neuhausen and Stuttgarrt, XV–VI.

Sherr, R. (1987) 'Performance Practice in the Papal Chapel during the 16th Century,' *Early Music* 15 (4), 454–62.

Stockigt, J. B. (2000) *Jan Dismas Zelenka. A Bohemian Musician at the Court of Dresden*, Oxford.

Weil, M. S. (1974) 'The devotion of the Forty Hours and Roman Baroque Illusion,' *Journal of the Warburg and Courtauld Institutes* 37, 218–48.

Willa, J.-A. (2014) '"Seele des Wortes" – Die Stimme im Gottesdienst,' in A. Gerhards and M. Schneider (eds), *Der Gottesdienst und seine Musik, Bd. 1: Grundlegung: Der Raum und die Instrumente. Theologische Ansätze. Hymnologie: Die Gesänge des Gottesdienstes*, Laaber, 63–75.

Zybina, K. (2020) *Die Litaneien von Wolfgang Amadeus Mozart und die Salzburger Tradition*, Wien.

Appendix 1

The textual basis of the Sacramental litany with English translation (a compilation of the Roman, Dresden, and Salzburg versions)[63]

No.	Line	Translation
1.	Kyrie eleison	Lord, have mercy
2.	Christe eleison	Christ, have mercy
3.	Kyrie eleison	Lord, have mercy
4.	Christe audi nos	Christ hear us
5.	Christe exaudi nos	Christ graciously hear us
6.	Pater de Coelis Deus	God the Father of heaven
7.	Fili redemptor mundi Deus	God the Son, redeemer of the world
8.	Spiritus Sanctus Deus	God the holy Ghost
9.	Sancta Trinitas unus Deus	Holy Trinity one God
10.	panis vivus de caelo descendens	living bread, that camest down from heaven
11.	Deus absconditus et Salvator	hidden God and Saviour
12.	frumentum electorum	grain of the elect
13.	vinum germinans virgines	vine whose fruit are virgins
14.	panis pinguis et deliciae regum	wholesome bread and delicacy of kings
15.	juge sacrificium	perpetual sacrifice
16.	oblatio munda	clean oblation
17.	agnus sine[64] macula	lamb without flaw
[17a]	[mensa propositionis][65]	[meal placed before us]
18.	mensa purissima	purest meal
19.	angelorum esca	food of angels
20.	manna absconditum	hidden manna
21.	memoria mirabilium Dei	memory of God's wonders
22.	panis supersubstantialis	super-substantial bread
23.	verbum caro factum, habitans in nobis	word made flesh, living in us
24.	hostia sancta	sacred Host
25.	calix benedictionis	chalice of blessing
26.	mysterium fidei	mystery of faith

---

[63] An adaptation of two following versions: Anon (1850), 657–59 and Petersen (2012), 119–20.

[64] In the Salzburg version: absque.

[65] In the Roman version only.

No.	Line	Translation
27.	praecelsum et venerabile[66] Sacramentum	most high and adorable Sacrament
28.	sacrificium omnium sanctissimum	most blessed of all sacrifices
29.	vere propitiatorium pro vivis et defunctis	true atonement for the living and the dead
30.	caeleste antidotum, quo a peccatis praeservamur	heavenly antidote, by which we are preserved from sin
31.	stupendum supra omnia miracula	stupendous miracle above all others
32.	sacratissima Domini Passionis commemoratio	most holy remembrance of the Lord's passion
33.	donum transcendens omnem plentitudinem	gift transcending all abundance
34.	memoriale perpetuuum divini amoris	extraordinary memorial of divine love
35.	divinae affluentia largitatis	affluence of divine largesse
36.	sacrosanctum et augustissimum mysterium	most holy and august mystery
37.	pharmacum immortalitatis	medicine of immortality
38.	tremendum ac vivificum Sacramentum	tremendous and life-giving Sacrament
39.	panis omnipotentia verbi caro factus	bread, made flesh through the omnipotence of the word
40.	incruentum sacrificium	bloodless sacrifice
41.	cibus et conviva	meal and guest
42.	dulcissimum convivium, qui assistunt Angeli ministrantes	sweetest banquet, whom the serving angels assist
43.	sacramentum pietatis	sacrament of piety,
44.	vinculum caritatis	bonds of love
45.	offerens et oblatio	offerer and offering
46.	spiritualis dulcedo in proprio fonte degustata	spiritual sweetness tasted in its own fountain
47.	refectio animarum sanctarum	refreshment of holy souls
48.	viaticum in Domino morientium	viaticum of those dying in the Lord
49.	pignus futurae gloriae	pledge of future glory
50.	propitius esto	be merciful
51.	ab omni malo	from every evil
52.	ab indigna Corporis et Sanguinis tui sumptione	from the unworthy reception of thy body and blood
53.	a concupiscentia camis	from passions of the flesh
54.	a superbia vitae	from pride of life
55.	ab omni peccato occasione liberet	from every occasion of sin

[66] In the Dresden version: admirabile.

No.	Line	Translation
56.	per desiderium illud quo hoc Paschacum discipulis manducare desiderasti	through that desire, with thy disciples manducare desiderasti, with which thou didst to eat the Passover
57.	per summam humilitatem, qui discipulorum pedes lavisli	through that profound humility, with which thou didst wash thy disciple's feet
58.	per ardentissimam charitatem, qua lux Sacramentum instituisti	through that most ardent charity, which instituted this divine Sacrament
59.	per sanguinem tuum pretiosum, quem nobis in altari reliquisti	through thy most precious blood, which thou hast left for us upon the altar
60.	per quinque vulnera hujus tui Corporis sacratissimum, quae pro nobis suscepisti	through those five wounds, on your most holy body, which thou didst receive for us
61.	peccatores	sinners we are, we ask thee
62.	ut nobis fidem reverentiam et devotionem hujus admirabilis Sacramenti augere et conservare digneris	that thou wouldst graciously preserve and augment the faith, reverence, and devotion in us towards this admirable Sacrament
63.	ut ad frequentem usum Eucharistiae per veram peccatorum confessionem perducamur	that thou wouldst graciously lead us through the true confession of our sins to a frequent reception of the Eucharist
64.	ut nos ab omni haeresi, perfidia et cordis caecitate liberare digneris	that thou wouldst graciously free us from every heresy, falsehood, and blindness of the heart
65.	ut in hora mortis nostrae hoc caelesti viatico nos confortare et munire digneris	that thou wouldst graciously protect and strengthen us in the hour of our death with this heavenly viaticum
66.	ut animabus principum nostratum omnibus fidelium defunctorum requiem aeternam donare digneris	that thou wouldst graciously grant eternal peace to the souls defunctorum requiem aeternam donare digneris: of our princes and to all the faithful people who are deceased
67.	Fili Dei	Son of God
68.	Agnus Dei, qui tollis peccata mundi	lamb of God, who taketh away the sins of the world
69.	Agnus Dei, qui tollis peccata mundi	lamb of God, who taketh away the sins of the world
70.	Agnus Dei, qui tollis peccata mundi	lamb of God, who taketh away the sins of the world

Appendix 2

Recorded versions of Mozart's Sacramental litanies

Year of issue	Litany (number according to Köchel's catalogue)	Conductor	Orchestra and choir	Soloists	Label
1955	243	Anthony Lewis	The Boyd Neel Orchestra, The St Anthony Singers	Jennifer Vyvyan, Nancy Evans, William Herbert, George James	*Forgotten records*, fr 1122
1974	243	Herbert Kegel	Rundfunk-Sinfonie-Orchester Leipzig, Rundfunkchor Leipzig	Renate Franck-Reinecke, Heidi Riess, Eberhard Büchner, Hermann Christian Polster	*Decca*, 0289 464 6602 5
1978	243	Herbert Kegel	Rundfunk-Sinfonie-Orchester Leipzig, Rundfunkchor Leipzig	Renate Franck-Reinecke, Annelies Burmeister, Eberhard Büchner, Hermann Christian Polster	*Philips*, 6768 018
1980	243	George Guest	Margaret Marshall, Margaret Cable, Wynford Evans, Stephen Roberts	Margaret Marshall, Margaret Cable, Wynford Evans, Stephen Roberts	*Decca*, 0289 458 3792 5

Year of issue	Litany (number according to Köchel's catalogue)	Conductor	Orchestra and choir	Soloists	Label
1981	125	Herbert Kegel	Rundfunk-Sinfonie-Orchester Leipzig, Rundfunkchor Leipzig	Mitsuko Shirai, Heidi Riess, Eberhard Büchner, Hermann Christian Polster	*Decca*, 0289 464 6602 5
1982	243	Günter Wand	Chor des Bayerischen Rundfunks, Symphonieorchester des Bayerischen Rundfunks	Margaret Marshall, Cornelia Wulkopf, Adolf Dallapoz, Karl Ridderbusch	*Profil Medien GmbH – PH05043, Edition Günter Hänssler*
1988	243	Peter Neumann	Collegium Cartusianum, Kölner Kammerchor	Patrizia Kwella, Ulla Groenewold, Christoph Pregardien, Franz-Josef Selig	*EMI*, 567–749379-2
1991	243	Nikolaus Harnoncourt	Concentus Musicus Wien, Arnold Schönberg Chor	Angela Maria Blasi, Elisabeth von Magnus, Deon van der Walt, Alistair Miles	*Teledec*, 9031–72304-2
1992	125	Nikolaus Harnoncourt	Concentus Musicus Wien, Arnold Schönberg Chor	Barbara Bonney, Elisabeth von Magnus-Harnoncourt, Uwe Heilmann, Gilles Cachemaille	*Teldec*, 4509–90494-2

Year of issue	Litany (number according to Köchel's catalogue)	Conductor	Orchestra and choir	Soloists	Label
1998	125	Tonu Kaljuste	Talliner Kammerorchester, Estnischer Kammerchor	Kaia Urb, Ave Moor, J. Roopalu, Tiit Kogerman, Mati Turi, Uku Joller	*Carus Classics*, 83–331
1998	243	Tonu Kaljuste	Talliner Kammerorchester, Estnischer Kammerchor	Kaia Urb, Ave Moor, J. Roopalu, Tiit Kogerman, Mati Turi, Uku Joller	*Carus Classics*, 83–331
2001	125	Nicol Matt	Chamber Choir of Europe, Süddeutsches Kammerorchester	Pamela Heuvelmans	*Brilliant Classics*, 99737/3

Tiziana Palandrani

SARDINIA'S FUNERARY LAMENTATIONS – THE *ATTITOS*, A CASE OF LITANY?

A number of instances of popular poetry share a number of characteristics with the litany genre and, as is the case for the latter, have appeared throughout time in different forms in various cultures. While some poetic forms have disappeared, there are others, such as the one discussed here, which are presently hovering on the brink. This paper deals with the funerary lamentation still current in today's Sardinia, called *attitos* (or *attitidos*) in the Sardinian language.

The performance of these songs is a strictly female prerogative, and the performers, called *attittadoras* in Sardinian, take part in the funerary rites as relatives or acquaintances[1] of the deceased. Their actions bring to mind the *preficae*, the professional mourners of the ancient world. While the practice of funerary lamentations is close to extinction, due to today's patterns of behaviour, no longer requiring such a solemn marking of death, it still survives in some parts of the island.

Ethnomusicological researchers find it difficult to listen to singing of the mourners, due to the unpredictability of the funerary event and the natural reserve which goes with it. The writer Grazia Deledda, who was steeped in the Sardinian culture whose practices and traditions she described, witnessed in person the insistence on reserve that goes with the performance of funerary songs outside their ritual context. Her own research, carried out toward the end of the nineteenth century, mentions that she found it impossible to convince the performers to sing an

---

[1] The performers' relationship with the deceased may be more or less close, but some level of acquaintance is always present, otherwise they would not be able to describe his or her life.

Tiziana Palandrani • Independent scholar

attitu[2] so that she could write down its lines.[3] Giuseppe Ferraro likewise found it difficult to research the *attitos* as soon as he arrived in Sardinia in 1888, eager to study a topic largely neglected by scholars.[4] Yet the extreme reserve of the Sardinian funerary context has enabled this archaic ritual to survive despite the hostility of the ecclesiastical power structure and the transformations brought about by modernity. Despite the difficulties, recordings have been made that do convey the specificity of Sardinian funerary lamentations, which we deem to possess important features akin to litany,[5] to such an extent that they should be considered to be a secular litany.[6]

Regarding their social role, it would be reductive to see the *attittadoras* as mere providers of a service, since their intervention involves a heartfelt participation and the conviction that they do escort the deceased in the passage to another world. Tradition demands that instead of a monetary reward[7] they sometimes receive gifts. Grazia Deledda however reports that in a Sardinian village 'esiste l'uso latino di pagare le prefiche di professione. Si sciolgono i capelli, si picchiano, si graffiano, cantano meravigliosamente ed in ultimo ricevono una quantità [...] di legumi e del miele'.[8]

The *attitos* are sung as an extra-liturgical ritual before the official religious ritual (the Catholic funeral), as a kind of funerary service that facilitates coming to terms with grief. The *attitu* (though not a prayer) is a monodic song, with one individual performer. The collective element emerges only through the supporting interventions, whereby the main mourner is joined by the other mourners, who either sing one by one or underline each line by means of groans and sobs, or repeat some words of the *attitu*.

---

[2] Singular of *attitos*.

[3] Deledda (1995), 184.

[4] Ferraro (1989), VII.

[5] That is, a litany in which the religious semantics, characteristic of the litanic verse, is not present (or is no more present, in case it was there initially).

[6] Cf. Marchi (2006), 52: 'Nel lamento sardo non solo non c'è conforto, ma non c'è, mai, nemmeno un richiamo formale alla divinità' ('In the lamentations of Sardinia no words of consolation are to be found, nor there is ever a formal mention of the divine').

[7] 'Nessuna prefica è prezzolata' ('No professional mourner is bribed'). Marchi (2006), 150.

[8] 'The Latin habit of paying the professional *preficae* still exists. They undo their hair, strike and scratch themselves, sing wonderfully, and in the end receive a certain amount of pulses, as well as some honey.' Deledda (1995), 184.

The Sardinian funeral lamentation consists of improvised poetry that is to be complemented by a sung discourse that follows certain rules of composition. Spatial relationships among people must likewise obey precise rules: the *attittadora*[9] takes pride of place next to the deceased, while the other women form a *sa ria* (a line or a circle) sitting around the latter.

This lamentation ritual has been described with a great deal of details by Father Antonio Bresciani, who considers it borrowed from Oriental cultures, on the grounds that it involves the recitation of the genealogies of the deceased 'a quella guisa appunto che ci nota la Bibbia delle prime stirpi de' patriarchi, ed Omero degli ascendenti degli eroi'.[10] The *attitu* is generally addressed directly to the deceased, whose qualities are praised, and the high points of their life are recalled with many images and details and by means of a variety of forms, melodies, and typologies. As the evocations of the sung discourse range from the age of the deceased to their social condition and type of death, the grief can reach different heights of intensity.

The writer Grazia Deledda, in a passage of her novel *La via del male*, relates that the *attittadoras* 'descrivevano la scena orribile della [...] morte, la desolazione della vedova; invocavano la vendetta e imprecavano contro l'assassino'.[11] Recent studies do not always mention this inducement to retaliation, cited in various Synods of the Church[12] from the sixteenth century on as one of the reasons justifying its ecclesiastical prohibition,[13] another reason being the behaviour of the mourners[14] (e.g. tearing out one's hair, yelling and floundering, scratching one's cheeks, etc.), deemed to be pagan and unseemly.[15]

---

[9] Singular of *attittadoras*.

[10] 'In the same way that the Bible lists the family trees of the patriarchs and Homer mentions the forefathers of the heroes.' Bresciani (1861), 416.

[11] '[...] described the horrible scene of the [...] death, the desolation of the widow; they invoked vengeance and cursed the assassin'. (trans. by R. Trippini). Deledda (1906), 257.

[12] Deledda (1995), 45–46.

[13] Bresciani (1861), 455.

[14] Bresciani (1861), 435–37.

[15] Giovanni Spano, a Canon and thus churchman, reports that already in his time (the nineteenth century) the *attittadoras* were few. He writes that: 'Grazie sia alla premura dei buoni Parrochi e dei zelanti Vescovi [...] e in qualche Diocesi con la scomunica, l'arte di quelle superstiziose femminuccie, riuscirono quasi del tutto a toglier di mezzo questo costume indegno nel seno del Cristianesimo'. ('Thanks to the diligence of our good parsons and zealous bishops [...] and in certain parishes through excommunication, the practices of these superstitious females, unworthy of Christianity, have been almost completely eliminated'). Spano (1995), 61.

Various etymological hypotheses have been put forward regarding the term *attitu*. In the Sardinian Etymological Dictionary compiled by Max Leopold Wagner, the verb *attittare* is taken to mean 'piangere il morto e fare il suo elogio, incitando nello stesso tempo alla vendetta, se si tratta di un uomo assassinato dall'avversario'.[16] This being an oral tradition marked by a paucity of documents, it is difficult to corroborate this interpretation, considered totally inadequate by the Sardinian scholar Giulio Fara,[17] who argues that the etymology in question refers to breastfeeding. He writes that 'unicamente nel dolore della perdita di un caro è da ricercare l'etimologia della parola *attittai* [...] il morto, cioè lo si piange, lo si ninna, lo si culla tenendolo al seno come pargolo, lo si loda anche, ma non lo si attizza e non lo si accende a odio o vendette, [...] perché il morto...è morto'.[18] Let us note how Fara's interpretation is implicitly confirmed by the ancient iconography. For instance, in representations of ancient Egypt the mourners are shown with bare breasts, something which Ernesto De Martino defines as gesture of high ethos, symbolizing 'il latte dato e perduto e al tempo stesso [...] invito al ritorno'.[19]

Another possible etymology, suggested by Dolores Turchi, brings up the cult of Attis:

> The cult of Attis was especially strong during the Roman occupation of Sardinia, [...] 'Attitare' must refer to periods of weeping prescribed for commemorating Attis' death, which by extension becomes a funeral lament for everyone.[20]

According to an oral tradition found in a village of the Barbagia[21] 'attittare vuol dire ninnare, cioé cantare nine nanne'.[22] All in all, we believe that the real function of these chants still eludes our full understanding.

[16] 'To grieve the dead and praise his life, at the same time calling for revenge, in case of a man killed by his enemy.' Wagner (2008), 133.

[17] Fara (1997), 182.

[18] 'Only the pain due to the loss of a loved one provides the etymology of the word *attittai* [...]; the deceased is mourned, is lulled, is embraced as if a small child held up to the breast, is praised but he is neither roused nor incited to hate or take revenge [...] because the dead... is dead.' Fara (1997), 181.

[19] 'The milk gifted and lost and at the same time [...] inviting to come back.' De Martino (2000), 104.

[20] King (1988), pp. 73–74.

[21] Region located in the centre of Sardinia.

[22] '*Attittare* means to lull, that is, to sing lullabies.' Pittalis (2007), 43.

As we shall see below, it is reasonable to think that they fulfil a protective and limiting function during a rite of passage, accompanying the grief-stricken during a transition which would otherwise be difficult to face alone. Once again Grazia Deledda reports on the unfolding of this ritual carried out by women:

> *Stanno per lo più tutte sedute per terra e alcune 'attitano' cioè cantano, improvvisando, narrando la vita e le azioni del morto. 'Attitano' anche le figlie, le sorelle, la moglie, e specialmente certe donne che sono in fama di 'attitadoras' (prefiche) e che in realtà improvvisano assai bene.*[23]

As to the overall structure, we note an eclectic versification which makes use of *settenari* (seven-syllable lines), *ottonari* (octosyllables) or *endecasillabi* (hendecasyllables), as fits the case. Given the irregular flowing of the lines, the emotional tension and the semantic density reside in the recurring rhythmic and melodic cells.

As we are dealing with improvised songs, we think that anaphora and epiphora play crucial functions. Besides contributing to the rhythmic organization of the text, the use of these rhetorical figures demands great proficiency and offers the performer the possibility to stretch time. The musical component is in fact that which structures the perception of time and augments its reception. In the oral tradition it is important to take into account such implications.

Many of these *attitos*, it must be said, have been transmitted over time (and thus have become to some extent crystallized[24]), but they were all born from the improvisation occurring at a specific moment, informed by recurring formulas deployed and adapted as the situation demanded. The *attittadoras* can avail themselves of a repertory of rhymes and formulas more or less stereotyped, but the final product is always something new, heard for the first time. This is possible because they are women with great poetic and improvisational skills: they are the female equivalent of the male poets, who in Sardinia use improvised poetry for reasons and situations other than funerary mourning. Writing in 1840 the Canon Spano insists the purely female role in the elaboration of these verses (or, at least, the progressive disappearance of the male component

---

[23] 'Most of them sit on the ground, with some of them singing (*attitano*), improvising a retelling of the life and actions of the deceased. So do the daughters, the sisters, the wife, and specially certain women known as *attittadoras* (*preficae*), who improvise very well.' Deledda (1995), 184.

[24] Even if their evocation does allow variations.

in the performance of the funerary lament, only occasionally alluded to, a component that in any case has left no traces).[25] The 'Sarde poetesse' writes Spano, 'hanno occasione di mostrare la loro abilità in due estremi punti della vita dell'uomo, cioè nella culla appena nato lodandolo, e nel feretro appena morto piangendolo con lugubri cantilene'.[26]

Since the performer is part of the performance, it would be of interest to examine more closely the reasons of the exclusively female role in the singing of the *attitos*. These songs are distinguished by their being exclusively dedicated to the event which gave rise to them. Unlike other types of singing, any change in their function would be unthinkable or at least ill-timed. This state of affairs explains their precarious survival as well as the difficulties faced by researchers when trying to convince the performers to reproduce the songs outside their traditional context.

Insofar as the improvisational techniques are concerned, we think that the litany-like structure sustains and facilitates the creation of verses by the *attittadoras*. It is reasonable to wonder whether they would be able to improvise verses for hours on end, as they do, if the *attitos* did not have a litany-like structure or use building tools akin to those found in litany.

We have already mentioned that the reserve which surrounds the funerary context has made this genre poorly documented. As a result, it has been largely studied on the basis of documentary evidence collected outside that context, relying on the good memory of the performers. This capacity to recollect long after the mourning is to be seen not only as an answer to the demands of the researchers but also, in our opinion, as revealing of other aspects. It may indicate the necessity to relieve suffering through repetition and reminiscence, two factors that generate a sense of safety. The *attitu* below, here quoted as an example, comes from an anthology first published in 1973 and recently reprinted:

E fizu ohi fizu meu
Chelzo a ti 'nde pesare
Sa prenda valorosa
E fizu ohi fizu meu
Mi chi mama no cheret
No b'andes a sa losa
E fizu ohi fizu meu

[25] Cf. Spano (1995).
[26] 'Sardinian women poets find the occasion to reveal their skills at the two extremities of a man's life, that is, celebrating the newborn in his cradle, and mourning the recently dead through lugubrious singsongs.' Spano (1995), 58.

Su dolore tou
Movet su coro duru
E fizu ohi fizu meu
No b'andes a sa losa
Chi inie b'at iscuru
E fizu ohi fizu meu
Beni a bolu columba
No b'andes a sa tumba
E fizu ohi fizu meu
Pro aer cussa sorte
Minore mortu esseres
E fizu ohi fizu meu
Beni a bolu columba
Mi chi mama ti cheret
E fizu ohi fizu meu
In coro apo fiama
E fizu ohi fizu meu
No b'andes a sa losa
Mi chi ti cheret mama
E fizu ohi fizu meu
Male postu in sa fasca
E fizu ohi fizu meu
Mi chi mama ti cheret
Benidinde pro Pasca[27]

In this *attitu* a son is mourned; not necessarily the son of the performer, as it is possible for the mourners to perform in the name of others. Accordingly, the fact that the mother is mentioned in the third person is hardly significant, for it could be a type of maternal expression, rather common in present-day parlance. In this case the projection would acquire symbolic meaning as an added value; in that respect, let us mention the ritual extending of the arm of the *preficae* in the course of the mourning, a gesture which has been practised by mourners since antiquity and

---

[27] Carpitella, Sassu and Sole (2011), 104. Reprinted with kind permission of the publisher. In the quotation above the text is modernized in spelling. (Translation: 'And son, oh, my son/ I want you to get up,/ My precious possession/ And son oh, my son/ Because your mum doesn't want/ You to go to the grave/ Son, oh, my son/ Your pain/ Moves the hardest heart/ And son, oh, my son/ Don't you go to the grave/ For it is all dark/ And son, oh, my son/ Take flight, you dove/ Don't you go to the grave/ Son, oh, my son/ To deserve this fate/ You'd have to be born dead / Son, oh, my son /Take flight, you dove/ Your mother wants you/ And son, oh, my son/ My heart is ablaze/ And son, oh, my son/ Don't you go to the grave / Your mum wants you/ And son, oh, my son / So badly bandaged / And son, oh, my son/ Your mum wants you/ Do come back for Easter').

is interpreted by De Martino as hinting at separation and relationship.[28] Among the elements that assign this improvised poetic happening to the genre of litany there are also enumerations. Another telling trait is the alternation of assertive and demonstrative lines (listing the characteristics and the qualities of the deceased[29]) on the one hand and emotionally involving verses, invoking and exhorting the deceased (to rise up or revive) on the other. As Diego Carpitella has underlined, during the wake:

> *Motivo del cordoglio viene ritualizzato con moduli protettivi verbali-musicali al fine di destorificare il dolore e di trovare una propria rassicurazione: motivi, questi, alternati a rievocazioni cronachistiche e biografiche che rientrano, appunto, nella meccanica delle 'distrazioni' rituali.*[30]

Also to be found are recurring techniques such as the use of lines with inversion (*versos retrogados* in Sardinian language), a compositional device widely used in Sardinian improvised poetry that allows to exploit all the possible rhymes of a given strophe. In the *attitu* in question, this technical device is exemplified by the line: '*mih chi mama ti cheret*',[31] which is subsequently repeated inverted: '*mih chi ti cheret mama*'.[32] The text is put together by means of a series of *settenari* strophes held together by the rhyming, which unfolds irregularly and rather freely, following the general tendency to be found among Sardinian singers to 'put together non-rhyming lines, each with different content'.[33]

We think that the crucial element that makes the *attitu* akin to litany is the presence of a recurring emotional refrain, which in the above-quoted example can be found in the first line. Indeed, the line *'E fizu ohi fizu meu'* between couplets provides a stereotypical but strongly emotional evocation.

Besides this type of stereotyped invocations, we can find in the *attitos* other phonic-rhythmic elements crystallized by tradition, namely,

---

[28] De Martino (2000), 339.

[29] The contents are drawn from the life of the deceased, whose actions are described with adjectives and similes of praise.

[30] 'The grounds of grief become ritualized through verbal and musical protective modules with the aim to de-historicize the pain and find reassurance; this is alternated with evocations of a factual and biographical nature which likewise belong to the logic of ritual "distractions".' Carpitella, Sassu and Sole (2010), 12.

[31] 'Your mother wants you'.

[32] 'She wants you, your mother'.

[33] Carpitella, Sassu and Sole (2010), 41.

periodic emotional syllables whose function is purely euphonic or nonsensical ('aah aah', 'oh oh', etc.), knowingly deployed by the *attittadoras* and referenced by Father Bresciani:

> *Questi carmi funerali son dalla Prefica declamati quasi a guisa di canto con appoggiature di ritmo, e intreccio di rima [...] Termina ogni strofa in un guaio doloroso, gridando: ahi! ahi! ahi! E tutto il coro dell'altre donne, rinnovellando il pianto, ripetono a guisa d'eco: ahi! ahi! ahi!*[34]

All these elements contribute to the creation of an auditive quilt and give a certain rhythm to the melopoeia which by means of repetition provides a degree of solace to the spectators and also helps mitigate any paroxysmal reactions on their part.

Therefore, if considered as a form of litany, the *attitos* acquire an extraordinary function, namely, to succour and brace the relatives of the deceased in a dramatic moment. This is what makes explicit the protective function of the lament.

As we have said, repetition is normative and generates a sense of safety, even a sort of toning. The healing and consoling function is sustained by the repetition of fixed formulas, as noted by the Canon Giovanni Spano, who defines them as 'intercalary' and places them among a series of lines in which rhyme is not always regular.[35]

The poetic and singing typology of the *attitu*, thanks to the presence of these protective verbal modules, was used in Sardinia also for rituals not strictly related to the funerary, namely, practices of a magical nature, such as the exorcisms of the *argia*,[36] related to the magical-religious practices of Tarantism.

Regarding the musical dimension of the *attitu*, the scholar Giulio Fara, in the first half of the twentieth century, pointed out the limited collection and transcription of the melodies as opposed to the far more substantial recording and accumulation of texts. What emerges is that even when the *attitu* unfolds as a free flow lacking a predominant rhym-

---

[34] 'These funeral poems are declaimed by the *preficae* almost as if they were songs sustained by rhythm and a rhyming texture [...]. Each strophe ends with a painful yelp: ahee! ahee! ahee! And the whole chorus of the other women reprise their crying and repeat like an echo: ahee! ahee! ahee!' Bresciani (1861), 404–05.

[35] Spano (1995), 59–60.

[36] The *argia* (*latrodectus tredecimguttatus*) is a venomous spider whose bite causes toxic shock, traditionally treated with a music and dance therapy known as 'Sardinian Tarantism'.

ing, or definite metrical technical devices, the obsessive repetition of its melodic cadences makes it kindred to the litany.

As we are dealing with an expressive speech that borrows and steals, the structure of the verses may be irregular and not always rhymed, but the presence of recurring structures, rhythmic and melodic, makes the listener perceive a compact and symmetrical whole. The principle of symmetry is that which presides over these songs, and it manifests itself by means of the geometric deployment of the various elements, through repetition or alternation. It follows that even if improvisation may generate a certain metric-literary asymmetry, the perception of symmetry is guaranteed by recourse to combinatorial rules whereby the variants get organized on the basis of fixed constants.

An important feature to keep in mind is that Sardinian popular poetry is sung and not merely recited, and therefore it is structured by music. The forms and modes of auditive execution are over time decoded by the community and thus play a central role in the oral transmission. However, it must be said that in the *attitos* a certain background 'monotony' due to the length intrinsic to their execution tends to push the performance of the text into a grey zone between recitation and singing, between the logogenic and the melogenic. The melodic and verbal modules are closely connected, and therefore, 'to a given phonetic-verbal chain there corresponds a related phonic-melodic chain'.[37] The musical component aggregates these recurrences, in that the conclusion of the rhythmic and syntactical period always coincides with the corresponding melodic ending.

In Sardinia, poetic quality is anyway assessed on the basis of the capacity to generate 'a sense of the geometry of the verses'.[38] Another recurrent element in funeral lamentations is the apostrophe; in the *attitos* it is very common to find the exhortation addressed to the deceased to rise up or to come back among the living (in the example quoted above this can be seen in the line *'Benidinde pro Pasca'*[39]). Characteristic are also the similes, which in the funerary lamentation are expressed as flattering paragons, often drawn from nature. The deceased is compared to noble animals (such as the dove), flowers or trees, and often to the palm tree[40] (*pramma* in the Sardinian language), a very useful word insofar as its ending with the vowel 'a' makes it possible to come up with very many rhymes, especially

[37] Carpitella, Sassu and Sole (2010), 9.
[38] Cirese (1988), 19.
[39] 'Do come back for Easter'.
[40] The Mediterranean dwarf palm (*Chamaerops humilis*) plays a prominent part in tradition, as its was once used to make corsets for women and to weave baskets.

in settings of rhythmic rest. Finally, Grazia Deledda[41] mentions the use of 'Oriental images' and 'Biblical metaphors', inserted to relate recount the virtues of the deceased and the grief caused by his passing away.

Regarding the origin of the structure of this type of song, it is possible to find similar elements in the Sardinian tradition, namely, the unfolding of certain recitative forms in the repertory of call-and-response prayers, sung in church. One example among many is the composition *'O tristu fatale die'*[42] by Bonaventura Licheri.[43] It belongs to the medieval tradition of the *planctus Mariae*, which came into being to counteract the practice of popular lamentations, considered by the Church pagan and inciting to excess; the mediation of the Madonna was meant to provide a symbolic figure who was nonetheless present on the earthly scene of human sorrow. Mary displayed the possibility of bearing with Christian fortitude and hope the death of a son, and therefore provided a didactic example to the faithful.

O tristu fatale die
oras penosas e duras
(Refrain)
Cagliadebos creaturas,
lassade piangher a mie.

A mie toccat su piantu
a mie su sentimentu,
depo pianpher de assentu
e giugher s'oscuru mantu,
ca so affligida tantu;
chie t'hat mortu e chie?

A mie toccat su dolu
pro chi su mortu est su meu,
a mie toccat su teu
a mie su disconsolu;
Fizu de mama consolu,
chie t'hat mortu e chie?[44]

[41] Deledda (1995), 184.

[42] 'Oh sad and inauspicous day'.

[43] A Sardinian writer who lived between the seventeenth and eighteenth centuries, among other things the historical period more prolific for choral litanies.

[44] Caria (1981), 172. In the quotation above the text is modernized in spelling. (Translation: 'Oh, sad and inauspicious day / hard and painful hours / (Refrain) Be quiet creatures, / let me cry. // I am the one who should cry / Who should anguis, / I must

The performance of the songs dedicated to the Madonna was generally antiphonal, with a soloist or a small group of soloists alternating with the rest of the faithful.[45] In Sardinia most of the texts dedicated to Mary were sung in a call-and-response form and were called *gosos*,[46] a poetic musical form held to be due to the Iberian influence,[47] consisting of strophes alternating with a refrain. In particular, *'O tristu fatale die'* reveals a litanic construction in its constant repetition of a line as a refrain at the end of each strophe. However, it also reveals the typical characteristics of the *attitos* by putting forward the collective nature of the deceased by means of the Madonna as the mother mourning the son,[48] and using the paragons of the *prenda*[49] and the *lizzu*.[50]

The participatory aspect of the mourning in the island can be seen in the fact that the *attittadoras* can take each other's place when they grow tired, and underline with their voices the various melodic formulas uttered by the principal mourner. The feasibility of this alternation underscores the litanic nature of the practice and probably indicates the survival of an original call-and-response recitation. At this point we must note the insistence of the Madonna on the question, purely rhetorical in this case, on who has killed her son ('Chie t'hat mortu e chie?')[51], which brings to mind the typical queries of the *attitos*, in particular those referring to violent deaths.[52] The queries addressed to the dead are a feature common to the funerary lamentations of various cultures.

Insofar as the structural elements are concerned, we think that the rhyming plays a fundamental role in the improvisation; it provides the primary structure of the whole as well as a method of oral composition. Rhyming helps the formation of structural models and is important in

really cry / And wrap myself in a mourning mantle, / because I am so afflicted; / who killed you, who? // I have to lament, / because the deceased is mine, / I have to mourn / I have got the sorrow; / Son, your mother's consolation, / who killed you, who?').

[45] 'This type of song has left traces in the Sardinian tradition also in the rites of Holy Week, when performing "l'*Attitu* della Madonna" [An *Attitu* of the Madonna], a funerary lamentation in Latin for solo voice and chorus.' See Sassu (2012), 96.

[46] Usually devoted to praising the saints.

[47] Notably the Catalan *goigs*.

[48] A theme also to be found in various *gosos*, the most famous of them being *'No mi giamedas Maria'* ('Do not call me Mary').

[49] Jewel.

[50] Lily.

[51] 'Who has killed you? Who?'

[52] The same question is quoted by Bresciani, referring to the *attitu* for a murder victim. Cf. Bresciani (1861), 452.

its own right for its aesthetic value and for its supporting the poetic creation. We can consider it as a sort of auditive 'laboratory' insofar as it allows the performers to make the most of their working memory, thereby becoming an essential tool of the improvised songs. Rhyming fulfils a useful function not only for the performer but also for the listener, making its memorization easier.

Regarding the reception, it is now possible to study *attitos* created in the past precisely thanks to the recollections of performers as well as of spectators, for this is what has enabled their preservation as living tradition.

It is to be noted that in the case of the *attitos* there has been an accumulation of standardized formulas that inform the rhyming or support it. For example, expressions such as 'prenda mia'[53] or 'coro meu'[54] are commonly used as an anaphora or epistrophe. In our opinion, the rhetorical figures of the *attitos* also fulfil another peculiar function: they make possible the triggering of trance-like or hypnotic states, not only in the performer but also among the spectators. Having said that, it might be better to speak of a 'psychic state of dreamy concentration'[55] on the part of the *attittadora*, as Ernesto De Martino defined it, or use Giulio Fara's description of a self-hypnosis condition that operates as 'anaesthetic of one's own grief in prolonging the lamentation'.[56] The condition seems to consist in a peculiar psychic state activated and sustained by the long unfolding of the lamentation, which makes the lived experience of those present atemporal (as is the case in many litanic performances).

In order to attain this liminal condition, the *attittadora* tends to keep her eyes closed, or else stares into the distance. We think that this state is due not only to the long time taken by the performance but also by activation of the prosodic memory needed to create the verse. This semi-oneiric state would enable the mourner to attain the concentration needed to access the 'reservoir' of her memory, which contains not only images and fixed formulas but also models informing the construction and elaboration of the lines. It follows that the skill of the mourner resides in her capacity to combine these phonic rhythmic modules in any way she decides,[57] since 'the performance implies competence. Be-

---

[53] 'My treasure'.
[54] 'My heart'.
[55] De Martino (2000), 188.
[56] Fara (1997), 180.
[57] Such skills are essential for improvised poetry. See Manca (2009), 196–97.

sides knowing what to do and say, the performance must also display a knowledge of how to be in time and space.[58] Such skills with melodic rhythmic formulas are an essential condition, more so if we consider the *attitos* as an instance of improvised litany.

In the light of all this, it is understandable that we find individual variations in production, depending on the performer and on her innate poetic and compositional capability, but also on the inheriting of relevant experiences; conceivably, many mourners evoke through their singing their first-person experiences of grief for their own dead beloved. It is in this sense that we can understand the concept of tradition, as in each *attitu* there persists the memory of the *attitos* which have preceded it. This referencing is underlined by the *attittadoras* not only through their voices but also through the physicality of their gestures and bodily actions. Let us note that percussive mimicry (using the chest, the thighs, or other parts of the body) and swinging and swaying movements, performed individually or carried out in synchrony by the mourners, are a universal trait of funerary rites since antiquity. In the case of the *attitos*, they also amount, in our opinion, to a visual representation of the litanic elements, such as the repetition *ad libitum* and the listings, that is, they visually illustrate the rhythm besides reinforcing it. This can be seen in the performances of the mourners, in the swinging and swaying of the bust and in their various hand gestures, which however fall short of the excesses of the classical world, such as scratching one's face or tearing out or undoing[59] the hair.[60]

Conclusions

The *attitos* embody a worldview so ancient that they come close to being archetypical within the collective imaginary. They emerge from a time in which poetry was conceived exclusively as singing (and not recitation), with repetition and symmetry as aesthetic and spiritual requirements. With the passage of time, we note a progressive transfer of the practice of funerary lamentations from the educated classes, which

---

[58] Zumthor (1984), 185.

[59] Mentioned by the Sardinian proverb 'Est pranghende a pilu isortu' ('She's crying with her hair undone'). Cf. King (1988), 75.

[60] Excesses did take place in relatively recent times; there are early twentieth-century Sardinian documents which describe such practices, likewise alluded to in Sardinian proverbs.

ultimately dispensed with it, to the poorer classes, which confined it to a domestic and private realm. It is in this most recent phase that the church attempts to extirpate the practice, deemed to be a pagan heritage, inducing to excess and deviant behaviour. The conservative nature of Sardinian culture has nonetheless allowed the practice of funerary lamentations to survive till our days.

In the traditions of the island we can find the use of repetitive formulas in other contexts and rituals, such as the previously mentioned spells and exorcisms of the *argia* or the spellbinding prayer *'Sas doighi paraulas de Santu Martinu'*,[61] assembled through a cumulative process and recited with apotropaic intent.[62] We think it is possible to discern an aspect of the funerary ritual tied to the latter's requirement of concreteness in the tradition of the *Dormitio Virginis*, an heritage of the Byzantine domination of the island in the high middle ages, which is widespread and has survived till today. Such a persistence in the representation of the Madonna *corpore presenti* on the deathbed, besides its purely religious significance, might be explained, we think, in terms of the characteristic need of the *attitos* for the physical presence of a body[63] serving as focus for energies, praises and prayers.[64] We think that the reference to the Madonna it is not casual, as she is a figure very present in the litanic context.

The aesthetic and ritual requirement for symmetry and repetition has taken litany-like form also in the visual arts, as seen in the dense colour rhythms of the funerary mat (*su tapinu de mortu*). Here we find

---

[61] 'The Twelve Words of Saint Martin' also known as *'Sas doighi paraulas mannas'* or *'adornadas'* (The Twelve Great Words, or Adorned); the adjectives 'great' and 'adorned' underline the importance of the repetition of a list of words so as to obtain a desired effect, but they also corroborate the value of the litanic word, insofar as adorned. This prayer, interestingly, takes the form of a dialogue between the devil and Saint Martin.

[62] Keeping away storms or the devil.

[63] If the body was not available, the custom was to *attitare* in the presence of the clothes or a picture of the deceased. We can find a reference to this custom in the lines of Antoninu Mura Ena (1908–1994), whose poem *'Chitto'* deals with the soldiers fallen in the first world war, on whose behalf 'candles were lighted around their empty clothes lying on the ground, and the mourners sang their lamentations, as if the body was there'. (Mura Ena (1998), 199).

[64] See Mura Ena (1998), 50. *'Pesadu in logu meu, happo connottu,/ dolu mannu e ispantu,/ attittidos e piantu/ (ohi, mortos in gherra!)/ subra s'ammuntonada/ de 'estimentas boidas/ remoidas in terra'.* ('Born and bred in my village I have known/ great pain and surprise/ crying and lamentations/ (oh, those killed in war!)/ over a pile of empty clothes/ lying on the ground.').

a notable example of visual litany, likely to be linked to the funerary tradition, instantiating the comforting role of repetition. If the rite of the lamentation is enacted to confront the experience of estrangement caused by death, which leaves powerless and desperate those touched by it, the *attitu* tends to configure itself in measured forms.[65] This happens when the 'the death is acknowledged and not hidden' and 'one doesn't react by fleeing'.[66] The litanic structure of the *attitu*, consisting of stereotyped rhymes and sentences, fulfils a comforting function insofar as it imparts order to the liminal situation of bereavement, keeping it between normality and chaos, using the 'resolution of the *planctus* in stereotyped refrains'.[67]

Thence the theatre of mourning is sustained by singing and is activated following a code stratified between psyche and body, individual and society, reason and instinct. The funerary lamentation is a special place for women, otherwise excluded from the rituals of the church, whose songs were in the past exclusively performed by the male faithful.

As music is the the key element to confront the enigma of human existence, we can find the reason of the need for the *attitu* in the Sardinian proverb *'mortu chene piangher non si ch'andat'*; the deceased cannot reach the afterlife unless he is mourned.

---

[65] Cirese (1951), 2.
[66] Gallini (2003), 210.
[67] De Martino (2000), 183.

Bibliography

Bresciani, A. (1850) *Dei costumi dell'Isola di Sardegna comparati cogli antichissimi popoli orientali*, Napoli.

Caria, C. (1981) *Canto sacro-popolare in Sardegna*, Oristano.

Carpitella, D., P. Sassu and L. Sole (eds) (2011) *La musica sarda, canti e danze popolari* [reprint of the 1973 edn], Udine.

Cirese, A. M. (1951) 'Nenie e prefiche nel mondo antico,' in *Lares* 17, 20–44.

— (1988) *Ragioni metriche*, Palermo.

Deledda, G. (1906) *La via del male*, Roma.

— (1995) *Tradizioni popolari di Sardegna*, edited by Dolores Turchi, Roma.

De Martino, E. (2000) *Morte e pianto rituale. Dal lamento funebre antico al pianto di Maria* [reprint of the 1975 edn], Torino.

Fara, G. (1997) *Sulla musica popolare in Sardegna*, edited by Gian Nicola Spanu, [reprint of articles originally published in *Rivista Musicale Italiana* (1909–26) and in *Archivio Storico Sardo* (1915–17)], Nuoro.

Ferraro, G. (1989) *Canti popolari in logudorese* [reprint of the 1891 edn], Cagliari.

Gallini, C. (2003) *Il consumo del sacro: feste lunghe di Sardegna* [reprint of the 1971 edn], Nuoro.

King, M (ed.) (1988) 'The "Attitos" of Sardinia: An Interview with Dolores Turchi,' *Folklore Forum Index* 21 (1), 72–76.

Manca, M. (2009) *Cantare in poesia per sfidare la sorte*, Nuoro.

Marchi R. (2006) *La sibilla barbaricina. Note etnografiche*, Nuoro.

Mura Ena, A. (1998) *Recuida* [Nicola Tanda (ed.)], Sassari.

Pittalis, F. (2007) *Rituali di morte e canti di prefiche in Sardegna – Bitti*, Mogoro.

Sassu, P. (2012) *Suoni della tradizione*, [*Musiche e musicisti in Sardegna*, vol. I], Sassari.

Spano, G. (1995) *Ortografia sarda*, [reprint of the 1840 edn], Cagliari.

Wagner M. L. (2008) *Dizionario Etimologico Sardo: Indici delle voci e delle forme dialettali compilati da Raffaele G. Urciolo* [Giulio Paulis (ed.); reprint of the 1964 edn], Nuoro.

Zumthor, P. (1984) *La presenza della voce. Introduzione alla poesia orale*, Bologna.

Jenny Ponzo, Francesco Galofaro,
Gabriele Marino

THE SEMIOTICS OF LITANIES FROM THE MIDDLE AGES TO THE YOUTUBE ERA

Interpretative, Intersemiotic, and Performative Issues

1. Introduction

Since their Medieval origins, litanies can be performed in a plurality of ways: in private or public occasions, employing verbal language only or a plurality of semiotic systems such as music and other symbolic resources engendering a complex and stratified process of meaning-making. The present paper aims at shedding light on this process by adopting a semiotic perspective centred on the performance of acts and their relationship with a corpus of multimodal texts (written, iconographic, and audio-visual/digital).[1]

In particular, we will look into three different ways of interpreting and performing litanies in Catholic culture. The first part (§ 2) presents considerations about the collective and oral performance of litanies in ceremonial occasions, by comparing contemporary ethnographic notes (based on two observations carried out in Poland and Italy) with Medieval testimonies. The second part (§ 3) looks into a written genre, i.e. into a corpus of nineteenth- and twentieth-century treatises in Italian, mostly authored by priests and exposing the results of an individual and intellectual meditation on the litanic text. The third part (§ 4) explores

---

[1] This paper is part of the project NeMoSanctI, which has received funding from the European Research Council (ERC) under the European Union's Horizon 2020 research and innovation programme (grant agreement No. 757314). Although the paper is the result of a close cooperation between the Authors, please consider paragraphs 1, 3, and 5 as written by Jenny Ponzo, paragraph 2 by Francesco Galofaro, and paragraph 4 by Gabriele Marino.

Jenny Ponzo • University of Turin
Francesco Galofaro • University of Turin and CUBE, Bologna, Italy
Gabriele Marino • University of Turin

The Litany in Arts and Cultures, ed. by Witold Sadowski and Francesco Marsciani, Turnhout, Brepols, 2020 (*Studia Traditionis Theologiae*, 36), pp. 273-302
© BREPOLS PUBLISHERS DOI 10.1484/M.STT-EB.5.119216

the role of new media in the semiotic elaboration of litanies by studying and classifying a corpus of YouTube videos retrieved via the Italian query *litanie dei santi* (Litany of the saints).[2]

Litanies constitute an integral part of Catholic liturgy, and liturgy in turn is an important factor for the construction of the identity of both the believing subject and the Church. Thus, the study of the different ways in which the litanic text is performed, meditated, interpreted, and remediated can contribute to an improved comprehension of some of the complex semiotic mechanisms that have shaped Catholic culture at least since the Middle Ages.

2. Ethnosemiotic Notes on Litanic Performance

2.a. Morpho-dynamical Hypothesis

In June 2016, we observed the Litany of the Sacred Heart of Jesus as performed in the Temple of Divine Providence located in Warsaw, Poland (see Figure 1). The temple was under construction, and the ceremony took place in the circular crypt beneath it, where important and honoured Poles would have been later buried, thus founding national Polish identity on Catholic Church. The Litany was performed after a Confirmation.[3] Being circular, the benches are located in the northern, southern, and western part of the crypt. The altar is a cube placed onto a wooden square basis in the middle of the crypt, whereas in the eastern part of it,[4] on the same axis of the altar, we find a lectern and the crucifix. The clergy's benches are in the background.

During the Confirmation, the disposition of the three involved actors ('clergy', 'worshippers', and 'altar') is mainly compliant with the Second Vatican Council's indications. The altar is the vertex of a quarter of a circle that constitutes the sacred space of the clergy, complementary to the three quarters of a circle that can be considered as the worshippers' profane space. The altar and its basis are between the two spaces, and clergymen are facing worshippers, with their back to the crucifix (which

---

[2] In Italian, the plural form is more common than the singular, both to refer to the litanic genre and to one specific text.

[3] In Poland the month of June is dedicated to the Sacred Heart and litanies are always performed after the rituals. Poland is officially devoted to the Sacred Heart from 1920.

[4] We refer to the liturgic East.

serves as the fourth actor). This implies that during the 'Our Father', while they address prayers to Jesus, the clergy and worshippers look at each other, also because the clergy is on the same line of sight of the crucifix. However, during the litany, the disposition of the space suddenly changes. Firstly, a deacon poses the monstrance on the altar, in the centre of the circle. Secondly, the clergy takes place between the altar and the worshippers, kneeling toward the monstrance, with the backs to the worshippers. Thus, both the clergymen and the worshippers look at the monstrance, which is on the same line of sight of the crucifix. Clergymen are at the first place, but they belong to the same space of the community. The altar is no more a frontier between two different semantic spaces, but it is the marker of the sacred space, delimited by its square basis. This disposition recalls the spatial structure preceding the Second Vatican Council.

Baumstark[5] proposed ten laws to explain the morphological change in liturgy in a diachronic perspective. In particular, law nine is the *law of the preservation of older usages in the more solemn liturgical seasons*: more solemn liturgical seasons tend to maintain older liturgical usages. Furthermore, as Taft[6] observes, the law can be extended to more solemn or less frequently celebrated liturgical services. A second important law (number eight) could explain how the ancient and the new disposition in space can coexist: newer elements may be juxtaposed for a certain time with older ones before ultimately supplanting them. Thus, the meaning produced by the old disposition of the actors in space can survive and be employed immediately after the new one, even if there is a strong contrast between them. According to this hypothesis, Baumstark's laws would not be relevant only to the verbal component of the litanies, but to the nonverbal ones too: in particular, to the semiotic relations between actors and spaces. In order to analyse the nonverbal features of the performance, we will apply a semiotic analysis to our ethnographic material, in an ethnosemiotic perspective.[7] The importance of a cooperation between Liturgical Studies and Semiotics has been pointed out by De Clerck:[8] from his point of view, liturgy is the place of the construction of the believing subject and the process which contributes to the formation of the Christians' identity and of the Church. Semiotics

[5] Baumstark (1958).
[6] Taft (2001).
[7] Marsciani (2012).
[8] De Clerck (2001).

helps to centre the analysis on the performance of the acts that we study, asking who the actors are, what programs they operate, what processes they follow, and what is their effect, as it is described in the texts or observable in behaviours.

Evidence supporting our interpretation of the reconfiguration of the space can be found in ancient descriptions of litanic performances, for instance in Beroldus:[9] 'Archiepiscopus flectit genua sua contra orientem. Tunc primicerius lectorum statim subinfert letanias'.[10] Beroldus, author of liturgical treatises, lived in Milan at the beginning of the twelfth century. In the quoted passage, he refers to the Litany of the saints as it was sung in the Ambrosian rite during the Eastern vigil, right after the baptism.[11] The liturgical East is to be considered the very position of the altar. The similarity between contemporary performances of the litany of the Sacred Heart of Jesus and Medieval performances of the litany of the saints is due to the fact that the latter, together with the litany of the Virgin, is the model to more recent litanies.[12]

2.b. *Thematic Roles*

Clergymen, considered as a collective actor in the performance, must take the first place between the worshippers. They are the first ones to invoke the saints and to propose petitions. They mediate between the worshippers and the divine manifestation, and between the two Churches (the one on Earth and the one in Heaven). The thematic role of the *mediator* is reflected in the structure of the litany of the saints, whose mediation is invoked before addressing petitions to God.

As structural analysis of medieval litanies shows,[13] the role of mediator between the profane space of the worshippers and the sacred space of *sancta sanctorum* is another feature inherited from ancient tradition. This role of the clergy is also confirmed by the architectural space of the early Basilica, where the two spaces were separated by the *Templon* – as we can observe, for instance, in the Church of Saint Mary in Cosmedin, Rome (sixth century) – and later gave the origin to the *Iconostasis* of

---

[9] Beroldus (1894).

[10] 'The Archbishop kneels to the East. Then the director of the lectors immediately starts the litany'. The primicerius was the first capitular after the archdeacon and archpresbyter, directing the liturgical functions and chant.

[11] Cf. Valli (2016).

[12] Cf. Sadowski (2011).

[13] See Galofaro and Kubas (2016) and Galofaro (2018).

orthodox churches. Thus, the space of the enunciation mirrors the structure of the enunciated space.

In order to achieve a better understanding of the role of the mediator, we can refer to classical analyses of ethnologic data,[14] according to which the permanence of values in the immanent universe implies the position of the source of values in a transcendent universe. *Senders* guarantee the participatory communication between the two universes and the circulation of values. Our case is actually more complex, since it involves a hierarchy of senders in the syncretic relation: the clergy is the sender in the space of the enunciation, while the Saints are the senders in the enunciated space. After the Second Vatican Council, when the position of the clergy changed, the role of mediator tends to disappear, or it is considerably weakened, and the relation between clergymen and worshippers becomes dialogic. This dialogic relationship between the priest and the assembly, which is evident, for instance, in the ritual of baptism, plays a strong influence on the meaning of the litanies, because it tends to underline the construction of the historical identity of the Church, rather than the ecclesiological relation between Heaven and Earth.

2.c. Formal and Semantic Variants

On 30 September 2018 we observed the performance of the litany of the saints during the Catholic baptism of two babies in Pordenone, a small city in the North-East of Italy (in the region of Friuli-Venezia Giulia). The priest added to the ceremony different explanations on the rite. Before the beginning, he explained why the ceremony starts at the beginning of the aisle. After the prayers of the faithful, he explained why the Saints are invoked, linking the entry into the family and into the church. At the end of the formula: 'I baptize you in the name of the Father ...' the minister asked worshippers to clap. Another explanation regarded the symbol of the paschal candle, the rite of the *ephphatha* – linked to Mark 7, 31–37. After the 'Our Father', before the final blessing, the priest explained that all humanity is one indivisible family. After the end of the official ceremony and the blessing, he gave two gifts to the babies: a shell ('Christian sign related to Santiago de Compostela') and a notebook ('to write the history of your life'). He then declared that it was possible to blow out the candle and said goodbye to everybody. In line with the 'modernising' character of the ritual, the litanies presented significant variants as well. This particular variant of the abbreviated version of the

[14] Greimas (1987).

litanies in use during baptism, in fact, does not comply with the traditional hierarchy. This is possible since the official baptismal prayer book of the Catholic church in Italy provides only a baptismal schema: the celebrant is invited to fill it with the names of other Saints, especially the names of the persons to be baptized and the patrons of the parish. Thus, in our case, after Saint Mary, John the Baptist, Peter and Paul, we find Martin, Francis, Clare, Thomas, the two names of the babies (Laurence and Irene), Edith Stein, Michael, Stephen, and the final invocation to all the Saints. After every name, the celebrant added an antonomasia. For example, Peter and Paul are the 'apostles of the Gospel and first eminent witnesses'; Saint Martin is 'rich with faith and he breaks bread with the poor'; Saint Francis is 'God's jester and greatly in love with life'; Saint Irene is called 'Life offered to the Lord for the Unity of the Church'; Saint Benedicta of the Cross, the only post-conciliar saint, is the 'strong and luminous witness of the beauty of the Gospel'. Basically, each apposition aims at resuming who the Saint was and why do we care about him or her. A literary model for such a practice could be identified in the litany of the Holy Virgin.

The variant is interesting in light of the relationship between form and morpho-dynamics. From the point of view of a narrative generative grammar,[15] a single grammar generates both the litanic genre featured by a list of Names (all the possible variants of the litany of the saints) and the one featured by a list of antonomasias (all the possible variants of the litany of the Virgin), provided that the grammar is equipped with the empty element [o]: this way the grammar can generate either the name *or* the antonomasia, *or* both. Thus, the variant can still be considered as a production of the *discursive configuration* of the litany.[16] The litanic grammar remained stable in the new litanies produced during centuries, and it is preserved even in the variant observed in Pordenone.

The apparition of appositions in the litany of the saints observed in Pordenone is an example of Baumstark's seventh law: 'Later liturgical prose develops in the direction of an increasingly oratorical form and becomes more and more governed by rhetoric.' More generally, the whole ceremony observed in Pordenone seems to support Baumstark's second general principle: 'Liturgical development proceeds from simplicity to increasing enrichment.' An example of such an increased semiotic complexity can be found in the new symbolic gifts, the shell and the book.

---

[15] Galofaro and Kubas (2016).
[16] Greimas and Courtés (1982), 49–51.

Possibly, something similar happened in early Christian baptism when new symbols (baptismal gown, eastern candle, blessed salt) were added to the immersion. Since in the observed case the new symbols appear after the very ceremony, as parting gifts, we can assume that elements as the gown could be originally involved in utilitarian actions and later charged of a symbolic meaning, according to Baumstark's tenth law.

The inserted appositions are related to the attempt to transfer knowledge to worshippers, which also motivates the comments on the ritual provided throughout the ceremony. This knowledge is not a necessary requirement for the rite performance, but the celebrants clearly attribute a great importance to the worshippers' awareness of the value related to litanies and to the other practices involved in the ceremony. This is probably due to the fact that their meaning entered a crisis. As we said, after the Second Vatican Council, the ecclesiological meaning seems weakened, and this could explain why, in our variant, the celestial hierarchy is not represented by the order of the invocations. The new sensibility is rather historical: in order to construct worshippers' collective memory, the priest must instruct them about who the Saints are, with particular reference to the lesser known (Irene, a martyr of Diocletian's persecutions) and to the newer ones (such as Edith Stein, one of the few post-conciliar saints who entered the list of contemporary litanies, together with Father Kolbe and Maria Goretti).

2.d. *Two Different Constructions of Time*

The historical sensibility accentuated in the twentieth century adds a linear notion of time to a cyclical conception that is connected in several ways to the tradition of the litanic genre.

This circular temporality is particularly evident in the litany of the saints, not only because the list of saintly characters connects the earthly Church with the Church on Heaven, but also because these litanies accompany both the beginning and the end of life. Thus, they are performed during the baptism, but also in last sacraments accompanying agony and death. For instance, the oldest litanies we found in the Ambrosian tradition are part of the ritual of the anointing of the sick and are sung also during funerals. This is a peculiar trait of the Ambrosian rite: the litany of the saints connects baptism to funeral, i.e. the beginning of the life of a Christian in the Church on earth to the beginning of the *real life* of the Christian in the Church on Heaven. Thus, the early meaning associated to the litany of the saints was ecclesiological. This explains also the syntagmatic position of the litany in the *preces mortuorum*. The rite is subdivided in five parts: (1) *Ad domum defuncti* (at home); (2) *In itinere ad ecclesiam* (during the procession from home to the church) (3) *In ecclesia* (in the church); (4) *In itinere de ecclesia ad sepulchrum* (from the church to the graveyard); and (5) Ad *sepulchrum* (in the graveyard). The litany concludes the part *In ecclesia*: ideally, it is the keystone of the whole ceremony and the link between two worlds. According to Magnoli,[17] litanies were originally sung during the anointing of the sick, and later became part of the baptism through the intermediate stage of the *baptismum gravitale*, addressed to babies in life-threatening situations.

Historical change of liturgy is seen as a way to preserve its meanings. This argument was frequently advanced after the Second Vatican Council. For example, during the second plenary session of the XLVI synod, 28 February 1967, while defending the maintaining of two distinct rites, the Roman and the Ambrosian, the Archbishop Card. Giovanni Colombo stated that the Ambrosian rite had to be reformed precisely to remain faithful to those pastoral values which inspired Saint Ambrose, because of 'the new needs of industrial society, which, with migrations and tourism, mixes and confuses the masses of the faithful'.[18] This implies a different, linear construction of time, in which the preservation of the identity of the Church is essential.

3. Written Meditations on Litanies

A kind of performance of litanies that differs from their recitation in ritual or ceremonial contexts consists in their individual meditation and in the intellectual elaboration of their content. Traces of this interpretative process, mainly carried out by the clergy, can be found in a genre of written treatises devoted to specific litanic texts. The corpus we focus on includes a sample of thirteen texts published in Italian between 1850 and 1999.[19] However, a similar literature also exists in other languages,

---

[17] Magnoli (1996).

[18] Biffi (1993).

[19] Andreoletti (1941); Anonymous (1933); Bergagna, Canziani, and Galbiati (1955); Bersani (1871); Cavatoni (1912); Cavedoni (1850); Mortarino (1938); Piccione (1896); Razzore and Mora (1931); Sandigliano (1923); Schuster (1953); Scippa (1999); Svampa (1913).

such as French,[20] and was produced at least since early modernity.[21] Our main interest lies in the paratext,[22] which expresses the aims and principles motivating these works.

3.a. A Moral, Popular, and Practical Genre of Treatises

In their paratexts, the treatises are defined as 'commentaries', 'explanations', 'instructions', 'thoughts', 'considerations', 'discourses', or 'sermons'.[23] They are all authored by clergymen, ranging from simple priests to high prelates (Svampa and Schuster, for instance, are cardinals). The readership designed in the prefaces and introductions is mainly composed by other clergymen, in particular preachers, who can find, within such books, new ideas for their discourses and sermons. Consequently, lay faithful are only secondary receivers, either as a minor fringe of readers or as the addressees of the homilies that the treatises report and/or inspire. All the treatises share a declared moral, popular, and practical character, as well as the aim of fostering the devotion toward the figure invoked in the litanies. The texts composing our corpus focus on three specific litanies: the Litany of the Blessed Virgin (or Litany of Loreto, nine texts), the Litany of the Sacred Heart of Jesus (three texts), and the Litany of St Joseph (one text). The recurring scheme of these books consists in presenting one discourse or meditation about each invocation.

It is possible to identify at least two reasons for the choice of particular litanic texts. The first is the intention of fostering a certain cult. Thus, a general goal expressed by the commentators of the Litany of Loreto is the promotion of the devotion towards the Virgin but, more specifically, a number of them assigns a prominent importance to the meditation and celebration of the dogma of the Immaculate Conception, proclaimed in 1854. For instance Piccione, instead of following the order of the litanic text, starts his discourses from the invocation '*Regina sine*

---

[20] See e.g. Cornet (1873) and Barthe (1858).

[21] The earliest treatise we found trace of is Fra Nicolò Riccardi's *Ragionamenti sopra le Litanie di Nostra Signora* (1626). This and other references for the early modern period can be found in Cavedoni (1850). It is reasonable to hypothesize that this literature was fostered since the Reformation period as a defence of litanies against the Protestant critique of vain repetitions.

[22] Genette (1982).

[23] Respectively: Scippa (1999), Cavatoni (1912), Andreoletti (1941), Schuster (1953), Anonymous (1933) and Svampa (1913), Piccione (1896) and Sandigliano (1923), Mortarino (1938).

labe concepta'.[24] Similarly, Sandigliano intends to promote the devotion towards St Joseph, especially after the abolition of his feast by Pius X and its recent restauration by Benedict XV.[25] In turn, Scippa, Andreoletti, and Svampa are careful in reconstructing the history of the cult of the Sacred Heart – which they date back to the Middle Ages – and to place their work in the frame of its most recent developments inside the Church.[26] The second reason is connected to liturgy. Especially the treatises devoted to the Litany of Loreto are conceived as propaedeutic tools for the celebration of the month of the Virgin (May), consisting in daily gatherings with the recitation of litanies accompanied by 'moral discourses' held by preachers. In this context, the meditations contained in the books could provide preachers with good material for their discourses and thus contribute to the edification of the faithful.[27]

3.b. Making the Litanic Meaning Explicit

Another feature characterizing the genre is the recurring idea that litanies contain a condensed theological sense that needs to be made explicit and explained. For instance, Sandigliano claims that the litany of St Joseph 'is wonderfully suited for the development of almost all the Christian morals',[28] while according to Svampa 'the Litany [of the Sacred Heart] is almost a brief and juicy [It. *succoso*] popular catechism where the most elevated truths of the Catholic dogma are proposed in brief and precise formulas.'[29] In reason of this complexity, authors are generally worried about the fact that, although the recitation of litanies is appreciated for their beauty and the consolation that they bring to the soul of the faithful,[30] they are not fully understood: 'Unfortunately, numerous Christians hear their chant and repeat them, without knowing what they are saying. And even though their heart feels a sort of piety and devotion, they cannot understand the meaning and the importance

---

[24] Piccione (1923), 15.

[25] Sandigliano (1923).

[26] Scippa (1999), Andreoletti (1941), and Svampa (1913).

[27] A similar argument is claimed by Sandigliano (1923) who wishes to promote the celebration of March as the month of St Joseph.

[28] Sandigliano (1923), XIII.

[29] Svampa (1913), 30.

[30] For instance, according to Andreoletti (1941), 13 the litanies of the Sacred Heart 'have a particular and most pleasing flavor, which leaves in those who recite them with devotion a deep impression of love and fervor. The invocations express the most beautiful titles of those that are suitable to our divine Savior.'

of each of those lauds and invocations'.[31] As a consequence, the treatises aim particularly at improving the faithful's comprehension of litanies.[32] This intention also determines some recurring formal features of the genre, such as the adoption of an argumentative style and the frequent conclusion of each argumentation with concrete examples (often taken from lives of the saints), as well as the use of a popular register, which entails the willing renounce to sophisticated theological disquisitions.[33] In some cases, however, fostering the conscious recitation of the litanies is not the sole goal, but the litanic invocations rather serve as the starting point (the pretext) for theological reflections that have a value per se.[34]

The idea of the condensation of meaning in the litanic text is well represented in the way our authors commentate the first invocation to the Virgin in the Litany of Loreto ('Holy Mary, pray for us'). Most part of the commentators assert that the very name of Mary contains all of her magnificent attributes. More specifically, authors such as Cavatoni and Mortarino refer to the tradition according to which the name of Mary was not originated by humans, but was attributed by God himself, thus bearing the sign of Mary's intrinsic qualities and of her predestination to be the Mother of God.[35] Each of these qualities are then individually described and discussed. The case of Mary is of course particular, but it exemplifies a more general belief in the evocative power of proper names: the name of the subject invoked in the litanies represents a summa of theological and moral meanings. This is true not only for litanies devoted to an individual subject, but also to those invoking a collective subject, such as the litanies of the saints. From this perspective, every saint represents a particular facet of the theology and the morals endorsed by the Catholic Church, or even a particularly significant moment of the Church's history. Therefore, the recitation of the sequence of saints should evoke in the mind of the ideal faithful a chain of coherent meanings. This concept is well explained by a sentence of John Paul II, who metaphorically defined 'litany' the list of the 512 lay men and women canonized and beatified in the twentieth century: the sequence of their names and appellations (such as *'mater familias'*, *'puer'*, and *'iuvenis'*) constitutes for the pontiff

[31] Bersani (1874), 14–15.

[32] For instance, the anonymous (1933), IX states: 'when one thinks that these litanies [...] are daily repeated by millions and millions of faithful [...] it must be a good thing to look into what they mean'.

[33] Cavatoni (1912), 2.

[34] See for instance Scippa (1999).

[35] Cavatoni (1912) and Mortarino (1938).

a sort of 'identity card' containing 'the history of the Church' and transmitting a message and an invitation to all the faithful. This is a further example of the importance of building an historical identity as one of the tasks of liturgy, especially in the contemporary Church.

Therefore, the comprehension of the litanies is an important part of their performance and clergymen seem attentive in disciplining the mental associations that the single invocations can raise. A number of our authors[36] stress the fact that the primary performance of the litanic text is their public recitation, and consequently that discourses and written comments are propaedutic to the moment of the oral and collective acting. However, the understanding of their meaning also necessarily entails a different kind of performance of litanies, a slower one, involving reflection and acquisition of knowledge. While for the faithful this secondary fruition mainly takes place by listening to the preachers' discourses,[37] written treatises can be considered as indexes of a kind of fruition of the litanic text peculiar to the clergy. The authors of such texts study the litanies, meditate about them, read the relative literature, and then rewrite them by developing and making explicit the meanings of each invocation. In turn, written works intend to help preachers, who then diffuse their ideas among the faithful. Therefore, the books in question are part of a hermeneutic cycle that involves a plurality of subjects. We could also argue that the treatises have a performative character[38] as far as they inevitably push the reader (and the listener to the derived sermons) to reproduce the logical and argumentative path of the writer's reflection. Ecclesiastic writers and readers of this genre are the protagonists of a performance of the litanic text characterized by a slow rhythm, an intellectual and contemplative elaboration. In this private interpretative process, the oral recitation is irrelevant. Despite its propaedeutic and ancillary character, this kind of performance is of primary importance for the preservation and the development of the meaning of the litanic text inside the Church. It is therefore reasonable to hypothesize that this written genre testifies an exegetic process and a kind of intellectual and meditative performance that parallels the oral and public one since the Medieval origins of the litanic texts, especially among the clergymen. This 'intellectual' execution does not contradict or ignore the aesthetic

[36] For instance Bersani (1974), Razzore and Mora (1931).

[37] In this case, regarding the Litany of Loreto the complete fruition of the text should take place in one month (May, the month devoted to the Virgin), according to the tradition of holding one moral discourse on one invocation per day.

[38] Austin (1962).

and multimodal components characterizing the litanic text. This integration of the aesthetic and intellectual components is evident in a particular sub-genre[39] where the verbal comments are accompanied by pictures[40] (see Figure 2). The preface to Razzore and Mora's illustrated book, authored by Cardinal Dalmazio Minoretti, underlines that the pictures are full 'of suggestion and instruction', that the written notes can help everybody to catch the meaning of the litanies, and that the work itself is suitable to meditation.[41] Similarly, the presentation of the illustrated book by Bergagna, Canziani, and Galbiati stresses that the work, which integrates beautiful pictures and wise words, fosters meditation and contemplation.[42] These multimodal works anticipate the contemporary multimodal reformulation – and performance – of litanic texts on the Internet.

4. Digital Renditions of the Litanies

4.a. YouTube as a Performative Ground

However huge it may be (being the first video-sharing platform globally), YouTube has to be understood as much more than an 'archive of recordings'. Indeed, the video has been employed as a key semiotic means of proselytism, at least since the age of cable-TV televangelists[43] and up to the age of spectacularized terrorism.[44] One can *do things with videos*, to paraphrase John L. Austin.[45] As suggested by Stephen D. O'Leary, in the wake of Brenda Danet,[46] 'technology can drive changes in our use of language and our concepts of symbolic action. If the creation of a written document can have the illocutionary force of a speech act, then it is not unreasonable to think that this force can be extended to

---

[39] This sub-genre is represented in our corpus by Razzore and Mora (1931) and Bergagna, Canziani, and Galbiati (1955).

[40] This sub-genre too has more ancient antecedents: Razzore and Mora (1931) mention an eighteenth-century German work by the Glauber brothers. Another antecedent can be detected into the manuscripts of litanies containing miniatures, which were produced since the Middle Ages (see e.g. Ferrari 2017).

[41] Razzore and Mora (1931).

[42] Bergagna, Canziani, and Galbiati (1955).

[43] Johnson (1998).

[44] Nauta (2013) and Leone (2015, 2018).

[45] Austin (1962).

[46] Danet (1996).

cybercommunication.[47] In this perspective, ethnographic research of online videos should not be limited to the analysis of video content (it should not only be the ethnography of an event happened in the past, which is observable thanks to recording); a whole new ethnography can be carried out, by investigating what happens 'on the screen' (what happens in the online interaction between the user(s) and the media content) and 'on this side' of it (what happens to the user(s) during the interaction with the media content). According to Stephen Pihlaja, this is why

> the video is only the beginning of the interaction: the ability to comment on and share the video across the web allows it to become a hub for interaction, both online on a variety of sites (on Facebook pages, Twitter feeds, blogs, etc.) and in offline interaction as users view videos together and comment on the content to one another.[48]

So, on the one hand, the performative nature of the platform lies in its interactive affordances.[49] On the other, it is granted by the fact that 'people are doing the rituals online and the participants are testifying to their efficacy'.[50] As scrupulously reviewed by Ronald Grimes,[51] along with 'rites being presented over the Internet' we can find

> online rituals that people view and participate in 'live'; rituals conducted in virtual reality environments; rituals and myths that people participate in during online gaming; magical rites in which the media device has become a fetish or icon; ritual activity that incorporates the computer as part of the altar space; ritual objects that are delivered 'online'; and cases where the ritual uses the computer as a tool around which its activities are built.[52]

Thus, 'changes in the way a ritual is presented, the way the rules are developed or changed, how people engage with the activity, and even the beliefs about where it can take place'[53] are key aspects the scholar has to take into account.

[47]   O'Leary (2004), 48.
[48]   Pihlaja (2015), 49–50.
[49]   A term popularized by perception psychologist James J. Gibson (1979) and his interpreters, meaning the features a given object or experience does offer to its potential user in order to be used.
[50]   Helland (2013), 37.
[51]   Grimes (2006).
[52]   Helland (2013), 37.
[53]   Helland (2013), 37.

4.b. A Typology of the 'litanie dei santi' on YouTube

The following explorative analysis aims at tracing the idea of the performativity of YouTube videos concerning the litanies of the saints, with a specific focus on the Italian context. Based on what we said about the meditations to be studied as a preparation to the performance of the litanies (see § 3) and the ethnography of live performances of the litanies (§ 2), our hypothesis is that no radical remediation[54] can be identified, but rather sporadic and yet key elements of what we may call a 'performative upsurge'.

The search on YouTube has been carried out as non-logged user, namely without being connected to any email account, in order to minimize the influence of the customization YouTube applies in the selection of the results as concerns navigation history (via cookies) and suggested or sponsored videos. With no systematic intent, nor employing quantitative tools of analysis, a selection of one hundred videos listed in the YouTube SERP[55] for the Italian query *litanie dei santi* ('litanies of the saints') has been watched, with the aim of outlining a – provisional and perfectible – typology; a brief description and elementary analysis of the most representative seventeen of them (see Videography) is here provided.

Whereas the English query 'litanies of the saints' returns 115k results and the Latin *'litaniae sanctorum'* a 17k, the Italian *'litanie dei santi'* is about 14.1k. Due to the functioning of the platform, many of these videos are ascribable to one or more of the following queries (and, therefore, categories), which are the first ten ones suggested by the autocomplete of the internal search engine: *litanie dei santi cantate in italiano, litanie dei santi in latino, litanie dei santi cammino neocatecumenale, litanie dei santi bose, litanie dei santi [canto] gregoriano, litanie dei santi italiano, litanie dei santi gelineau, litanie dei santi frisina, litanie dei santi veglia pasquale, litanie dei santi cantata.*[56]

---

[54] As defined by Bolter and Grusin (1999).

[55] Search Engine Results Page, the list of results selected by the algorithm as pertinent to the query.

[56] As of Oct. 23, 2018. Autocomplete is a form of automatic word completion provided by online search engines; Google and YouTube's search predictions 'are possible search terms you can use that are related to the terms you're typing and what other people are searching for' (bit.ly/gytautocomplete; accessed Oct. 31, 2018). Predictions are made based on factors, like the popularity of the search terms, namely the number of times in which people have entered them as a query on the engine.

Despite its relatively small dimension and the non-systematic character of our analysis,[57] the selected corpus allowed us to outline a typology of six kinds of videos that may constitute a good basis for further in-depth studies.

4.b.1. TV Broadcast

The uploaded video, a recording of a litanic performance, is an extract from a TV broadcast. In this case the remediation is double, since the litanies passed from the live event, to their televised version, to the sample put online on YouTube.

In the video *'Litanie dei Santi - processione del Conclave (2005)'* (see Videography), this two-step remediation process is made explicit via paratextual clues such as the superimposed text 'Replica' and the symbol of the TV channel.

Even though *'LITANIE DEI SANTI – GELINEAU'* does come from a TV broadcast (one can find editing, shots from different angles, transitions, etc., but no paratextual signs), it presents detailed information about the event itself,[58] rather than about its televised rendition. This is due to the fact that the user who uploaded it is the very performer – the organist – in the video; this also explains the focus on the composer of the music (Joseph Gelineau), whose surname is included in the video's title.

4.b.2. Published Music

The uploaded video presents music from a published record, whose editorial metadata are usually automatically identified by the YouTube algorithm; the main difference between the many videos of this kind is the usage of one still image or more images, constituting a slideshow that may be synchronized or not to the recited or sung verbal text.

'Litaniae Sanctorum + Litany of the Saints / Litanie dei Santi'[59] stands as the blockbuster in the series, being the most viewed one in the

---

[57] Due to space restrictions, it was not possible to focus on users' comments, nor on a series of interesting cases of anonymous, misattributed, or ambiguous content.

[58] *'Sabato 30–09-2017 / S. Messa di Professione Perpetua / di Fr. Domenico Morello / Basilica Pontificia Santa Casa di Loreto / Coro della Cappella Musicale Cattedrale di Macerata / Direttore Carlo Paniccia' / Organista Marco Agostinelli'.*

[59] The YouTube automatic metadata retrieval info reads: *'Brano: Litaniae Sanctorum – DNC / Artista: Saint Bernard Choir / Album: Kyrie: Chants from the Soul / Concesso in licenza a YouTube da: HAAWK for a 3rd Party (a nome di Naive Records) e 1 società di gestione dei diritti musicali.'*

whole YouTube SERP for our query; it displays one single picture, a portion of Beato Angelico's depiction of the saints from his famous Fiesole Altarpiece (1424 circa).

'*Litanie dei santi*', with a Polish description ('*Litania do świętych*') and no automatic metadata displayed, employs a peculiar still image, namely what seems to be a stock photo[60] for the query *inkwizycja stosy* ('inquisition piles'; see Figure 3).

Another video called '*Litanie dei santi*' presents quite a postmodern series of pictures of very different kinds and from very different sources, most of them being unrelated to the saint isotopy at all, including apocalyptic images such as an atomic explosion (see Figure 4); the grim tone of the images is mirrored by a user's comment which reads *Dio mio vieni a salvarmi, Signore vieni presto in mio aiuto* ('Make haste, O God, to deliver me; make haste to help me, O Lord!').

'*Litanie dei fiori*' matches a version of *Ave Maria di Lourdes* by Giancarlo Silva (as identified by Google and YouTube's metadata) to a slideshow visualizing the *Litania Mariana dei Fiori* written by Suor Chiara Immacolata Trigilia,[61] so that hundreds of pictures of flowers, their romanticized descriptions, and the subsequent invocations are displayed to the user as the music goes on.

4.b.3. Video-recorded Event

The uploaded video stands as a devotional document of a live performance, with a prominent focus on the local, communitarian dimension, so that there is a proliferation of litanies as in the tradition of specific orders (e.g. Dominicans) or devoted to specific figures (the litanies of *Santissimo Sangue, Vergine Maria*, etc.). Recorded events may include ordinations of priests, presbyteries, and deacons, synods, consecrations of the Virgins, funerals of religious figures, regular liturgy, and ceremonies of various kinds, such as the Easter-related ones or patron's holidays.

'*Litanie dei Santi – Professione Perpetua – Chiesa San Pietro, Viterbo*' is an extract from a perpetual profession of vows; it is featured by the typical enunciational traits of the amateur or found footage video genre, such as the shaking, side shot. A title in the video description and a comment from a user make it legitimate to think that the video is mainly addressed to the local Romanian community.

---

[60] A stock image commercially available via specialized online repositories.

[61] A Clarisse at the Santa Chiara monastery in Biancavilla, Catania. The litanic poem was published in 2005 by the publishing imprint of the monastery.

'Festino dell'Assunta 2011 a Novara di Sicilia – Canto delle Litanie' testifies the momentum from the procession that takes place during the town's patron holiday referenced in the title (August 15); the video has devotional and memorial purposes only, as inferable by the watermark of the freeware software employed for the conversion of the video file from camera to computer that pops up cyclically along the reproduction.

4.b.4. Original Content

The video presents a piece of user-generated content that was most probably created on purpose for being posted onto YouTube as its primary medium. In such cases, the personal and devotional value is of prominent relevance, together with a strong sense of authorship.

As we can deduct from paratextual elements such as the comments, '*LITANIE LAURETANE (illustrate)*' presents the reciting voice of the YouTube user himself, paired with a music composed by a 'former student' of his and pictures from various sources synchronized with the text. A rich textual and hypertextual apparatus is provided in the description: the text of the litanies, links to other videos made by the user, and to his website.

'Litanie al Preziosissimo Sangue di Gesù' features a reciting voice, with a slight Slavic accent, performing the litanic text in what seems to be a recording realized *ad hoc*; this video is particularly interesting because it testifies how users do interact with the multimedia content via comments, which are meant to be invocations or proper prayers (one can find a lot of comments by different users reading 'Amen!'), and because it was uploaded by a quite prolific and followed YouTube channel, which publishes videos on a daily basis, and more than once a day, specifically devoted to online prayers and ceremonies.[62]

4.b.5. Didactic Video

This category is the most sub-articulated one. By 'didactic' we mean here a video providing the YouTube viewer with a quantity of semiotic and paratextual resources so as to reconstruct or simulate the live rendition of the litanic performance or to study and learn the litanic text and performance practices, in order to re-enact them in turn. In other words,

---

[62] On the early hours of Oct. 23, 2018, the latest video, uploaded '7 hours ago' (youtu.be/uuCeWhf95Ho), already has 336 likes, 7 dislikes, and 3491 views.

we define as 'didactic' the slideshow videos that pair the recited or sung text of the litanies with pictures, captions or subtitles, and scores or musical notes, more or less synchronized, in order to provide the name of each saint with his or her visual representation and the recorded performance with the corresponding series of musical notes.

'*Litanie dei Santi in latino*' presents a slideshow employing three pictures only, so that there is no actual synchronization between the recited text in the soundtrack,[63] which is in Latin (as suggested by the title), and what the YouTube user is seeing. The focus of the slideshow is rather the indication of the response that the user-believer is supposed to utter (*'ora pro nobis', 'orate pro nobis', 'te rogamus audinos'*, etc.): contrarily to the pictures, responses are synchronized with the sound. It is interesting to notice that, diversely from the other videos uploaded by the very same channel ('Blog Cattolici'), the comments were disabled; one can assume that this happened due to a controversy of some kind (maybe concerning the usage of Latin instead of Italian).[64]

'*LITANIE DEI SANTI per la Veglia Pasquale (Diego Montaiuti)*' presents an original audio content, namely the piano tune of the title, written and performed by the user who owns the YouTube channel; the recording is acoustic, so that we can hear the sound of the hands hitting the keys. The instrumental music, conveyed through a passionate but imprecise performance (particularly, as regards rhythm), is matched to a slideshow with the score, the notes (for those who would not be able to read notation), and the lyrics of the invocations.

'*Invocazione dei Santi 1*' matches a field recording of 'the Acclamations adopted during the Mass in the parishes of Sammartini, Caselle, Ronchi, Bolognina, Dozza, Calamosco, within the diocese of Bologna' (as the description reads) to one single slide featuring a summary of the notes and the lyrics; despite this limitedness, it is clear that the aim of the video is not only testifying the practice, but also making online users 'sing together' (which is also the very name of the YouTube channel in Italian, *insieme cantiamo*). The recorded performance features guitar, organ, and flute, as regards the musical part, and a male and female lead vocals, for the call, and a small choir, for the response.

'*Litanie dei Santi. Coro Unacum Angelis. Dirige R. Caiazzo, all'organo P. L. Marino, solista A. Perrella*' presents a live recording,

---

[63] '*Canto Gregoriano Desde Jerusalem by Monjes de Santos Sepulcros as published by Producciones AR/The Orchard Music*' as the automatic metadata specify.

[64] See Ponzo (forthcoming).

datable thanks to the information in the description (Easter Vigil 2015), with a prominent focus on authorship (we are given the full detail of the interpreters in the title); the subtitles and captions flow in sync with the invocations of the litanic text (with no formal distinction between call and response) and, occasionally, still pictures from the Easter celebrations are inserted in the flow of the live footage.

'*LITANIE GREGORIANE DEI SANTI*', employing the very same musical piece of '*Litaniae Sanctorum + Litany of the Saints / Litanie dei Santi*' (see § 4.b.2.; perhaps the most standard musical version in usage), presents a slideshow of synchronized pictures from different pictorial sources and the related identifying captions (e.g. '*Sancte Basili et Gregori*') and invocations ('*orate pro nobis*').

The same type of semiotic resources is featured in '*LITANIE SANTO ROSARIO*', with the difference that both the recited and the written text is in Italian. Furthermore, there is a prominent focalization on the actions evoked by the invocations; at 05:30, for instance, the picture of a soldier kneeling before Jesus and hugging him in cry, with the Golgotha in the background, is employed as a figurativization device, to provide the response *Perdonaci o Signore* ('Forgive us, Lord') with a visual companion.

4.b.6. Reinterpretation

Technically, the videos included in this cluster would belong either to the type at § 4.b.2. or § 4.b.4., since they happen to include published music or content created *ad hoc* for the YouTube upload; nevertheless, we chose to create a dedicated group due to the specificities of some notable tokens, as to highlight the relevance of the transtextual[65] levels in action.

'*Litanie dei Santi (Rock) – I Maddalen's Brothers*', for instance, proposes a song by a Christian band, the Maddalen's Brothers, that recontextualizes the invocations to the saints in a folk-Medieval sort of soft-rock style, including the refunctionalization of the calls and responses as lines and refrains and the usage of a vocoder/autotune-filtered male vocal part. As noted by a user (whose comment reads 'Perfect timing:-*'), the video was purportedly uploaded in coincidence with the All Hallow's Eve, so that it is possible to hypothesize an – extra-liturgical – ritual usage of the song.

---

[65] Genette (1982).

4.c. From Recording to Remediation

Through our survey, we have identified videos that diversely stress or feature one or more of the following aspects: intersemiotic translation (still image or slideshows for recorded music), authoriality (original uploads), remediation (TV footage), devotional and community values (footage of live events), performativity (didactic videos), and transtextuality (re-interpretations).

Our main focus concerned mediation; in this respect, there are at least two main aspects to be addressed: the first one is the multimodal encoding of the litanies and the second is the elasticity of the medium in channelling performative affordances. Both aspects are part of a communication strategy aiming at conveying immediacy through hypermediation and transparency through opacity;[66] in other words, the analysed videos build up layers of interfaces and semiotic resources in order to give the user the illusion of an immediate religious experience, that is the simulation or the substitutive experience of a live, face-to-face litanic performance.

As concerns the litanies, the most interesting case is the one of the slideshows; pictures of the saints are being synchronized with their recited or sung names (in a kind of 'mickeymousing'),[67] as an attempt of widening the semiotic resources at stake. Thanks to the visualization of the saint figure, such digital renditions make it possible the recognition of the saint (e.g. his or her traditional iconography, the circumstances of the death, etc.), which is key to the functioning and the effectiveness of the litanic performance. The perlocutionary effect[68] aimed at by this kind of videos is the same as in the case of the variations introduced during the baptism observed in Pordenone (see § 2) as well as the written and illustrated treatises on the meditations (§ 3).

As concerns YouTube specifically, it is possible to identify digital renditions of the litanies that rely on the features of the medium in order to reconstruct the conditions of a litanic performance and, therefore, summon the latent presence of the user-believer and his or her agency; it is the case with what we have called didactic videos, which propose a kind of call-and-response or karaoke-style litanic reading.

---

[66] Bolter and Grusin (1999).

[67] The practice, perfected and popularized by Disney cartoon studios (hence the name, alluding to Mickey Mouse), to synchronize the moving images with the music that would have served as their soundtrack.

[68] The perlocutionary component of a given speech act, as defined by Austin (1962), concerns its consequences on the listener (e.g. persuading, scaring, etc.).

5. Conclusions

Despite the fact that the oral and collective recitation is generally perceived by believers as the main model of litanic performance, our enquiry shows that other kinds of enactment and remediation play an important role in shaping both litanic performative features and meanings. Litanies are at the centre of a complex dialectics between private and public performance, and their identity depends on a multifaceted interaction between different media, from speech to written text, from picture to video.

The relationship between words and pictures is particularly interesting and deserves further analysis. While in the illustrated treatises the iconography appears to be traditional and responds to the stereotyped collective imagery connected to saintly figures, the analyzed videos display a proteiform iconography, characterized by the proliferation of non-traditional subjects and sources.

The re-elaboration of the litanic text is detectable in each of the litanic renditions that we analyzed (the variations introduced in the oral performance, the comments and images in the treatises, and the interplay between text, music, and images in online videos). The semiotic expansion of the litanic text is often due to the widespread idea that litanies, under the surface of their substance of expression and their rigid formal structure, hide a deep richness of meanings that needs to be expressed explicitly. The perlocutionary effect presupposed by this explicitation of implicit meanings is to provide participants with the cognitive competences enabling them to fully understand the litanies. This understanding is not strictly necessary for the felicity of the performance of the text per se, but it is fundamental at two deeper levels: it is crucial, firstly, for the fulfilment of the narrative program contained *in nuce* in the litanic text (narrating the identity of the invoked characters and, consequently, of the Church) and, secondly, for the efficacy of the litanies in shaping the identity of the believing performer.

In addition to this explanatory function, the online renditions of litanies also display another peculiar and unprecedented function, which consists in freely expressing and sharing subjective mental associations connected to the litanic text. This is evident for instance in the videos associating litanies to apocalyptic or inquisitorial imageries. While the recitation of litanies in ceremonial gatherings and the meditations expressed and fostered in the treatises are 'mediated' by the Church, Internet allows a non-mediated public exposition of individual and unconventional ideas associated to the litanic texts.

Semiotic complexity is undoubtedly a constitutive feature of the litanic genre. However, the changing equilibrium between performative options, interpretative trends, and kinds of remediation depends on historical and cultural circumstances. This is evident not only in the above-discussed dialectics between the ecclesiological and the historical identity-building value attributed to the litanic acting, but also in the variable and growingly blurred relationship between private and public performance. Indeed, the prominence attributed to the public recitation of litanies can be traced back to the Council of Trent, which prohibited silent prayer in order to avoid heresy and regulated the occasions when private prayer was admitted, based on a restricted corpus of liturgical texts, rigorously in Latin. These rules contrasted with the aristocratic tradition of the private prayer based on the 'Books of Hours',[69] widespread in the Middle Ages. The nineteenth- and twentieth-century treatises demonstrate a renewed acceptance of private practices of prayer and meditation, especially because they do not exclude the lay faithful as readers and therefore interpreters who can meditate and perform litanies in private contexts. The twenty-first century digital remediation of the litanies tends to dilute the border between public and private fruition: even though an individual watching a litanic video on YouTube typically sits alone in front of a screen, the overall fruition of a video should be considered as set within a communitarian dimension; indeed, users share an experience by the very fact of watching the same video and interact with each other through comments, tags, and posting.

---

[69] Rozzo (1993).

Bibliography

Andreoletti, M. (1941) *Le litanie del Sacro Cuore: commento e riflessioni pratiche con esempi storici* [2nd edn], Monza [Ancora].

Anonymous (1933) *Il più bel fiore del paradiso: considerazioni sulle litanie lauretane* [3rd edn], Vicenza [Società anonima tipografica fra cattolici vicentini; 1st edn 1904].

Austin, J. L. (1962) *How to do things with words*, Oxford [Oxford University Press].

Barthe, É. (1858) *Monument à la gloire de Marie. Litanies à la Très-Sainte Vierge illustrées – accompagnées de meditations*, Paris [Librairie Catholique de P.-J. Camus].

Baumstark, A. (1958) *Comparative Liturgy*, Westminster MD [English edn from the 3rd French edn of *Liturgie comparée*, Chevetogne, 1953].

Bergagna, E. R., L. Canziani and L. M. Galbiati (1955) *Cantico mariano: sussidi alla contemplazione delle glorie di Maria SS. secondo le litanie lauretane*, Milano [Scuola Beato Angelico].

Beroldus (1894) *Beroldus sive ecclesiae Ambrosianae Mediolanensis kalendarium et ordines saec. XII: Ex codice Ambrosiano*, Milan [Magistretti].

Bersani Dossena, A. (1871) *Il mese di maggio: discorsetti ad onore della Vergine*, Lodi [Tipografia vescovile di Carlo Cagnola].

Biffi, I. (1993) 'La riforma del rito ambrosiano,' *La Scuola Cattolica* 121, 367–86.

Bolter, J. D., and R. Grusin (1999) *Remediation: Understanding New Media*, Cambridge, Massachusetts [MIT Press].

Cavatoni, A. (1912) *Le litanie della SS.ma Vergine Maria: spiegate al popolo con discorsi istruttivi e morali* [3rd edn], Trento [Tipografia Editrice Artigianelli].

Cavedoni, C. (1850) *Le litanie lauretane della Beata Vergine Maria Madre di Dio dichiarate coi riscontri delle sacre scritture e de' santi padre*, Modena [Soliani].

Cornet, N. J. (1873) *Les litanies de la Très Sainte Vierge: explications, exemples, traits, notices relatifs au culte de la Sainte Vierge: ouvrage utile au clergé at aux pieux fidèles* [3rd edn], Paris [Libr. Internationale Catholique].

Danet, B. (1996) 'Speech, Writing, and Performativity: An Evolutionary View of the History of Constitutive Ritual,' in B. L. Gunnarsson, P. Linell and B. Nordberg (eds), *The Construction of Professional Discourse*, London [Longmans], 13–41.

De Clerck, P. (2001) 'Les lois de Baumstark, l'evolution de la liturgie,' in Taft and Winkler (2001), 233–49.

Galofaro, F. (2018) 'Le Litanie ai Santi: tempo, memoria, gerarchia,' in S. M. Barillari and M. Di Febo (eds), *Calendari. L'uomo, il tempo, le stagioni*, Monza [Virtuosa-Mente].

— and M. M. Kubas (2016) 'Dei Genitrix: A Generative Grammar for Traditional Litanies,' *Open Access Series in Informatics* 53, 12:1–12:8.

Genette, G. (1982) *Palimpsestes. La littérature au second degré*, Paris [Éditions du Seuil].

Gibson, J. J. (1979) *The Ecological Approach to Visual Perception*, Boston [Houghton Mifflin].

Greimas, A. J. (1987) 'A Problem of Narrative Semiotics: Objects of Value,' in *On Meaning: Selected Writings in Semiotic Theory*, Minneapolis [University of Minnesota Press].

Greimas, A. J., and J. Courtés (1982) *Semiotics and Language: an Analytical Dictionary*, Bloomington [Indiana University Press].

Grimes, R. (2006) *Rite Out of Place: Ritual, Media, and the Arts*, Oxford [Oxford University Press].

Helland, C. (2013) 'Ritual,' in Campbell (2013), 25–40.

John Paul II (2000) *Il Giubileo dell'Apostolato dei Laici. 26 novembre 2000: l'Omelia e l'Angelus di Giovanni Paolo II e le litanie dei 521 santi e beati laici canonizzati e beatificati nel XX secolo. Supplemento all'OsservatoreRomanodel 26 novembre 2000*, Vatican City [Editrice l'Osservatore Romano].

Johnson, E. (1998) 'The Emergence of Christian Video and the Cultivation of Videoevangelism,' in L. Kintz and J. Lesage (eds), *Media, Culture, and the Religious Right*, Minneapolis [University of Minnesota Press], 191–210.

Lapidge, M. (1991) *Anglo-Saxon Litanies of the Saints*, London [Henry Bradshaw Society].

Leone, M. (2015) 'Propaganda mala fide: Towards a comparative semiotics of violent religious persuasion,' *Semiotica* 207, 631–55.

— (2018) 'Conversione e complotto. Il reclutamento del fondamentalismo religioso violento,' in A. Prato (ed.), *Comunicazione e potere. Le strategie retoriche e mediatiche per il controllo del consenso*, Roma [Aracne], 63–78.

Magistretti, M. (ed.) (1897) *Monumenta Veteris Liturgiae Ambrosianae* [vol. 1], Milano.

— (ed.) (1905) *Monumenta Veteris Liturgiae Ambrosianae* [vol. 2], Milano.

Magnoli, C. (1995) 'La liturgia funebre nella tradizione del rito Ambrosiano,' *La Scuola Cattolica* 123, 217–57.

— (1996) 'Un nuovo rituale di iniziazione cristiana ambrosiano?,' *Ambrosianus* 72, 500–21.

Marsciani, F. (2012) 'Il discorso della preghiera,' in *Minima semiotica*, Milano-Udine [Mimesis].

Ferrari, M. (2017) 'I rotoli delle litanie triduane Ambr. Z 256 sup.,' in *Miscellanea Graecolatina* [vol. 5], Milano [Biblioteca Ambrosiana – Centro Ambrosiano], 231–46.

Mortarino, G., (1938) *La Vergine invocata nelle litanie lauretane: sermoni per il mese di maggio con varie citazioni e numerosi esempi* [2nd edn], Vicenza [Società anonima tipografica fra cattolici vicentini; 1st edn 1934].

Nauta, A., (2013) 'Radical Islam, Globalisation and Social Media: Martyrdom Videos on the Internet,' in M. Gillespie, D. Herbert and A. Greenhill (eds), *Social Media and Religious Change*, Berlin [De Gruyter], 121–42.

O'Leary, S. D. (2004) 'Cyberspace as Sacred Space: Communicating Religion on Computer Networks,' in L. Dawson and D. E. Cowan (eds), *Religion Online: Finding Faith on the Internet*, London [Routledge], 37–58.

Piccione, G. (1896) *Mese di maggio: le grandezze di Maria SS. Svelate nelle litanie lauretane: brevi discorsi compilati con figure, fatti ed esempi tratti alla S. Scrittura e SS. Padri* [2nd edn], Alessandria [Tipografia Giovanni Jacquemod].

Pihlaja, S. (2015) 'Analysing YouTube interaction: a discourse-centred approach,' in S. Cheruvallil-Contractor and S. Shakkour (eds), *Digital Methodologies in the Sociology of Religion*, London [Bloomsbury], 49–58.

Pierno, F. (ed.) (2015) *The Church and the languages of Italy before the Council of Trent*, Toronto [Pontifical Institute of Medieval Studies].

Ponzo, J. (forthcoming) 'The representation of Latin and liturgy in 20th-century Italian narrative,' in *Ancient and Artificial Languages in Today's Culture*, Rome [Aracne].

Razzore, D., and D. Mora (1931) *Le Litanie Lauretane in onore della Vergine Madre di Dio*. Acquasanta, Genova [Santuario N. S. Acquasanta].

Rozzo, U. (1993) *Linee per una storia dell'editoria religiosa in Italia 1465–1600*, Udine [Arti Grafiche Friulane].

Sadowski, W. (2011) *Litania i poezja. Na materiale literatury polskiej od XI do XXI wieku*, Warszawa [WUW].

Sandigliano, G. (1923) *Corona di fiori sul capo del glorioso S. Giuseppe ossia tracce di discorsi sulle litanie del San Patriarca per un mese di predicazione in suo onore*, Casale Monferrato [Unione Tipografica Popolare].

Schuster, I. (1953) *Pensieri mariani su le litanie lauretane*, Milano [STEM. Pontificia editrice arcivescovile Giovanni Daverio].

Scippa, V. (1999) *Le litanie del Sacro Cuore. Un cammino di catechesi per il terzo millennio.* Casale Monferrato [Piemme].

Svampa, D. (1913) *Le Litanie del Sacro Cuore di Gesù: studio storico e teologico e considerazioni divote*, Milano [R. Ghirlanda].

Taft, R. F. (2001) 'Anton Baumstark's Comparative Liturgy Revisited,' in Taft and Winkler (2001), 191–232.

— and G. Winkler (eds) (2001) *Comparative Liturgy Fifty Years After Anton Baumstark (1872–1948)*, Roma [Pontificio Istituto Orientale].

Valli, N. (2016) *Il triduo pasquale ambrosiano*, Roma [Edizioni liturgiche].

Videography

All the videos were accessed on October 31, 2018.

'Litanie dei Santi – processione del Conclave (2005)', youtu.be/GYlrh4JKccE, 09:57 minn., uploaded on Apr. 6, 2012, couting 125,928 views.

'LITANIE DEI SANTI – GELINEAU', youtu.be/GqplcGzZXgo, 14:02 minn., Nov. 25, 2017, 2506 views.

'Litaniae Sanctorum + Litany of the Saints / Litanie dei Santi', youtu.be/KiM9uJIN64g, 08:08 minn., June 16, 2008, 1,058,048 views.

'Litanie dei santi', youtu.be/hOwNEtg7V94, 08:02 minn., March 22, 2012, 6879 views.

'Litanie dei santi', youtu.be/oEiSw-ZjEcI, 03:53, March 22, 2015, 8558 views.

'Litanie dei fiori', youtu.be/s8eozWMLYX4, 06:15, Apr. 22, 2009, 985 views.

'Litanie dei Santi – Professione Perpetua – Chiesa San Pietro, Viterbo', youtu.be/O8HJr9sPl6k, 08:97, March 11, 2018, 208 views.

'Festino dell'Assunta 2011 a Novara di Sicilia – Canto delle Litanie', youtu.be/4vhkSor3nAE, 09:35, Aug. 21, 2011, 1681 views.

'LITANIE LAURETANE (illustrate)', youtu.be/AuSFgFLQcyE, 02:55, Feb. 12, 2017, 12,600 views.

'Litanie al Preziosissimo Sangue di Gesù', youtu.be/sOHPgL3_-Xs, 04:21, Feb. 28, 2018, 2848 views.

'Litanie dei Santi in latino', youtu.be/Wm-IMjXis4A, 06:25, March 8, 2015, 5085 views.

'LITANIE DEI SANTI per la Veglia Pasquale (Diego Montaiuti)', youtu.be/2OAOI55Uh60, 07:47, Feb. 21, 2015, 9278 views.

'Invocazione dei Santi 1', youtu.be/VTtCKJmy9Io, 09:10, Aug. 10, 2014, 843 views.

'Litanie dei Santi. Coro Unacum Angelis. Dirige R. Caiazzo, all'organo P. L. Marino, solista A. Perrella', youtu.be/mN3aPqLzZpM, 05:44, Apr. 5, 2015, 916 views.

'LITANIE GREGORIANE DEI SANTI', youtu.be/scHLnPKw7Wo, 08:15, Aug. 14, 2018, 227 views.

'LITANIE SANTO ROSARIO', youtu.be/xnZGHIWSTDI, 06:40, Aug. 22, 2012, 5006 views.

'Litanie dei Santi (Rock) – I Maddalen's Brothers', youtu.be/KnEUC7yjGYA, 04:18, Oct. 31, 2017, 1547 views.

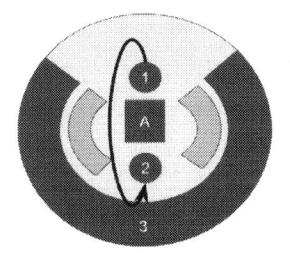

Figure 1. Temple of Divine Providence, Warsaw. Map of the crypt by Francesco Galofaro.

Figure 2. '*Sancta Maria Ora Pro Nobis*', Table 6 from the treatise by Razzore and Mora (1931).

Figure 3. Inquisition-styled still image employed as the visual companion for the YouTube video '*Litanie dei santi*' (youtu.be/hOwNEtg7V94).

Figure 4. Apocalyptic stock image employed as a visual companion for the YouTube video '*Litanie dei santi*' (youtu.be/oEiSw-ZjEcI).

INDEX

Scriptural Index

1 Chronicles 94
    1 Chr 6:31 96
    1 Chr 13,15,16 92
    1 Chr 14 94
    1 Chr 15–16 92, 94
    1 Chr 15:29 93
    1 Chr 16 96
    1 Chr 16:7–36 94
    1 Chr 16:31–33 94
    1 Chr 16:35 94
    1 Chr 16:37–42 94
    1 Chr 16:43 94
    1 Chr 17 94
2 Chronicles
    2 Chr 36:23 96
1 Corinthians 131
    1 Cor 2:9 138
    1 Cor 9:27 136
    1 Cor 14:7 96
Daniel
    Dn 2:18–19,28,37,44 96
    Dn 3:52–90^{deut} 22
Deuteronomy 98
    Dt 6:5 131
    Dt 12:5,11,21 90
    Dt 14:23–24 90
    Dt 16:2 90
    Dt 26:2 90
Exodus 96, 97
    Ex 2:13–15 131
    Ex 15:20 93
    Ex 19:11 89
    Ex 30:6 91
    Ex 40:31–34 90
Ezra
    Ezr 2:1 96
    Ezr 5:11–12 96
    Ezr 6:9–10 96
    Ezr 7:12,21,23 96
Galatians
    Gal 5:16 137
Genesis 96, 97
    Gn 24:3,7 96
Jonah
    Jon 1:9 96
    Jon 4:24 92
Joshua 98
    Jo 3:3–5 90
    Jo 3:14–17 90
    Jo 4:19 90

Jo 5:10   90
Jo 6:8–14   91
Jo 6:20–21   91
Jo 7:6   91
Judges   98
Leviticus
   Lv 16:2   91
   Lv 19:18   131
Luke   98, 131
   Lk 10:27   136
   Lk 18:20   136
   Lk 6:27   137
   Lk 6:31   136
   Lk 9:23   136
Mark   131
   Mk 7:31–37   277
   Mk 10:19   136
   Mk 12:30–31   136
Matthew   131
   Mt 5:10   137
   Mt 5:44   137
   Mt 7:12   136
   Mt 16:24   136
   Mt 19:18   136
   Mt 22:37–39   136
   Mt 23:3   137
   Mt 24:30–31   94
   Mt 25:36   136
Nehemiah   99
   Neh 1:4–5   96
   Neh 2:4,20   96
Numbers   96, 97
   Nm 4   92
   Nm 4:15–20   92
   Nm 4:19   92
   Nm 7:9   92
   Nm 12:8   89
1 Peter   131
   1 Pet 2:17   136

1 Pet 3:9   136
Philippians   131
   Phil 3:3   92
Psalms   5, 11, 98, 99, 108, 200–204, 218
   Ps 100:1–5   93
   Ps 105, 96   94
   Ps 106   99
   Ps 136   94–97, 98, 99
   Ps 136:5–9   95
   Ps 136:10–24   95
   Ps 149:3   93
   Ps 150:4   93
Romans   131
   Rom 12:11   137
   Rom 13:9   136
1 Samuel   98, 99
   1 Sm 4:22   91
   1 Sm 6:14   93
   1 Sm 14:18f   91
   1 Sm 16:6   93
   1 Sm 16:7   93
2 Samuel   98, 99
   2 Sm 6   92, 94
   2 Sm 6:1–4   93
   2 Sm 6:4,16   93
   2 Sm 6:5,15   93
   2 Sm 6:12,18   91
   2 Sm 6:14,16   93
   2 Sm 7:1,9   92
   2 Sm 7:2–4   92
1 Thessalonians   131
   1 Thes 5:15   136
1 Timothy   131
   1 Tm 3:3   137
Titus   131
   Ti 1:7   137
Tobit
   Tb 4:16   131, 136

Index of Manuscripts

Berlin
    Ägyptisches Museum und
        Papyrussammlung
        P. 3027   34
    Staatsbibliothek
        Mus.ms.autogr. Mozart,
          W.A. 243   237

Cambridge
    Magdalene College
        MS 1236   199, 217

Dresden
    Sächsische Landesbibliothek —
        Staats- und Universitäts-
        bibliothek
        MSS Bibl.-Arch. III H b 787^d
          (Zelenka's scores)   232, 243
        Mus. 2358-D-55 (Zelenka's
          scores)   232
        Mus. 2358-D-56 (Zelenka's
          scores)   232

Dublin
    Trinity College Library
        KK.k.55 (*Processionale...*
          Sarum, 1525)   199

Florence
    Biblioteca Medicea Laurenziana
        Pluteus 29.1 (monophonic
          conducti)   144–148, 153, 156, 158, 162–165

London
    British Library
        Add. MS 34191   208–209, 219
        Add. MS 36881 (*De monte
          lapis scinditur*)   143, 161
        Add. MS 49999 (Book of
          Hours)   202

    British Museum
        EA 10554 (*The Greenfield
          Papyrus*)   35
    Lambeth Palace Library
        ****H.5142.P.1545*
          (*Processionale... Sarum*,
          1545)   199, 200, 211

Munich
    Bayerische Staatsbibliothek
        Mus.ms. Mm 779   242
        Mus.ms. Mm 781   242

New York
    Public Library
        *MSS Mus. Res. *MNZ
          (Chirk)*   212

Oxford
    Bodleian Library
        Auct. T inf. III.17
          (*Processionale... Sarum*,
          1525)   199
        MS Rawl. liturgy. e. 45
          (*Processionale... Sarum*,
          1525)   199
        MSS Mus. Sch. e. 420–22
          (*Wanley Partbooks*)   209

Paris
    Bibliothèque nationale de France
        latin 1139 (*Resonemus hoc
          natali*)   143, 161
        latin 5267 (Marian
          litany)   143, 165
        Rés. B. 1852 (*Processionale...
          Sarum*, 1545)   200, 211

Tours
    Bibliothèque municipal
        MS 927 (*Salve virgo
          virginum*)   143

Vatican
    Biblioteca Apostolica
        MS Barberini lat. 4184 (*olim* XLVII.55) (Palestrina's scores) 226
        MS Capella Guilia *XIII.24* (*olim* Cod.60) (Palestrina's scores) 226

Washington, DC
    Folger Shakespeare Library
        STC 16237 (*Processionale... Sarum*, 1528) 206–209, 216

Index of Ancient and Medieval Names

Abydos, Seti I kinglist 28
Abydos, Seti I litany 28
Alas! Wise Lord, Counselor 54, 57, 80–81
Alma redemptoris mater 144
Ambrose, Archbishop of Milan 131, 280
Amduat 35, 38, 40
Amenhotep III, Pharaoh 29
Anonymous works[1]
Athanasius of Alexandria 131
Augustine of Hippo 131
Ave Maria virgo virginum 144, 146–155, 158–159, 163, 166
Basil of Caesarea 131
Benedict of Nursia 4, 125–136, 180
Beroldus of Milan 276, 296
Book of Caverns 38
Book of Gates 38
Book of the Dead, spell 15 31
Book of the Dead, spell 125 part B 31
Cantigas de Santa Maria 143
Cassian (John Cassian) 131
Constantine V, Emperor 106
Constantine VII, Emperor 4, 102–104, 107, 109–114, 119, 121
Cyprian of Carthage 126, 131
David, King of Israel 91–94, 96–97
De monte lapis scinditur 161
Devastating Combat-Impulse 52

Dialogue of a Man with his Soul 34
Dominic de Guzmán 180
Egeria, pilgrim 3, 188–189
Elevated Ox of the Land 56–57
Emesal Litany of the Gods 76
Enki, a liturgical prayer to 81–82
Enki/Marduk, a lamentful prayer to 59
Enlil and Ninlil 48–49
Enlil, a liturgical prayer to 84
Epic of Gilgamesh 72
Esna, Osiris litany 27
Evagrius of Pontus 131
extispicy omens 49
Fashioning Man and Woman 56, 59, 63
Fashioning Man and Woman 60
Francis of Assisi 180
Geoffrey de Vinsauf 156, 167
George Pachymeres 106, 121
Gregory Pakourianos 111, 121
Haymo of Feversham 182, 191
Hermann of Reichenau, see *Alma redemptoris mater*
Honored One, Wild Ox 55
Ibn Rustah (Ahmad ibn Rustah Isfahani) 106, 121
Ignace of Smolensk 105, 121
In the Steppe, in the Early Grass 60–61

[1] All such texts are indexed under the first word of their common title.

Irene Doukaina 111, 121
Isaac Komnenos 116
It Touches the Earth Like a Storm 53, 58
Jerome of Stridon 131
Johannes de Grocheio 158, 167
John II Komnenos 111, 121
John Malalas 121
John Skylitzes 113, 121
Karnak, Tuthmosis III Contra-temple 29
Law of Manou 126–127
Litany of the Sun 35–38
Liutprand of Cremona 121
Louis VII of France 105
Luxor, Ramesses II Great Litany 28–29
Manuel II Palaiologos 105
Manuel of Stroumitza 111, 121
Marduk's Address to the Demons 49
Michael Attaleiates 111, 113, 121
Michael Psellos 113, 116, 121
Michael V, Emperor 113
Nabû, a liturgical prayer to 83
Neilos of Tamasia 111, 121
Nergal, a liturgical prayer to 77–80
O summi regis mater inclita 144–148, 155–161, 166
Odo of Deuil 105, 122
Oh, brickwork of Ekur 58, 63
Passio Juliani 125
Pelagius, British monk 131
Pepin the Short 106
Pérotin the Great 145
Peter the Magistros 102
Philip the Chancellor 145
Philotheos, Protospatharios 102

Poetical Stela of Tuthmosis III 33
Porphyry of Tyre 131
Pseudo-Dionysius Areopagite 117–118, 122
Pseudo-Kodinos 102
Pyramid Texts, 573 32
Pyramid Texts, 601 30
Rabanus Maurus 183
Resonemus hoc natali 161
Rule of Master 126
Salva nos, stella maris 144, 146–155, 158–159, 163, 166
Salve regina celorum 153
Salve regina, Mater misericoriae 202
Salve virgo virginum 143–144, 146–155, 158–159, 163, 164, 166
Sentences of Sextus 125, 131
Senwosret III, Hymns to 32–33
Sergius I, Patriarch of Constantinople 102
Sextus (believed to be Quintus Sextius the Elder), see *Sentences of Sextus*
Sokar, Ritual of 31
Solar Litany, Tomb of Ramesses IX 38
Sulpicius Severus 131
The Defiled Apsu 53
The House Is Encircled Like a Cattle Pen 59, 61
The Lowing Cow 55–56
The Raging Sea 51, 57, 62
Timothy Evergetinos 111, 122
Urra 48
Vinaya 126
Yahya Harun ibn 106
Zoe Porphyrogenita, Empress 113

Index of Modern Names

Abitz Friedrich 37, 38, 42
Addamiano Antonio 18

Adlgasser Anton Cajetan 236, 244, 245

Adrom Faried 44
Ahrweiler Hélène 106, 122
Akyürek Engin 122
Allen James P. 30, 32, 42
Amiet Robert 175, 191
Anderson Gordon A. 148, 167
Anderson Michael A. 144, 167
Andreoletti Maurilio 280, 281, 282, 296
Andrieu Michel 184, 185, 191
Angelov Dimiter 122, 123
Angermüller Hannelore 242, 244
Angermüller Rudolph 242, 244, 245
Aplin John 209, 217,
Aranda Doncel Juan 16
Assmann Jan 4, 25, 26, 31, 32, 35, 38, 40, 42
Astier Colette 9, 16
Atlas Allan W. 226, 228, 244
Austin John L. 284, 285, 293, 296
Auzépy Marie-France 117, 122
Avraméa Anna 123
Bács Tamás Antal 23, 29, 42
Bailey Terence 200, 217
Baines John 30, 42
Bąkowska-Czerner Grażyna 42,
Baldick Chris 101, 122
Baldovin John F. 101, 122, 181, 191
Baltzer, Rebecca A. 146, 167
Bandy Anastasius 121,
Barchie, D. 93, 98
Barillari Sonia Maura 297
Baroffio Giacomo 6, 16
Barta Winfried 38, 42,
Barthe Édouard 281, 296
Bataillon Lionel 15, 16
Bauer Franz Alto 123
Bauer Wilhelm A. 242, 244
Baumstark Anton 2–3, 16, 22, 275, 278–279, 296, 297, 299
Bekker Immanuel 121
Benedict XV, Pope 282

Benzinger Immanuel 89, 98
Berg Adam 221, 223
Bergagna Ernesto R. 280, 285, 296
Berger Albrecht 102, 122
Bernard George W. 197, 217
Berry Virginia Gingerick 122
Bersani Dossena Angelo 280, 283, 284, 296
Bianchi Lino 226, 228, 229, 244
Biffi Inos 280, 296
Bishop Edmund 3, 16
Bitterman Helen Robbins 106, 122
Black Jeremy A. 49, 50, 67
Blackburn Bonnie J. 223, 244
Blasi Angela Maria 252
Blazey David Anthony 6, 16, 226, 244
Böck Barbara 68
Boeckmann Aquinata 126, 129, 135
Bolter Jay David 287, 293, 296
Bonney Barbara 252
Boone Graeme M. 170
Boring M. Eugene 96, 98
Bornert René 118, 122
Boudinhon Auguste 168
Bougard François 121
Bourmont Clément de 10, 16
Bourriau Janine 44
Bowers Roger 197, 199, 202, 203, 205, 217
Bradshaw Murray C. 223, 244
Braga Carlo 124
Branner Robert 146, 167
Bresciani Antonio 257, 263, 266, 271
Brockett Clyde W. 161, 167
Brown Howard Mayer 228, 244
Brubaker Leslie 101, 122
Bruun Mette Birkedal 168
Büchner Eberhard 251, 252
Bugnini Annibale 175, 191
Bukofzer Manfred F. 161, 169

Burkard Günter   25, 31, 42
Burmeister Annelies   251
Butterfield Ardis   148, 167
Byrd William   6, 210–211, 218
Cabezón Antonio de   7, 210, 213–215, 218
Cable Margaret   251
Cabrol Fernand   2, 16
Cachemaille Gilles   252
Caldwell Mary Channen   7, 146, 147, 153, 156, 158, 167
Camargo Martin   167
Cameron Alan   104, 123
Campa Carmona Ramón de la   16
Cancik-Kirschbaum Eva Christiane   68
Canziani L.   280, 285, 296
Capelle Bernard   188, 191
Caplin William E.   241, 244
Caria Clemente   265, 271
Carlson, Rachel Golden   144, 161, 167
Carpitella Diego   261, 262, 264, 271
Carranza Bartolomé   217
Case Steve   98
Catanzaro Christine D. de   236, 244
Cavatoni Angelo   280, 281, 283, 296
Cavedoni Celestino   280, 281, 296
Chaguinian Christophe   167
Chaouachi Slaheddine   20
Chapman Roger E.   244
Charles Sydney Robinson   199, 217
Chavasse Antoine   181, 191
Cheruvallil-Contractor Sariya   298
Cheynet Jean-Claude   113, 123
Chiesa Paolo   121
Chiţoiu Dan   101, 123
Chiu Remi   223, 244
Christian Ed   93, 98
Chrulska Elżbieta   16, 147, 168

Chrysos Evangelis   123
Ciampini Emanuele Marcello   27, 42
Cirese Alberto M.   264, 270, 271
Civil Miguel   47, 67
Clark Ève Vivienne   116, 123
Clark Herbert H.   116, 123
Clark Suzannah   80, 86
Clay William Keatinge   205, 217
Clement VIII, Pope   225
Clercx-Lejeune Suzanne   22
Coens Maurice   3, 16, 186, 187, 191
Cohen Mark E.   49, 51, 52, 53, 55, 56, 59, 60, 61, 67
Collier Mark   32, 42
Colombo Giovanni   280
Cornet N.-J.   281, 296
Courtés Joseph   278, 297
Cowan Douglas E.   298
Cranmer Thomas   201, 203–206, 208–209, 210, 213
Crossley John N.   167, 169
Cuming Geoffrey J.   203, 217
Curtis Gareth   199, 217
Cuva Armando   3, 16
Cymbrykiewicz Joanna   12, 16, 17
Czarnowus Anna   12, 17, 147, 168
Czövek Ágnes   13, 17
Dąbek Stanisław   6, 17
Dagron Gilbert   102, 103, 104, 106, 123
Dahlhaus Carl   241, 244
Dallapoz Adolf   252
Danet Brenda   285, 296
Daressy Georges   29, 43
Darnell John Coleman   35, 36, 37, 38, 43
Dawson Lorne L.   298
Day Juliette J.   176, 191
De Clerck Paul   275, 297
De Martino Ernesto   258, 262, 267, 270, 271

Delaunay Isabelle 14, 17
Deledda Grazia 255–257, 259, 265, 271
Delnero Paul 49, 67, 74, 82, 86
Deshman Robert 14, 17
DeSilva Jennifer Mara 225, 244
Deutsch Otto Erich 242, 244
Dhennin Sylvain 45
Di Febo Martina 297
Diehl Patrick S 9, 13, 17
Dindorf Ludwig 121
Donovan Claire 202, 217
Dornn Francisco Xavier 20
Dreuille Mayeul de 126, 127, 128, 129, 130, 135
Drocourt Nicolas 106, 123
Duchesne Louis 2, 17
Dudek Katarzyna 12, 17
Duffy Eamon 200, 202, 203, 213, 217
Duncan J.M. 6, 17
Edward VI of England 205
Edwards John 213, 217
Elizabeth I of England 205, 217
Ellinwood Leonard 162, 168
Emerit Sibylle 118, 123
Engelhardt Markus 246
Enmarch Roland 5, 34, 43
Erdbeer Robert Matthias 22, 68
Erler Mary C. 202, 217
Evans Nancy 251
Evans Wynford 251
Everist Mark 144, 145, 146, 148, 162, 168, 169
Faburel Guillaume 118, 123
Failler Albert 121
Fara Giulio 258, 263, 267, 271
Fassler Margot E. 148, 168
Faulkner Raymond O. 26, 31, 43
Fayrfax Robert 212
Featherstone Michael 106, 123
Federhofer Hellmut 22, 223, 236, 242, 244

Federhofer-Königs Renate 223, 236, 242, 244, 245
Fellowes Edmund 209
Fenlon Iain 199, 218, 246
Fernandez Marie-Henriette 164, 168
Ferrari Mirella 285, 298
Ferraro Giuseppe 256, 271
Festa Costanzo 221, 243, 245, 247
Fijałkowski Michał 12, 18
Firchow Otto 30, 43, 45
Fischer Balthasar 178
Fisher Alexander J. 6, 18, 162, 165, 168, 223, 245
Flamm Christoph 246
Flusin Bernard 121
Foley Edward 71, 86, 169
Fowler Joseph Thomas 206, 218
Fox Michael V. 34, 43
Fradejas Lebrero José 10
Franck-Reinecke Renate 251
François Wim 191
Fretheim Terence E. 89, 98
Gabbay Uri 4, 18, 49, 50, 51, 52, 54, 58, 60, 63, 64, 67, 71, 72, 73, 75, 76, 77, 79–81, 82, 83, 84, 86
Gaebelein Frank E. 99
Galbiati L. M. 280, 285, 296
Gallini Clara 270, 271
Galofaro Francesco 15, 273, 276, 278, 297, 301
García Turza Claudio 19
Gardiner Alan H. 29, 30, 43
Gasse Annie 35, 43
Gattermann Günter 246
Gautier Paul 121, 122
Geffray Geneviève 242, 245
Geldhof Joris 3, 176, 191
Geller Markham J. 49, 67
Genette Gérard 281, 292, 297
Gennrich Friedrich 147, 168
Gerald Abraham von 22
Gerhards Albert 247

Gibbs Daisy May   209, 212, 218
Gibson James J.   286, 297
Gillespie Marie   298
Gillespie Timothy   93, 98
Gillgren Peter   246
Giraudo Cesare   192
Głażewski Jacek   12, 18
Goeje Michael Jan de   121
Goelet Ogden   32, 33, 43
Gorczyńska Małgorzata   13, 18
Gordon Robert P.   93, 98
Graef Hilda C.   144, 168
Grapow Hermann   30, 43
Greenhill Anita   298
Greimas Algirdas Julien   277, 278, 297
Gressmann Hugo   89, 98
Grimes Ronald L.   286, 297
Groenewold Ulla   252
Grusin Richard   287, 293, 296
Guest George   251
Guglielmi Waltraud   26, 43
Guidotti M. Cristina   44
Guizot François   121
Gunn David M.   91, 98
Gunn Steven J.   217
Gunnarsson Britt-Louise   296
Gutmann Joseph   89, 98
Guzmán José Antonio Peinado   14, 15, 18
Haar James   246
Haberl Franz Xaver   246
Haikal Fayza   41, 43
Hakham Amos   95, 98
Harley John   211, 212, 218
Harnoncourt Nikolaus   242, 252
Harper John   71, 86, 169, 221, 246
Harrison Frank Llewellyn   198, 218
Hartwell Herbert   99
Hasbrouck John Baptist   135
Haseloff Arthur   15, 18
Hassler Hans Leo   223
Haug Andreas   157, 168

Haydn Johann Michael   236, 241
Hays Harold M.   32, 43
Heil Günter   122
Heilmann Uwe   252
Heinemann Joseph   4, 18
Heinemann Michael   226, 245
Helck Wolfgang   42, 43
Helland Christopher   286, 297
Henry VIII of England   7, 197, 203–206, 217, 218
Herbermann Charles G.   168, 169
Herbert David Eric John   298
Herbert William   251
Herbin François-René   31, 43
Herrick Jennifer A.   95, 98
Herrin Judith   106, 123
Heuvelmans Pamela   253
Hickman David   200, 218
Hickmann Ellen   34, 43
Hiley David   161, 168
Hilsey John   203
Hochradner Thomas   246
Horn Wolfgang   232, 236, 245
Hornung Erik   36, 40, 43
Huglo Michel   71, 86, 164, 168, 169
Human Dirk   95, 98
Jackson Mark   124
James George   251
James T. G. H.   42
Jeffe Sara   247
Jeffery Peter   176, 188–189, 191
Jeffreys Catherine   167
Jeffreys Elizabeth   121
Jeffreys Michael   121
John Paul II, Pope   283, 297
Johnson Eithne   285, 297
Johnson Timothy J.   170
Johnstone Andrew   197, 206, 210, 212, 218
Joller Uku   253
Jong Mayke   122
Juhásová Jana   10, 11, 18

Jungmann Josef Andreas 3, 18, 178, 188, 192
Kaldellis Anthony 102, 105, 112, 113, 121, 123
Kaljuste Tonu 253
Kantorowicz Ernst H. 13–14, 18, 161, 169
Karagiannis Christos 5, 89, 98
Kazdan Alexander P. 101, 123
Kegel Herbert 251, 252
Kelly Thomas Forrest 169
Kendrick Robert L. 6, 18,
Khitrovo, B. de, Sofiia Petrovna Khitrovo 121, 123
Kim Eun-ju 6, 16
King Martha 258, 268, 271
King Robert 241
Kintz Linda 297
Kippenberg Hans G. 42
Kircher Armin 236, 245
Kitchen, Kenneth A. 31, 44
Kitzinger Ernst 14, 19
Kläger Florian 22, 68
Knott Bill 93, 98
Koch Ulla Susanne 48, 67
Köchel Ludwig von 236
Kockelmann Holger 30, 44
Kogerman Tiit 253
Kohlhase Thomas 232, 236, 245
Kowalska Magdalena 12, 13, 16, 17-24, 45, 68, 126, 135, 147, 157, 164, 168-170, 247
Krallis Dimitris 121
Kraner Johannes Günther 223, 245
Krecher Joachim 49, 50, 61, 67
Kreyszig Walter 223, 245
Krutmann Johannes 236, 245
Krzywkowski Isabelle 8–11, 19
Kubas Magdalena Maria 7, 12, 16-24, 45, 68, 126, 135, 168, 170, 247, 276, 278, 297
Kuhl Adrian 223, 245
Kutscher Raphael 49, 57, 67

Kwella Patrizia 252
La Chapelle Skubly Jacqueline de 169
Laiou Angeliki 123
Lambert Wilfred G. 68
Landsberger Benno 48, 67
Lapidge Michael 3, 14, 19, 187, 192, 297
Lasso Orlando di 223, 243
Lathrop Gordon W. 188, 189, 192
Lauinger Jacob 67, 86
Laurent Vitalien 121
Leahy Anthony 42
Legg John Wickham 200, 218
Leitz Christian 27, 44
Leone Massimo 285, 297
Leopold Silke 247
Lesage Julia 297
Lesure François 245
Łesyk Lesław Bogdan 20
Lewis Anthony 251
Licheri Bonaventura 265
Lieberman Stephen J. 69
Limberis Vasiliki 102, 123
Linell Per 296
Lippe Robert 191
Liszt Franz 6
Llewellyn Jeremy 155, 168, 169
Löhnert Anne 49, 50, 63, 64, 67
López Calderón Carme 14
López Poza Sagrario 20
Loprieno Antonio 42, 43
Lörke Tim 22
Lossky André 102, 124
Louth Andrew 103, 124
Luerssen Jade 91, 98
Luisi Francesco 18
Lütteken Laurenz 170
Macrides Ruth 122
Magee Diana 44
Magistretti Marco 297
Magnoli Claudio 280, 298
Magnus Elisabeth von 252

312

Magri-Mourgues Véronique 116, 124
Majeska George 121, 124
Mâle Émile 14, 20
Maliaras Nikos 106, 124
Maloney Linda M. 95, 98
Manassa Darnell Colleen 35, 36, 37, 38, 43
Manca Maria 267, 271
Manolopoulou Vicky 101, 124
Maraud André 9, 10, 20
Marchi Raffaello 256, 271
Mariette Augustine 28, 44
Mariot Nicolas 117, 124
Marsciani Franceso 275, 298
Marsh Dana 197, 200, 203, 218
Marshall Margaret 251, 252
Marvin Clara 226, 245
Marx-Weber Magda 170, 221, 226, 236, 239, 245
Mary I Tudor 7, 197, 205, 211, 213–214, 217, 219
Maschke Eva M. 144, 169
Massenkeil Günther 246
Mathieu Bernard 25, 44
Matt Nicol 253
Maul Stefan M. 49, 59, 65, 67, 68
McCarthy Daniel P. 179, 192
McCormick Michael 104, 124
McFarland Jason J. 6, 20
McKinnon Leigh 167
Mears Natalie 203, 218
Meersseman Gilles Gérard 3, 20, 144, 165, 169
Méndez Rodríguez Daniel M. 40, 44
Mershman Francis 161, 169
Mews Constant J. 167, 169
Meyer Wilhelm 6, 20
Miles Alistair 252
Miller Patrick D. 95, 98
Milsom John 209, 218
Minoretti Dalmazio 285

Mirelman Sam 5–7, 49, 52, 68, 74, 75, 76, 78, 79, 82, 83, 86
Moers Gerald 26, 44
Moffat Anne 121
Moniuszko Stanisław 6, 17
Monson Craig 211, 218
Montandon Alain 20
Monterroso Montero Juan Manuel 14, 20
Monteverdi Claudio 6
Moor Ave 253
Mora Dino 280, 284, 285, 298, 301
Moran Neil 105, 124
Morenz Siegfried 33, 44
Morgan Nigel J. 20, 202, 218
Morlacchi Francesco 241,
Morley Robert 211–213, 215
Mormando Franco 123
Mortarino Giuseppe 280, 281, 283, 298
Mozart Leopold 6, 236, 246
Mozart Maria Anna 241, 245
Mozart Wolfgang Amadeus 6, 8, 225, 236–242, 244-247, 251
Mullally Robert 164, 169
Munitiz Joseph A. 122
Mura Ena Antonio 269, 271
Nauta Arjen 285, 298
Necipoğlu Nevra 122
Nesbitt Claire 124
Neumann Peter 242, 252
Nicholson Sydney 209
Nielsen Eduard 89, 98
Nims Margaret F. 167
Norberg Dag 148, 169
Nordberg Bengt 296
Nutter David 71, 86, 169, 221, 223, 246
O'Connell Matthew J. 191
O'Leary Stephen D. 285, 286, 298
O'Regan Noel 226, 246
Ödekan Ayla 122

Oesterley William Oskar Emil   93, 94, 98
Olivési Stéphane   116, 124
Olleson Edward   219
Orsenigo Christian   43
Osieczkowska Celina   13, 20
Østrem Eyolf   168
Otto Eberhard   43
Page Christopher   163, 169
Palazzo Eric   176, 192
Palestrina Giovanni Pierluigi da   6, 7, 223, 225–229, 231–233, 236, 241–242, 243-247
Parkinson Richard B.   34, 44
Parpola Simo   69
Parr Roger P.   167
Pärt Arvo   6
Patanè Massimo   25, 44
Paulis Giulio   271
Pentcheva Bissera V.   118, 124
Perrot Sylvain   118, 123
Peryn Alexander   211–213, 215
Petersen Nils Holger   168, 223, 225, 226, 246, 248
Petit Louis   121
Pfannkuch Wilhelm   22
Philip II of Spain   205, 213, 215
Piacentini Patrizia   43
Piccione Guglielmo   280, 281, 282, 298
Pierno Franco   298
Pihlaja Stephen   286, 298
Piłat–Zuzankiewicz Marta   2, 12, 20, 21
Pioletti Antonio   19
Pistoia Alessandro   124
Pittalis Francesca   258, 271
Pius V, Pope   179
Pius X, Pope   282
Pius XII, Pope   175
Polster Hermann Christian   251, 252
Pongratz-Leisten Beate   65, 68

Ponzo Jenny   15, 273, 291, 298
Porta Constanzo   215, 216, 223, 243, 245, 246
Prałat Emilian   13, 21
Prato Alessandro   297
Pregardien Christoph   252
Pröbstl Volker   95, 99
Procter Francis   200, 218
Pruett Lilian P.   223, 246
Pruzsinszky Regine   86
Quack Joachim Friedrich   28, 30, 35, 44
Quirke Stephen   27, 31, 32, 40, 42, 44
Rabaté Dominique   16
Rabatel Alain   116, 124
Rachmaninoff Sergey   6
Ragavan Deena   86
Ragazzoli Chloé   30, 45
Rakusa Ilma   9, 21,
Rapisarda Stefano   19
Razzore Domenico   280, 284, 285, 298, 301
Reiske Johann Jacob   102, 121
Reisner George   59, 68, 76, 77, 87
Renaud Émile   121
Renwick William   218
Reynolds Christopher   226, 246
Rhijn Carine van   122
Richards Jeffrey   144, 169
Richter Thomas   68
Ridderbusch Karl   252
Riedel Friedrich Wilhelm   246
Riess Heidi   251, 252
Ritter Adolf Martin   122
Robbins Landon Howard Chandler   244
Roberson Joshua   38, 45
Roberts Stephen   251
Robertson Anne W.   145, 169
Robledo Luis   213, 214, 218
Roccati Alessandro   42
Rochberg-Halton Francesca   67

Rodríguez Miranda María del Amor 18
Roesner Edward H. 145, 169
Roopalu Juta 253
Rosati Gloria 44
Rosen Charles 241, 246
Rosenthal Karl August 236, 246
Roth Joachim 6, 21, 223, 226, 246
Rothenberg David J. 144, 169
Roti Grant C. 169
Rozzo Ugo 295, 298
Rubin Miri 144, 164, 170
Ruszkiewicz Dominika 12, 21
Ryrie Alec 218
Sadowski Witold 2, 3, 4, 5, 9, 11, 12, 13, 15, 16-18, 20-24, 25, 45, 50, 57, 64, 68, 126, 135, 147, 157, 158, 168, 170, 223, 247, 276, 298
Sahlin Margit 163–164
Saint-Saëns Camille 6
Saltzstein Jennifer 153, 170
Sanders Ernest H. 148, 170
Sandigliano Giovanni 280, 281, 282, 299
Sandler Lucy Freeman 202, 218
Santi Angelo de 144, 164, 165, 168
Sassu Pietro 261, 262, 264, 266, 271
Sauneron Serge 27, 45
Sawicki Bernard 4
Saxby Michael 123
Schafer Raymond Murray 118, 124
Schanzlin Hans Peter 6, 22
Schermann Theodor 2, 22
Schick Hartmut 236, 247
Schidenhofen Joachim Ferdinand 241–242, 244
Schlager Karlheinz 170, 224, 247
Schlötterer Reinhold 226, 247
Schlüter Arnulf 44
Schlüter Katrin 44
Schmid Manfred Hermann 241, 247

Schmoll-Barthel Jutta 247
Schneider Matthias 247
Schott Siegfried 26, 28, 45
Schubert Franz Anton 241
Schubert Franz Peter 6
Schuster Ildefonso 280, 281, 299
Schuster Joseph 241
Schützeichel Harald 245
Schwens-Harrant Brigitte 9, 22
Scippa Vincenzo 280, 281, 282, 283, 299
Scot Stefan 212, 219
Scott Roger 121
Seay Albert 221, 245, 247
Selig Franz-Josef 252
Sermet Joëlle de 16
Sgavicchia Siriana 19
Shakkour Suha 298
Shehata Dahlia 86
Sheppard John 212, 219
Sherr Richard 228, 247
Shirai Mitsuko 252
Sirleto Guglielmo 179
Skinner David 197, 203, 219
Smith David 98
Snickare Mårten 246
Sodi Manlio 175, 176, 192
Soen Violet 191
Sole Leonardo 261, 262, 264, 271
Somaglino Claire 45
Sorci Pietro 179, 192
Spangenberg Johann 206
Spanke Hans 148, 163, 170
Spano Giovanni 257, 259–260, 263, 271
Spanu Gian Nicola 271
Spar Ira 68
Spinks Bryan D. 178, 191, 192
Stankowska Agata 22
Sterne Jonathan 118, 124
Stierstorfer Klaus 22, 68
Stockigt Janice B. 232, 241, 247
Streck Michael P. 48, 68

Stroumsa Guy G.   42
Summerly Jeremy   209, 219
Svampa Domenico   280, 281, 282, 299
Świerzowska Agata   42
Szczurko Elżbieta   7, 22
Szöverffy Joseph   144, 170
Szymanowski Karol   6, 22
Taft Robert F.   3, 6, 22, 101, 124, 275, 297, 299
Tall Maxeme   121
Tallis Thomas   6, 7, 206, 210–213, 215, 218, 219
Tanda Nicola   271
Taverner John   212
Telicki Marcin   22
Temperley Nicholas   209
Theuws Frans   122
Thompson Emily Ann   118, 124
Thorel-Cailleteau Sylvie   19,
Tillyard H. J. W.   112, 124
Toboła Łukasz   4, 22, 30, 45, 47, 68
Toniolo Alessandro   176, 192
Tortora Massimiliano   19
Triacca Achille Maria   175, 192
Troelsgard Christian   112, 124
Trowell Brian   198, 199, 200, 219
Truman Ronald   217
Tsiknopoullos Ioannis P.   121
Turchi Dolores   258, 271
Turi Mati   253
Urb Kaia   253
Urciolo Raffaele G.   271
Vadé Yves   16
Valli Norberto   276, 299
Van Dijk Stephen Joseph Peter   191
Varille Alexandre   29, 45
Vasiliev Alexander A.   121
Vaux Roland de   91, 98
Veldhuis Niek   47, 68
Vélez Marín Manuel   2, 23
Vernier Léa   15, 23
Verpeaux Jean   122

Vettori Alessandro   157, 170
Victorinus Georg   222, 223, 224, 243
Vincent Alexandre   118, 123
Vogel Cyrille   176, 183, 185, 192
Vogt Albert   105, 121
Vogüé Adalbert de   125, 128, 135
Volk Konrad   49, 68
Vos Cas J. A.   98
Vyvyan Jennifer   251
Wagner Andreas   44
Wagner Max Leopold   258, 271
Walt Deon van der   252
Walter-Jochum Robert   22
Wand Günter   252
Wantuch Ewa   12, 23
Wasserman Nathan   47, 68
Wathey Andrew   199, 217
Weil Mark S.   225, 247
Weiser Artur   95, 99
Wellesz Egon   106, 112, 124
Werning Daniel A.   38, 39, 45
Westendorf Wolfhart   42
White James F.   177, 192
Whiting Robert M.   69
Whittaker Gordon   49, 69
Wilcke Klaus   48, 62, 69
Wilkus Aleksandra   7, 12, 16, 23
Willa Josef-Anton   242, 247
Williams Carol J.   167, 197,
Williamson Magnus   3, 7, 213, 219
Winitzer Abraham   48, 50, 69
Winkler Gabriele   22, 297, 299
Worcester Thomas   123
Wordsworth Christopher   200, 218
Woźniak Maria Judyta   12, 23
Wright Craig   12, 145, 170
Wrightson James   209, 219
Wulkopf Cornelia   252
Yamazaki Naoko   34, 45
Youngblood Ronald F.   93, 99
Yoyotte Jean   29, 45
Zacharia Cesare de   223, 244, 245

Zaluskowski Corinna   35, 45
Zamponi Stefano   19
Zańko Aldona   12, 16, 17
Zelenka Jan Dismas   7, 225, 232–236, 239, 241, 242, 243, 245-247

Ziegler Georgianna   206
Żmuda-Trzebiatowska Marta   12, 23
Zumthor Paul   157, 170, 268, 271
Zybina Karina   7–8, 236, 239, 247